Governor
Alexander Martin

Governor Alexander Martin

Biography of a North Carolina Revolutionary War Statesman

CHARLES D. RODENBOUGH

Foreword by Lindley S. Butler

McFarland & Company, Inc., Publishers
Jefferson, North Carolina, and London

The present work is a reprint of the illustrated case bound edition of Governor Alexander Martin: Biography of a North Carolina Revolutionary War Statesman, *first published in 2004 by McFarland.*

LIBRARY OF CONGRESS CATALOGUING-IN-PUBLICATION DATA

Rodenbough, Charles D., 1932–
    Governor Alexander Martin : biography of a North Carolina Revolutionary War statesman / Charles D. Rodenbough ; foreword by Lindley S. Butler.
        p. cm.
    Includes bibliographical references and index.

ISBN 978-0-7864-4919-4
softcover : 50# alkaline paper ∞

    1. Martin, Alexander, 1740–1807.   2. Governors—North Carolina—Biography.   3. North Carolina—Politics and government—1775–1865.   4. North Carolina—History—Revolution, 1775–1783—Biography.   5. United States—History—Revolution, 1775–1783—Biography.   6. Legislators—United States—Biography.   7. United States. Congress. Senate—Biography.   8. Martin family.   9. Rockingham County (N.C.)—Biography.   I. Title.
F258.M35R63   2011
975.6'03'092—dc22   2003025326

BRITISH LIBRARY CATALOGUING DATA ARE AVAILABLE

© 2004 Charles D. Rodenbough. All rights reserved

No part of this book may be reproduced or transmitted in any form or by any means, electronic or mechanical, including photocopying or recording, or by any information storage and retrieval system, without permission in writing from the publisher.

On the cover: Pastel portrait (c. 1793) of Alexander Martin by James Sharples, Sr. (Independence National Historical Park, Philadelphia, Pennsylvania)

Manufactured in the United States of America

McFarland & Company, Inc., Publishers
  Box 611, Jefferson, North Carolina 28640
    www.mcfarlandpub.com

For Jean

For her years of understanding and love

Contents

Foreword by Lindley S. Butler 1
Preface 3

1. Martin's Youth and Education in New Jersey 9
2. Martin's Arrival in Salisbury, North Carolina 19
3. The Unrest of the Regulators 28
4. A Move to Guilford County 35
5. War against the British and the Incident at Germantown 44
6. Martin as Speaker of the Senate and as President of
   the Board of War 54
7. Martin's First Term as Governor 67
8. A Time of Peace, Independence, and Rebuilding 75
9. The Cession of Western Lands 90
10. Martin's Personal Life at Danbury 104
11. The U.S. Constitutional Convention in Philadelphia 110
12. Debate over Ratification of the Constitution 121
13. Elected Governor Again 132
14. The Development of the First State University 141
15. Washington's Southern Tour and the Establishment of
    a State Capital 151
16. Martin as United States Senator 161

17. Martin Becomes "Wonderfully Federal" 173
18. Martin's Final Role as Governor 186

Epilogue—The Final Resting Place of Alexander Martin 199
Chapter Notes 205
Bibliography 225
Index 235

Foreword
by Lindley S. Butler

Contemporaries as well as historians of the late eighteenth century have noted the exceptionally talented men who launched the American Revolution and created a federal republic whose constitution preserved the revolutionary natural rights ideology in a centralized nation-state. To Pulitzer Prize–winning historian Joseph J. Ellis, the "founding brothers" were truly "the greatest generation of political talent in American history." Scholars have been appropriately awed by Washington, Jefferson, Adams, Franklin, Madison, Hamilton, and their compatriots. However, to comprehend fully the remarkable depth and breadth of the nation's leadership at its birth, it is necessary to delve beneath the national scene into the states, where the people's sovereign power was represented until transferred to the national government in 1788–1789. Within the individual states, extraordinary men engaged in subversion of Crown authority, promulgated constitutions, governed, defended borders, and served as representatives in the Continental Congress.

Like its fellow colonies, North Carolina had a pantheon of revolutionaries who guided the emerging state through the war and into the Federal Union. The isolated state's political persona, unlike that of its neighbors, was grounded in a strong affinity for egalitarian self-government. The colony's chaotic proprietary period and the backcountry Regulator insurrection segued into a deeply rooted Anti-Federalism that initially rejected ratification of the Federal Constitution because it included no guarantees of individual rights. The state's leaders mirrored the key actors on the national stage, and on the state level they transformed the nation's aspirations into practical political solutions.

In North Carolina, Alexander Martin shines in a constellation of revolutionary politicians, soldiers, and statesmen. Born in New Jersey to a middling Scots-Irish

Presbyterian family, Martin was better educated (an A.M. degree from Princeton) than most of his contemporaries; yet he chose to seek his fortune among the flood of settlers in the Carolina backcountry. Landing in Salisbury, North Carolina, in frontier Rowan County in 1760, the 22-year-old Martin opened a store, acquired a plantation on the Dan River near Virginia, and as a magistrate and attorney quickly entered the county governing elite. During the Regulator upheavals in 1770, Martin was assaulted at the Hillsborough Court riot, an uprising against a corrupt provincial government. When violence was threatened the next year in Salisbury, he successfully negotiated an end to the crisis and thereafter remained sensitive to the egalitarian proclivities of his frontier neighbors.

Active from the outset in the Revolution, Martin was a delegate to provincial congresses, colonel of a North Carolina Continental regiment, long-time member and speaker of the State Senate, six-term governor, delegate to the Federal Constitutional Convention, U.S. senator, a founder and first president of the trustees of the state university, and sometime poet, dramatist, and scientist. He was equally at home in a rough-and-tumble backcountry political rally, a militia muster, the serene Moravian religious community of Salem, the worldly streets of Philadelphia, and the erudite meetings of the American Philosophical Society. The aspect of his character that illuminates the nation's formative years is that he bridged the Anti-Federalist/Federalist dichotomy, not to manipulate his personal power but to be consistent with an intellectual commitment combined with daily experience in practical politics. Martin's life demonstrates what insight can be gained about our national origins from those who may appear to be secondary figures on the national stage but indeed are central "founding brothers" in their respective states.

Preface

There is a considerable body of recent nonfiction advancing the critical importance and unique circumstances that gathered a particular "band of brothers" in colonial America to initiate a revolution and create the first democratic republic of the millennium. With broad popular support for that view of the miracle of the American Revolution, a conspicuous parallel assertion would be that, in order to propagate this miracle, throughout a vast and often querulous chain of colonies, there must have been a subset of leaders who carried grievances into action and theory into law. Without access to more modern forms of communication, there must have been, in every colony, leaders who were trusted by local populations, who fought alongside military commanders and republican revolutionaries and served with them in the constitutional conventions, who protected and articulated the minutiae of local anxieties, and who ultimately delivered their constituencies into the melting pot of nationhood. It was these people, this second level of founding fathers, who rejected the languid lure of demagoguery and led poorly educated and previously persecuted subsistence farmers and laborers to trust in a future based on self-government where, in principle, everyone was willing to sacrifice something for a common good.

In the dazzle of the phenomenon of the moment, which brought this galaxy of leadership into a common enterprise that was without any historical precedent, there was this secondary cadre of command, men who similarly risked everything and led their neighbors to vest their lives and families in this experiment in popular government. In modern vernacular, these were the commanders who led their companies out of the trenches or onto the beaches of another time in defense of the principles their leaders had defined.

This biography is an attempt to capture the likeness of one such leader who stood just off center stage throughout the separate acts of this political play. Because he was better educated than most and had been born and raised in the middle colonies and rose to political power in the Southern colonies, Alexander Martin is particularly important to the understanding of the role that this secondary leadership played in the formation of the union. His Princeton education and Presbyterian roots perhaps typecast him for the role of a revolutionary, but it was his decision to locate on the edge of a frontier and to become the spokesperson for the dispossessed. It was the honing of his skills at persuasion and his pragmatism that allowed him to transcend the regional gulf between east and west, between merchant and farmer, and between *noblesse oblige* and popular sovereignty within the colony of North Carolina.

Among Britain's Atlantic colonies, North Carolina displayed an understated character. Its treacherously barricaded coastline discouraged the development of ports, and its elongated shape dictated a dependence on ultimate colonial expansion to the west. Alexander Martin arrived in North Carolina coincidentally with the emergence of the Carolina frontier as the idyllic destination of thousands of dispossessed Protestant farmers from Germany, Ireland and Scotland. Attracted to the abundant promise of colonial America, they had been unwanted in the already populated middle colonies, hustled along through the rapidly filling valley of Virginia, and broadcast like seed across the Carolina Piedmont frontier. Unaccustomed to the orderly accumulation of land title, they acquisitively took possession as squatters or claimants and tore at the earth to own their inheritance.

The passage of colonial North Carolina from the domination of tidewater, mercantile elite to reflect the insular demands of an impoverished frontier majority materialized as a political reality in the course of the rebellion against British colonial rule. This shift in internal character was, therefore, in some way masked by its more public transition from colony to state. Martin's emergence as a politician was a reflection of this metamorphosis of North Carolina. Having rejected military service as his revolutionary role, he committed his energy to the vigorous pursuit of public service as a civil officer. When the war moved south in 1781, he was in the vortex of a civil war of international dimension. His response defined him as a leader. Later, Alexander Martin stepped onto the national political stage at propitious moments prepared to contribute to the urgency of the occasion but never to seize the moment for personal aggrandizement. Attributing this nobleness of purpose to Martin does not ignore his human frailties. Instead, it recognizes the formative influences of his vigorous family along the Delaware, the doctrines of the Presbyterian Church, and his education, particularly his years at Princeton, which challenged his capacity and cast his character.

I would propose that North Carolina, at the end of the Revolution, was a state made up of an underclass majority, as were no other seaboard states, and that only as statehood moved west did America see similar underclass majorities take charge. Early writers of North Carolina history too frequently attempted to emulate the record of the Virginia or South Carolina tidewater aristocracies, and attributed to the North Carolina elite these states' characteristics of oligarchic leadership. Such efforts begged only humiliation as historians sought by feeble comparison to contradict the reality that there was no comparable Washington, Lee or Pinckney. Why was there no North Carolinian among the trusted leadership under those first administrations of Washington, Adams or Jefferson? The answer was because the underclass eschewed leadership as a characteristic of domination and therefore saw it as suspect.

What historians have tended to ignore about Alexander Martin was his impact on the national agenda as a voice of this particular underclass. These people did not seek to advance a political system or a philosophy of government beyond minimalism and a suspicion of leadership in direct proportion to the distance between the government and the governed. Hence, at the Constitutional Convention there was no North Carolina Plan and debate was more important than regionalism to the winning of the state's vote. Martin was recognized as one of the few delegates to the convention who represented the farmer of the frontier, so his voice in discussion—formal and informal—had a resonance that others knew they had to respect if they expected their work to be ratified. His intellectual training gave him the capacity to translate the popular expectations into political reality. It is evident that if a more dedicated opponent of central authority, such as a Patrick Henry or Luther Martin or Sam Adams, had been in North Carolina at the time of the ratification conventions, he might have succeeded in breaking the unity of the chain of original states as many in Britain were predicting would happen. It was the more pragmatic antifederalism of men like Richard Caswell and Alexander Martin that bridged the gulf and brought the state into union. They succeeded at their task less by advocacy and more by judicious representation to navigate through pettifoggery toward the practical reality that made a nation of united states. That mission was more difficult to discern than the committed support of more acknowledged Federalists, but it was critical to the eventual ratification by the frontier dispossessed of North Carolina.

Martin's single most consequential action as a United States senator, his championing of a Senate open to the public, accomplished the final break with class government of the British style. Although the federal government was to be representative, the actions of that government were to be taken in accessible debate before the people who were the ultimate source of power. Over time, even these citizens, previously marginalized by every country and government they had even known, came to cherish the independence into which they had been delivered, although they continued for over 200 years to struggle with the duty of freedom as responsibility or license.

Between the end of the Revolutionary War and the turn of the century, no North Carolinian approached Martin's record of public service. During those 17 years, he served consecutively in one or the other of the three highest offices in the state, except in 1787 when he was a delegate to the Constitutional Convention. That record has not been replicated. He literally was a founding father, not only because he was a delegate to the Constitutional Convention, but by virtue of his service in many other capacities. He was the first person from the frontier elected governor and so was the founding voice of that dominating, isolationist constituency although he spoke as a recognized advocate of ratification. He was the first governor of North Carolina elected after the Revolution. The book asserts that he was a founding father of the first state university and of education in North Carolina in general. He was a founding promoter of commerce and internal improvements, and was a champion of political and religious dissent—all issues that were anathema to the dispossessed. He saw all of these causes aggressively pursued in his lifetime and viewed with dismay, at the end of his life, the slide of North Carolina into an age of debilitating isolation and inactivity.

In an age stingy with its recognition of merit, Martin was one of the first Princeton graduates to be awarded an honorary doctorate. He was an active Mason, an honorary member of the Society of the Cincinnati, and only the second North Carolinian made a fellow of the American Philosophical Society. This last honor came to him by a vote of the intellectual leadership of the nation in 1798. He had enjoyed some success as a writer but it was as a Princeton-trained former governor, friend of Philadelphia society, delegate of the Constitutional Convention, and United States senator that Alexander Martin was escorted into that elite company.

Throughout this text I have attempted to use specific modifiers to characterize Martin's political approach at that moment to those circumstances. Thus, he progresses from particularist to anti-federalist to Anti-Federalist. Note that in the early part of this book, "anti-federalist" is treated as a common noun (no capital letters) because for the time period covered in those chapters, the term was an informal descriptor. Only later did it become an official party name, a change reflected in this book by a change to capital letters. As a delegate to the Constitutional Convention, Martin was the representative of the frontier west (of North Carolina), whose population of subsistence farmers were suspicious of all government, their suspicions increasing in direct proportion to the physical distance of the government. In that sense, representing that constituency, Martin was anti-federalist, generally cautious of any centralized power. By the time he reached the Senate and party labels had been attached to all politics, he was counted as part of the national Anti-Federalists.

I held it as critical to an understanding of his political influence to recognize that Martin was forming his relationships to a democratic, federal system as that system was being created. At some moments he had personal influence on the formation itself. On those occasions he tended toward deliberation rather than initiation. He represented a single state, but his scope of analysis exceeded all but a few of his contemporaries. When he spoke, he typically sought to move beyond details to reflect the broader field of common ground. Historians have been responsible for the confusion of his political affiliation, some listing him as Federalist and others as Anti-Federalist. In his time, although he was inclined to discount the necessity of political parties, it was his kind of attachment to representative government that made the development of political parties inevitable.

Martin emerged as a leader at the same time that colonial government was giving way to an independent state government, and he became a singular voice for an evolving but immature majority. The eastern elite viewed him alternately as a pariah speaking for ignorant farmers whose right to the franchise was debatable or as an educated and cultured voice that could be a link to obstreperous neighbors. Martin learned to navigate between the shores of these opinions with the certainty of a river pilot. He confounded his critics in an age when there was no measure of propriety on personal attack, when the scarcity of a press encouraged delivering the most offensive personal insults upon public figures. Martin was never welcomed as part of the eastern establishment, only as a sometime ally; thus, when the establishment history of North Carolina came to be written, Martin's contribution was measured more by caustic diminutives than by a reflection of his accomplishments. Moreover, Martin's private correspondence has been lost to history, depriving him of an equivalent interpretive voice. (His public nemesis, William R. Davie, left his papers, did his own interpretive writing, and had a family that sought to enhance his reputation after his death.)

To compile a biography under such circumstances, without personal papers and saddled with inaccurate research, it was necessary to go beyond the conclusions of early historians. It was necessary to understand Alexander Martin in the broad context, as a reflection of his age, then with logic and perception to move through the details and attempt to sift impurities. Back and forth, the matrix was filled.

Since I worked for such an extended period on this text, there have been many who have made their contribution to its completion. I want to make particular mention of Charles Martin, Lenora Sutton, and Bob and Tom Upshur, all of whom are descendents of Col. James Martin, and Francie Lane, a direct descendent of the governor, who helped so much with family details that had never been part of the public record. Francie was the source of much original research, and I always found her thoughts to be accurate and insightful. Then there was Bob Carter, Rockingham County Historian, who always watched the details and made certain I did not assume too much. Dr. Lindley Butler, for many years historian-in-residence at Rockingham Community College, was my academic guru and particular friend. When I got bogged down, his enthusiasm for the project was always what restarted my engine. Finally, my family, particularly my wife, Jean, humored me on "my project"; Jean took many hours from her busy schedule to proof various versions. I hope all these people, and others I have not singled out, feel some satisfaction in seeing this biography in print.

"A jealousy of their ruler ought to subsist in all free Governments as the grand check that freedom hath over tyranny."

— *Governor Alexander Martin,*
December 22, 1791

1

Martin's Youth and Education in New Jersey

The Continental army began its move south toward Germantown at 7:00 A.M. on the 3rd of October in 1776. General Washington's complicated plan of attack would have been a bold challenge to an experienced army, depending as it would have on a precise timetable of prearranged maneuvers. Alexander Martin, senior colonel under General Francis Nash, and the North Carolina brigade were to be part of the reserve force commanded by General William Alexander, Lord Sterling. According to the plan, units were to have moved into their respective positions within two miles of the enemy by 2:00 A.M. and there they would rest until 4:00 A.M. Unfortunately, they were not even in position until 5:30 as the sun began to rise. The stealth with which Washington planned to initiate his attack was evaporating. The rising sun revealed a heavy fog that Washington welcomed as a natural element of surprise to shield his movements. Sullivan initiated the bayonet attack in the center just after 6:00. The impenetrable fog at first masked the movement in forces and the Americans strained to hear the sounds of firing that would announce that the battle was joined. The British, at first unwilling to appreciate the report of their own pickets that the Continentals were attacking in force, finally initiated several unsuccessful counterattacks. For an anxious 20 minutes Washington waited, listening to the firing increasing on left, right and in his center, and receiving dispatches from his commanders. Finally, certain that his attack had the enemy in retreat, he moved forward to press the advantage.

The North Carolina and New Jersey brigades held their reserve position but pushed in behind the center, keeping pressure on the retreating British. Just beyond St. Michael's Lutheran Church a hasty, perhaps parting, shot from a British Light Infantry six-pounder passed over Sullivan's Pennsylvanians and over the heads of

Washington and his staff, falling among the reserves. The ball struck a signpost, then ricocheted through the neck of General Nash's horse and tore into the general's thigh. Passing on, it struck Major James Witherspoon in the head, killing him instantly.[1] As Nash's horse fell dead, the general was caught beneath the animal. Martin and the remaining staff stood shattered by the bloody slaughter that had erupted in their midst. Nash was reported to have brought immediate order, declaring his own wounds not serious and ordering them to push forward.[2]

The battle now centered around Cliveden, the massive home of Benjamin Chew, that had been strategically and hastily fortified like a castle by the British. Eight artillery pieces were firing on the house from front and rear, some of the shots arcing over their target to fall among their own American troops. The smoke of battle mixed with the morning fog to shroud the field. General Anthony Wayne's Pennsylvania brigade had advanced beyond Cliveden, toward Germantown, but, hearing the increase in shot and shell to their rear, they wheeled about and countermarched toward the musket sounds. The brigades lost contact with each other's movements in the dense fog. Suddenly, General Adam Stephen's troops from Nathaniel Greene's division faced a battle line approaching in their direction and opened fire. There was a withering fusillade in response. The Americans were firing on their own troops with appalling results. In the confusion, units began to break up. Some had run out of ammunition. Others had lost all perception in the smoke and fog, and the army, which Washington had thought was on the verge of an important victory, was consumed in the panic of retreat. "Faces blackened with powder, breaths shrieking from nostrils, shoulders beating against the sides of his horse like so many huge bats," Washington's men fled.[3] Their path of flight was through the North Carolina brigade, no longer held in reserve but firing from the north. Officers beat back the terrified soldiers caught up in the panic. Alexander Martin, having only recently been witness to the mortal wounding of his commander and friend, Francis Nash, now was among those striking at terror-stricken troops, pulling them cowering from behind trees and trying to stop the rout. The desperate efforts resulted in a less than orderly retreat toward Pennypacker's Mill. Three days later, Washington advised Congress that his investigation had confirmed that his army had been on the point of victory when it had suddenly broken and fled.

Blood-spattered and mud-spattered, Colonel Alexander Martin, suffering unspeakable fatigue, led the North Carolina brigade from the field. In the recrimination that inevitably followed defeat, General Stephens was cashiered for drunkenness. Accusations were made against other officers, including Colonel Martin. Several officers of the fourth regiment brought charges of cowardice, specifically that in the heat of the battle Martin pulled a soldier out of hiding in a tree truck and hid inside it himself. Martin demanded a court-martial be convened, which cleared him of the charges. The question of choosing a brigadier to replace the slain Nash consumed the Carolinians in the wake of the Germantown defeat. The politics of the military, particularly at this stage in the creation of a professional American army, were routinely conducted through character assassination. Men who risked their lives in battle were subjected to scurrilous attacks on their personal character. Martin had his enemies among the officers of the North Carolina Brigade. His position, as the senior colonel of the brigade, meant that the only way for any other colonel to gain the vacant position of brigadier was to bring him down, and some had demonstrated the extent to which they were willing to go to accomplish that purpose. Refusing to undergo this inevitable assault on his reputation, Martin resigned his commission on November 22, citing his physical exhaustion.

As the army prepared for winter quarters at Valley Forge, Alexander Martin and his manservant, Ben, rode south. The court-martial had given official vindication to his actions at Germantown but leaving the army at that critical moment in the crucible of revolution was a sad and disheartening choice he felt he had to make. His return to North Carolina initiated that portion of his life that would determine the wisdom, merit and virtue of his action at Germantown. His commitment to a bold re-entry into state politics was not a factor in his resignation; it was a product of those lonely hours riding home in that bleak November. Approaching the age of 40, he could resume his practice as a circuit-riding frontier lawyer and allow his military record to define his life. Instead, he committed himself first to the certainty of national independence. Then he made the personal commitment to take as crucial a part in the formation of the state of North Carolina and its integration into a free nation as his abilities would allow him. It was the only choice available to him if he was to be true to his own integrity and heritage.

To understand Martin's heritage and his willingness to fight for independence, it is important to know about his upbringing and education. Alexander Martin was born in 1738 in Lebanon Township, Hunterdon County, New Jersey.[4] His parents were both born in Ireland of Scottish descent: Hugh Martin, his father, in 1697 in County Tyrone and his mother, Jane Hunter, in 1717 in County Antrim. The earlier generations of the Martin family had left Scotland only a few years before Hugh Martin's birth. Perhaps following the death of his first wife, Hugh Martin's father, Alexander, had brought his children to Ireland. There he again married, this time to Martha Coughran, and Hugh was the eldest child of this second marriage.[5] Along with the Scots' exodus had gone the Presbyterian Church, which, in Ulster, was the Scot's "peculiar institution, his mark of distinction from other people in Ulster, his proud heritage."[6] In this tradition, the first Alexander Martin was a ruling elder in Ireland in the Presbyterian Church.

Ireland was becoming overcrowded and the English were growing hostile to the economic rivalry that the presence of the Scots represented. The Great Plantation, begun in the reign of James I as a way to tame the rebellious Irish by imposing upon them the Scots whom the pale soil of Scotland could not support, had become too successful. The Scots were concentrated in six of the nine counties of the province of Ulster, and by the end of the Glorious Revolution in 1688, they were in excess of 100,000. In the course of the revolution, it was claimed that Ulster was nearly colonized anew by Scottish settlers and Protestant camp followers.

In the next decade, "eighty thousand small Scotch adventurers" came to Ulster.[7] It was in this last period of migration that Alexander Martin, the emigrant, and his family crossed the Irish Sea. In spite of great numbers, the Lowland Scots, now Ulster Scots, found themselves in the midst of the hostile Irish whom they despised, and who hated them in turn as aliens and usurpers. Spurred in new directions through contact in Ulster with English Puritans, French Huguenots and Dutch Reformers (like themselves held in contempt), they became more adaptable, less traditional and clannish. These Scots were as apt to be businessmen, tradesmen or manufacturers as they were to be farmers.

In Ireland, Alexander and Martha Martin bore a family that, in addition to Hugh, included daughters Agnes and Ester and sons Robert, Thomas and Henry. Alexander was not a rich man, but in spite of increasing adversity he prospered. The emigration of Ulster Scots to America began soon after the Martins reached Ireland. In 1699, the English passed the first restrictions on Irish trade initially forbidding the export of woolens, a staple industry of Ireland, to any part of the world except England and Wales. There followed more restrictions on commerce, then the practice of rack-renting and, most abhorrent, restrictions on religion. The erection of Presbyterian churches was limited, Presbyterian marriages could be declared illegal, and the Test Act of 1704 excluded the Ulster Presbyterians from all civil or military offices. This religious persecution came not from the Irish Catholics, whose animosity surrounded them, but from the established Church of England. All these causes exacerbated the exodus of the Ulster Scots, but two periods of severe famine in 1727 and 1740 produced two of the largest waves of emigration.

It was about the time of the first wave that the Martins decided to leave Ireland. Hugh, the eldest son, was sent by his father to "explore America and inform him if it would suit to move there with his family."[8] Such an investigation to evaluate the wisdom of the move could only be the luxury of a family of some means. Alexander was probably reluctant to move his family to yet another land of promise after his first migration had proved unsatisfactory. The report Hugh brought his father, added to the ever-tightening repressive laws and crop failures, was enough to precipitate the voyage to America that ended at New Castle on the Delaware.

Hugh reported on a land of vast size, something neither Scots nor Irish had ever experienced. There were already large numbers of their own living on better land than they had ever seen in their islands. They could not be immediately certain that there would be religious toleration because there was little organized religious structure. Government power rested far away and was as yet not exploitative. Local government was popular, as opposed to autocratic rule, and so lightly organized that much of the law lay within the hands of individuals. There were few signs of privilege and many individual stories of success. It was already a competitive land, but the Scots were experienced competitors given the opportunity of contest.

The Hunter family, soon to be allied with the Martins, was still later in their move from Scotland to Ulster and arrived about 1700. They were an extensive family, a conclusion reached because one sister, perhaps old enough to be married, was left in Scotland, and Jane Hunter was not born until 1717 after the family was already in Ulster. Nothing is known of the parents and little can be concluded from circumstantial evidence. They lived in County Antrim, perhaps near Belfast, the principal town. Between 1735 and 1738, three of the Hunter children, Jane, Alexander and John, immigrated to America. According to the family record these "were all" that came of the family. They, like the Martins, landed at New Castle, and came up the

Delaware into New Jersey where Jane Hunter, a young girl, met Hugh Martin, a 40-year-old Scotch–Irish bachelor.

The Hunter brothers settled on the Delaware six miles above Easton and Hunter's Settlement was named for Alexander, who appears as the leader of a concentration of Scotch-Irish in that area.[9] A family tradition, recalled by his nephew, touts the strength of this Alexander Hunter, who was so admired for his athletic prowess by the Indians that they searched among several tribes to find one of their own strong enough to best him at wrestling. There were a number of contests that Alexander won and as a result the Indians behaved "in a very submissive manner when he was in their company."[10]

The Martin family turned to the east side of the Delaware and settled in New Jersey. Having situated his family in Hunterdon County, Alexander Martin soon died there. It is known that at least some of the children of each of his marriages came to America. Of the children of the first wife, James and William, as adults, established their own families. William went to South Carolina where he died and although he left several daughters, family contact was lost. James Martin, however, settled two miles from his father on the south branch of the Raritan River. He married Annie Drummond, who was the daughter of James Drummond. They had two sons and three daughters.

Of the children of Alexander's second wife, Martha, Robert was for a time a teacher and he later went to Northampton County, Pennsylvania, across the Delaware. Thomas was a stonemason and accumulated considerable property. Daughter Agnes married a Quaker named Dawson, who was a farmer, and they lived near Carroll's Ferry on the Delaware in Pennsylvania. The other daughter, Ester, married Francis Mason, also a farmer, and they located in the forks of the Delaware.

The youngest son was Henry Martin, who came to Hugh, as the eldest brother, asking for financial help so that he might attend college. The Martins' emigration was concurrent with the first Great Awakening, that extensive series of emotional religious revivals that swept the colonies and resulted in a schism in the Presbyterian Church. A new college had been established at Elizabethtown, New Jersey, in 1747 and after a very short time was moved to Newark as the College of New Jersey.[11] It was this college, under vital Presbyterian doctrine, that Henry Martin entered in 1751. A graduate in 1754, he was licensed as a clergyman by the Presbytery of New York. He married and had several pastorates before his early death in 1764.[12]

This was the extended family that surrounded Hugh Martin and his wife, Jane. The Hunter and Martin families had not known each other in Ulster. They were, after all, part of a large movement of people. There were similarities in the pattern of their history. Both families came late from Scotland to Ireland making them sojourners, much more Scots than Irish. The Martins left grown children in Scotland. They were in Ulster at the end of the period of plantation settlement, after the Crown had lost its concern for the value of colonization and when ugly acts of discrimination were being passed by Parliament. Ulster had already become the explosive theater of Protestant and Catholic prejudice that it has remained to this day, with the Protestants a belligerent minority. The Catholics, however, without political control, could express their hatred only in attitude and a deep-set animosity. Both families, though not considered wealthy, had the means to extricate themselves from this hostile land. The move from Scotland to Ulster may have been such a disappointment for the Martin family that, as dour Scots, they were not willing to cross a vast ocean on promise alone, hence the trip of exploration by Hugh Martin to determine if indeed they would find a forgiving land of opportunity.

Of the initial settlement of the Scotch-Irish in New Jersey between 1709-1715, it was said that "they were Presbyterian and Calvinist to the core, independent to a man, and blessed with few scruples about squatting on vacant land."[13] This tenacious attitude toward land acquisition was the source of the prejudice that grew up among the English toward the Scotch–Irish. In New Jersey, however, for the Martins, it was the Germans who were the near neighbors in Sussex and Hunterdon counties. The arrival of Germans in the fertile valley of the Raritan River was concurrent and coexistent with that of the Scotch-Irish. Both peoples were hardworking and proud. The native Indians, whose lands they had acquired by treaty, were established ominously on the horizon and they were, for the whites, a source of ever-present concern and occasional life-and-death fear.[14] As a colony parted by two proprietary interests, New Jersey was divided into East Jersey and West Jersey. It was a natural division that in many ways still remains, East Jersey attaching its natural interests to New York, and West Jersey attaching more to the interests of Pennsylvania. William Penn became the chief influence among the group of Quakers who came to acquire the West Jersey proprietary interests.

Hunterdon County lay in West Jersey and it was into this social and political environment that the first child of Hugh and Jane Hunter Martin was born. They named him Alexander after his grandfather. The only known reference to his early life came from his brother, an ironic jest: "I have heard my Mother say he never spoke a word until he was four years old."[15]

Alexander soon had brothers—Thomas, James, Samuel and Robert—and sisters, Martha and Jane. The New Jersey of their youth was known as one of the "bread colonies," because of its rich farmland and Hunterdon County was called the "bread basket," producing more wheat than any other county in the colonies.[16] Their parents had known young years spent in lands of periodic famine while their children's memories were to be of abundance. Then, as Alexander approached his teens, armed conflict broke out on the colonial frontier between England and France and the defeat of General Braddock in 1755 raised the specter of Indian ravages. Across the Delaware, the Moravian town of Gnadenhutten was burned and a family named Swarthout was murdered in Sussex County. In October 1758, at Easton, a treaty was signed between the various tribes of the Delaware and Governor Denny of New Jersey and representatives of Pennsylvania, by which the Indians gave up all claims to land in New Jersey.[17] The active potential for conflict was finally removed from New Jersey.

Although the excitement of fighting Indians may have absorbed his youth, it was to be education that set Alexander Martin apart for all his adult life. Wherever Scotch-Irish settled, they build churches first in communities; schools then followed.[18] Within the Martin family there was perhaps an even higher respect for education than was typical among the Scotch-Irish. His father had taught an English school for several years after he emigrated and before he married. Hugh Martin required of his sons an application to study but he respected the individuality of their aptitude, allowing them to seek their own interests. It was this dedication to education that connected Martin to the Scottish period of enlightenment that so deeply influenced the political and social evolution of the United States.

Alexander was considered to be a good student. His Uncle Henry was at college and soon would become a Presbyterian minister, a profession that may have been planned for Alexander. The Rev. Francis Alison, in 1741, had established a classical academy at his pastorate in New London, Pennsylvania. It was taken over and supported by the "Old Side" Synod of Philadelphia and became a preparatory school that trained not only ministers but also many who became physicians and political leaders. In this academy, Alexander Martin was prepared to follow his uncle into the college at Newark.

There was much concern among the "Old Side" Presbyterians because support of the Alison Academy seemed to contradict their principled opposition to the classical academies of the "New Side." In 1749, the Alison Academy was abandoned.[19] The Rev. Alison moved to an academy in Philadelphia, which later developed into the University of Pennsylvania, and Martin may have followed him there.

In further preparation, Martin, for a time, was a student under the Rev. Samuel Finley at his "Log College" at Nottingham on the Pennsylvania-Maryland border.[20] Students "were required to study the standard Latin and Greek authors as well as logic, arithmetic, geography, geometry, ontology and natural philosophy."[21] Benjamin Rush, Ebenezer Hazard and William Tennent were also prepared for college at Nottingham and later entered the College of New Jersey.[22]

Martin's preparatory education ended when he was about 15 and he entered the college at Newark. In many ways it was a parochial atmosphere at the college where the Rev. Aaron Burr had a new wife, the young daughter of the well-respected New England divine, Jonathan Edwards. Martin was only six years older than Esther Burr. He was the child of parents who likewise were considerably different in age. For impressionable, intense young men, it was natural that the respect that they held for the Rev. Burr was distinct from the affection they could imagine for Mrs. Burr. She was a mother and sister. When her children were born, they were reminders of younger brothers and sisters at home.[23]

Burr was a "New Side" Presbyterian, intimately involved in the Great Awakening. Francis Alison had been "Old Side," so Martin's education was early coming under the influence of each of the fierce, competing schools of Presbyterian theology. Within the "New Side" school of thought, the Rev. Burr was considered a moderate; he believed in a religion marked by personal contact with God and the necessity "for a formally and traditionally educated ministry."[24] His energy and untiring effort on behalf of the College of New Jersey took ultimate form and substance in the decision to move the college to the tiny town of Princeton in the year Martin entered the college. The cornerstone of the college building was laid there in 1754 with great satisfaction. Two years later, Martin received his bachelor's degree and entered on his masters program as part of the first class at Nassau Hall. This was an impressive college building as was the adjoining president's house, designed by Robert Smith, architect of the Pennsylvania statehouse later known to Martin and other delegates as Independence Hall. According to Esther Burr, Nassau Hall was the largest man-made structure "upon the Continent": 176 feet by 54 feet, three stories and a basement, of uncut native stone.[25]

Martin was an advanced student in the first class to enter this expanded institution. As such he was a tutor for the younger boys as he had been for his younger brothers. The student tutors were assigned to the three lower classes and the president instructed the seniors.[26] In Nassau Hall, students were quartered three to a room; each room was 20 square feet. There was a student dining hall presided over by a steward. The Prayer Hall was for services and was used for general meeting purposes. Alexander's room included the books he had purchased as a student, including the works of Watts, Plato, and John Locke, as well as the sermons of the Rev. Burr.[27] As an advanced student, he commanded the respect of the younger students, which he considered a formal responsibility. Burr had instilled the strict Presbyterian call to enlightenment as a moral duty, expecting the prodigality of youth to be held in restraint. Students attended classes in academic robes in the Scottish style. Sixty percent of the graduates became clergymen in the Presbyterian or Congregational churches. The rest became lawyers, physicians or public officials. Since his Uncle Henry was already a Presbyterian divine, it was natural that such a profession was considered for Alexander.

The influence of the Scottish Enlightenment, however, was also present and accelerating as the school was moved to Princeton. Through Princeton the connection was made between the Scottish intellectuals and the American experiment. For Martin, the clash between the strict influence on his adolescence of the church, rigid and unyielding, was merged with the application of the power of self-interest and the surrender of personal freedom to create the common good of community. It was at Princeton that these forces came into tension and where Martin formed the base of his political attitudes.

Alexander began his day at 5:00 A.M. when the bell rang in the cupola of Nassau Hall. By 6:00, students and faculty assembled in the Prayer Hall for prayer and scripture. There was an hour of study before breakfast of porridge and coffee or tea. Classes began at 9:00, interrupted at 1:00 by a plain dinner with a little cider or beer. A free hour followed, then two additional class hours. The bell called the students to evening prayer and psalm singing. Study followed until 9:00 when the steward checked students into their rooms to be asleep or studying.[28] For a graduate student, there was more latitude to accompany his greater capacity.

On February 20, 1757, the pastor of the Presbyterian Church at Newark, Elihu Spencer, delivered a sermon at Princeton that had a highly emotional effect on some of the students. As a "New Side" institution, the college put considerable store in personal religious experience and it is not surprising that these young men should have been so overcome. Burr was summoned and according to Esther Burr, "found about 20 young men in one room Crying and Begging to know what they Should do to be Saved, & of them under deepest Sense of their wicked Hearts & need of Christ."[29] Martin's name is not among those who had participated in the outburst. His senior position would have made such actions anathema. Martin's preparation

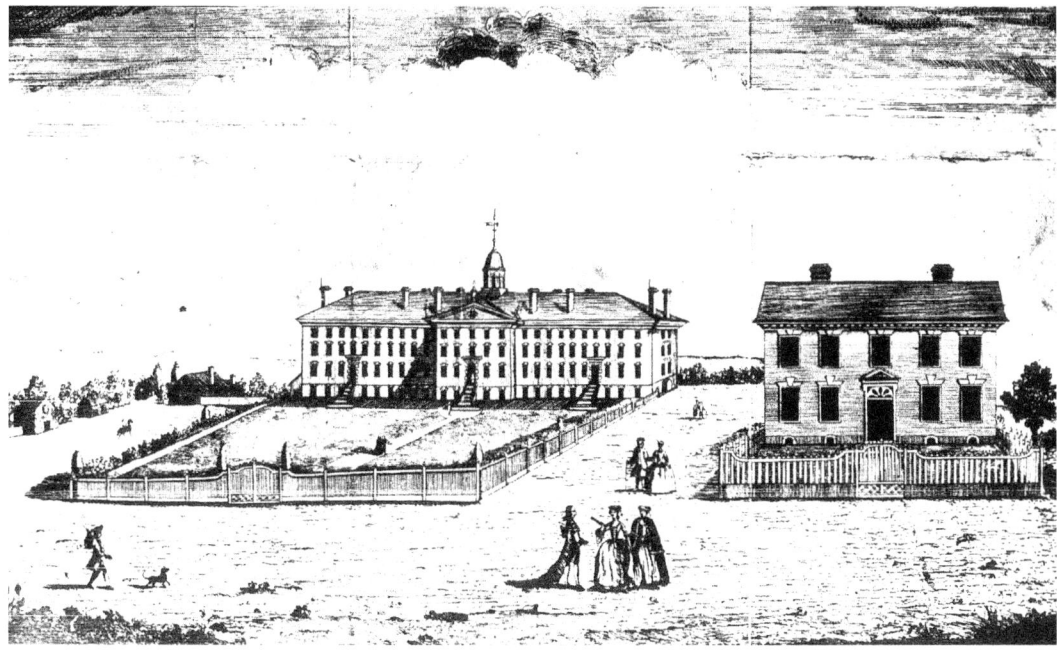

Princeton as Alexander Martin knew it. The College of New Jersey was relocated from Newark to Princeton in 1756 during Martin's tenure as a student. He lived in Nassau Hall, one of the largest buildings in colonial America.

for college first came under an "Old Side" influence that did not hold with such overt outbursts. At Nottingham and in college he had been under "New Side" influences but he could see in this incidence the terrible, unsettling result of loss of self-control. For the remainder of his life, Martin was seldom identified with his religion's affiliation or doctrine.[30] Essential to his formative years, the Presbyterian Church faded as a personal influence even as it became a major institutional influence on government.

The Rev. Burr was tireless in his efforts to raise funds to support the Princeton institution and to pay for its move and its new accommodations. Between his responsibilities as father of a young family and the administrative demands of president, he wrote letters to churches and wealthy patrons soliciting contributions. He traveled throughout the middle colonies preaching and making speeches. In September, returning from one of these tiring trips, he learned that one of his supporters, New Jersey Governor Jonathan Belcher, had died. Although he was already ill himself, he prepared and preached the funeral oration. On September 24th, the Rev. Aaron Burr was dead.[31]

The shock felt by all the students was no less traumatic for the administrators of the struggling school. The trustees, concerned about any break in leadership, two days after his death, chose Burr's father-in-law, Jonathan Edwards, as his successor. Burr had been the driving force, the inspiring spokesman. Edwards was a scholar and writer who considered himself ill-suited to the task of college president. He did, however, accept the appointment. He left his congregation at Stockbridge, Massachusetts, and arrived at Princeton on February 16, 1758, in the middle of a smallpox epidemic. Dr. William Shippen of Philadelphia was in town giving inoculations to the students and townspeople. A friend of both the Edwards and Burr families, his son, William, Jr., had been in the class of 1754 and another son, John, was to enter Princeton in the fall. President Edwards and his widowed daughter were inoculated.[32] Edwards developed a "secondary fever" and he died on March 22. In less than a month, Esther Burr died. Nassau Hall, thus deprived of the personal commitment of the Burr-Edwards family, was virtually cut adrift. Impressionable young men must have keenly wondered at these trials and the capricious nature of life.[33] Martin had been immersed in the lives of the Burrs, and this was the greatest tragedy of his young life. His mourning was internalized, however, becoming part of the motivational drive that directed his life to attainment in service. As his youth was concluding, he had dramatic examples in his family history and in the lives of Aaron and Esther Burr, of the power that could be directed toward a purpose, the necessity of knowing the obstacles and the determination to maneuver through adversity.

For the rest of Alexander Martin's life, the experiences and associations of the years at Princeton were a constant and recurring thread. He came from a people who respected education as essential for fulfillment of responsibility. He made his home in a frontier where his education set him apart. His public life and accomplishments were frequently enabled by and through his Princeton years.

2

Martin's Arrival in Salisbury, North Carolina

During Alexander Martin's final year at the College of New Jersey, the school was without a president and the sequence of emotional trials it had gone through threatened its continuation. Had the Rev. Aaron Burr not succeeded in completing the construction of Nassau Hall, the school might have closed. Inordinate pressure was exerted on the faculty and the older students to maintain continuity.[1] Under these uncertain circumstances, the trustees of the College of New Jersey turned to Samuel Davies, considered one of the Apostles of Dissent in colonial Virginia. He was one of the divines who had labored hard in the support of the college by preaching and raising funds throughout England and Scotland. At first, Davies, like his predecessor, was reluctant to leave his congregations in Hanover Presbytery but he finally accepted the post in July 1759.[2] Although Alexander had only a brief association with Davies, it was through the Virginia minister that he received his first employment. He accepted a masters degree from the College of New Jersey in 1759 and traveled to Cumberland County, Virginia, where he served as tutor for the son of N. Davies.[3]

Alexander was in a position at graduation to return to New Jersey to assist his father as a merchant or to assume duties on the family farm. Those choices seem never to have been under serious consideration despite the fact that his father was a successful man and there was by now a large and supportive family of Martins and Hunters on both sides of the Delaware River. After a year in Virginia, Alexander did return briefly to New Jersey to make a final decision on his future and to confirm it with his parents.

His Uncle John Hunter had left Pennsylvania as early as 1749 and settled in what was then Albemarle County, Virginia.[4] Five years later, another uncle, Alexander Hunter, had moved to the same region.[5] Alexander Martin visited his uncles when he was tutoring in the county immediately east of their home. They each had growing families with children that were Alexander's contemporaries. It was through the Hunters that Alexander Martin became part of the migration of the Scotch-Irish from the Delaware River to Virginia and into the frontier of North Carolina. The motivation for this extended migration was always more and cheaper land. Much of this movement of Scotch-Irish was by impoverished, landless people, many of whom had been indentured. The Martins and Hunters were neither landless nor poor. They accompanied the migration as part of the natural leadership that had become weary of contesting the political control held by the Quakers in Pennsylvania and had sought more tolerant circumstances in Virginia. The outbreak of the French and Indian War in 1754-1755 placed the Virginia frontier in even greater jeopardy from marauding Indians than the Delaware Valley had experienced earlier. By 1758, the people of the frontier were war-weary.[6] The Hunter brothers were inclined to move their families into North Carolina to remove them from harm's way. Alexander Martin's visit with his Hunter cousins was when the move was in process. They would be crossing the border into the part of the province of North Carolina under legal title to Lord Granville.[7] Confused land titles encouraged squatters but it also offered choice land to persons willing to risk a modicum of uncertainty.

In 1760, Martin left Hunterdon County, again heading south. He traveled first to Charleston, where he purchased a store of goods and then moved inland.[8] His plan was to move north to Salisbury, the county town of newly created Rowan County.[9] Five years earlier, Colonial Governor Arthur Dobbs, passing through Salisbury, had found the frame courthouse complete and "seven or eight log houses erected."[10] Salisbury had been where the Great Wagon Road, the principal immigration route from Pennsylvania to the Carolinas, converged with the ancient Indian Trading Path, the primary route of trade used by the Indians in the 17th and 18th centuries. Its location was at the vortex of a funnel of trade and population flow. Martin arrived in Salisbury much as his father, Hugh, had arrived at New Castle 20 years earlier, ready to test the potential of the frontier. At Salisbury, and along the Yadkin River, he found concentrations of Scotch-Irish, English and German settlers, an ethnic distribution not unlike that of his Hunterdon County birthplace.

He met John Frohock, who was considered to be "the wealthiest and most influential inhabitant of the northwest Carolina frontier."[11] The two men had arrived in Rowan County about the same time; Frohock was from Bucks County, Pennsylvania, by way of east-central North Carolina.[12] Alexander Martin had close associations with Frohock and his brothers and, through them, with the McCullochs. Martin was not a land speculator on the grand scale of either of these friends but he was attracted by the opportunity represented by the abundance of cheap land and the rapid settlement of the frontier.

On December 10, 1761, an advertisement appeared in the *Pennsylvania Gazette*: "Notice is hereby given to Alexander Martin, merchant, in Salisbury, N.C., that his father, Hugh Martin of Hunterdon County, New Jersey, died 9th March last, and left him and his brother James executors of his will; wherefore, said Alexander Martin, if not inconvenient to his business, is desired to return home, to settle his late father's affairs, but if his coming should be attended with disadvantages to him, he is required not to come by his mother, Jane Martin."[13] Alexander Martin had been making his passage from home through Charleston to Salisbury for most of the year. He was not able to receive news of his family nor had his Hunter uncles, so he did not know of his father's death. Hugh Martin was buried in Lebanon and a marble stone noted his birth in County Tyrone and his age.[14]

> Here lie the remains of Hugh Martin, who lived in this vicinity many years, during which, possessing the confidence of his government and his fellow-citizens, he discharged the duties of several offices of profit and trust with integrity and honesty. In the practice of the private and public virtues, eminent; as husband, father, relative, and friend, beloved; as a magistrate, revered. To religion a support, to science a patron, and to the poor, a friend. He was born in Ireland, County Tyrone, and died March 7, 1761, aged 63.
>
> > Let sculptured marble vainly boast,
> > And birth and titles scan;
> > God's Noblest work, of value most,
> > Here lies an honest man.
>
> His weeping sons in North Carolina pay this tribute to his memory.

The last phrase indicates that the stone was erected after Hugh Martin's widow and children had been moved to North Carolina and after the Rev. Thomas Martin had died. His will had listed his eldest sons, Alexander, James, and Samuel as executors. Hugh Martin left six slaves including "a negro boy called Prince," who was willed to James but at some point later became property of Alexander. They shared close life experiences and Prince ultimately survived his master dying a free man in Tennessee.

The will reflected once more the value Hugh Martin placed on education. His sons, Thomas, Alexander, and James were already demonstrating a predilection toward education, at the time the will was constructed, and to this end they were to have £20 each. James, however, seemed to be vacillating about his desire for an education so he was included with Samuel and Robert who, in lieu of education, were to divide their father's real estate.[15]

Eleven days after the notice appeared in the *Gazette*, Alexander Martin acquired his first land in Rowan County, a grant from Earl Granville, and witnessed two grants made to his cousin, Joseph Tate.[16] The Hunter family had word of the death of Hugh Martin and when they were finally in contact with Alexander, they gave him the sad news. Martin's purchase of the 436 acres on Jacobs Creek of Dan River, surrounded by the Hunter relations, represented a place where he could move his widowed mother and his siblings if they chose to leave New Jersey.

In the early months of 1762, Alexander returned to New Jersey. James Martin had completed most of the work of the executor. At the time of their father's death, Thomas and James were students at Princeton. The will allowed James to "choose rather to come home and work the farm." By the time Alexander reached home, James had probated the will and inventoried his father's personal property.[17] Alexander, therefore, found James in competent control of their father's estate and as co-executor; he was needed only for support. As the eldest son, however, he was

Anthony of *Thomas Boone* Esq *Captain General Governor* in Chief in and over His Majesty's Province of **New-Jersey**, and Territories thereon depending in **America**, &c.

To all to whom these Presents shall come or may concern, Greeting.

KNOW YE, That at _____ on the Day of the Date hereof, before _____ being thereunto delegated and appointed, the last Will and Testament of _____ Deceased, (a Copy whereof is hereunto annexed,) was proved; and is approved and allowed of by me. The said Deceased having while he lived, and at the Time of _____ Death, Goods, Chattels and Credits within this Province, by Means whereof the Proving the said Will, and the granting Administration, of all and singular the said Goods, Chattels and Credits, and also the auditing, allowing, and finally discharging the Account thereof, doth belong unto me, And the Administration of all and singular the Goods, Chattels and Credits, of the said Deceased, and any Way concerning his Will, was granted unto _____ in the said Will named, being first duly sworn Executor _____ well and faithfully to administer the same, and to make and exhibit a true and perfect Inventory of all and singular the Goods, Chattels and Credits, and also to render a just and true Account of _____ Administration, when thereunto lawfully required.

IN TESTIMONY whereof, I have caused the Prerogative Seal of the Province of *New-Jersey*, to be hereunto affixed, this _____ Day of *May* _____ in the Year of Our Lord One Thousand Seven Hundred and _____ concerned about the future care of his mother who was not yet 45 and in good health. James had come home from college to run the farm. The land Alexander had purchased, in the midst of his mother's Hunter relations in North Carolina, represented an alternative home for the Martin family. For the time being, however, the choice of the family was to remain in New Jersey where the younger children could have access to better education. Alexander was not abandoning his responsibility when he returned to North Carolina. He was continuing to make more viable the opportunity his family would have if they moved south. After he returned to Salisbury, he determined on the law as a profession although he continued to be a merchant. He read law, and since John Dunn was the only lawyer living in Salisbury in 1762, he benefited through the elder lawyer's encouragement.

In 1765, Martin received appointment from Governor Tryon as a justice for Rowan County and bought a lot and storehouse.[18] The governor had observed that North Carolina was growing more rapidly than any other colony. He marveled that in the "autumn and winter about one thousand wagons with families accompanying them passed through Salisbury."[19] A year later, Martin received his appointment as attorney for the Crown and in the same court; he produced his commission from the attorney general, making him deputy King's attorney.[20] He purchased one-fifth of lot 5 in Salisbury as a location for his law office.[21]

All his life, Alexander Martin had lived on the edge of European settlements threatened by Indians. In North Carolina, it was the Cherokee who represented this threat in the west. The French and Indian War was over but continued encroachments of white settlers on the Indian ancestral hunting lands raised the level of resentment of the Indians. Daniel Green likened this clash between settlers and Indians to a Greek tragedy. He concluded, "The settlers had to have farmland or else cease all attempts at settlement. The Indians could not and would not become farmers. Therefore they had constantly to be pushed westward."[22] The two groups wanted the same land for different purposes. The vast region of Tennessee and the trans-Allegheny was a twilight zone, penetrated by whites. The angered native Indians struck back with increasing incidents of murder and deprivation.

In the summer of 1767, Governor William Tryon, in an attempt to bring a greater degree of peace to his western lands and show his authority to subjects over whom he had been given governorship in 1765, marched from his capital at New Bern to Salisbury. On his arrival in the village, an ingratiating letter was delivered, signed by four of the leading citizens as spokesmen for the inhabitants: John Dunn, the attorney; John Mitchell, a merchant; John Frohock, and Alexander Martin. Martin had risen rapidly in this frontier setting and now found himself a spokesman for his neighbors. In terms elevating the governor to demiroyalty, the petition begged that he "not pass unnoticed the borough of Salisbury," which they thought at maturity might "be the future seat of a flourishing people situated in this remote part of

Opposite: **Appointment by Governor Thomas Boone of the Province of New Jersey of Alexander, James and Samuel Martin as administrators of the last will and testament of their father, Hugh Martin, May 12, 1761. Owned by Dr. Thomas Upshur of Charlottesville, Virginia. (Courtesy of Dr. Thomas Upshur.)**

the world."[23] The governor assembled about 100 people at Salisbury, including a regiment of militia each from the counties of Rowan and Mecklenburg, 16 servants and assistants and 2 surveyors, and marched them all west. He met with the Cherokee, impressed them with his office and presented them with abundant gifts.[24] Then he set his party to running a boundary line beyond which purchase of land was forbidden.[25] It was a grand show but an unrealistic solution in the face of the inevitable. One of the commissioners for running the boundary line was John Frohock.[26] Martin was an observer to this meeting with the Indians and the experience was a later influence on his own dealings with the Cherokee.

During the time in Salisbury, before and after the expedition to the Indians, Governor Tryon and his wife were proudly entertained by the locals and Alexander Martin took advantage of the opportunity to come to know the governor and his retinue. Salisbury had become a crossroad for dynamic frontier energy. The opportunity presented to this age was one of immigrant discovery and exploitation, and the Scotch-Irish were a perfect people for the time. They were infinitely acquisitive and self-sufficient. There were those among them who were born adventurers. They penetrated the frontier, to be followed rank on rank by their fellows.

Daniel Boone became the epitome of this frontier pioneer. Although part of this Scotch-Irish migration, Boone was actually of English ancestry. After a Pennsylvania sojourn, the Boones had located at the Bryan Settlement on Yadkin River near the Shallow Ford. Frequently present in Salisbury, Boone was one of the rugged, rowdy youths often at odds with locals. In lower courts, Martin defended Boone several times for these excesses.[27]

In 1763, Daniel Boone made his first exploration for the Henderson Company. Henderson, Thomas Hunt, and John Williams formed Richard Henderson and Company for the purpose of land speculation. In the spring of 1769, John Findley, John Stuart and Daniel Boone were in Salisbury attending court and, on March 5th, Judge Richard Henderson arrived. At this time plans for the exploration of Kentucky were concluded.[28] Alexander Martin was present in Salisbury, and, through his association with Boone, he was consulted on the plans for exploration and settlement.[29]

Martin himself was planning another trip to New Jersey. As he had prospered in Salisbury, his brothers and sisters had matured and it was time to make a family decision. Alexander Martin was committed to his future in North Carolina. Brother James, however, had married and started a family in New Jersey.[30]

Thomas Martin, Alexander's third brother, a minor at the time of his father's death, was recognized as a good student and his father's will had provided for his education.[31] Through some influence outside the family, and presumably even beyond his education by Presbyterians, Thomas became an Anglican cleric. He was ordained to the priesthood in the Chapel Royal, St. James Palace, London, on June 24, 1767. On July 8th, he received the King's Bounty, which was the money provided him as a priest, to return to America.[32] He became rector of the Brick Church, St. Thomas Parish, in Orange County, Virginia.

Late in 1767, he added to his duties the task of tutor to the family of James Madison, Sr., at Montpelier. There were three sons and a daughter in the Madison household and the eldest, sixteen-year-old James, had completed his study with a

Virginia schoolmaster.[33] Martin was responsible for the completion of James Madison's college preparatory education and logically became involved in the choice of the school Madison was to attend. It had been common for a scion of one of Virginia's plantation aristocracy to attend William and Mary but, during the past decade, that college "had fallen upon unstable and contentious times."[34] The senior Madison, though a vestryman, was opposed to the episcopacy as William and Mary represented it. The new Anglican rector presented an alternative. He had been at the College of New Jersey at the end of the presidency of Samuel Davies, whom James Madison, Sr., had known personally.

The family debate over the choice of colleges was still in process in June of 1769 when, on his way to New Jersey, Alexander Martin stopped to visit his brother at Montpelier. Irving Brant says that "noted as Alexander Martin was in later years for moderation and persuasiveness, his mature counsel may have won the elder Madison to a course on which the others already were agreed."[35] Alexander spoke with enthusiasm about the Scottish scholar, author, preacher and church leader, the Rev. John Witherspoon of Paisley, who now presided at Princeton.[36] The debate transcended theology, centering instead on the anti-church-power for which Princeton had become noted under the recent presidencies of Davies and Samuel Finley. With Alexander Martin leading a persuasive discussion the elder Madison could speculate with pleasure on the championship "of orthodoxy and strict pastoral conduct" for which Witherspoon was renowned, while his son could be swayed by the picture of Witherspoon as "a perpetual rebel against church authority."[37] James himself referred to Alexander as one who had helped make the family decision for the College of New Jersey.

Within a month, James Madison, accompanied by Alexander Martin, the Rev. Thomas Martin, and a Madison slave named Sawney, took the road to New Jersey. The routing was by way of Fredericksburg, Alexandria, Baltimore, and Philadelphia. Crossing rivers on poled ferries, they rode their horses along roads that were frequently little more than stump trails through the woods.[38] By August 10th, Madison was speaking of himself as a student at Nassau Hall when writing to Thomas Martin.[39] Thomas and Alexander were visiting their mother and preparing to return to Virginia. Thomas Martin's health had suffered under the stress of travel. With all the family together, the choices were laid out. With the same effective persuasion he had used in the debate at Montpelier, Alexander urged his mother to come to North Carolina. James, at this point, had no intention of leaving New Jersey but he now had his own family to look after. Thomas advanced an alternative. He had no family and his circumstances were splendid at Montpelier, supported as he was by the Madison patronage. His mother had already met young James Madison and she knew that she would be welcome. The alternative was agreed to as the best choice and plans were laid for the family moves. Between August and November, the Martins left New Jersey and relocated at the Brick Church's Glebe House, Orange County, Virginia.[40] With his family much nearer to him, Alexander Martin was back in North Carolina for the winter (November) term of Rowan County Court.[41]

All biographies of James Madison, beginning with the monumental work of William Cabell Rives, emphasize the contribution made to the forming of Madison's political thought by the years at Princeton. An analysis of these influences, as they

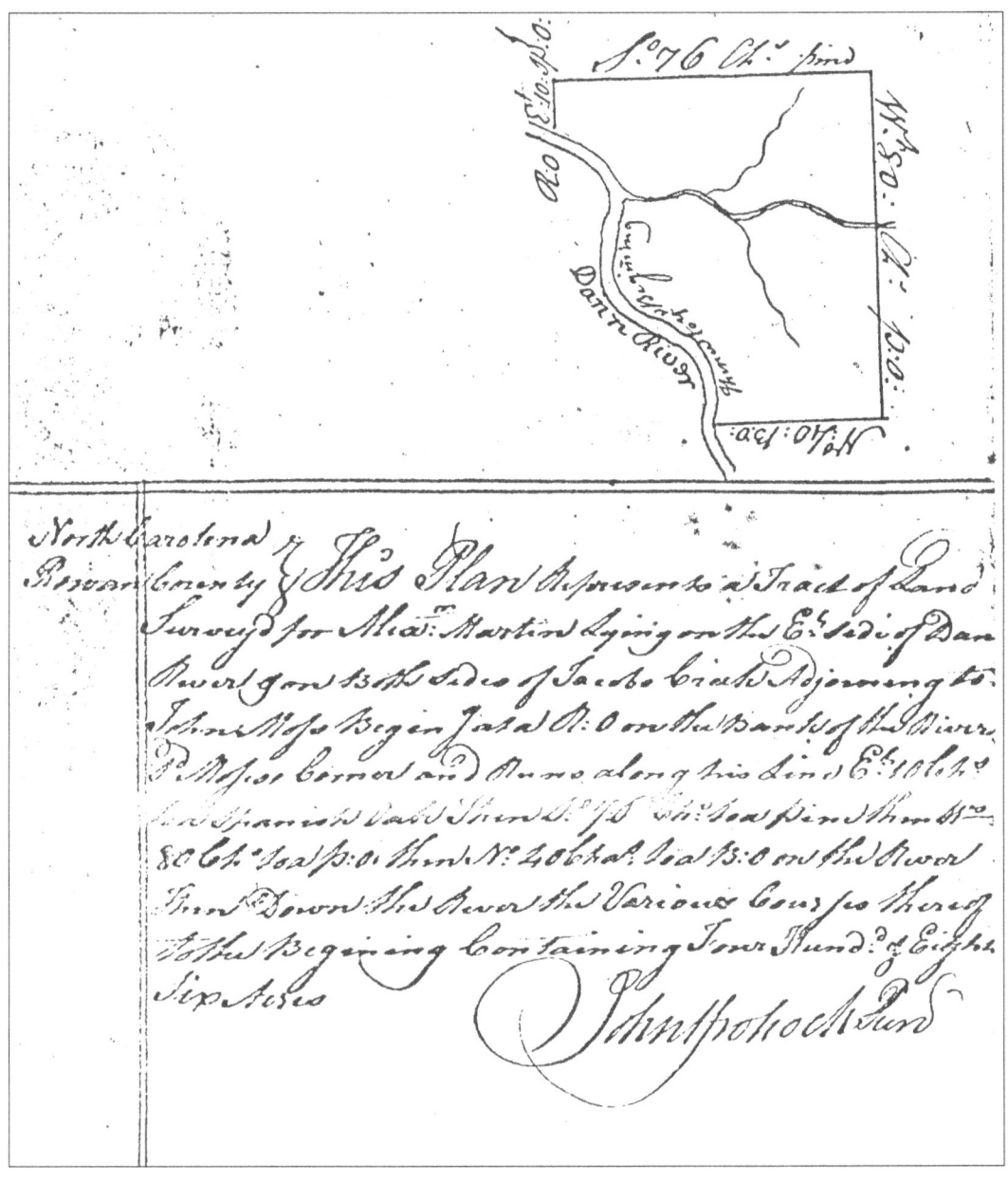

Plat for "Danbury"

coursed through his life and thinking, belongs in a Madison biography. For this study the conclusion must be made that Alexander and Thomas Martin had a pivotal connection with James Madison. Only nine years separated student and tutor, and Madison and Thomas Martin were obviously congenial. The relationship for both to Alexander Martin was that of elder and respected brother. Alexander's influence, however, may have had its greatest impact as the bridge between the Madisons, Senior and Junior. Alexander Martin and James Madison would have a friendship for life, as do people who share the significant moments in their lives.

James Martin continued to operate the family estate in New Jersey, at first in association with his brother-in-law, Samuel Rogers. There was a regular flow of Martins and Hunters between New Jersey and North Carolina and the Glebe House at Montpelier was a stopping point on this route. The Madisons took advantage of this interchange, occasionally sending their slave, Sawney, as contact with James at Princeton.[42]

The school that the Rev. Thomas operated at the Glebe now included his younger siblings, Samuel and Jane. Although Jane Martin seemed well pleased with the location, she was concerned about Thomas' poor health. He complained he was "as sickly and crazy as any aged Man, and in what Manner to account for it I know not." His mother, who was to be cared for, now found herself caring for her son. In August 1770, Thomas Martin died.[43]

Any plan that the Martin family had for an extended stay in Virginia was over. They were destined to locate on Alexander's 436-acre grant on Dan River at Jacobs Creek. With the help of the Hunter relations, Alexander built a home suitable for his mother, his two sisters and his youngest brother, Robert.[44] It was also commodious enough to be his home away from Salisbury. The site was on a modest bluff on the south side of the river and to the west of Jacobs Creek.

While preparations for the move to North Carolina were being made, Mrs. Martin became, by default, the tutor for the Madison children and moved from the Glebe into Montpelier.[45] By February 1771, Alexander was quoted as having located on Dan River.[46] In October, James Madison wrote his father from Nassau Hall that James Martin had been at the college for commencement where he had news of "his brothers and friends in Carolina by a young man lately come from thence.... You may tell Mrs. Martin he left his family at home all well."[47] Within the next year, accommodations were complete enough so that Jane Hunter Martin and her daughters moved to the Dan River location. Sojourners no more, the Martin family had completed its journey from Scotland to Ulster to Hunterdon County, New Jersey, to Orange County, Virginia, to the Dan River in North Carolina.

3

The Unrest of the Regulators

    The brawl at Hillsborough Court on the morning of September 24, 1770, erupted out of such modest provocation that it is certain the Regulators present fully intended mischief in the face of authority. Men were armed with clubs and whips and switches. Judge Richard Henderson opened the court with a pseudo-formal manner, but there was cautious uncertainty in the order that was demanded of the citizens packed in and straining for a view in this small, rustic public room. All morning, people had milled about the dirt streets of the Orange County town shouting and bellowing, building their courage. The entry of the judge was like a curtain rising and no sooner than he had seated himself upon the elevated bench than Jeremiah Fields stepped forward declaring he had something to say before business proceeded. Recognizing this as no time to consider contempt, Henderson agreed and Fields, speaking for the Regulators, declared their determination to be heard on their charges against the court. They would be heard now or heard later but they would be heard and, if the judge preferred order, he had better listen now. Henderson responded with groping platitudes attempting to defuse the moment and maintain his dignity. The judge knew full well how to reason with the mob before him, as it was made up of the Scotch-Irish rustics who had been his neighbors and his emissaries to Kentucky. The judge debated the matter for half an hour, then someone in the crowd cried out "Retire, Retire, and let the Court go on."

    Briefly separated by this action, the Regulators looked for a strategy and the court officers measured their minority situation. Inopportunely, a lawyer, John Williams, chose this moment to attempt to enter the courtroom. Obstreperous Regulators seized this act as sufficient provocation and fell on Williams with sticks and clubs. Running from the mob, he found refuge in a nearby storehouse and, now vitalized, the Regulators turned back to the courthouse to drag Edmund Fanning, the court register, from behind the lawyers' bench where he hid in the crowd. Fanning was an arch-villain to the Regulators, his registration charges for legal documents singled out as exorbitant though confirmed by the provincial attorney general in London. In desperation Fanning broke free and bolted for the door, escaping his now frenzied pursuers. At that moment Judge Henderson considered himself the vulnerable next-best target. James Hunter, one of the identified leaders of the Regulators, attempted to reassure him that he would not be harmed provided he was willing to hold court on their grievances. Self-preservation displaced all court decorum in Henderson's disingenuous assurance that he would hold such court, but he considered his deceit honorable because these same Regulator leaders stipulated that no lawyers would be allowed in the court except the King's Attorney.

For more than four hours, the rampage surged through the courtroom and into the town. Lawyers Alexander Martin, Thomas Hart, Michael Holt, and John Sitterell, clerk of the Crown, were all listed as victims of severe whippings from the mob while other lawyers, including Colonel Gray, Major Lloyd, Francis Nash, John Cooke, and Tyree Harris, were barely able to escape the same fate.[1]

Henderson escaped in the night. Edmund Fanning was declared a prisoner of war and the mob intended to put him to death the next day but cooler heads prevailed. He was discarded into the street with the disdainful verdict that he was "to run until he should get out of their Sight." Still unsatisfied, they cut his Hillsborough house off its sills and tore it apart, destroying every piece of furniture, his wine cellar, and burning his papers and all his personal belongings.

In the "mischief" of the Hillsborough Regulator incident, Alexander Martin experienced the unleashed fury of force beyond law. It was certain discomfort to be the object of such unreasonable passion, but Martin had decided to be an instrument of the law and, when that authority became exploitive and corrupt, he became a common object of the rage of the people. Whipping, aside from the pain engendered, was considered an act of contempt but it is doubtful that any of those whipped by this crowd felt any shame. Each represented colonial authority acting, under Governor Tryon, as agents of the Crown. In the decade of revolution that was beginning, each of the lawyers and court officers, with the lone exception of Fanning, emerged as leaders of the rebellion.

Alexander Martin seems to have been profoundly disturbed by this experience. The Regulators were his neighbors and clients. They shared with him a common heritage. Like him, many of their families had fled Scotland and then Ireland because the Crown authorities were harsh and corrupt. Rack-renting in Ireland had an obvious exploitive parallel to the exorbitant fees some colonial officials charged for land transfers. Martin had been eager to become an influential leader in colonial North Carolina, but he had to decide if such leadership was to be at the price of betrayal of his friends and neighbors. On the other hand, if he were to aspire to even higher elective office in the colony, he would have to do it under the rubric of colonial government, set by Governor Tryon and the Board of Trade in London and in cooperation with the same elite legal leadership that had sat cowering with him on that Hillsborough court bench. Add to these pragmatic considerations the personal paradox that James Hunter, a leader of the Regulator mob, had presented the petition to Judge Henderson at the start of the court session and may have been Alexander Martin's first cousin.[2]

It was probably these unstable conditions provoked by the Regulators that prolonged Jane Martin's stay at Montpelier. Alexander, however, pressed forward with acquisition of land at Salisbury, purchasing five lots in the town and thirteen acres nearby in Rowan County.[3] He became a town commissioner.[4] The meeting of the colonial assembly in December saw the passage of the Riot Act by which ten or more people who gathered for a riot and who refused to disperse when challenged would be declared felons and be subject to the death penalty. That assembly also passed many bills addressing the more obvious Regulator grievances and a bill creating Guilford, Wake, Chatham, and Surry counties that attempted to defuse the concentration of the Regulators.[5]

In the spring of 1771, the Regulator crisis came to Salisbury with the March term of Superior Court. On the 6th, as court was prepared to sit, between 400 and 500 Regulators were assembled between the town and the Yadkin River. Three companies of armed militia headed by Major Dobbins, Captain Rutherford, and Captain Berger defended the townspeople. They were joined by two companies of militia from Mecklenburg: 70 or 80 men, headed by Colonel Alexander and Captain Polk.[6] The size of the Regulator encampment was a larger population than that of Salisbury but the town had a significant militia defense. The militia was made up of the same types of frontier farmer (largely Scotch-Irish and German) arrayed against them as Regulators. Ambiguous and untested loyalty made for indecision on both sides and Salisbury feared their court would be more explosive than had been the fall court at Hillsborough. Militia officers were confident that they could defend the town and they itched for the opportunity to roust the rabble once and for all.

Faced with this volatile situation, two men, Alexander Martin and John Frohock, rode out to meet with the Regulators as delegates of the town and the court. The Regulators as exploiters of the civil court system targeted both men. What had happened to Edmund Fanning at Hillsborough was certainly demanded by some as just action against each of these men. Frohock, as one of the wealthiest men in the neighborhood, had much property to protect. In this situation Martin was the key man because he faced a concentration of his fellow Scotch-Irish neighbors. He had already been singled out for the lash and tasted the bitter rage of his friends.

Martin and Frohock were the source of the report Governor Tryon received explaining the next several hours. When asked their purpose, the Regulators had replied that they did not intend to interrupt the court or to injure people. They hoped "to petition the court for a redress of Grievances" against the court officers. Their arms represented only defense if they were assaulted by the militia. These were the claims of the leaders, recited to a loud counterpoint harmony of the crowd's menacing threats of whipping. When told that, because of their threatening presence, there was to be no court, the crowd was disappointed, thinking their stage for protest had been removed. They insisted they intended no harm to the judge but they made no assurances concerning other lesser officials. The Regulators in force were faced with a public debate with two of the court officers who were the target of many of their grievances. The experience was without parallel because there was a good-faith attempt to lay the foundation for a negotiated settlement to the conflict. Frohock and Martin attempted first to validate their position as negotiators by insisting that if they or any of their fellow court officials were the ones against whom the Regulators had justly founded complaints then they would be willing to return full satisfaction. The response from the crowd was that they were indeed the object of the complaints but the Regulators would show their commitment to the preservation of order by appointing a committee from their number to meet more formally and in an atmosphere of eased confrontation. In the representative tradition of the Presbyterian leadership among them, a committee was formed which in turn formed a smaller committee that would meet on the third Tuesday of May at the house of John Kimbrough on the Uwharrie, "to settle every differences between us whatsoever."[7]

Notified of the terms of the agreement, the rest of the Regulators marched through the town, gave three cheers and returned to their homes. Two men had faced a crowd of 500, had reasoned effectively and had avoided violence directed both toward themselves and presumably against the court and a frightened village. The official report they wrote of the encounter made no claim concerning the public adulation that must have been given in relief to their success. That was left to the imagination.

Alexander Martin's actions on this day set him apart from much of the colonial elite that was soon to make a revolution. He was committed to function within the law but he believed that the law could become alternately arbitrary or feeble in times of public panic. At such a time a leader had a moral duty to act in the best interests of the governed to restore public order. The law, fairly applied, was the only real guarantee of civil order but the law had to be a product of the consent of the governed. In Martin's actions at Hillsborough and Salisbury it is possible to see the maturation of the personal philosophy that he would finally articulate when faced with the ultimate choice between the Tories and Rebels in 1775. It is also possible, out of the public actions at Salisbury, to glimpse Martin's ability to bridge issues in such a way as to defuse hostility and engineer debate.

Richard Henderson, when similarly threatened, had promised the mob whatever they demanded, with no intention to honor his commitments. Martin intended to honor his promises after hearing complaints that he realized had a reasonable basis in fact. He and Frohock were, however, quick to justify themselves, being certain that in a fair examination they could prove they had not been guilty of charging extortionate fees. The militia units assembled at Salisbury were therefore not used to crush the Regulators under terms of the Riot Act. Instead Frohock and Martin had negotiated, presumably for higher authority, the basis for a meeting on "the third Tuesday in May next."

Now they had to report formally to that higher authority in such a way as to convey the wisdom of their representative action, given the situation they faced. In treating with the Regulators, they had committed public authority to an action. They made no claim that their commitment, although made under threat, had been an act of expediency or that it lacked significance, as had Henderson. Instead, they contended that they had negotiated an equitable agreement and defused the danger, simultaneously producing a matrix for at least partial settlement of the broader dispute. They reasoned that the Regulators, through outrages and excesses already committed, had overplayed their hand and forfeited their public support. They assured the governor that "this deluded people begin to grow sick of Regulation and want peace upon any tolerable terms."[8] Martin and Frohock were thus presuming to advise Governor Tryon as if they had some official status on his behalf.

Their proficient logic in communicating the accomplishments of their negotiations contrasts farcically with the flowery, pandering tone of the 1767 letter to Governor Tryon, that Frohock and Martin had signed, representing the people of Salisbury. Tryon had grandly accepted the previous petition, but he found the brief on this latest confrontation with the Regulators to be meddling with the will of the governor. His first response came on March 30th when he informed Frohock that he was being replaced as commanding officer of the Rowan regiment of the militia, which would, by the way, be part of the force that the governor was assembling to march against the Regulators. In sarcastic and demeaning terms, he attributed Frohock's purpose, in his late conduct with respect to the Regulators, to saving his own property and to conscience over having himself been guilty of taking excessive fees. He added to this rebuke an official response to Frohock and Martin dated April 5th. The governor opened this letter with a simple command. If you are guilty, "give Satisfaction and make Restitution to the injured."[9] Tryon affirmed no respect for men guilty of extortion. Secondly, the governor insisted that the court officers had no constitutional authority to make agreements with insurgents. He judged the Salisbury council as "Dishonorable to Government."

Tryon discounted the importance of the Salisbury incident because he was already committed to a military campaign to destroy the Regulators as a cohesive force. On the day that Frohock and Martin penned their report to Tryon, the governor and council had determined to raise a force to march against the Regulators.[10] The conference that Martin and Frohock had arranged for Kimbrough's was therefore redundant but Tryon, unwilling to betray his intensions, suggested that plans for the conference proceed. The governor forwarded the report of the activities of Frohock and Martin at Salisbury to Lord Hillsborough, secretary of state for the colonies in London, along with the governor's response. Tryon also included his plan to raise forces under General Hugh Waddell and to "cheerfully offer [his] Zealous Services" against the insurgents.[11]

Tryon finally faced the Regulators at Alamance Creek on May 16th with a force of 1,452 men, mostly militia from Orange and Rowan counties. Instead of the conference that Frohock and Martin had negotiated for May, the Governor faced 2,000 Regulators whom he was prepared to crush. In the official reports and incidental stories about the events surrounding the Battle of Alamance, only one author, the Rev. Eli Carruthers, recounts the tale of the effort of a Presbyterian divine, the Rev. David Caldwell, and Alexander Martin to prevent the battle of that day. Caldwell and Martin had known each other as students at Princeton and would be close personal friends all their lives. Martin was, if not a member by profession, at least a regular worshiper of Caldwell's at Buffalo and Alamance Presbyterian churches in Guilford County.[12] Three years earlier, when David Caldwell had been but six months at his church at Buffalo, he had joined with three other early Presbyterian ministers in a letter to Tryon, pledging their support of the governor against those they called the insurgents.[13] In that letter they had enclosed a copy of an open letter to Presbyterians of North Carolina wherein they had urged the loyalty of their denomination for the "Protestant Succession in the present royal Family," and asked that any who had taken an oath in support of the Regulators break it as an unlawful oath.[14] Without any sanction possible within the polity of the denomination, this letter was the strongest possible support that Presbyterian clergy could have offered to the government of the Crown. In reward, the provincial assembly approved an act to allow Presbyterian clergy in the colony "to solemnize the Rites of Matrimony." In his pragmatic justification of this action, Governor Tryon told the Bishop of London that he was "sensible the Attachment the Presbyterians have shewn to government merit the Indulgence of this Act." He was also conscious of the political reality that "the Presbyterians were the strongest party in that House."[15]

The night before the battle, Caldwell had a conference with Tryon. The governor also received a petition that night from the people of Orange County presenting their grievances. Caldwell claims that he had the assurance of the governor "that he [Tryon] would not proceed to extremities or fire on the Regulators until he [Caldwell] had made a fair trial of what could be done by negotiations."[16] On the day of the battle, Tryon rejected the earlier petition as long as the petitioners stood before him in insurrection. Meanwhile, Caldwell passed back and forth between the two armies and sometime in this period was joined in the negotiations by Alexander Martin. Tryon had delayed long enough. General Waddell, with still more militia to join the governor, was delayed under siege at Salisbury. The Regulators were calling out in derision, "Fire and be damned!" An old Scotchman yelled at Caldwell to get out of the way and Tryon, exasperated by more delays, called out to the militia, "Fire, fire on them or on me." As the volleys opened from each side, Robert Thompson, a Regulator, who was a member of Caldwell's Buffalo congregation and had somehow been restrained within Tryon's camp, broke through and dashed for the Regulator lines only to be cut down by fire said by some to have come from the governor.[17] Ensign William Bryan, clutching the Royal standard, was felled by a Regulator sharpshooter. Aside from the many friends from Buffalo and Alamance, Martin that day had certainly reasoned with his cousin, James Hunter, who was a strong influence in this army without a commander. In the brief, intense battle Tryon's army prevailed with the Regulators in undisciplined rout. Many of the leaders, including James Hunter, temporarily fled the state. Tryon set fire to the homes of some Regulators who lived nearby, including that of one James Hunter on Stinking Quarter.[18] Then he ceremoniously returned to New Bern and soon after departed to become the last royal governor of New York.

In the span of less than a year, Alexander Martin had been directly involved as the Regulator protest came to open warfare against civil government. Martin observed the entrenched power of the eastern North Carolina colonial elite and their ability, when unified on a single self-interest, to sustain their will. If he were to rise within colonial government, it would be these people and their rooted hegemony over regional politics with which he would have to bargain. His constituent base, however, would be these rough, strong-willed, and opinionated Scotch-Irish who were filling the frontier of the colony and inevitably would wrest numerical control of North Carolina from the easterners. Unlike many of his kith who in future generations would gain power within this political base through demagoguery,[19] it was Alexander Martin who sought to understand the nature of the government they sought then to establish and to interpret laws and a court system to protect that philosophy of government, maintain order, and protect the disadvantaged. These people always sought less government and, since their generations in Scotland, they were suspicious of their rulers in proportion to the distance they were removed from the seat of government.

Simultaneous to the political influences that were shaping his view of civil government, Alexander Martin was embracing the influences of the Presbyterian Church as his religious heritage and Princeton and the Scottish Enlightenment as his educational bias. Time and again in his life it was the influence of his religious background or the college or the two in tandem that defined Martin's actions.[20] These influences are first publicly evident at the time of the Regulation—the image of David Caldwell, the Presbyterian minister, and Alexander Martin, fellow Princetonians, moving between the forces of the royal governor with his colonial gentry and the angry, dispossessed, acquisitive insurgency on the frontier.

4

A Move to Guilford County

The colonial assembly, attempting to defuse the concentration of Regulator forces in the frontier counties of Orange and Rowan, determined that subdividing those counties would weaken the Regulator resolve and divide their leadership. Out of Orange County came Chatham and Wake and out of Rowan came Surry.[1] Between Orange and Rowan, between Hillsborough and Salisbury, they directed that a new county be formed and called Guilford. The eastern third of Guilford was from Orange and the remainder from Rowan. Alexander Martin was chosen as a commissioner to employ the workmen and run the boundaries of the new county that included Martin's grant on Dan River at Jacobs Creek. Martin was spending enough time there with his brothers that the Moravians noted him as living on Dan River.[2] In a few months, they would be joined by their mother and sisters and the move from New Jersey, by way of Virginia, would be complete. Martin's brother, Samuel, located in Mecklenburg County and become part of its leadership. Alexander kept his interests in Salisbury and was there for long periods of time. He was elected to the bar of the new Guilford County in 1772. The operation of the county government was completed with Thomas Henderson as the first clerk and Sam Martin as county register.[3] On March 6, 1773, the clerk of the Crown certified the election of Alexander Martin and John Kimbrough to the colonial assembly.[4] Martin replaced a Regulator, William Fields. Kimbrough was the man whose house had been chosen by Martin and Frohock as the site of the unrealized meeting with Governor Tryon and the Regulators two years earlier.[5] A significant bill appeared in the assembly in 1773 concerning the election of vestrymen in Guilford County. When the county was proposed, a new parish of the established church, Unity Parish, was to encompass the same boundaries. This was a normal practice to abet the growth of the Anglican

Church. The attempt to have the Freeholders of the Parish of Unity meet to elect vestrymen was aborted. At a meeting called for the purpose, so few members of the established church were present that the body elected Presbyterians as vestrymen. Martin and Kimbrough then introduced, and the governor signed, an act to dissolve the vestry. The governor advised Earl Dartmouth that the act was necessary "in consequence of an illegal election made of the Vestry to the great disquiet of the Presbyterians in the said Parish."[6] Tryon had succeeded in concentrating the Regulators who were predominantly Quakers or Presbyterians. Guilford County sent a warning that the frontier would not be a welcome field for the growth of the Church of England.

Alexander Martin, throughout his life, had a close relationship of mutual confidence with the Moravians, a religious brotherhood that had settled an extensive tract they called Wachovia between Salisbury and Martin's home on the Dan. First, as a youth in New Jersey, he had been familiar with the Moravians in Northampton County, Pennsylvania, across the Delaware River.[7] On his arrival in North Carolina, he found them his near neighbors and he soon became a frequent guest in transit. Their chief town was organized in 1771 and named Salem. Unlike many of his covetous neighbors, who were always suspicious of the self-contained Moravians, Martin considered these people essential to the frontier and a trust grew into a friendship of critical value.

Important to the Moravians at this moment was the creation of Surry County out of Rowan. Martin became their confidant on the developments, supplying them information about the political decisions being made. Their religious isolation made it improbable that any of their members would be elected to be part of a civil government even though that authority might be making decisions having direct bearing on them and their property. Martin respected their beliefs and he understood that they would always be an island of economic success on a frontier populated as his was by historically landless farm laborers, "forced off their land by Enclosures; Highlanders exiled by the Clearance; and Irishmen fleeing from famine or evicted by their landowners."[8] Martin saw the Moravians as capable of an essential service as frontier merchants.

When William Tryon departed for New York, Josiah Martin, son of a sugar planter from the Leeward Island of Antigua, replaced him. Martin had advanced from an uneventful military career to his new office through the continued advocacy in London of his brother, Samuel. He approached his appointment eagerly, hoping to pacify the Regulators and improve the lot of the colony through closer ties with England.[9] Josiah Martin, soon after his arrival in the colony, initiated a grand tour during which he attempted to become acquainted with the regional leadership and to demonstrate his accessibility. In the neighborhoods of the Regulators, he took particular pains to listen to the details of the grievances and on occasion freely expressed his opinion that the action of his predecessor had shown "folly, extravagance and cruelty."[10] His demeanor won over much of the Regulator leadership that, having finally been defeated by the Crown representatives and forced to take an oath of loyalty, were determined to honor that oath. This was particularly true of those he met in the southern third of Guilford (the part that later became Randolph County).

The second colonial assembly under Josiah Martin convened at New Bern on January 23, 1773. The formalities that qualified the delegates and certified the election of the leadership were designed to imitate those used by the King and Parliament, confirming the order of sovereignty. With John Harvey in the chair as Speaker, the assembly considered the two proposals provided by the governor in his speech to the delegates. The first was a general pardon and oblivion for those who had been involved in the Regulator uprising. On this issue perhaps no one in the assembly was better informed than Alexander Martin. His presence at Salisbury as a negotiator with the Regulator force and a few months later his efforts with the Rev. David Caldwell to prevent bloodshed at Alamance made him an informed and credible authority on the issues and the campaign. He represented the county geographically at the heart of the controversy. He also shared either the religious belief or the cultural roots or both of many of the Regulators. The eastern elite had precious little understanding of the concerns of the Regulators, viewing them as the uneducated poor of the frontier. In his person Alexander Martin contradicted their disdainful judgment. What they did not recognize early was that Martin represented the Scotch-Irish Presbyterian who would support the developing revolution on the North Carolina frontier in tandem with the eastern economic establishment. It was not the Regulators who would evolve into revolutionaries. Their perspective was too selfish, too clannish. They tended not to trust any attempt at community and distrusted any laws, especially those that sacrificed self-interest for the public good. Martin understood their hostility, and he became adept at pacifying their self-indulgence so as to marginalize their political impact. In this assembly, he became their advocate in support of Governor Josiah Martin in the passage of the laws that pardoned their earlier transgressions.

Alexander Martin served on the Committee on Military Claims that heard from those who had provided service, provisions, or livestock for the government campaign against the Regulators. When the assembly committee on pardon and oblivion presented the list of "persons concerned in the late Insurrection," they had struck off the names of James Hunter, Samuel Deviney and Ninian Bell Hamilton. The council objected.

The other recommendation that Governor Martin made to the assembly concerned the so-called court laws. Alexander Martin was placed on the committee to draft the new court act that would replace the one passed under Governor Tryon in 1768 that was expiring.[11] Governor Martin made his recommendations on reform based on his own study of the colonial system. He suggested that the council appoint seven magistrates in each court division to hold court of pleas and quarter sessions in their counties. He made other less critical recommendations but the sticking point in the court bill was not so much the makeup of the courts as the authority to be given to particular courts in the colony.

The 1768 court bill had established a system of courts through which creditors could attach property, within the province, of debtors who did not live in the province. This was a reasonable avenue of recovery but when the act was received by the Board of Trade in London, it was approved only because it included a clause allowing it to lapse in three years. This was not an issue unique to North Carolina. London opposed so-called foreign attachment.

Under these conditions, Governor Martin urged the assembly to omit any clause concerning foreign attachment and its concurrent system of courts. Like all other colonial governors, Martin had been advised to reject any court bills containing foreign attachment unless they included a clause that suspended their application until approved by the Crown.[12]

The bill reported out of the committee was the first to have Alexander Martin's legislative input. Passed by the assembly, it included the attachment provision and was vetoed by the governor. The assembly then passed a bill applying it only for six months—an attempt to buy time—and the council rejected it. Pressure was building on the assembly at the prospect of collapse of the court system. Finally, a court bill was sent forward including attachment but suspending its application until the "pleasure of the Crown." The governor and council approved it but, still containing the attachment clause, it was rejected in London.

By March, North Carolina was essentially without courts. "Litigation ceased, large debts could not be collected, and criminals escaped arrest and punishment."[13] Fear was rising in the assembly that order would be swept away, particularly in the frontier counties so recently involved in insurrection and containing a larger proportion of the lawless and dispossessed. Aside from his concerns about order, Alexander Martin had particular self-interest in the continuity of the court system. The courts were his professional stage and his chief source of income. His political base in Rowan, Orange, Surry and Guilford counties laid in his official status as a lawyer, an officer of the court. He had no conflict with the tradition of the English law.

Alexander and Josiah Martin were diligent in seeking compromise. The governor claimed the Royal prerogative and appointed justices to hold courts of *oyer* and *terminer* for hearing pleas in criminal cases. When the third assembly met in December, William Fields replaced John Kimbrough as a representative for Guilford County.[14] The governor presented a compromise on the court bill suggested by Lord Dartmouth that would allow the attachment provision if the clause would be applied within the colony, showing proof of the intent of the defendant to abscond beyond the law to avoid payment of just obligations. This was the same form of attachment allowable in the commercial cities of England.[15]

Under the leadership of John Harvey, the assembly was becoming more combative. He placed letters from Committees of Correspondence in other colonies before the assembly that urged North Carolina to establish its own committee of intercolonial correspondence. When such a committee emerged, its members were all from the powerful eastern establishment. They were the "artful and designing men," whom the governor complained were leading the assembly.[16]

The assembly rejected the compromise on attachment that had come from London, finding that the protection was inadequate for merchants, and they rejected the governor's authority to establish courts of *oyer* and *terminer*. They made their case, passed again their old court bill with foreign attachment, and the council rejected it. Governor Martin's response was to prorogue the assembly. Assembly members returned home to measure the fears of their constituents, and the governor attempted once more to persuade London to approve attachment as it had been passed in New York, Virginia, and Pennsylvania. Alexander Martin preferred compromise on the issue of attachment but the power lay with the eastern merchants. They were determined that London would not succeed in placing them at a legal disadvantage to which the neighbor colonies were not held.

When the assembly reconvened in March 1774, the governor asked the assembly to pass the court bill, omitting attachment that he suggested would be passed in a separate bill, as was the precedent in other colonies. Supported by the council, he was rejected by the assembly, which claimed they had consulted their constituents and found enthusiastic support of the firm position of the assembly on attachment. The court bill was thus being held hostage at the price of the attachment clause although the assembly did allow the establishment of inferior courts limited in their authority to cases involving less than £20 proclamation money, and they established courts of *oyer* and *terminer* and general bail delivery, all of which was approved by the governor. Again, the governor prorogued the assembly to meet again in two months.

The stagnation of the colonial court system found sheriffs forbidden, by the assembly, from collecting poll taxes that were the means of paying the public debt while the governor was issuing specific directives to the same sheriffs to make such collections.[17] Alexander Martin accepted appointment by the governor as a judge of the court of *oyer* and *terminer* at Salisbury in 1774 and again in 1775.[18] Law and order still dominated his perception.

Word was received in the east that the first of the so-called Coercive and Intolerable Acts, the bill closing the port of Boston, was being debated in London. Then the rumor spread that the governor would not call an assembly blocking the possibility for North Carolina to choose delegates to a Continental Congress. Speaker Harvey countered that possibility by issuing a handbill calling for a provincial assembly to meet at New Bern on August 25, 1774.[19] There were no delegates seated at this first provincial assembly from Guilford, Surry or Wake counties, an indication that the radicals had yet not forged a broad-enough alliance to bring the colony into revolution.

This provincial congress met only three days at New Bern in front of the governor and in spite of him. They professed loyalty to King George III but rejected the right of Parliament to impose taxes on any colony—a right they reserved to the colonial assemblies. They elected delegates to the Continental Congress called for September and adopted an economic boycott of England in the form of a nonimportation, nonexportation policy. The three-day Congress effectively established self-government in the colony in defiance of royal authority. Although they were sparsely represented and thus peripheral to the debate, it was obvious to the westerners that North Carolina was in the hands of the Whig elite.

For potential leaders like Alexander Martin it was a difficult situation. He was not a firebrand by nature. He was an advocate, a man who carefully examined the issues, options, and character of a situation. He could not be called an opportunist but he knew the value of timing for any action. Throughout his adult life, more adventurers and rough frontiersmen than gentlemen surrounded him, but he was at home with either. He did not pledge his support in bold strokes, by jumping onto an issue and leading the advance, but he confirmed his commitment by years of reliable and consistent support. Therefore, he was seldom the hero, which, as a role, made him uncomfortable. Instead, he represented dependable experience that his associates, neighbors, and the state repeatedly turned to in confident expectation.

The First Continental Congress established a continental association that was instituted provincially by a system of Committees of Safety. Before such committees were authorized by the second provincial congress, Alexander Martin denounced before the Rowan County committee two members of the Rowan bar, John Ross Dunn and Benjamin Booth Boote, questioning their loyalty and recommending their expulsion from the colony.[20] Dunn had helped Martin in the latter's first years in Salisbury but as early as 1771 they had clashed over the question of the location of the courthouse in newly established Surry County. Dunn supported Gideon Wright, a local Tory, on whose land the court had originally been located. Martin supported the brothers Martin and John Armstrong, local Whigs, who became good friends of Martin, in their advocacy of a tract three-quarters of a mile east that they owned.[21] Martin may have only acted as an ad hoc prosecutor in this action against Dunn and Boote but the public accepted him as a Whig.[22]

Although the early county records are sparse, the question of the location of the Guilford County Courthouse was similarly contested, leading to speculation over time that "skullduggery" was involved.[23] In February 1773, John Kimbrough presented a petition to the assembly, altering the place originally chosen for the courthouse. A counterproposal was filed by 248 signatories and was approved by the next assembly and the governor in 1774. The county at this site purchased an acre from John Campbell.[24] The conflict continued. It was Alexander Martin who advanced the bill to relocate the courthouse according to the final petition, and a year later he and Thomas Henderson had bought the 100 acres on which the courthouse had already been built. They named the place Martinville.[25]

Through actions of Alexander Martin at the three courts in Rowan, Surry, and Guilford it is possible to observe his evolution as a Whig and his efforts to establish himself in the contest for power in the county governments. His political development is concurrent with the assumption of the Scotch-Irish Presbyterians of political power on the North Carolina frontier. It can be seen as a direct result of the Regulator insurrection that an alliance was forged between the tidewater elite and these Presbyterians and that alliance constituted the heart of the Whig coalition in the state.[26] Governor Josiah Martin contended correctly that most of the Regulators, having sworn a new oath to the Crown following Alamance, would retain their loyalty in the face of the extending Whig influence. This view was particularly applicable to the concentrations of Regulators, who were also Quakers, as in southern Guilford. It did not hold among the Regulators, who were Scotch-Irish Presbyterians, mainly because these people were influenced by the leadership of such men as Alexander Martin, James Hunter, James Martin, John Armstrong, Thomas Henderson, and particularly the three Presbyterian ministers, David Caldwell, Hugh McAden, and Henry Patillo. These last three had so ardently pledged their loyalty and that of their congregations in 1768 to Governor Tryon. Out of this group it was Alexander Martin who was assuming greater political leadership.

In defiance of the governor, John Harvey called the second provincial congress to meet at New Bern the day before Josiah Martin had summoned the assembly into session in the same place. Guilford County was not recorded in attendance in the assembly. This may have been an oversight but more likely it was a declaration on Martin's part. He was recorded as the lone Guilford delegate at the provincial congress that confirmed North Carolina as a member of the Continental Association.[27]

Operating as one of the Scottish merchant/traders that so concerned the provincial assembly was Charles Gallaway, who lived just ten miles down Dan River from Martin. As early as 1765 he had located on the south side of the river adjoining the celebrated 26,000 acres that William Byrd II had claimed as the "Land of Eden."[28] There he traded in land and kept a store at a settlement called Sauratown purchasing tobacco, hides and livestock to send to the Scottish merchant representatives in Petersburg, Virginia. In the face of the suspicion directed by the Whigs against such representatives of the Scottish merchant houses, Gallaway became a member of the local Committee of Safety, establishing himself in the Whig cause.

James Parke Farley was building a mansion on the Eden plantation that his father had purchased from the Byrds. He was married to the daughter of William Byrd III, who was considered one of the outspoken Tory sympathizers in Virginia. Farley had been born on the island of Antigua and was well acquainted with Josiah Martin. Wrestling with these contesting loyalties, Farley joined Alexander Martin and Thomas Henderson as part of the Guilford County delegates to the critical third provincial congress in August.

On June 2, 1775, Josiah Martin left the seat of royal power in the colony, the Governor's Palace at New Bern, and took refuge at Ft. Johnston near Wilmington. With the remaining loyal members of the council, he attempted to preserve his authority in form while devising means of restoring his government and the rightful claim of the Crown.

On the first day of June, at the opening session of the Rowan County Court after the oath to the Crown was administered to the court officers, Alexander Martin, as presiding judge, made a speech that attests to the tenacity of his belief in the law and in maintaining public order.[29] These were not the words of a revolutionary.

> If revolution and civil commotion arise in our state, do you, gentlemen, endeavor to calm their boisterous effect by a spirit of loyalty to his majesty's government in your several spheres of influence on the true principles of the constitution of Britain and this province. Let not violence, rapine, and licentiousness under the cloaks of liberty stalk round you with impunity while so large a share of the reclaiming and chastening powers of justice is lodged in your hands.
>
> Let me dismiss you then, gentlemen, with this serious injunction: to support and maintain and defend as far as in you lies, the constitution and the laws of your country, the just prerogatives of the crown, and the declared rights of the people. This is liberty, this loyalty. Do you thus, loyal gentlemen, and you will be free.[30]

Martin was yet refusing to accept the collision course between the two stanchions of liberty that he was defending — the prerogatives of the Crown and the declared rights of the people. He still viewed them as compatible when all around him circumstances were declaring that they were not.

Before the end of this spring session of court, however, a dramatic declaration made by the citizens of Mecklenburg County to the Continental Congress ultimately ignited the frontier. A rider arrived in Salisbury, James Jack, on his way from Charlotte to Philadelphia with a dispatch of resolves. A "Declaration of Independence," the authenticity of which remains fiercely debated, may have supplemented the Mecklenburg Resolves of May 1775.[31] Martin probably knew Jack who had settled with his family west of Salisbury in 1770. He saw among the signatories to the resolves some Princeton friends, Hezekiah James Balch ('66), Ephraim Brevard ('68), and Waightstill Avery ('66), and he was told that Brevard had authored the resolves.[32] He did not see the signature of his brother, Samuel Martin. The resolves were read in open court, arousing the Whig forces, but the court continued to administer justice in the King's name.[33] When Jack reached Philadelphia, he received a cautious reception from the delegates who considered the Resolves, that declared among other features that Crown laws and authority were null and void, to be premature.[34]

Martin, continuing to act as an advisor to the Moravians, attempted to assist them in understanding the parties to the rebellion. Gideon Wright of Surry and his brothers, he told the Moravians, were "obstinate enemies" of this country.[35] The Moravians knew about the Dunn-Boote incident at Salisbury and of Martin's involvement. The fact that letters of these gentlemen to associates in Britain had been seized, opened and used against them became a warning to Moravians. "From this time on we will have to be careful about our correspondence."[36] They were wisely reluctant to be seen as partial to any of the belligerents.

The third provincial congress was assembled at Hillsborough on the 20th of August at a location that removed the delegates from the observation of Governor Josiah Martin and that recognized the importance of the frontier to a broad-based Whig leadership. There were seven delegates from Guilford County: George Cortner, William Dent, Ransom Southerland, Nathaniel Williams, Thomas Henderson, James Parke Farley and Alexander Martin.[37] Martin's brother, Samuel, and his close friend, Waightstill Avery, were also delegates from Mecklenburg County. The governor had fled and this was the first North Carolina assembly to call itself a provincial congress, however, the colony was ambivalent about the commitment to the united colonies. Parliament, seeking to punish those colonies for disorders of the spring, approved a restraining act that cut off colonial trade with Britain and the West Indies but exempted North Carolina from the prohibition.[38] Josiah Martin campaigned for a policy of redemption, based on anticipated Tory support anchored on the Highlanders of the Cape Fear and the Regulators of the Piedmont.

An initial act of the congress was the appointment of a committee of 13 to confer with the Regulators to undermine their loyalty to the crown. The congress had heard that "Hunter, the Regulator," threatened to bring 1,000 men from Guilford County to interrupt the proceedings.[39] The Guilford County delegates were therefore threatened by their own neighbors—a demonstration of how narrowly the Piedmont was divided.

The congress proposed a test oath for its members that professed loyalty to the

Crown while declaring Parliament had no right to impose taxes. The delegates were bound to the acts of the Continental Congress. Alexander Martin was assigned to the committee to regulate "Internal Peace, Order and Safety in this Province," the committee on intelligence, and the committee to investigate the loyalty of a certain member of the Congress and to receive petitions of Congress.[40]

The provisional government that was established at Hillsborough has been called the most elaborate on the continent. It established a congress of five delegates from each county that elected a 13-member provincial council that in turn held the chief executive and administrative power. The royal governor and council were effectively replaced although the congress, with each act, proclaimed that, with redress of grievance, the colony would gladly resubmit to royal authority.

Alexander Martin was positioned to assume a leading civil appointment within the new government,[41] but at this critical moment he abandoned the civil for the military. The congress ordered two battalions of Continentals to be raised in the colony. Each battalion was to contain 500 men under the command of James Moore of New Hanover and Robert Howe of Brunswick as Colonels. Alexander Martin was selected as second in command under Howe as lieutenant colonel of the Second North Carolina Regiment of Continentals.[42]

5

War against the British and the Incident at Germantown

As it had been possible to observe Alexander Martin's progressive transition from court official for King George to Whig, it was impossible to have anticipated the next life choice he made in public leadership. The provincial congress on September 1, 1775, authorized the formation of two regiments to be incorporated into the Continental army. Of the 1,000 men raised for the two regiments, 400 were to be stationed in Wilmington and 200 each at New Bern, Edenton, and Salisbury. When the regiments were organized, they elected James Moore of Wilmington and Robert Howe of Brunswick as colonels, and Francis Nash of Hillsborough and Alexander Martin of Guilford as lieutenant colonels. Moore and Howe had each seen service in the French and Indian War and they and Nash had served as part of Governor Tryon's artillery at the Battle of Alamance. Only Alexander Martin can be said to have had no military training nor could any previous experience be said to have prepared him for the military. He had served with Howe and Moore on key committees of the congress establishing the test oaths and the committee to regulate internal peace, order, and safety: each a significant step in the organization of Whig control of the government. Nash was from Hillsborough where the provincial assembly was in session but it was really Martin who represented the people of the frontier on this military high command.

Alexander Martin, having navigated deftly into prominence as an educated, articulate representative of the people of frontier North Carolina, found himself in the vortex of revolutionary fervor. The Whig elite directing the evolution of this new government badly needed a token representative of the frontier in the top leadership of its new army, particularly one who could embody the Scotch-Irish Presbyterians they viewed as their most likely allies. Alexander Martin fit the mold and he was present at that moment of decision. Sombe militia commanders from the west, like Thomas Polk of Mecklenburg, were present at the congress and available but they already had positions of established political and military power in North Carolina that they would have to give up to become part of this new army. Concerned as he must certainly have been, Alexander Martin could do nothing more than accept this new role with the same bravado that was infecting all the Whigs.

Martin acted quickly to assemble men and supplies. Captain John Armstrong had been at the Hillsborough congress with a volunteer company of Surry men to protect the delegates from any hostile Tory action. He arrived back in Salem with an order from Alexander Martin directing the Moravians to furnish articles of clothing for the new enlistees. The invoice was for "70 yards of Osnabrugs, 1½ yards Russia Drill, 12 yards Russia Duck, one string of button Molds and 10 Ounces of Thread."[1] Payment was to be in the new continental paper currency, which presented a dilemma for the Moravian merchants. The paper was to be equal to silver and gold and to be retired in two years.[2] The brethren knew better, as did the delegates who declared that anyone who refused the currency, or talked against it, lost the right to trade and would be considered an enemy. In 1775 there were but 77 people in Salem; throughout the war, however, the Moravians were regularly required to provide supplies for both sides as battle lines waxed and waned. They were being paid constantly depreciating currency so that every sale was a loss, but they endured.

For a brief time following the congress, Martin returned to his family on the Dan River to prepare for the war. The military assignment that he had assumed might mark his family for attacks by local Tories and any organized military force. He brought with him an appointment, signed by Samuel Johnston as president of the provincial congress, for his brother, James Martin, as commander commandant of the Guilford regiment of militia.[3]

All that was military was new to most of the colonials. In Surry County, men who had enlisted in the Continental Line thought they would remain at home. Martin had to explain that they "may be called to Virginia, South Carolina or even Boston." His enlistees for the district were to be stationed at Salisbury and from there they were to be trained in arms and marched to the frontier "to learn the Motions of the Indians." Some men arrived without guns and had to be reminded that their enlistment gave them "5¾ p month," but on the understanding that they had to have their own guns.[4] Ever the conciliator even as he prepared for a fight, Martin proposed a test oath for the Tory, Gideon Wright, and his brother that he hoped they would sign. He declared, "I mean to show as much Indulgence as possible to ignorant people I would have no man used ill."[5]

On October 4, the men Martin had enlisted in Guilford County marched through Salem on their way to Salisbury. Untrained, ill-equipped, and inadequately clothed, his force was not calculated to convince the Moravians that it was formidable enough to challenge British regulars. Martin did not arrive in Salem until later in the day. He remained overnight and attended the evening Bible reading and attempted to be reassuringly friendly to the Moravians whom he knew too well he would need as a crucial source of supplies.

Tory hostility abounded, and the Tories attempted to counter every act and effort made by the colonels to assemble a fighting force. James Henderson recounted the efforts of Tory William Moore to interrupt recruiting, as he "likewise told the people who would have enlisted as Minute Men, that he could not see how they would come at their pay as there was no regular Committee or Congress, thereby prevented the people from enlisting, & also in telling said that Col. Martin was a rogue and a fool, & ruining the country by virtue of his present proceedings as a Colonel for Liberty, and told the people that if they took none of the public money, they would have [none] of it to pay."[6]

In the early winter, with training incomplete, Howe was ordered to move against Governor Dunmore of Virginia who was attacking and burning property around Norfolk.[7] Martin was left behind to continue the training and recruiting on the frontier. In December, the two companies he had training at Salisbury under Captains George Davidson and John Armstrong were ordered to join the Mecklenburg militia under Colonel Thomas Polk, the Rowan militia under Colonel Griffith Rutherford, and the Tryon militia under Colonel Thomas Neal and move south against a band of Tories identified as Scovillites in up-country South Carolina.[8] It was called the Snow Campaign because of a severe early snow that made the movement of forces treacherous. The North Carolina troops joined with forces from South Carolina at the Saluda River and came under the command of General Richardson of South Carolina.[9] The combined forces moved against the Tory concentration under the command of Cunningham and Fletchall at the fort at Ninety-six. Under the cover of the freak snowstorm on December 22, the Tories attempted an escape but were overtaken and defeated by the Patriot forces. About 400 Tories were taken prisoner and the royal cause was left in disarray in much of South Carolina.[10] The campaigns against Norfolk and against the Scovillites in South Carolina were the first occasions in the war when one colony came to the military aid of another.

The sally into South Carolina by the new recruits from the frontier gave them a first experience with battle even though it was against mostly irregular troops. The timing for them was fortuitous since, within little more than a month, the Tories in North Carolina were planning a similar challenge to the sovereignty of the provincial congress. Josiah Martin, still claiming his authority as governor, issued a proclamation calling upon the king's faithful subjects to rally to the royal standard. The governor had devised a four-part offensive in the colony that had received support from London. He proposed to raise within the state a force of 3,000 Highland Scots, 3,000 Regulators, and 3,000 Tories. Lord Cornwallis was to bring seven regiments of British regulars to the state. Sir Peter Parker was to accompany Cornwallis with a fleet of 54 ships. In the final element, Sir Henry Clinton was to bring 2,000 seasoned regulars from Boston. All were to rendezvous at Brunswick no later than February 15, 1776. Had it been possible to bring all these parts into junction, the force would surely have destroyed the Whig campaign in North Carolina and it would have driven a wedge that would have divided the possibility of a continental union.[11]

Robert Howe, at Norfolk, was soon to be promoted to brigadier general and Alexander Martin was confirmed in command of the Second North Carolina Regiment. He still had only those troops he recruited after Howe had departed for Norfolk but he continued to recruit and train and the Snow Campaign had given him a degree of experience in battle. It was the First North Carolina Regiment under General Moore that was considered the only drilled Continentals available to the defense of North Carolina. On February 19, Wilmington Minutemen and Duplin Rangers reinforced Moore and his regiment below Cross Creek.[12] Other Whig irregular troops were en route including the Guilford militia under Colonel James Martin.[13]

Alexander Martin was ordered by the provincial congress to order out the militia forces of western North Carolina and to rendezvous at Cross Creek. Earlier in the winter many of these men had trained at Salisbury under Martin. Now they were the nucleus of these rough militia units.

The militia of Wilkes County set out on the 13th under Captain Jesse Walton and a few days later they joined Colonel Martin Armstrong at the head of the Surry County militia near Richmond Courthouse. When they reached Randolph County, they joined Alexander Martin en route "with a small body of troops under his command."[14]

The march of the Guilford militia was less orderly and it demonstrated the independence that these citizen soldiers displayed in the face of command. On the 23rd at Cross Roads, on the way to Cross Creek, Captain Alexander Hunter openly deserted his command and behaved "in a tyrannical and lawless manner" to his men. James Martin, contrary to law but perhaps with a mutiny on his hands, issued a warrant to one of his officers to tie up several of his men and to levy £10 upon their estates "without hearing any excuse or admitting them to a trial by a Court Martial."[15] Both apparent abuses of power were brought under control before they reached their destination.

Most of the troops from the western counties arrived at Cross Creek a day or more after the battle at Moore's Creek Bridge. Part of their contribution to the action was their confirmation of the defeat of the Tory/Highlander expectations. The arrival of these men from the west validated the claims of the Whigs to have control of the colony.

The troops under Alexander Martin were assigned to round up the defeated Highlanders and their sympathizers. Richard Caswell ordered that all suspected persons, all Highlanders, and all Regulators were to be disarmed. Scouts following the flight of the defeated Tories reported a concentration in flight toward Cross Creek, and Colonel Martin was directed to intercept them.[16] James Martin concluded: "Said Colonel Martin and myself took most of their head men and imprisoned them and then I was ordered home with my regiment."[17] The raising of the militia had consumed about two months and had the effect, on the western militias and the Continentals under Alexander Martin, of being more like a training exercise.

Moore's Creek was one of the first absolute decisions won by American arms, and "the abilities of the North Carolina colonels, even those who played minor roles, reached astronomical heights in northern eyes." The president of Yale penned this praise in his diary: "The Colonels Moore, Martin, Caswell, Polk, Thackson, Lillington & Long, have great Merit; any one of these Gent, in this Country would be an over match for a Howe, Burgoyne, or a Clinton."[18]

A month later, Martin took formal command as colonel of the Second North

Carolina Regiment when Robert Howe received his promotion. That action was taken by the fourth provincial congress meeting at Halifax in April, which added four new Continental regiments.[19] The Second Regiment under Martin was officered by Lt. Colonel John Patton and Major John White.

On April 12, the provincial congress reported out resolves that empowered the delegates of North Carolina in the Continental Congress to declare independence in harmony with delegates of the other colonies, to form foreign alliances, to form a constitution and laws, and to appoint delegates to future assemblies of the colonies. It was the first public expression of the right and desire for independence approved by any colonial assembly.[20] It was a month before Virginia followed suit. The passage of the Halifax Resolves is more remarkable because it came in the colony that contained perhaps the highest proportionate concentration of loyalists and was therefore, according to the London Board of Trade, thought to be the weakest link in colonial resolve. The decisive action can be directly attributed to the success of the Moore's Creek Campaign.

On April 13, the day after the passage of the resolves, Samuel Johnston informed the state's delegates in Philadelphia that General Henry Clinton had arrived in the Cape Fear area with perhaps 400 British troops. The forces of Lord Cornwallis and the fleet of Sir Peter Parker joined him there. This formidable gathering represented the linchpin of the grand strategy advocated by Governor Josiah Martin, but it was pathetically out of sequence and doomed. With no one to greet them and shadowed at each turn by General James Moore, the British weighed anchor and sailed toward Charleston, abandoning for now their effort in North Carolina.

The threat to Charleston resulted in a call from South Carolina for support, and General Lee immediately dispatched the First and Second North Carolina Regiments to their defense. They reached Charleston on the 11th of June and twelve days later the British fleet attacked Fort Moultrie. Sir Peter Parker's overconfident certainty of the invincibility of the fleet led to a humiliating defeat before British land forces could be effectively dispatched. The North Carolina troops had been stationed on the mainland in defense of the city and looked on at the ten-hour bombardment between the fleet and fort until the shattered British withdrew. Although they had seen action only of the periphery, the North Carolina regiments were highly praised by Lee for their "zealous and spirited" action.[21]

In New Jersey, sometime in the late summer, the Rev. Robert Martin died; he was Alexander Martin's uncle and had preceded him at Princeton. It had once been a family hope that Alexander would follow him into the Presbyterian ministry. A childless widower, Robert Martin divided his estate among the families of his siblings. Alexander's brother, the minister's namesake, was left £50 and Alexander was given £20. The most unusual aspect of his will was his gift of "all the remainder of my estate principal and interest for the education of the poor and pious youth who may design with the blessings of heaven, to enter into the ministerial character of the Presbyterian denomination, in North Carolina." The Rev. Martin may have been personally committed to the growth of the Presbyterian Church in North Carolina through mission efforts that were strong in the church in New Jersey and Pennsylvania. Since only Robert and Alexander, of those specified as legatees of his will, had settled in North Carolina, they were in a position to see the benefit of this very specific gift. It would also suggest that Robert and Alexander were still involved in the Presbyterian Church rather than the Anglican Church of their late brother, Thomas. As revolution broke over barriers, a Scots Presbyterian infused the mission cause with one last directed encouragement.[22]

The fifth and final provincial congress convened at Halifax on the 12th of November. A committee was formed to create a constitution and bill of rights for the governing of the state of North Carolina. Richard Caswell, in the chair as president, was credited with leading this convention in the establishment of the state government in a period of a dozen days. It was still the Whig elite of the east that controlled the action of this assembly. Alexander Martin was absent in command but his Princeton friend and Presbyterian minister, David Caldwell, allowed himself to be elected, although he considered it inappropriate for ministers to be elected as representatives to future state assemblies. Influenced by the rigid Scotch-Irish Presbyterianism of the frontier, and as an example of the desperation of the need of the Whigs for the support of the Presbyterians, the assembly approved the Rev. Caldwell's exclusionary clause on religion to be added to the Constitution:

> No person who shall deny the being of God, or the truth of the Protestant religion, or the divine authority of either the Old or New Testament, or who shall hold religious principles incompatible with the freedom and safety of the State, shall be capable of holding any office or place of trust or profit in the civil department, within the State.[23]

This incident is important because it illustrates the righteous, rigid, and self-absorbed attitude of the Scotch-Irish frontier that traditionally had to be kept in check by men like Alexander Martin. Contrary to an expression of Scottish Enlightenment, this zealous intolerance was a Presbyterian counterbalance that Martin would not confirm. In this case the eastern Whigs had to accept the uncompromising view of David Caldwell as the price of larger support for the cause. They did so knowing that men like Thomas Burke, a Roman Catholic, could be excluded if the clause was applied, but they were pragmatic enough to believe that, if they continued to control the real power, they could apply such clauses as they saw fit. This was no solution. It was an accommodation that at some future time would have to be addressed.

The defeat of the British southern strategy to break the colonial chain at Moore's Creek, and then at Charleston, had the effect of closing the southern theater of war. Although General Howe continued to petition the Continental Congress, predicting that the British would return to the south in even stronger force, the real danger was now in the north where Washington was holding on at Morristown and the Continental Congress had abandoned Philadelphia. By late March, General James Moore was organizing an expedition of the North Carolina regiments to reinforce Washington. Wisely reflecting uncertain realities, he "thought it prudent [not] to order out any Troops from the Counties of Cumberland, Chatham, Guilford & Anson where most of the late Insurgents came from, as they may be necessary to prevent those people from any further Attempts to disturb the peace of the country by disarming & securing the disaffected Ministerial Emissaries."[24] Moore and Martin advised the Council of State of "sundry medicines" that had been brought into the state by Monsieur Renusson; they suggested that these would be needed by the army.[25] Unfortunately, General Moore returned briefly to his Cape Fear home where his brother was ill. By the 15th both he and his brother were dead.[26] General Francis Nash, who continued to gather the Continentals at Halifax, succeeded Moore.

Alexander Martin remained at Salisbury for most of the year following the Moore's Creek conflict and continued to grow the army, train new recruits, and stabilize the frontier.[27] Captain John Armstrong of his command became the acknowledged protector of the Moravians along with Charles Gallaway, their friend and Martin's Dan River neighbor.[28] Martin was in position with the Continental Line when Nash moved them north to Georgetown, where all were inoculated against smallpox.[29] Martin wrote John Hancock, president of the Continental Congress, as the troops waited inoculation near Fredericksburg, advising the Congress of the condition of his men. "We are badly armed, and would beg a supply at some proper place. The arms we have we propose sending back to N Carolina as they are scarce worth bringing."[30]

Most of Alexander Martin's Carolina farm boys had never seen a town bigger than Salisbury. Their wonder as they became part of this moving army can hardly be imagined. On their arrival, Washington wisely restricted access to Philadelphia by permit only, an acknowledgment as much of the provincialism of the troops as it was the terror of the citizens in the face of these ruffians.

The regiments were moved to Trenton where Lt. Colonel Ingram of the Eighth North Carolina Regiment resigned. The field officers were convened by Colonel Martin, as the senior regimental commander, to pick a successor.[31] There was already much infighting among the officers, most of whom had never been part of an army. Commanders were dealing with desertion and insubordination, female camp followers, and the insufficient equipment and clothing they had brought from North Carolina. More disruptive at this point were members of the Congress, like Thomas Burke, who considered themselves divinely gifted with military and political insight on all issues. Burke made himself the gadfly of every activity involving the North Carolina regiments. He was fed provocative information by every side. This citizen army, lightly tested in battle or command, was more infected by the cabals of personality than the scourge of smallpox. Martin's position represented a coveted target.

Washington moved south after it became obvious that the British under Lord Howe intended to take Philadelphia. Although he wondered at the impression that his ill-clothed and irregularly trained Continental army would make on the threatened civilians of Philadelphia, he could at least demonstrate some courage in numbers. As his army marched through the city, its "free style of marching and lack of uniforms" aside, Washington showed his men to best advantage and the crowds cheered apprehensively.[32]

Howe landed at the head of Elk River and Washington decided to block his march at Brandywine Creek, aware that, if he failed, the way was open to the Schuylkill River. The North Carolina regiments were part of William Maxwell's corps of the division commanded by Nathaniel Greene.[33] The initial British attack at Chadd's Ford in the face of Washington's concentration was by a party of Hessians who were repulsed by Maxwell with heavy losses. Appearing to be reinforcing the Hessians, the British succeeded in an outflanking maneuver by crossing at the upper fords of the Brandywine. Sullivan, Sterling, and Stephens were rushed in to repulse the crossing but without high ground they could not hold. It was only the arrival of Greene that prevented a rout and allowed withdrawal.[34] At night Washington fell back toward Chester. Only the failure of Howe and Cornwallis to press their advantage prevented an even heavier American defeat. Alexander Martin was in the midst of the battle at Brandywine Creek. He was at one point sitting on his horse only a short distance away from where General Lafayette was wounded.[35]

British officer's gorget which has come down in the Martin family with the information that it was picked up on the battlefield at Germantown, October 4, 1777, by Alexander Martin. Owned by Dr. Thomas Upshur of Charlottesville, Virginia. (Courtesy Dr. Thomas Upshur.)

Washington had failed to stop the British move toward Philadelphia. In the vicious infighting among the officers, blame was spread widely, almost costing Generals Sullivan and Maxwell their commands. A former subordinate, Major William Heath, said of Maxwell, "we had opportunities and anybody but an old woman would availed [sic] themselves of them—He is to be sure a damned bitch of a General—."[36] Not to be left out, Thomas Burke directly charged General Sullivan. "I was present at the actions at Brandywine and saw and heard enough to convince me that the fortune of the day was injured by miscarriages where you commanded."[37]

Howe camped his main body of troops at Germantown, leaving Cornwallis to occupy Philadelphia. Washington had reconnoitered Germantown thoroughly and he was familiar with the British position. He determined to attack using a battle plan that had not worked well for him at Trenton. He had 8,000 Continentals and called up 3,000 militia. Howe had 3,000 men in Philadelphia and 8,000 at Germantown.

The American defeat at Germantown ended Alexander Martin's military career. In the fratricide now routine with defeat, he was charged, demanded a court-martial and was found innocent. The death of General Francis Nash was a crushing loss to the North Carolina troops. Alexander Martin said "the genteel figure of his person, added to his easy and engaging manners, gained him the affections of all those who had the pleasure of his acquaintance."[38] That seems an obtuse description from a man who had seen the shell (the same one that had lopped off the head of John Witherspoon) fatally wound Nash in front of him.

Martin confessed that the sorrow of defeat and death was "almost too much for my constitution."[39] On November 7, as commandant of the board of field officers of the North Carolina brigade, he presided over action to fill the vacancies occasioned on the death of Lt. Colonel Irvine of the Fifth Regiment and the resignation of Lt. Colonel Lockhart of the Eighth Regiment. The death of Nash brought on the reorganization of the North Carolina Line and under such circumstances reputations were open to the most savage political assaults.

John Penn, then a North Carolina delegate to Congress, reported to Governor Caswell that "Colonel Martin was arrested for cowardice." The accusation made on the 4th of October by Colonel Martin's detractors asserted that, in the confusion at Germantown, Martin saw "a soldier slip into a hollow of a gum tree, ordered him out, threatened to run him through with his sword. The soldier obeyed, and our gallant colonel took shelter from danger by getting into his place." [40] Demanding a court-martial to clear his name, Martin appeared at the same court that heard charges against General Adam Stephens of Virginia. Stephens, who had fought alongside Washington as early as the French and Indian War, was found guilty of "unofficerlike behavior" and "drunkenness" and he was dismissed. Martin was acquitted of the charges against him, but he resigned on November 22.[41]

Cornelius Harnett informed Thomas Burke that "Col. Martin has again been so unfortunate as to meet with censure." The use of the modifier "again" in this quote seems to indicate that there had been other occasions on which Martin had received criticism. Harnett may have been implying the source of that criticism as he continued, "I am told by several officers that should Colonel Martin be appointed, many resignations would take place, as several of the Colonels, etc., are much dissatisfied with his conduct."[42] A few days later Harnett reported Martin's acquittal but he added: "Our Brigade, the high officers of it, are exceedingly anxious to have a General officer appointed." He noted that the colonels in seniority were Martin, Sumner, Polk and that there was strong support among the officers for Sumner and Clarke and Martin's appointment "might cause several resignations."[43]

Martin communicated his feelings to Governor Caswell. "I am almost worn down with fatigue," and he concluded, "I am determined in a few days to resign, and return to Carolina, and leave the command to Col. Sumner."[44] He described the atmosphere in the North Carolina Line with which he refused to continue to contend: "I have had censures liberally bestowed on me by some officers in the 4th Battalion[45] of my conduct at Germantown, but with pleasure I can inform you I am honorably acquitted by a Court Martial and am sorry to inform you that a censorious spirit too much prevails in the army, that the conduct of almost every General and Commanding officer has been arraigned by those of inferior Rank, & generally acquitted, particularly Sullivan, Stephens, Wayne, Maxwell and Col. Maryland."[46]

Although the charge of cowardice has a taint even to this day, Alexander Martin left the army because he lost the struggle for command. He had accepted, even sought, military command in an incontrovertible dedication to the Patriot cause. As long as regimental activities stayed within the south, he was successful in assembling support for the cause on the frontier, in converting recruits into serviceable troops, and in commanding troops during regional fighting. Experienced as he was by the time he moved his men north to join Washington, he was unprepared for the merciless factionalism of a military force in defeat. Civil politics had an order and a decorum that the politics within the newly formed American military had not yet achieved. He had two choices: stay and battle this "censorious spirit" or return to North Carolina, where an elite that considered him among its leadership was forming the new government.

Was Alexander Martin guilty of the charge of cowardice? Nothing in his military career or in his life before or after Germantown reflected a man who would cower in a tree trunk in the face of an enemy. The source of that story also claimed Martin was found guilty by court-martial and sent home with a wooden sword—embellishments that confirm the lie.

On his return to North Carolina, Martin was immediately trusted with the highest positions in civil leadership at a time of extraordinary national crisis. Later, he was selected as a member of the Society of the Cincinnati, the select club of the officer corps of the Revolution. This action would have been impossible had this group considered Martin as an officer to have been deservingly discredited by any actions at Germantown.

6

Martin as Speaker of the Senate and as President of the Board of War

Alexander Martin's resignation from the army was the most difficult decision of his life and he lived to see the vindication of his choice. He was physically exhausted. He had been accused by fellow soldiers of the most odious act of cowardice. He could face the enemy before him but he could not tolerate the internal quarrels that indiscriminately attacked personal character. Martin's military career was sacrificed in that cauldron of tumult out of which Washington forged an army. Revolutions by their nature have too many amateurs and the measures of heroism and cowardice are difficult to define when standards of performance are determined in the fog, fury, and terror of battle.

Martin did not recover rapidly from the physical effect of the war on his constitution. When Georgia and South Carolina, fearing another British incursion along the coast, requested troops from North Carolina, he was appointed to command a "regiment raised from the New Bern Brigade to march on the Southern expedition," but he was forced by his poor health to resign this appointment on November 13, 1778, before the Council of State.[1]

The Martin family on Dan River had remained safe in the face of the partisan attacks that flashed along the frontier. Martin's younger brother, Robert, lived at home and was active in the militia. Sister Anna Jane was her mother's companion. Thomas Henderson, who had given up the position of clerk of court in Guilford County and assumed the same post in Rockingham, was courting her. They were married in March 1778. Thomas Henderson had become Alexander Martin's closest political confidant.

Alexander's brother, James Martin, as commander of the Guilford County militia, was heavily engaged in countering the Tory sentiment that bubbled just beneath the surface in his district. In the summer James and General Rutherford were appointed by the assembly to investigate the disaffected, including several prisoners of war in the county who had broken their parole and rejoined the British.[2] James was also actively making land entries in Surry County on the upper reaches of the Dan River where mineral deposits had been uncovered.[3] The provincial congress in 1775 had provided for a bounty of £250 to encourage the mining of ore. As young men in Hunterdon County, the Martin brothers were familiar with the nearby Union Furnace and Ironworks.[4] Along with their brother-in-law, Samuel Rogers, they now entered claims they hoped contained sufficient ore.[5]

Although he repeatedly encouraged James and other members of the family toward investments in the iron business, Alexander Martin was only a sometime investor. James acquired another section on Snow Creek of Dan River that included a lime kiln built by James Duncan. This was the place where James would move his family at the end of the war and where he built a forge that he named the Union Forge in reflection of that of his youth. The ferrous deposits of magnetite and brown hematite ore found exposed by erosion along the tributaries of the Dan River were mined and first produced into ingots and bars in small forges using ore, limestone and charcoal. James Martin's lime kiln was the only source of burned lime in the area.[6] Charcoal was available from the forests and the state provided large grants, excused from taxation for as long as they remained unimproved and were used only as a source of charcoal to support the furnaces.[7]

While Alexander Martin had been active as a commissioned officer of the Continental Army, North Carolina had become a state with a new constitution. Richard Caswell, president of the fifth and last provincial congress, had been chosen as governor. The provincial congress had been replaced by a general assembly of two branches. As a regimental commander, Martin had been in regular communication with Caswell and the government. He had now left the army. It is possible, at this defining juncture in his life, to glimpse the emergence in Alexander Martin of a concept of the machinations of civil government that made him an unwitting progenitor of the American politician. There is a scholarly consensus that politics in the first years of the republic "was closer to eighteenth-century patterns than to the voter-oriented, mass party politics of the 1840s and after." Parties were "still viewed as inherently pernicious."[8]

The war was raging with no end in sight. Framers, scholars and farmers, were creating governments and constitutions. Martin had just extricated himself from the suffocating experience of military politics in an army that had not yet achieved manageable levels of order and discipline. At the age of 40, he could look in retrospect on a youth of comfort and affection in an extended family that over several generations had endured the disruption of persecution and exile in defense of their religious beliefs and their independence. In support of his own capacity for learning, he had been provided an education that prepared him for an enlightened future of leadership in a land of expanding opportunity. As a young man he had chosen to leave the security of a more economically developed colony to settle in North Carolina on the edge of a frontier. In accordance with his preparation, within a decade he established himself in business and as a district leader in politics by gaining the confidence of a populace made up chiefly of farmers and dispossessed squatters, many of whom shared with him a Scotch-Irish heritage. As an elected county official, he was chosen to represent his neighbors in the colonial government where he faced the reality of power concentrated in a Whig elite in the populated eastern section of the colony. Advancement at the colonial level, in the face of the reality of this power block, was stymied but the flow of people into the North Carolina frontier pointed to the inevitable redistribution of civil power in the state. War was the catalyst of the initiation of this redistribution and in Martin was manifest the effect of this recognition that the eastern Whigs could no longer go it alone and ignore the power of the people of the frontier. Martin was offered his commission in the Continental Line from North Carolina, not because of his military experience but because he was a rising political spokesman from the west, and, in order to prosecute successfully a war of revolution in North Carolina, the Whigs had to have the support of the most populous and aggressive block of people on the frontier. When Martin returned home in 1778, this was the accumulated experience on which he built his personal prospectus for his political future. There was no indication that he formalized any targets to be achieved or any offices he intended to win, but from this point it was possible to see an undeniable structure to the way he achieved success in public office. There was a consistent pattern to both the way he fashioned a constituency and the way he fashioned a majority in the face of the reality that both economic and electoral power was in the hands of the eastern elite. His personal success was a manifestation of the pure principle of republican politics when few in America could even theorize about the direction of the political system that came out of independence would take and before political parties could sprout out of the democratic soil. It was Martin's ability, at this very early date and throughout his life, to fashion a constituency and assemble a majority through a thorough understanding of the range of forces that could be brought to bear at any given time for a single purpose. That ability sets him aside as one of America's first successful exponents of the "art" of politics. As the innovator he would not have analyzed his activities in contemporary terms of party politics, but in following his life it is possible to see that he innately knew how to build a broad base, keep a close ear to local issues, trade support on regional issues, avoid rigid positions that he might later regret, and listen intently to all arguments in a debate so that he could discover new issues and find the points of compromise. This was the essence of the emerging politics of the nation. In contrast to the reality within the united colonies, Alexander Martin was closer in ideas and practices to the voter-oriented, mass party politics of the 1840s than he was to the eighteenth-century patterns of the early republic.

Within a year of his return from the army, Alexander Martin was elected to the upper branch of the assembly by the landowners of Guilford County. Ralph Gorrell had been elected the first senator from Guilford in the new assembly, but by the time he was re-elected the following year he had also accepted the county office of entry taker. His seat was declared vacant when it was noted that the state law forbade double officeholding. A new election was held and Alexander Martin was elected.[9] He took his seat four days after the assembly had convened at Hillsborough on August 8. His cousin, the sometime Regulator James Hunter, chosen as a delegate for the House of Commons by Guilford, joined him.

His return to elective office proved the support he could assemble in a county so evenly divided between Whigs and Tories. Martin could expect the support of his Scotch-Irish neighbors in the upper part of the county along the Dan River and the Presbyterians of the Buffalo and Alamance communities. His attempts at mediation on behalf of the Regulators may have gained him some votes, as would his personal support of nonconformist Quakers at New Garden, Centre, and Deep River. It was a breadth of acceptance among the yeoman farmers no other political figure in the county could assemble. This was the constituency to which Martin was loyal for the rest of his life. They were never easy taskmasters. At times they held to fundamental beliefs with such tenacity that they risked realizing the potential of both freedom and independence. It was Martin who would lead them repeatedly through this abyss of clashing beliefs to understand the value of a common good.

During his abbreviated attendance at the Hillsborough assembly, Martin was added to four committees, including that to review the Confiscation Act passed by the first assembly.[10] The original act was particularly severe, pressed by the more radical Whigs coveting the opportunity to divide the spoils. The first difficulty was to define the enemy. Tories were required to take an oath of allegiance or accept banishment. Loyalist merchants were given three months to sell their goods and depart the state. Persons found aiding the enemy were to be imprisoned for the duration of the conflict and half their lands were forfeit. In the more populated east and in the towns, such definitions of loyalty might be applied and in the structure of the community, although often inevitably partisan, law could be sustained. On the Piedmont frontier, however, the structure was the family unit or the ethnic or religious community where any political diversity was submerged and only merchants, lawyers and elected officials were easy targets of partisanship.

The third assembly met at Halifax.[11] Martin was assigned to ten committees, reported for two committees and authored two bills. He also was nominated as a delegate to the Continental Congress but was defeated.[12] This short session and another at Smithfield in May, dealt with the extension of the boundary with Virginia and the formation of more western counties including the separation of the southern third of Guilford into Randolph County.[13] The Regulators were heavily concentrated in this new county and their separation from Guilford gave Alexander Martin an even more favorable majority in the county. The sessions continued the debate on confiscation. Martin reported the 1777 act and moved its implementation after loyalists were given reasonable opportunity to pledge support to the state constitution. He advanced another modification that would protect women and aged loyalists from being left destitute by confiscation. The fall assembly at Halifax made a list of 68 persons whose property was declared confiscated.[14]

At the end of 1779, Richard Caswell had completed three single-year terms as governor, the maximum consecutive terms allowed by the new constitution. He stepped aside and accepted command of the North Carolina militia; 8,000 troops had been committed to the defense of South Carolina.[15] Caswell's son, William, had served under Martin as a young ensign. Abner Nash, the Speaker of the Senate, succeeded Caswell as governor.

When the assembly met at New Bern in April, Nash resigned his post as Speaker and the Senate elected Alexander Martin.[16] The mounting threat of British assault on South Carolina was an equal threat to North Carolina. At this crucial moment Martin had the combined strengths, as a candidate for this influential position, of his leadership experience within the military and his representation of the Scotch-Irish Presbyterians. He was the first political leader from the western part of North Carolina to reach this level of elective power in the state. The constitution qualified the Speaker of the Senate as next in succession to the governor.[17] He could view his selection as Speaker as a massive stroke of luck or as a formula for electoral success that he had successfully executed.

Within a month of his election as Speaker, the fall of Charleston cost North Carolina almost her entire Continental troops and about 600 members of the state militia as prisoners. Having secured their major southern victory, Sir Henry Clinton and Lord Cornwallis, in command of a British force of 8,000 men, initiated their campaign to complete the conquest of South Carolina and moved to invade North Carolina. Kenneth Roberts observed that "even on the strength of the partial records that still remain, the Revolution, after it moved to the South, was one of the dirtiest civil wars ever fought."[18]

North Carolina faced an unnerving dilemma. Her unswerving support of the defense of Charleston had cost her the best-trained forces available to provide her own defense. If she now mounted a defense against the advancement of the British, would her neighbors come to her aid with equal enthusiasm? The Whig leadership stood firm and in June, Baron DeKalb arrived at Hillsborough with 1,400 men from Delaware and Maryland.[19] A month later, Horatio Gates, victor at Saratoga, assumed command of the Continental army in the South.

Virtually the entire command of the state militia was by members of the recent assembly and their commander, Richard Caswell, who had been governor. These same men had voted for the commitment of men and resources to meet the threat and now they were ready to take command. Alexander Martin was the only member of the state assembly with senior military command experience who did not leave civil government at this time to accept a military assignment. Although his health was not robust, this inaction is in stark contrast to his eagerness to command in 1775. Back then, he had a splendid opportunity to attain fame and glory. In 1780 he was the second most powerful elected official in North Carolina brought to office by a sequence of circumstances not always available in state government. His opportunity to contribute to the successful prosecution of the defense of North Carolina against the British lay in the civil as opposed to the military theater, and in coming to this conclusion he made the correct choice. The state retained a man near the top who understood the vagaries of command and the insatiable demand for provisions for an army on the move.

Taking little time to evaluate his command or organize his troops at Hillsborough, Gates moved directly into the disaster at Camden where on August 16 he met Lord Cornwallis and suffered the worst American defeat in the South and one of the worst of the war.[20] Losing almost 1,000 prisoners, and with several hundred of his own men killed, Gates also succeeded to abandoning all his baggage, stores, equipment, guns, and ammunition. Unable to rally his command, and without leaving orders for a place of reassembly, Gates left every man for himself and fled to Charlotte on his way to Hillsborough—to "that town he rode as if engaged in a steeple chase."[21] General Caswell was unable to rally the North Carolina militia and he rode off in desperation. In the next few weeks Piedmont North Carolina, heard about the defeat from ragged, half-starved, disorganized bands of Americans in full retreat. There was not an organized force left in the state to face the British invasion and, of equal concern, the Tory sympathy, submerged since Moore's Creek, had a revival of hope.

While the Americans were being decimated at Camden, Alexander Martin was attending court in Surry County at Richmond. Recent word was that the British had been driven back after an attack at Hanging Rock in South Carolina earlier in the month. News about Camden arrived on the 19th.[22]

On August 30, the second session of the 1780 assembly convened at Hillsborough, which also happened to be the new headquarters of General Gates. North Carolina's Continental line had been lost at Charleston and now its militia had been lost at Camden.[23] Cornwallis seemed poised to invade. The state's resources of food and equipment had been seriously depleted. Bands of light horse cavalry were ranging through neighborhoods on Tory hunts.[24] A defeated general camped at Hillsborough.

Governor Nash claimed that he lacked the freedom to act with authority in the emergency. He considered his authority to have been breached in the appointment of Caswell to command of the state militia. Nash further claimed that the legislature "violently intruded upon his [Nash's] rights" as governor when they created a Board of War.[25] The Continental Congress had created a Board of War in 1776 and a year later Washington had it reorganized as a "new expedient to ease the internal army bickering."[26]

In North Carolina the justification for the Board was the "calling forth [of] the powers and resources of this state."[27] The Board represented the assembly's answer to the repeated frustration of Governor Nash in attempting to mobilize his state, threatened as it was with invasion, when the Council of State seemed destined to "neglect of their duties." The legislative solution, enacted at the suggestion of Nash, was the creation of a Board of War.[28] The Board of War was given authority to remove and appoint officers in the state departments; to survey routes and defense; to raise, organize, and equip troops; and, when the assembly was not in session, to supervise the application of all public money. The act was an emergency assumption of executive power by the legislature. Appointed to the board were Senators Alexander Maclaine of Brunswick, Oroondates Davis of Halifax and Alexander Martin of Guilford; General Thomas Polk; and John Penn, delegate to the Continental Congress.

The Board of War had a thankless task at a desperate time. Maclaine was a conservative from the Cape Fear elite who was suspected in some quarters as harboring Tory sympathies. Polk was acting commissary general for provisions for North Carolina and commissary of purchases for the Continental troops under General Gates.[29]

His military duties paralleled many of the functions of the Board. Penn was the link to the delegates in Congress. Davis was an effective senator who had actively sought adequate revenue in the legislature to carry on the war. Martin, as Senate Speaker, already had a position second to the governor and he assumed greater influence as the Board took further executive power from Nash. Maclaine and Polk simply did not attend meetings. The Board elected Martin as president at its first organizational meeting on September 3.[30] The assembly ended on the 13th, intending that the Board should act in continuity between sessions. Martin assumed his task as if he had been commissioned an officer in an army. In preparation for the assignment he and Penn returned briefly to their homes to put their business in order.[31] The Board reassembled to select a commanding officer for the North Carolina troops. The rout at Camden and his own rapid personal retreat had seriously tarnished General Caswell's reputation and he was "at that time prevented ... from taking the Field."[32] The Board chose General William Smallwood of Maryland to assume command. Martin wrote from the "War Office Hillsborough" to General Sumner, who was infuriated at not receiving this command. He had obviously been General Gates' choice but he had not gained the pleasure of the assembly or the Board. Martin reminded the general that Sumner had been glad to serve under Caswell but when the Board had found General Smallwood, "whose Military Fame is great," available to serve, they had offered him Caswell's position in order to prevent Smallwood's return to Maryland. Martin was sure Sumner would serve under Smallwood if he had been willing to serve under militia General Caswell. However, if he was not, Martin said he was certain that "a brave and virtuous Soldier" would not "for a few little Punctilios of Honor Suffer his Country to be given up into the Hands of a merciless Enemy."[33] There is a powerful irony at work in those words that was not lost on Sumner.

Abner Nash described the schedule of the Board of War: "It sat continuously at Hillsborough sometimes with one member, sometimes with two, and very rarely with three, from September 14th until December 1st, 1780, and then continuously at Halifax, with one or two members, until January 30th 1781."[34] The Board was advised by Governor Jefferson that Virginia was unable "to furnish a Single Stand of Arms for the use of your troops." Soon they "expect that 5,000 to 5,500 Regulars and Militia will march from this state to yours" but they had advised Washington they would need to be re-supplied.[35]

The assembly had organized the state commissary by selecting a purchasing commissioner for each county, who reported to a district superintendent, who had the task of storing the provisions. The district superintendents operated under the Board of War, which soon recognized the arrangement was not effective and asked the governor to appoint a commissary general.

On October 14, General Nathaniel Greene of Rhode Island replaced General Gates, who had lingered at Hillsborough since his debacle at Camden. General Washington ordered Greene to assume command of the army in the South. For the first time, this American army had a wise and capable leader who could blend in adequate proportions a "native intelligence and acquired skill."[36] North Carolina had at least 5,000 men in the field but they were inadequately supplied. Rations were in such short supply that additional militia calls were delayed. At the same time western lands were being set aside as bonus lands as incentives for enlistment. This was the status at the time Lord Cornwallis crossed into the state near Charlotte.

The tasks assigned the Board of War as crisis managers in a moment of potential humiliation were assumed as duties and at personal sacrifice. Given the critical task of supplying provisions, its members were constantly bombarded by General Greene for more of everything. No matter how they struggled to meet his needs, they could not do enough for a general desperately defending against a better-trained army. Overlooking the reality of the circumstances, most 19th-century historians of the period have accepted the acerbic judgment of William R. Davie of the Board and its members.

> Nothing could be more ridiculous than the manner this Board was filled. Alexander the Little,[37] being a Warrior of great fame, was placed at the head of the Board—Penn who was only fit to amuse children, and O. Davis who knew nothing but the game of Whist composed the rest of the Board.

Sour grapes sometimes makes catchy copy. John Penn had been a signer of the Declaration of Independence. He had risen rapidly in state politics and as a member of the Board practically controlled the military forces of the state. He was considered the most active member of the Board.[38] Davis, although cognizant of his lack of military experience, was tireless in the efforts to supply the army. He candidly explained that the board "would not be able to furnish suitable mounts for Davie's cherished project of a personal cavalry unit," which strikes close to an explanation for Davie's later animosity.[39] William R. Davie shared many parallels with Alexander Martin. Both came from Scottish families, although Martin's family had spent a generation in Ireland on the way to America. They were raised within families of strong Presbyterian doctrine, although neither had very active association with the denomination in later life. Although Martin was 18 years his senior, both had graduated from Princeton. Each served in the Continental army, would be instrumental in the founding of the University of North Carolina, and served as governor of the state.

Davie had been headed for Camden on August 16 when he met the fleeing men of Gates' defeated army. Recognizing the probable extent of the debacle, he attempted to recover what he could of supplies and baggage and to usher scattered troops toward Charlotte. Untainted by the defeat, he was everywhere the rallying force while Gates skulked toward Hillsborough.

Greene's arrival brought immediate action to secure adequate provisions for an army. He wrote to Governor Thomas Jefferson that the North Carolina troops had "no magazines or provisions..., but depend upon daily collections for support; and this state has been so ravaged by the various militia ... that it is a doubt ... whether, with the great industry and best dispositions any considerable magazines can be found." He persuaded the Board of War that a reluctant Davie should be made general superintendent of the state commissary. Davie feared it would tarnish his reputation. It was the predictable outcome of a forced marriage. The relationship between Davie and the Board was at best acrimonious.[40] Greene was pressing the Board of War to appoint a young man who demanded plenary power that at the time they held.

Hillsborough was the supply depot for the efforts of the Board of War. Governor Nash described it.

> It [the Board] collected hides and leather wherever to be found, and made the tannery at that place work its full capacity for the government, pressed into service every one who could make a shoe, and put them all to work shoe-making for soldiers. Tailors also, and needle-women, under its command, made or repaired much-needed clothing for the army. It wrote to everyone everywhere, who had arms or ammunition, to hurry them forward. The army needed salt and it must have salt. It then made itself a nuisance to all whose dilatoriness or neglect had caused this condition. It wrote to its captains of hundreds, and to its captain of thousands, and instructed them how to fight if the enemy approached, how to retreat, if retreat should be necessary, and where to take position for a final stand if any position was to be taken. In short, its management was Ubiquitous and minute. It was too energetic and zeal-inspiring, if not in all particulars wise. It had no holidays of holy days. It worked Sundays as well as Mondays, and its individual members seemed, if only the enemy could be defeated and driven out of the state, to be perfectly willing to answer for their conduct before any tribunal—the true spirit in such a crisis.[41]

As president of the Board of War, Martin corresponded with the Continental Congress, advising delegates of the pitiable condition of supplies in the state.[42] General Greene asked him to visit General Smallwood in the east to help coordinate the military action in the state.[43] The Board of War was to be short-lived, because it was not the answer to the circumstances it had been created to meet. When the assembly convened in January 1781, with Martin again in the chair as Speaker, Governor Nash submitted the ultimatum that he would resign "unless you restore it [executive power] to a condition as respectable as it was when you did me the honor to confer it upon me." He repeated the demand in a more peremptory manner on February 1.[44]

General Greene wanted no state high command to interfere with his prosecution in what he considered a continental war. In spite of his complaints about the Board, Governor Nash needed a working, available council to administer state government in the face of the immediate crisis to help him govern and assemble supplies. The assembly recognized the probability that Cornwallis' presence would ultimately interrupt the function of state government. A mobile council, attached to the governor, would be needed to act swiftly. The assembly created a Council Extraordinary "to advise the Governor in all cases whatsoever." The Council was to be made up of "three persons of integrity and abilities, such as the General Assembly can place the greatest confidence in."[45] In joint-balloting, the two houses chose Richard Caswell, Allen Jones and Alexander Martin, who was the lone holdover from the Board of War. All three members had military experience that gave them credibility with Greene. The same law that created the Council Extraordinary abolished the Board of War.

The Council had all the "authority heretofore vested in the board of war and the council of State." The act enumerated broad-ranging responsibilities, including the blanket authority to "exercise all other rights, powers and authorities, which the council of state might have exercised in a state of war."[46]

The Council with all these authorities was expected to function when public order was nowhere secure. Public officers felt "left altogether in the lurch" when the assembly could not pay allowances. Samuel Spencer, a Superior Court judge, took the position under these circumstances that "I shall never budge another Foot in their Service, at least as a civil Officer, till they make proper Provision for my Support. I have no Doubt other Judges will do the same."[47] The work of the Council, by its very nature, appeared to be peremptory "in commandeering supplies and in general measures of impressments," and it soon lost popular understanding that further undermined the public confidence in state government.

The assembly, mindful of the difficulty Governor John Rutledge in South Carolina had in trying to create civil government after the fall of Charleston, took the conditional step of providing for legislative continuity in case it was prevented by the British invasion from re-assembling in April for the next scheduled meeting. They gave to the governor and Council Extraordinary the option to call the assembly into session at another time and place.

Two days after the assembly convened at Halifax, a British force under Major James H. Craig occupied Wilmington, an occupation that would last until the surrender at Yorktown. The eastern elite was outraged and threatened. William Hooper characterized "a Country on the verge of ruin—a corrupt or what is worse an Idiot Assembly, an Indolent executive—Treasurers without money—a Military without exertion—Punctilios superseding duty."

Earlier successes of American forces at King's Mountain had the effect of cooling Tory enthusiasm for the Cornwallis invasion. In terms of reputation, he still had the superior force in the field but Greene's organizational efforts were creating a stronger American army than he had previously faced. The assembly reduced the battalions of the state's Continental Line from six to four and began refilling the ranks. The Council Extraordinary authorized requisition of supplies, receiving from "every inhabitant a fifth part of his provision for the use of the army." Impressment was ordered of "every man who abandoned his post in the last action [Camden]," and they were to be "enrolled in the continental army for 12 months."[48] Cornwallis, maneuvering with predictable deliberation, sought to maintain pressure on Greene. He occupied Salisbury and then camped at the Moravian towns. In February he began to be more aggressive. As he pressed Greene ever north toward Virginia, the armies were engaged in a race to cross the Dan River. In spite of high water, Greene, who had made himself a student of the terrain in the central Piedmont, outfoxed the British and brought his army across the river to continue the process of military reinforcement. Alexander Martin's home on Dan River was in the midst of this maneuvering of the armies and his entire family was at risk. His plantation lay at Lone Island, one of the upper fords used by Greene particularly in moving his baggage.[49] Local history mentions that the plantation was burned by the British and, if true, it is likely that the fire occurred at this time.[50]

Cornwallis was briefly left in command of North Carolina. He dropped down to occupy Hillsborough, recent locale of the state assembly and the Council Extraordinary and recent headquarters of Gates and Greene. There he raised the King's standard in the second test of the strategy advanced several years earlier by former governor Josiah Martin. Greene, unable to leave the ground to Lord Cornwallis for too long, recrossed the Dan River on February 23. Cornwallis broke camp at Hillsborough on the 26th. With no force to hold that position, the Tory camp followers who had responded to his rally moved out in his train. Within a few days, the state government had returned. On March 15, Greene and Cornwallis met at Guilford Courthouse. Although Greene refused to give credit outside the army, the Council Extraordinary and the Board of War had done much to assemble troops and supplies in the six months since Camden. It was possible for Greene to put in the field an American force of 4,000 men from many regional militias.

The scene of the battle was the site of the county courthouse that had been used for the first time the previous month.[51] It was also the center of Alexander Martin's political base from which he had fashioned his rise within the Whig government. This day it was his brother, James Martin, as colonel of the Guilford militia who, under the command of General Greene, faced the British regulars. The North Carolina militia units had been placed in the forward line with the order to fire three rounds then they had Greene's "free permission to retire from the field."[52] The militia took their rounds, some breaking early, and then they all took flight, many flying all the way to their homes.

Also at Guilford Courthouse, which was very near his residence, was the Reverend David Caldwell. Before the battle, the British and their Tory supporters actively sought the Presbyterian minister as a chief enemy of the Crown. In the course of that search, his home, school and library were all destroyed. He was on the battlefield ministering to the wounded and dying immediately after the fight, and he retreated with the army.

Alexander Martin as a member of the Council Extraordinary had critical personal knowledge of the neighborhood over which Greene and Cornwallis struggled. Greene has been widely credited with having a scholar's knowledge of the terrain of the upper Piedmont that gave him a tactician's advantage over the British army. That advantage was buttressed by the resources Martin could provide the civilian government concerning that neighborhood and his neighbors. Although they were in tension over the requisitioning of the meager resources remaining on the land, Greene's army and the civil government were able to maximize this parochial advantage.

In the aftermath of the battle, Greene fell back to the ironworks at Troublesome Creek that he had fortified as a precaution in case of a retreat. Cornwallis, however, with only half the force that the Americans had placed in the field, was so decimated at Guilford Courthouse that his claim of victory was recognized, even at home, as hollow. Greene rested his army and tended the wounded at Troublesome Creek and Sauratown. Cornwallis likewise reassembled at Guilford Courthouse, then moved east to join Craig at Wilmington.

The April assembly meeting, in such question when that body adjourned in February, was called at New Bern under the rumors and threats of British assault.[53] There was no quorum. The Council Extraordinary, which was to cease at the end of this scheduled meeting, continued now under questionable authority that satisfied neither the legislators nor the exasperated governor. The six-month enlistments of the militia were ending and this farmer army was determined to return home to their spring planting. Greene shrewdly held his criticism of the state government. He was aware that North Carolina was exhausted of men and material. General Sumner, however, on the 25th ordered the line officers of the state to Hillsborough and they reported moderate success in refilling the manpower of depleted units. General Caswell was indisposed at his Kinston home and did not appear at Hillsborough.[54]

With Caswell unavailable, the Council Extraordinary was in limbo until the assembly next met. Greene broke off his tactics of shadowing Cornwallis and pushed into South Carolina. With him went Major William R. Davie, who considered his position as commissary chief for the general a priority over his commissary responsibilities in North Carolina.

The assembly finally gathered on June 23 at Wake Courthouse. Alexander Martin was re-elected as Speaker. Governor Abner Nash, however, who was ill and thoroughly disillusioned by his clashes with the Council and the complaints of General Greene, declined to allow his name to be placed in nomination. Thomas Burke, a delegate to the Continental Congress and a radical, then defeated conservative Samuel Johnston.[55] Burke, an Irishman, arrived in North Carolina in 1775. He located at Hillsborough as a lawyer.[56] Learned and egotistic, he was saluted as Dr. Burke and had opinions on everything; he considered the natives generally uneducated and rude. As a delegate to the Continental Congress in 1776, he served as a less than solicited volunteer officer at Brandywine Creek, where he authored some scathing criticism of several other officers. In Congress he was an unswerving champion of the rights of the individual states and introduced into the Articles of Confederation a resolution that guaranteed that those powers not expressly delegated to the Confederation be retained by the states. This same safeguard was later incorporated into the Federal Constitution as the Tenth Amendment.

Martin, on behalf of himself and the assembly, pledged full support to Burke. "Nothing shall be left undone on the part of the Legislature which may tend toward the General Defense and make your Administration very happy and honorable."[57] It was a pledge having particular importance in the face of the civil strife abroad in the land.

The June assembly gave the governor temporary authority to commission judges of courts of oyer and terminer in any district. The act was necessary in order to prosecute the numerous acts of treason in a state that was sharply divided. That need was exacerbated by the reluctance of some judges to serve when they were not being paid. Similar frustrations abounded. Delegates to the Congress were not able to pay the inflationary expenses of Philadelphia. Lesser officers, both civilian and military, were not sufficiently compensated. The assembly passed acts regulating officer's pay and set new salaries for senior public officials. These actions were balanced by those requiring complete disclosure of the collections of public money and for the levying of a Specific Provisions Tax for one year.

Instead of easing the tension in the state, the departure of the armies of Greene and Cornwallis only served to drive the war down to perhaps its most barbaric forms. Except in the area around Wilmington, the Tories of North Carolina understood that the British army had abandoned them. The Continental army, however, was no longer near enough to support the local Whigs. The state government had wrung virtually every material resource from the citizens. The Tories had diminished prospects on their own but they also recognized that the destitute conditions in the state gave them their last chance at some form of victory. In the end, the laws of treason and confiscation made it clear that there was no compromise and that the victor would exact harsh retribution.

The most dramatic success of the heightened determination of the Tory efforts came on September 12 when Colonel David Fanning and his second-in-command, "One-eyed Hector" McNeill, rode a band of 1,200 Tory partisans into Hillsborough in broad daylight and "after a brisk skirmish" captured Governor Burke, the Council of State, members of the assembly, the governor's military guard, and 71 Continental soldiers. About 400 militiamen under General Butler ambushed the loyalist column the next day at Lindley's Mill. The battle that followed was one of the largest of the war in the state. Although Fanning was wounded and McNeill was killed, the loyalists managed to reach Wilmington with their captives.[58] From there, Governor Burke was sent to Charleston and ultimately to James Island.

Had the Council Extraordinary not ceased to exist by act of the assembly at the end of the last session, Alexander Martin would no doubt have been among those captured. Instead, as Speaker of the Senate, he became acting governor of North Carolina.

7

Martin's First Term as Governor

Within a period of six months North Carolina had splintered in civil war, a circumstance that Josiah Martin had held as possible since 1776.[1] Fanning's raid, coming in 1781, was not part of the long-discussed coordinated plan of invasion, but it restored spirit to the Tory loyalists.

State legislatures typically held precedence over the executive branch as the source of power because they were directly tied to the vote of the people. The executive, governor and Council of State, however, was looked to as the source of the continuity of civil order. Had Fanning's raid occurred while Josiah Martin was still in the state with Cornwallis, the former governor might have been put forward as a legitimate alternative to the captive Governor Burke. The Whigs, at the beginning of hostilities, had vigorously sought to capture Josiah Martin as the symbol of royal government. When he fled the Governor's Palace, the Whigs held as justified the establishment of a patriot state government.

As armies marched through North Carolina and Tory bands were emboldened and reinforced, there was no effort to secure the few state officials who remained free or to make secret their whereabouts. Alexander Martin rode the court circuit appearing at Salisbury, Richmond (Surry), and Guilford Courthouse. Although he was recognized as holding "the second position in the government of this state," in these courts he was considered to be just another lawyer/assemblyman.[2]

Ten days after Burke's capture, Alexander Martin, as acting governor, wrote to Major James Henry Craig requesting the release of Burke on parole pending a prisoner exchange. Martin argued that Burke, as a state official, could not be a prisoner of war—a position Craig refused to accept subject to overrule by his superiors.[3] Martin was provoked by Craig's response, which in effect made Martin governor. In later instances this assumption of office by Martin subjected him to charges of being opportunistic. At the moment, however, even Burke was grateful to Martin for his efforts on his behalf; Burke wrote to Martin in November from James Island that "Col. Lyttle and Capt. Reed will be so Good as to furnish you with any paper which may be necessary to clear me, and you may be assured Sir, that to repay you will be the least of the Obligations I shall hold myself under to you."[4] Burke gave Martin no advice on government, which would have been in character. He was interested only in release, which he obligated Martin to continue to pursue. Martin was understandably reluctant to assume the office of governor. Under the siege circumstances, the real risks to life, and the lack of precedent for an orderly transfer of authority, led to the conclusion that this was not, at the moment, a post devoutly to be wished.

Greene maintained pressure on the state through his commissary officers, never satisfied that civilian authorities were doing all in their power to feed and cloth his army. Davie echoed his concerns but there is little to support their claim of indifference among North Carolinians to their needs. According to R. D. W. Conner, "during this period North Carolina was the victim of a carnival of pillage, rapine and murder that surpassed that of the era of Reconstruction."[5] Such an analysis serves as an explanation of why North Carolina, the third most populous state and one with good agriculture, could support only a small army in the field.[6] The acting governor advised the president of the Continental Congress of his temporary situation.[7] He understood by various letters received, that the Congress did not know who the governor of North Carolina was and that he could expect little supply support from sister states. He warned he had a "body of Militia on Foot, for the purpose [of] quieting the present internal insurrection and, if possible, expelling from our Borders the power and Influence of Great Britain."

The first part of October found Martin at Bute Old Courthouse, perhaps visiting General Jethro Sumner who had recently commanded the North Carolina Continental Line at the victory of Eutaw Springs.[8] Martin was eager to remain in close contact with the important leader, to keep him informed, and to gain implied authenticity.

The act creating the Council Extraordinary had anticipated the need for emergency measures that would sustain the state government in case of some sort of Tory raid or British breakthrough. When the assembly, with the insistence of Governor Burke, abrogated the Council, these procedures were simultaneously annulled. Therefore, there was no plan in place for the capture of the governor, which would seem particularly short-sighted since, in June, Governor Thomas Jefferson in Virginia had only narrowly escaped capture, with his assembly, by Colonel Bannistre Tarlton in a raid very similar to Fanning's.

Martin met the available members of the Council of State in Granville County on October 5 and took over the office of governor. The atmosphere was one of heightened concern and equal determination to continue to maintain the government. Fortuitously, Martin had visited his friends the Moravians at Salem in July in his capacity as Senate Speaker to persuade them to host a session of the assembly. The first plan was for using the *Saal* in the *Gemeindehaus* but the Moravians found that prospect too intrusive on their daily order. Instead they offered the still-house, "which is light and roomy, and the adjoining room."⁹ They depended on Martin to advise them on what they should do and what would be expected of them. The unassuming Moravians, caught between two sometimes cruel and crude belligerent forces, recognized this opportunity to witness to their beliefs "if with all modesty we hold to our chief purpose, if our conduct shows all people that we are children of God, and if we treat them in an orderly manner and with courtesy, then the Savior will turn to good the evil that was intended against us."[10]

In August Martin detailed the requirements of the assembly. He would do all in his power to leave the *Saal* free for the Moravians for their services. Four or five rooms would be needed "for the Governor, Speaker, etc." On November 4 the Speakers of both houses would arrive to make final arrangements and the members would arrive "a good while after that." The Moravians would attend to gathering necessary provisions and it was understood that all the members could not be fed at the same time or place. No one could have suspected then that within a month Martin would be back in Salem as governor.

To this peaceful island of people of faith that Alexander Martin had protected, and thereby gained mutual respect, he came now as governor to try to restore a functioning government. On September 26, one of Martin's earliest acts as governor was to visit Salem and to provide them a "protection" against demands by militia units for food that the Moravians had set aside for the use of the scheduled meeting of the assembly.

Martin needed to make contact with the army to establish some relationship in the present uncertainty. With a small escort, he rode to Wilmington in October and visited General Griffith Rutherford, his friend from Rowan, who was reconnoitering the possibilities of driving Major Craig from the city.[11] On October 30, before the assembly meeting, news arrived that Lord Cornwallis had surrendered at Yorktown 11 days earlier. The news was stunning but it was not understood at that moment that it was a conclusive victory and did little to lessen the lawless danger that remained in North Carolina.

On the evening of November 8, Governor Martin arrived at Salem with two companies of soldiers.[12] He was given a private lower room in the *Gemeindehaus*. In the next few weeks, members of the assembly began arriving. The governor was making this the temporary seat of government. He ventured to the Surry County Court at Richmond on the 14th and a day later one of the North Carolina delegates to the Continental Congress, William Sharpe, arrived to see him. As usual, the delegates to Congress were without direction from the assembly.[13] Burke, as a former delegate to Congress, had been perhaps more sensitive to their complaints of lack of direction. Sharpe sought to determine the attitude that the acting governor and his assembly might manifest.

A watch was placed on the *Gemeindehaus* on the 21st. Until then Martin had apparently moved without a guard. The members of the assembly met for the first time that day and found they did not have a quorum. The next day former governor Richard Caswell arrived with military officers, including officers from Greene's army. They welcomed the news that, on the 19th, Major Craig had evacuated Wilmington by moving his 400-man force to Charleston. The last British force had left the state.

On Sunday, an alarm brought memory of the Hillsborough raid. "A party of Tories had been seen on the road to the mill" only half a mile from town. The militia was assembled and quickly stationed before the *Gemeindehaus* "where the Governor is Lodged" but the rowdies turned out to be horse thieves who fired some shots when challenged by a sentinel. The relieved assemblymen were invited by the Rev. Friedrich Wilhelm Marshall to his room for "a hot drink and cold cake" at which time the Moravians had a chance to answer "many modest questions about [their] organization, which [Marshall] explained to them until day broke and they separated."[14] Truly agitated, the assemblymen found Marshall's explanation a welcome distraction and the Moravians cemented their position in the young state as acceptable nonconformists. By Thursday, after other attempts to assemble, the Senate stood 10 short and the House of Commons 28 short of a quorum. The members reluctantly decided to go home.

The majority of departing assemblymen agreed that the January meeting should be at Salem. It was not welcome news for the Moravians who had been hard-pressed to provide for their pleasure and comfort the first time, but they saw it as the Lord's will. The accounting between the Moravians and the assembly committee for this session, and the terms of payment for the next, were formal and stiff.[15]

At this aborted meeting of the North Carolina government, it was dynamically clear that Governor Alexander Martin represented the only functioning branch of the state government. As the war waned, neither branch of the legislature could raise a quorum. The elected governor was a captive on a South Carolina prison island along with most of his council. The militia was irregularly occupied in containing the last bitterness of the defeated Tories. The court system continued to preserve a semblance of legal order, which was as much as many citizens demanded of government. The Moravians, as the assembly retired on November 29, "humbly thanked our dear Lord for His gracious ordering of events."[16]

Briefly the acting governor went home to "Danbury," then spent most of December at Halifax. From there he issued a Proclamation of Pardon on Christmas Day, which he signed, with all the accumulated authority he could add to such an act, "Speaker of the Senate, Capt. General Governor and Commander in Chief."[17] State law forbade the holding of two offices simultaneously, so where was the authority to take exception to the tasks that Martin recognized as his responsibilities? He was serving only as the elected Speaker of the Senate. The office of governor was his by default and he functioned only in Burke's incapacity. Nowhere in the history of the state is there a similar time when the functioning offices of state government were so represented by one man. If something happened to Martin, there was no provision in law for a successor to the office of governor. It was this understanding of the structural weakness of the state government, the empty treasury and commissary, and the still-strong Tory sentiment that had led David Fanning to expect the capture of Burke to terrorize the Whigs and devastate the government.[18]

The Proclamation of Pardon initiated the efforts of the victorious Whig government to close the wounds of war and re-unite the people. Had the legislature convened, the pardon might have been their action. Martin acted on the proclamation after the Salem assembly failed. At the time of his capture, Burke was in the process of preparing a very inflexible proclamation that included sending the families of recalcitrant Tories out of the state. It was his view that a civil government must be "composed entirely of Citizens who own allegiance" exclusively to that government.[19] This severe intent, that he had already made public, was a reason for Burke to fear that in captivity the Tories would take his life. At first Martin too intended the bitter persecution of the Tories, believing that only punitive action would demonstrate to Tory malcontents that they would not be tolerated. Under the circumstances, he was acting only as an agent of Burke's intentions. He advised the Council of State that Tory families were "nursing up serpents in our own bosoms for our own destruction." He concluded that: "Tho' humanity feels for the distressed, and pleads the cause of the poor women and children yet does not policy suggest and point out this measure tho' rigorous that they be banished from among us."[20] Jeff Crow concludes that "Martin's Christmas proclamation showed more Whig vindictiveness than Christian charity."[21]

At Halifax he was able to share the proposed proclamation with political leaders who had not been at Salem. Consideration had to be given to timing. A bold action was needed to re-establish authority and to undermine the threat of the Tories to rampage in the vacuum. The proclamation was directed to the "deluded" citizens who "revolted and withdrew themselves" from their country and "now find themselves deserted by our feeble and despairing enemy."[22] Pardon was granted to any man who, before March 10, 1782, surrendered and immediately enlisted in the Continental battalions for 12 months. Those guilty of murder, robbery, and house breaking were precluded and were subject to the courts, and special courts were created to handle the actions taken by civil authority in application of the proclamation.

There was continuous pressure placed on General Greene by state leaders to intervene on Governor Burke's behalf to obtain his "enlargement." Davie pressured from within Greene's command. A few days after the proclamation, General Allen Jones, Martin's friend and Davie's father-in-law, wrote Greene, "I know no one who can so well draw out the resources of the State or who has more Activity and Zeal."[23] Jones recognized that any acts by Martin were, at best, functions of a caretaker. One other action intended by Burke and prosecuted by Martin was the relief of Wilmington. Martin dispatched General Rutherford and General Butler at the head of 1,100 men to liberate the city.[24]

Martin chose Pleasant Henderson as his private secretary and as clerk of the council, a position that the young man would continue to hold for the next three years.[25] Henderson was the younger brother of Judge Richard Henderson and had seen action at Moore's Creek and Guilford Courthouse.[26] Thomas Henderson was also his brother and in 1786 Pleasant married the governor's niece, Sarah Martin.[27]

Alexander Martin arrived at Salem on January 25, 1782, as did the Speaker of the Commons, Thomas Benbury of Chowan, and several members of the assembly, all hoping that a quorum could be reached. Daily, more members arrived but the Moravians were glad to see that there were fewer observers and military. It was promising, in their view, that "most of them were those who were not here for the first session."[28]

Quite unexpectedly, on the evening of January 30, Governor Burke appeared.

He had been incarcerated at James Island in South Carolina on his honor not to escape, as a prisoner on parole.[29] The island was a haven for Tories who made life miserable for Burke, and he later claimed that he considered his life in danger. One evening a shot fired through a window and killed a man sitting beside him. He fled the island and in doing so he broke the terms of his parole. He made his way to Salem. His arrival was celebrated and the Moravians noted that "he was now free." Quickly, however, his freedom was questioned as a matter of ethics. Colonel Steward, a deputy from General Greene's army, and Major Taylor, a deputy from the Virginia assembly, were at Salem and they were the source of news of Burke's escape as it found its way back to military headquarters.

Governor Burke was restored to his office at Salem as Martin vacated the office immediately. He turned over official papers and a résumé of his actions taken during Burke's captivity, although Burke would later complain that he had been left uninformed as to actions taken in his absence.[30] It was an ingenuous complaint, considering the absence of a seat of government and the consequential mobility forced on Martin as the only functioning branch of state government. Even records kept by the secretary of the council were stored in various locations in the state to preserve them from capture by Tories or by the British who might make "incursions and marches in the state."[31]

Burke returned from captivity to immediate controversy and his reaction to criticism was to imagine enemies in all directions. Martin made Burke's list of enemies because he had assumed his role as governor. That was unfair but Burke was demonstrating a kind of irrational paranoia. In contrast to Burke, the brilliant but impetuous and imperious Irishman, Martin was emerging as a politician of prudence and ingenuity. In his brief interim, and under the worst of conditions, he had visited camps and sought to cheer the troops.[32] His proclamation gained the support of the radicals, but Burke was critical of its promulgation even though it was based on his own planned document.[33] Martin had been careful to consult the council whenever he could on all important actions, and he was solicitous of the members of the assembly although he could hardly report officially to an assembly that could not gather a quorum. Burke was patronizing and patrician and, although delivered the opportunity to be the object of popular worship as a hero, he was unable to interpret the popular mood. He retained the support of Davie and most of the eastern Whig establishment including Johnston, Hooper, Iredell and Willie and Allen Jones but it was with the army, and particularly General Greene, that his escape raised serious questions. Breaking parole was unacceptable. Davie advised Burke that the opinion of Greene and a court of inquiry, headed by Major General St. Clair, was that "the Enemy have legal claims upon you as a prisoner of war, that your leaving Head Quarters before matters could be settled or adjusted, taking the government under those circumstances is considered highly reprehensible in you, and dishonorable to the State."[34] Greene could accept Burke's escape from James Island because of a threat to his personal safety in order to serve out the terms of his parole in a safer place. When he reassumed his position as governor, however, he broke parole and that Greene could not afford to condone.

Martin had expressed no misgivings about the efficacy of Burke's escape. He was relieved to restore the governor's office to Burke and to retain his Senate speakership, pending action of a sitting assembly. On February 3, the members present met to debate whether they would wait another eight days for a quorum; the decision was to give up and go home and to reassemble in April in Hillsborough.

Burke plunged into vigorous efforts to supply the commissary needs of Greene's army, closely cooperating with Davie.[35] He expedited the Specific Act passed by the last seated assembly that authorized a four-shilling tax on each pound value of taxable property and four more shillings per pound on monies held in the state. Moravians, and others who had claimed exemption from military duty, were taxed under the act at 12 shillings per pound value. The act sought to rebuild the state treasury. Greene's interest in the act was in a one-year tax in kind on specific crops that would go to rebuild the commissary. The Moravians and other nonbelligerents were to be taxed at three times the basic rate.[36]

Martin's reluctance to prosecute the Specific Act was based on his sympathy with the destitution of the people and was compounded by his support of the Moravians. Pragmatically, he could reason that the Whig elite would support his inaction since they had most of the taxable value in the state. Burke's appeal in the state was his drive, intellect and preemptive opinion on every subject. He was no Federalist believing in the integrity of individual states but he accepted the necessity, in this crisis, to support a concerted effort to defeat the Tories. Critically, it was in his best interests to satisfy Greene's aims in order to recover the general's blessing over the matter of his broken parole.

Davie, in a letter to Greene, found the Specific Act a "stupid policy" because it made provision only for bread. Beef on the hoof, collected by Davie on Martin's orders in November, had still not reached the army in April because Davie did not have enough feed or grass to fatten the livestock.[37] Greene still complained.

Burke's defense of his actions in breaking his parole appeared self-serving in the face of a military opinion that his actions were "reprehensible" and "dishonorable to the State." His mystique was rapidly eroding, a frightful reality for a proud man. As a young man, he had fought duels to defend his honor. A month after his return to office, he suggested to Davie that he did not know how long he would remain governor "but that period, I hope, will not be long."[38]

After nine months of legislative inaction, the assembly met at Hillsborough on April 15. Burke made a complete report of vindication for his actions as a captive. He had concluded that he did not want to be re-elected, suspecting that he did not have sufficient support anyway. The day before the start of the assembly, he sent Major McCauley to visit "the different rooms occupied by members of the Assembly" to test his support.[39] Although McCauley found support, he acknowledged much disaffection over the parole issue. Facing what he saw as the inevitable, Burke declined to let his name stand when it was placed in nomination the next day. Samuel Johnston, Congressman William Sharpe, John Williams and Alexander Martin were nominated. The contest narrowed to Martin and Johnston, the powerful Chowan politician who had been defeated a year earlier by Burke. On the 23rd, in a close vote, Martin was elected governor of North Carolina.

Moore, in his history, charges that "Colonel Martin and his friends, for his own gain," smeared Burke's reputation and caused his defeat and indirectly his premature death. This charge was influenced by the opinion that Martin's actions "justified the contemptuous opinion entertained by Colonel Davie and the Continental line, as to the old Regulator's courage and principles" and this has undermined public judgment of Alexander Martin for two centuries.[40] Superficially, it is uninformed since Martin was never a Regulator. This conclusion, however, which depicts Martin as the character assassin, written years after the election, is part of the elite eighteenth century history of the state that has only recently been re-assessed. Burke destroyed his own reputation by breaking his parole. He failed to consult Greene on a matter of military justice. Having reclaimed the government, his judicious prosecution of the Specific Act did not regain Greene's blessing but brought into question Burke's role as the staunch defender of the interests of the people of North Carolina. Had Burke felt truly wronged by Martin, his attack would have been malevolent. Had he considered Martin as the source of his public scorn, his abuse would have been withering. Burke's rejection by the assembly brought from him a complete repudiation of democracy and a declaration that there could be no equality in a political society.[41] He considered himself universally rejected and in abject bitterness he died an agonizing death the next year.

8

A Time of Peace, Independence, and Rebuilding

The assembly installed Alexander Martin as governor with considerable ceremony and formality. "He was brought forth before the Assembly in a eulogistic address; the Bill of Rights and the State Constitution were committed to his keeping."[1] Richard Caswell in a profusion of eloquence said, "It gives me particular pleasure to have at the head of the Executive department a gentleman on whose dignity, Firmness and Integrity we can relie with the utmost confidence."[2] The governor-elect responded with deference then outlined the objects of his administration: the need to control commerce, to create public credit, to continue support of the army, and to arrange for the proper use and appreciation of the soil of the state. A particular plea, obviously a personal priority, was for attention to the education of the youth of North Carolina.[3]

With deliberate steps, the victorious Whigs were consolidating their victory and structuring the institutions of popular government. Only a few months earlier, it was the attitude of the frontier that "there is Scarce the Shadow of civil government exercised in the state." Martin himself was pragmatically declaring that "the Civil operation of Law ... must cease for a moment till the Government be restored to calmness."[4] In Virginia the state constitution had been so ineffective in the face of the British effort to capture the executive and dislocate the legislature that there was a serious effort to seek the appointment, through Washington or Greene, of a dictatorship to stabilize the institutions.[5] As the conflict withered, the incredible public incubation of popular democracy took root throughout a network of independent colonial governments. The eight-year interactive debate preceding the Constitutional Convention began to be waged in 13 states eager for the opportunity for independent action each claimed to have won.

In North Carolina, since the declaration of its independence, the reality continued to be the control of economic and political power in the east but the drama, in these early acts, was the emerging majority of the small farmers along the western frontier. At closer examination, driven primarily by self-interest, the merchants and lawyers across the state took conservative positions in opposition to paper money and the confiscation of loyalists' property, while the farmers and laborers assumed a more radical view by favoring the outlawing of the British debt, cession of western land, and opposition to the judiciary.[6] These were the issues in the state during this prelude to a federal constitutional government. Conservatives and radicals in North Carolina did not constitute political parties but they foretold their emergence. Identifiable among the conservatives were Samuel Johnston, James Iredell, Joseph Hewes, Thomas Jones, Hugh Williamson, Archibald Maclaine, William Hooper, William R. Davie, Allen Jones and John Steele. They tended to an almost patrician belief that they were "the natural leaders of the people." Radical leaders were Willie Jones, Thomas Person, John Penn, Timothy Bloodworth, Matthew Locke and Samuel Spencer. Alexander Martin and Richard Caswell could best be considered moderates who avoided the entanglement of either political identification.[7]

It was asserted, by those who had opposed Martin's election, that he was "crammed down their [the legislature's] throats" by Richard Caswell.[8] This obvious partisan simplification ignores Martin's position as Speaker of the Senate and his commendable performance during Burke's seizure. He was able to parlay that reputation, with the support of the former governor and militia general, to defeat Samuel Johnston. Confirmed as governor, Martin resigned the speakership of the Senate and was succeeded in that office by Caswell.

Since the Guilford Courthouse battle, the state militia was a less than secure defense. There was an understandable disagreement between Caswell and Martin that arose from their military experience. General Jethro Sumner, recognizing the unreliability of the militia, had offered his command services through General Greene. Martin had served with Sumner. In fact, it was to Sumner that he had turned over his command after Germantown when he had resigned the army. He agreed that an officer of the regular army could instill the order and discipline and order of command needed by the militia. Martin was thoroughly qualified on this issue, but Caswell, former commander of the North Carolina militia, took exception. Governor Martin wrote to Sumner in January 1782: "I flatter myself with the great advantage this State will derive from having the honor of Continental officers in its service at this important period which may finally blast the hope of a despairing enemy and cause them to fall an easy prey to our arms."[9]

The assembly had to exercise immediate attention to the restoration of the ranks of the Continental battalions and to pay for the troops of the line. Operating in the vacuum between sessions of the legislature, the state quartermasters and commissaries had become agencies of theft and confiscation operating outside the law. Both quartermaster and commissarial departments were abolished. Accounts were demanded within three months and the individual county commissioners were restored in an effort to recover civil authority.

The Confiscation Act was promulgated, repeating the enemy list of 1779 with some additions.¹⁰ Two Scottish merchant houses included on this list—Dinwiddie, Crawford and Company, and Buchanan, Hastie and Company were associated with Martin's Dan River neighbor, Francis Farley.¹¹ By the end of the war the colonial branches of these Scottish trading houses disappeared with considerable loss to all associates. To this war-weary state everything British or anything that could be connected as British, was anathema.

Turning to the restoration of public revenue, the assembly restructured the tax base and redefined taxable property, dividing each county into tax districts with tax listers to make accountings. Recognizing the lack of money, the Specific Provisions Tax was extended another year to accept agricultural products as payment against value. A revenue tax was added of one penny for each one-pound value of taxable property. This tax also could be paid in kind, the dissenters, as before, paying an extra two pence per one-pound value. The comptrollers' office was established with ten districts governed by boards of auditors.

The bickering of public officials and judges about lack of pay brought about a restructuring of salaries for public officers as an effort to restore public faith. With echoes of the Regulator crisis still within memory, the salary act equated adequate reward with accountability. The governor's salary was to be the highest, at £1,000 specie. Delegates to the Continental Congress received £80 per month traveling to and from and while attending Congress. Members of the Council of State received 20 shillings per day attending council meetings.¹²

The long struggle of the Moravians to gain recognition as citizens ended with this assembly, when title to all their lands was finally vested in the Rev. Frederick William Marshall of Salem for the *Unitas Fratrum*. Up to this final step, men like Alexander Martin had to defend these dissenters from the avaricious efforts of opportunists to have them included in the Confiscation Act.¹³ Martin represented the Moravians in their title quest in 1782 after gaining for them, the Quakers, Dunkards and Mennonites the "Right of Citizens" from the assembly in August 1779.

The governor rode the court circuit as an attorney. In July he was at Salisbury, in August at Richmond, and in September at Salisbury again, each time passing through Salem, usually spending the night and attending religious services.¹⁴ In April, three Tory leaders were indicted for high treason at Rowan Superior Court. Colonel Samuel Bryan, Lt. Colonel John Hampton, and Captain Nicholas White were all members of the regiment of North Carolina loyalists. They had given up their cause after Yorktown and were arrested on April 15. They were represented by Richard Henderson, John Penn, William Kinchen and Col. William R. Davie, who rested their case on the argument that if the state owed no defense to the prisoners, and if the prisoners owed no allegiance to the state, then there could be no treason. Community agitation ran particularly high and Martin was forced to dispatch an armed guard for the court. The Tories were convicted and sentenced to execution. A direct appeal was made to the assembly, still in session. The governor, in one of his first acts, signed the pardon at the direction of the assembly and the prisoners were part of a later officer exchange.¹⁵

There were other convictions and executions throughout the state in the early part of 1782. David Fanning sought to establish a superior bargaining position for his Tory band by attacking Whig leaders in remote locations, killing those who would not surrender, burning their homes and farm buildings, and generally terrorizing the surrounding location. He marched into Randolph Courthouse on the day of the election for the assembly with the intent of negotiating with "the Gentleman Representatives." Instead he prevented the election when all the freeholders scattered. During the first week in May, Fanning crossed into the Pee Dee region of South Carolina and the last major Tory force abandoned the state.

On June 15, Governor Martin issued a second Proclamation of Pardon with much the same wording as that of the proclamation in December. The difference was that those who refused this opportunity of pardon would be deemed prisoners of war if captured and would be subject to exchange. With this modification Martin sought to advance normalcy since this treatment of belligerents was more in keeping with the accepted rules of war.

The governor could be a staunch architect of civil law but he was not above a pragmatic use of punishment as a public deterrent in spite of the law. Middleton Maubley had terrorized Wilmington during the British occupation. When Iredell asked for a pardon in Maubley's behalf, Martin declined, saying he had "fully made myself acquainted with that criminal character." While he claimed that "every tender feeling I possess for humanity revolts at the idea," of this execution, "public justice calls for satisfaction." He thought "the example may deter others of those wretches from committing those common atrocious offences which they consider necessary in their military character against us." Finally Martin posed this interesting expedient: "I think, that the justice of this country, which has long been offended with impunity, should at this time receive some reparation, to convince our enemies we have a Government, and will support it against all oppressors whatsoever, and that no British Commission shall give a sanction to the crimes of our citizens, or those living among us, when they fall into our power."[16]

This incident provides an interesting point of character study. Alexander Martin considered his public trust to place on him the necessity of a decision that he could not make out of personal preference. His actions could be construed as simple political expediency, but this was the man who risked his life and reputation to mediate a settlement at Alamance, who pardoned the Rowan Tories, and who would later make one of his first acts on hearing of the British acceptance of peace the pardon and reconciliation with former enemies. Martin's actions in this case, both his public actions and his privately expressed preference, could have been defended with equal impunity by the Reformed religious traditions under which he had been raised and educated but they would be hard-pressed to be justified in the philosophy of the Scottish Enlightenment.

At the end of the war, North Carolina had a population of 350,000 people, nearly a third of whom were slaves, settled chiefly in the east. Its population distribution, however, was more balanced than in either of its two neighbor states. The radical majority that had framed the state constitution in 1776 had provided for a broader electorate than was enjoyed in Virginia or South Carolina, both of which tended more toward an officeholding caste. The North Carolina lower house of the assembly was elected by free men paying public taxes while the Senate required a freehold of 50 acres for voter eligibility. Members of the Commons had to own 100 acres; senators had to own property of at least 300 acres.[17]

North Carolina stretched from the Atlantic Ocean to the Mississippi River. As late as 1790, there was no post except between the seaboard towns. News from Halifax to Hillsborough, a distance of 100 miles, took a fortnight. Pairs of towns—such as New Bern and Edenton, Guilford and Salem, and Salisbury and Charlotte—seemed to communicate more freely.[18]

The office of governor required a freehold in lands and tenements of £1,000. Reflecting the fear of tyranny in 1776, the office had little power independent of the assembly or the Council of State. Burke and Nash had chafed at the extralegal limits on their functions. Martin was experienced in the assembly and, moving between the offices of governor and Speaker of the Senate almost uninterrupted for 13 years, there was little practical difference in the power and influence available to the two offices he held. There was public respect for the office of governor, but the man holding the office was not broadly known outside the political venue of court circuits and assembly sessions.

Order out of chaos was the challenge for Governor Alexander Martin and the assembly. There were leaders in every state anxious to pontificate or postulate on the structure of a democratic republic. In Virginia, Jefferson could dream of "a 'natural' aristocracy of talent and virtue."[19] Thomas Burke had foreseen that at the end of the conflict "all pretense for continuance of a Congress" would disappear and the states would reassert their independence.[20] Local legislative and judicial government was necessary to restore public confidence. There would be time for theory and debate later.

An example of the frustrations faced by the governor in this first-things-first approach to restoring economic and political order is expressed in a letter Martin wrote to General Greene continuing to justify the shortfall in state commissary procurement: "The Executive [is] fettered with restrictions in the Acts of the Assembly [he] walk[s] on ticklish ground if they [he] deviate in any uncommon exertions not authorized by law; which renders it difficult for me to supply the wants of the army immediately as you request."[21] The elimination of the state commissary departments had not significantly improved the collection by the tax districts and the Specific Provisions Tax was not due for collection until September. By then Martin was no more successful in his pursuit of supplies for the army. He wrote the commissioner of supplies that "the Assembly have not levied any [tax] I am tired out with apologizing, and am reduced to Silence...." Sounding the familiar complaint of his predecessors, he continued, "The Assembly have neglected and flung the whole burden on the executive.... The Assembly have not done their duty, and the Executive for want of support cannot do theirs. The fault will not be at my door ... if the Assembly will provide us no other way to collect supplies of this kind, but by impressments.... It must be executed at last, however disagreeable by the army itself."[22] This argument was political hyperbole. The last thing that Martin desired, or the assembly could permit, was for the army to be foraging for food throughout the state.

The Whig leadership continued to exert itself with mild indifference. The prospect of a new nation seemed to be an important reality only to the extent that the states could be left alone, farmers could attend their crops, and merchants could have better access to European markets. There was little eagerness or anticipation at the prospect of creating the world's first popular democracy. Public service, when the state coffers were bare, had limited attraction. In November and again in January, an assembly was called but in neither case was a quorum met. By early April, information was arriving aboard ships that a Preliminary Treaty of Peace had been signed in Paris on January 20, 1783. Lafayette himself had dispatched news of the signing that had arrived in Philadelphia on March 23.[23]

The election to the spring assembly lacked several of the leaders of the previous session. Alfred Moore, Joseph Blount, Willie Jones, Nathaniel Macon, Hugh Williamson, Richard Dobbs Spaight, and William Hooper were all absent when a quorum was finally declared on April 18. For the lawyers among them it was an unfortunate reality that election to the assembly did not pay. On top of that there were few paying clients at the court session, "owing to the great scarcity of money." Iredell confided, "I should be much mortified had I been the only unsuccessful lawyer [at court]." He feared that "until the peace makes it flow in, our profession will not be much benefited."[24]

Governor Martin was always remote from news when he was at his home on the Dan at "Hoop-hole Bottom" as Iredell derisively called his plantation.[25] He could not overcome the fact that when he was home he was largely cut off, by the poor roads and the lack of a post, from the population centers. His compensation was to correspond regularly with other state leaders and to keep his council informed and active. There was a rumor when he arrived at Hillsborough that he already had some conclusive news about peace that he thought would be exciting news for the delegates, but it was only a copy of the speech King George had made acknowledging American independence.[26] It was, therefore, with a supercilious manner, that other lawyers and delegates from the eastern counties informed him of "an official account of Count D'Estaing's dispatches," referring to the recounting of the Preliminary Treaty of Peace sent by Lafayette.

Martin was joyous as he opened the assembly. "With impatience I hasten to communicate the most important intelligence that has yet arrived in the American Continent," he began, retelling, for historic moment and effect, news which his listeners had already received and had actually told him. Martin captured the dynamics that he hoped this news would inaugurate. He foresaw that "nothing now remains but to enjoy the fruits of uninterrupted constitutional freedom, the more sweet and precious as the tree was planted by Virtue, raised by Toil and nurtured by the Blood of Heroes." Martin moved immediately to challenge the assembly to action: "To you, Gentlemen, the representatives of this free, sovereign, and independent State, belongs the task, that in sheathing the sword, you soften the horrors and repair those ravages which war has made, with a skillful hand and thereby heal the wounds of your bleeding country." He proposed an immediate revision of the act of pardon and oblivion to put old bitterness aside. Finally, he placed his faith in a free people exercising the rule of law. "Let the laws henceforth be our sovereign; when stamped with prudence and wisdom, let them be riveted and held sacred next to those of Deity. … Happy will be the people, and happy the administration when all concerned …

contribute to this great end."²⁷ It would be a government of laws, not of men, thus confirming the British law of precedence over the Scottish emphasis on reason. After more than two centuries, this prophecy is like a battle cry designed to rally the troops to the possibility that was now open to them. Like most of his contemporary leadership, this was what they were waiting for. To this point they had been winners on the battlefield but they had not been able to even speculate beyond that because the future was so uncharted.

This was the euphoria that only an unqualified underdog could appreciate at the moment of triumph. In the celebration of victory, only the naïve and unsophisticated could expect a single purpose to emerge. The strength of the system, to whose birth they were privileged to be present, would lie in its diversity. This reality would be proven in time, but, for many of Martin's contemporaries, it began as a vague and shadowed obstruction.

Many conservatives and radicals still looked on Martin as a lightweight who represented a frontier populated by subsistence farmers with little power and less capacity to rule. However, in the elections of the spring of 1784, he proved his cunning, wisdom, and durability. In reference to that election, Norman Risjord believes it is possible to measure the beginning of party formation in North Carolina. He credits a resolution drawn by James Iredell and approved at a public meeting in Edenton in August 1783 as the "first announcement of a coherent political program in the Chesapeake states." Risjord sees the renewed effort of established lawyer leaders to return to the assembly as the linchpin around which a single party initiative developed.²⁸ A more pragmatic view of the return of the lawyers to the state government is that they could no longer let their concern for the guarantee of their own compensation keep them out of the assembly that was considering and enacting laws of governance and court reform.

Caswell, who had supported Martin as a straw man the previous year, was ready to reclaim the governorship. He was eligible again under the 1776 constitution to seek that office.²⁹ The conservative Samuel Johnston, having been defeated by both Nash and Martin, did not covet a third rejection. He and the conservatives could, however, deny the office to Caswell, who had effectively done the same to them. Under "the aggressive leadership of the able and vitriolic [Alexander] Maclaine," they charged that Caswell, since he first held the office of governor, was "a man who had basely abandoned his important trusts, and deserted his colors in the hour of distress."³⁰ He employed the ultimate political weapon of the time by charging Caswell with undefined courageous shortcomings—apparently with reference to his hurried retreat after the debacle at Camden and his subsequent resignation from command of the state militia.

Maclaine reversed his opinion on Martin. A year earlier, he had considered Martin as a man of poor mentality.³¹ In February, he had accused Martin of being a caterer after office whose hand was in the public purse.³² The conservatives intended to hoist Caswell on his own petard. Caswell advised his son that they were "saying I had crammed him [Martin] down their throats last year and they were now determined to keep him there."³³

Martin's support in the election was broader than simply as a foil to Caswell"s aspirations. Some votes came to the incumbent "from principle," as Maclaine observed. Such support came ordinarily when all other factors were equal and only from fair-weather friends. There was a pocket of support for Martin from the Cape Fear region, resulting from his support at that particular moment for Cross Creek (Fayetteville) as the site of the state capital. Martin has been criticized by some historians as superficially opportunistic on this issue, assuming that his natural regional interest would be for keeping the capital in Hillsborough. That conclusion overlooks Cross Creek as the commercial center for the Guilford/Mecklenburg Piedmont. All these factors were in play but Martin succeeded in mobilizing the western support for his candidacy and for the first time the west held the balance.[34] The lawyers had returned to the assembly but they did not coalesce around a single candidate for governor because, as a lawyer, Martin was acceptable at the time. The assembly cast 66 votes for Martin and 49 for Caswell. In this election Martin had finally consolidated his reputation and after this election he was a recognized political power in state politics. He also had integrated the formula necessary for a westerner to retain statewide office in North Carolina without creating an adversarial atmosphere between the geographical regions of the state.

At his second inauguration, the assembly praised Martin for the "justice, rectitude and moderation of your Excellency's Administration...."[35] Martin responded with gratitude for re-election and reiterated the limits on his office that made effective cooperation with the legislature necessary. "Though my exertions be feeble, when supported with Legislative aid, they will become strong. Laws tempered with wisdom carry with them almost their own coercion and require only formal powers of the Executive."[36] In his message to the assembly, Martin placed emphasis on the revision and codification of the state laws—many of which, passed in the duress of war, were flawed, conflicting, or confusing to the courts.

The Council of State, appointed by both houses of the assembly, functioned with the governor as the executive branch of state government. Under Martin, the members of the council were increasingly from the western part of the state, reflecting not only his influence but also the practical consideration of logistics when gathering the council to meet. Spruce Macay served on the council from 1781 to 1783. He and Martin had practiced law together at Salisbury. Among the many young men who read law under this jurist were William R. Davie and Andrew Jackson. Philemon Hawkins, Sr., of Warren County served all three years of Martin's administration. His son had been in Thomas Burke's council. At the Battle of Alamance, Hawkins had been aide-de-camp to Governor Tryon. Warren County was also the residence of Nathaniel Macon who was just beginning his political life as a member of the council in 1783. Like Macay, he was a Princeton man. Thomas Eaton was the third member of council from Warren, elected in 1781. He served throughout the Revolution and as a militia general at the Battle of Guilford Courthouse. John Penn, like Macay, was a holdover from the Burke council. He had a close relationship with Martin from the days of the Board of War. Several friends of Governor Martin served single terms on the council. Richard Henderson was brother of the clerk of the council, Pleasant Henderson. Griffith Rutherford was a popular leader in the senate and one of the chief spokesmen for the farmer/debtor faction, and he led that group's continued opposition to restoration in any form for North Carolina loyalists.[37] Thomas Polk was the first member of the council from Mecklenburg County. He served with distinction throughout the Revolution and had been active during the writing of the Mecklenburg Resolves. James Saunders was in the senate from Caswell County and had been colonel of the county militia. Perhaps the most unusual member of council in this period was the Marquis de Bretigny, the only titled person to serve in a state office. A French officer, the Marquis was North Carolina's most successful purchasing agent. He operated out of Martinique through the New Bern merchants Van Scheelebeck and Marshall, who were his factors.[38] By the end of the war, he had located at New Bern and, during Martin's terms, he was the only councilmember from the coastal counties. These were the men who advised Martin and together provided the executive leadership of the state. With the erratic functioning of the legislative branch at this time, the governor and council were a more determinative influence on the course of the North Carolina government than the constitution envisioned, not because they usurped power but because it was theirs by default.

The early histories of North Carolina, written as they were by the heirs of the Whig elite, viewed Martin and the council that surrounded him as a rural, unrefined majority that was poorly equipped to govern or to organize the emerging state government. That perspective is still found in some contemporary history. "There is no evidence of organization. ... Their few surviving letters are barely literate. ... They led an overwhelming popular majority, and they held their position because they shared its intellectual limitations and its prejudices."[39] For this school of North Carolina history, the heroes were Samuel Johnston, James Iredell, and William R. Davie, whom they saw as far more articulate because they published broadsides and tended to collaborate on public legislation and coalesced into a political party. That view of state history, however, always elevated this minority, articulate as they may have been, at the expense of the reality of what North Carolina was as a people. This governor and council cannot be characterized by either intellectual limitations or prejudices. They spoke for the overwhelming popular majority that had limitations and prejudices and they succeeded, through debate and stump speech and retention of the public confidence, in maneuvering the state into the assumption of its intended role within the new government.

The assembly turned its attention first to relief of the veterans, some of whom had been elected representatives. A public printing of £100,000 of paper money was authorized to begin payment to the men of the Continental Line. Each veteran could receive a quarter of his pay in this new issue and they were given a certificate for the balance due in specie.[40] Companion legislation assigned bounty land in the western counties as compensation to Continental soldiers with at least two years of service. The state boundary lines were extended to the Mississippi, and the lands of the Cherokee were determined with borders, and the bounty lands were inscribed in the northeast corner between the Cumberland and Tennessee Rivers.[41] The act specified that Alexander Martin and the commissioner to the Indians, Assemblyman David Wilson, were each to receive 2,000 acres of this bounty land and Halifax was established as the place for redemption and settlement of claims arising. Colonel Martin

Armstrong was appointed surveyor of the bounty land claims. A year earlier, Armstrong had delivered to the assembly a petition from inhabitants already settled on the Cumberland for recognition of their claims and titles. Many petitioners were veterans or widows of veterans who feared the intension of the assembly was to set aside the best land, some of which they had already claimed and cleared, for officers and soldiers.[42] In North Carolina after 1780, enlistment in the Continental Line carried with it a promised bounty of 640 acres of land in the west.[43] The estimate is that North Carolina had about 6,000 men in the Continental Line.

The lawyer/creditor and farmer/debtor divisions within the assembly manifest the parties that would find their roots in this assembly. Neither dominated and each found reason to be satisfied that they had support within the government. The assembly passed a series of acts that tidied up some of the conditions left from the war: a depreciation schedule tied to the rapid depreciation of the currency so that there was at least an equitable basis for the settlement of suits and protections from "vexatious suits" against overzealous Whigs for their acts of lawlessness during the war (an act that legalized some severe cruelty). The equal application of the tax laws finally relieved dissenters of the three-fold penalty they paid in lieu of militia service. Specifically reflecting the impoverishment resulting from the war, a poor tax of a shilling per pound was to be levied in each county for the support of the poor, and prosecution and judgments were suspended for a year against debtors in recognition of the many who were destitute.

Immediate attention was applied to negotiations with the Chickamauga and the Cherokee. The governor was given sole authority to grant all licenses to deal with the Indians and Joseph Martin, a Virginian, was appointed agent of the state.[44] Joseph Martin had been trading with the Indians since the end of the French and Indian War. Prior to the Revolution, he had settled in Henry County only 20 miles north of Alexander Martin and in 1777 Governor Patrick Henry had put him in charge of Cherokee affairs for Virginia.

In the 1782 assembly, there was the first recognition of the counties across the mountains in the bills and directives.[45] The Salisbury Court District was divided because it was found that the "great extent of these counties west of Salisbury makes it extremely inconvenient for the parties."[46] The reality of peace initiated the further reality that, since the western lands were only tacitly represented in the assembly, they were also ignoring, with impunity, laws passed by the assembly including tax laws. Their remoteness, and resulting independence, had to be brought within civil authority. The eastern Whigs, except for those like the Blounts who had vested interest in the western trade, viewed such concerns with indifference.

Concurrent with the election of the westerner Martin as governor, the question of the administration of the land across the mountains became a public concern in the state. In June, Martin forwarded to Congress, by way of William Blount, "a Map or short sketch of the outline of the State extending to the westward far as the Mississippi the boundary formed by the Treaty of Paris." Martin contended, however, that the state did not consider itself "absolutely bound by [that treaty] having a previous right by the Charter of Charles the Second ... to extend from sea to sea, that is from the Atlantic to the western ocean."[47] He was about to become a negotiator and he was advising Congress of the perspective from which North Carolina would begin consideration. This is a neglected aspect of Martin's influence as governor. He was, after all, a westerner in a state where the political and economic power still lay in the east. Now, as concerns leaped across a vast mountain barrier to double the size of the administration of the laws of the state, the definition of who constituted a westerner became confused. The option was open for Martin to flaunt his westernness, but he would thereby alienate all support from the eastern leadership he had cultivated. Martin's choice was to act as evenhandedly as possible, defining himself as a leader in the middle, who was able—through his appreciation of the leadership of the lawyer/creditor east and his natural affinity for the small farmer/debtor west—to negotiate and reflect the broad scope of issues without being beholden to any narrow faction or philosophy. Modern parlance may view him as attempting to be all things to all people but it is a reality that, at this stage of the creation of an independent nation, few leaders viewed the institution of defined political parties as necessary. Having taken on the role of impartial spokesman/mediator on the issue of the western counties, it was afterwards impossible for Martin, even secretly, to become a speculator in western land, as did men like the Blounts, the Armstrongs or even Richard Caswell.

The Confederation Congress recognized that the advancing settlement in the western lands of Virginia, North Carolina, and Georgia was producing a demand for independence in the region. In 1782, Congress approved a resolution under which these regions, if released by their respective states, could become member states in the Confederation. From that point, the evolution to statehood could be said to be inexorable.

One of the governor's more significant connections with western settlement was through the family of his brother-in-law, Thomas Henderson. Richard Henderson had failed in his pre-war Transylvania project, the "most romantic enterprise" of its period.[48] Henderson's establishment of the form of state government that sent delegates to the Congress at Philadelphia in 1775 was a precursor of the statehood now being considered in the west. The Transylvania Company failed in the course of the Revolution, and the 1783 assembly compensated Henderson and his partners for their "great expense, trouble and risqué" in the purchase of land from the Indians and their attempted settlement by granting them 200,000 acres in the Powell River valley.[49]

Yet another Henderson brother, Samuel, returned from Boonsborough, Kentucky, and located in Guilford County a few miles west of the governor's plantation. He too had been active in the efforts of the Transylvania Company, although not a partner, and in 1780 had been a signatory of the Cumberland Compact.[50] He was well known in the west even after he lost all his property there in 1782.[51] The governor was to use him as his official emissary to leaders in the western territory.

North Carolina lawmakers looked on the resolution of Congress, that of approving the future creation of states in the west, as interference. The assembly, by defining the western boundary as the Mississippi, setting the boundaries of the bounty lands and redefining the boundaries of the Cherokee lands, established what the state intended to govern. The westerners, who until now had been busy conquering a wilderness, saw liberty and license, which they assumed would be theirs, threatened. Colonel Arthur Campbell drew a petition to Congress that requested separation of the Cumberland into a state but the congressional delegations of both Virginia and North Carolina were quick to object.

In 1782, William Blount and Hugh Williamson had written to Martin as congressman in support of cession of the western lands. The governor had rejected the suggestion, as had that assembly.[52] Martin's response to the Campbell petition was a proclamation of his own of reason and assurance directed at all North Carolinians. He avoided the assertion of absolute authority, which would have inflamed the rising cycle of anger, when he urged, "The spirit of our government is so moderate and the general disposition of our western inhabitants is so good, that our subjects will be the last to riot."[53] Such sophism in the face of reported acts of rage against tax collectors and passive responses to calls to the militia or official correspondence attempted to mask the urgency of the issue and to counter the efforts of William Blount and the lawyer/nationalists who were on the side of cession. To the congressional delegation Martin confided more pragmatically, "it would not surprise me, if citizens of the new counties, which now number five and continue to grow, resort to armed insurrection to gain their freedom from us. I deplore their inconsistency. They affirm their fealty to North Carolina before leaving the older parts of the state, and at that time they still recognize the validity of the state's claims to her western lands. Let them but spend three months in a new homestead, however, and these loyalties are cast aside. I sometimes wonder whether there is some quality in the very air of the western counties that breeds disaffection. No matter. Let them fulminate, we will not relinquish that which rightly belongs to us."[54]

As Martin knew North Carolina to be drained, from the ravages of war, the western lands represented a necessary means of economic recovery. Cession at this point might mean default on the bounty warrants the state had given to its citizen soldiers. The assembly had also put aside the unsettled portion of the western lands as guarantee against their £100,000 currency issue.[55]

John Gray Blount had maneuvered legislation through the spring session of the assembly in 1783 that reopened a land office in Hillsborough, which offered western lands as far as the Mississippi at £10 in depreciated North Carolina paper currency. The act flagrantly violated all Indian treaties and further confused existing titles throughout the west. It was, however, an enormous benefit for merchant speculators who had been collecting North Carolina paper currency. The estimate is that three million acres were taken up under this act. Although limiting individual purchases to 5,000 acres, speculators grouped claims and bought military warrants. Companies organized by the Blounts and other individuals, like Richard Caswell, obtained hundreds of thousands of acres of land.[56]

Martin wrote from Guilford Courthouse to the congressional delegation: "It will not be to our interest or policy to make a cession of our Western Lands on any terms yet proposed by Congress." The governor was not closing the door on cession but the terms were not yet good enough. In his opinion, the proposal from Congress was "the same as to urge an Individual to give up to a stranger without compensation part of his land he is daily improving with husbandmen and husbandry."

The price that Martin sought, if the state were to approve cession, was compensation for the expedition against the Indians, liquidation of existing land claims, guarantees of the boundaries, and assumption, by any newly created state, of its proportion of the public debt charged to North Carolina.[57] This was a negotiation that could only be conducted in an atmosphere of normalcy and order, so it was necessary to pay attention to a second story line playing on the same stage.

In January 1782, John Sevier and his western troops returned to the Watauga, and their enlistment period being complete, they were disbanded. Farmers, who had hesitated until hostilities were over and mindful that the western settlements were lightly defended, now pressed close on the heels of this returning army over the mountains. The Cherokees, as interested observers, were quick to recognize this influx and sent immediate notice of their concern to the governor. Martin wrote Sevier concerning the Indians' complaints.[58] He noted he was "distressed with the repeated complaints of the Indians respecting the daily incursions of our people on their lands beyond the French Broad River." He directed Sevier to warn them off. By mid-March, however, if they had refused to oblige, Sevier was ordered to "draw forth a body of your militia on horseback, and pull down their cabins, and drive them off, laying aside every consideration of their entreaties to the contrary."[59] These were unforgiving orders to his military commander in the field but if Martin were to be recognized by the Indians as the leader of the government, he had to be able to control his people. The governor said as much, advising Sevier further that he had goods on order from Philadelphia, which had not yet arrived, and that he intended to "send them to the Great Island and hold a treaty with the Cherokee."[60] It was the same logic employed by Martin in a communication to the legislature when he objected to the consideration of repeal of a section of a negotiated treaty. "They [the Indians] will have little faith in what may be urged on them in the future from this state; as I shall not only falsify the assurances on this subject which I have already given them, and the State of Virginia, who hath interested herself in their behalf."[61]

Alexander Martin does not appear to have had any serious humanitarian concerns for the plight of the Indians; this attitude mirrored the attitudes of his contemporary politicians and most frontiersmen. His view was perhaps closer to that of Thomas Jefferson, who at the time of the Louisiana Purchase thought he had purchased from France only the right to negotiate the settlement of the west with the Native American nations. Martin repeatedly acted from a position that recognized Indian treaty rights to land, although there was always the implication that Indians were constituted as vassal nations of the governing white state. Throughout his first three one-year terms as governor, even as he negotiated with the Indians, Martin consistently directed his attention toward the evolution of a state west of the mountains.

In September, the governor delegated Joseph Martin, then a member of the assembly from Sullivan County, to treaty with the Indians on the Great Island. Spain had stepped in to take advantage of the Indian concerns about the encroachments of white settlements on treaty lands. At Pensacola in June, the Spaniards had advised "that 'the Americans had no King and were nothing of themselves and was [sic] now like a man that was lost and wandering about in the woods.'"[62] Joseph Martin therefore met the Cherokee under the serious threat of hostilities on the frontier against the Creek and Chickamauga in alliance with the Spanish.[63] At Chota, Old Tassel spoke for the Indians. He complained, "Your people from Nollichucky are daily pushing us out of our land. We have no place to hunt on. Your people have built houses within one day's walk of our towns." The Indians sought no quarrel and Old Tassel couched his plea in the tenderest terms of human aspiration. "We, therefore, hope our elder brother will not take our lands from us; that the Great Man above gave us. He made you and he made us; we are all his children, and we hope our elder brother will take pity on us, and not take our lands from us that our father gave us, because he is stronger than we are."[64]

The distribution of the state's bounty claims became more urgent with the receipt of news that elements of the Pennsylvania line had left their barracks at Lancaster and had surrounded the statehouse in Philadelphia, where both the Continental Congress and the Pennsylvania Executive Council were in session. The soldiers were refusing to disburse until arrears in pay were met. General Robert Howe of North Carolina, with 1,500 men, was sent against the dissidents.[65] The report of this protest from Benjamin Hawkins was not lost on the governor, who recognized that it was the western lands that underwrote the state's ability to honor its responsibility to its veterans.

Like all his predecessors, Martin had an indifferent relationship with the delegates to the Continental Congress and that is nowhere more obvious than in the period when cession lay as an unsettled contention between the state and Congress. The delegates had a standing complaint that they were "absolutely without information" concerning issues upon which they were supposed to vote in the interest of the state.[66] Hugh Williamson said he found himself "in the usual ignorance concerning anything going on in North Carolina."[67] Distances and the condition of roads made it impossible to keep informed and co-coordinated efforts at action were always a muddle. The tension between Martin and his congressional delegation, however, had an edge beyond that created by impossible communication. Unlike Caswell and Burke, Martin never chose to be a delegate himself; even Nash became a delegate after serving as governor, therefore there was an unproven logic to the feeling that Martin could not fully appreciate their plight. When the assembly repeatedly failed to gain a quorum to do the business of the state, it was necessary for Governor Martin to advise the congressional delegates that he was "under necessity to decline [returning] the answers" that they expected as often as they expected.[68] The assembly had advised the delegates in 1781 that they were "authorized and empowered ... to sit and vote ... upon all matters at their discretion," unless they received "particular instructions from the General Assembly."[69] The riddle faced by the delegates was that they had authority for independent action but this was always subject to the shifting political attitudes at home. Add to such a lack of definition the difficulty of finding the means to pay the delegates regularly and there was ample reason for the delegates to feel deserted. Benjamin Hawkins decried, "Surely it can never comport with the dignity of a Sovereign State, to let their Delegates depend on such Humiliating and precarious means of support."[70]

Nationally, the issue of cession was debated in relation to the actions and interests of other states with or without western territory. It was debated in western North Carolina courtrooms and sometimes by rump gatherings claiming legal authority. Finally, it was debated on the east side of the Appalachian, superimposed on the evolution of the structure of state government and the emergence of political parties.

The other issue debated nationally during Martin's first term was the public debt. Each state government held myopic views for retirement of the debt that lay as an albatross over nationhood. For North Carolina, the debt issue was inexorably connected to the question of cession. Insolvent as the state was, Martin was adamant that the western lands could not be ceded unless previous agreements of the sovereign state were honored, particularly the commitment to bounty lands made during the war as part of the enlistment contract. Martin could accept cession as inevitable and honorable, given the unilateral cessions by other states with western claims, but he refused to surrender that card without an adequate *quid pro quo*.

Martin's influence in the Moravian community can be observed in 1783 when he issued the first "state order" for celebrating Independence Day on the 4th of July. The people of Salem, ever-conscious of their need to demonstrate their loyalty to the new government and equally solicitous of their reputation, showed their patriotism was second to none.[71]

9

The Cession of Western Lands

On the last day of January 1784, the stunned Moravian community at Salem watched as fire consumed their brick tavern.[1] No guests were staying the night but several families of the town were displaced. The distressed brethren gave thanks that all had been spared from the fire but this was an added economic burden in a difficult time. A month after the fire, when Governor Martin visited Salem on his way to Salisbury court, he stayed in a private home. The brothers were still honored to have the governor in their midst and he attended the evening service. He visited the ruins of the tavern and heard the woes that the community faced and their plans to rebuild. Continuing to Salisbury, he was present for the election to the assembly and the business of the court.[2]

Some historians have seen in the election of delegates to the spring assembly of 1784 the seed of an emerging political party. There was yet no name so it is difficult, except by analyzing voting patterns on key issues, to isolate groupings. The breakdown of conservative and radical labels, used to differentiate the breadth of political philosophy seen in the state during the revolution, no longer sufficiently applied to the lawyer/merchant/creditor politicians who responded to the manifesto drawn the previous fall by James Iredell. Under the veteran leadership of Samuel Johnston, Archibald Maclaine, Benjamin Hawkins, and Richard Dobbs Spaight, these politicians sought a controlling voice in what they recognized as an opportunity for setting the course of North Carolina within an evolving nation.[3] Rallying support through mass meetings and pamphlet warfare, these lawyers advocated fiscal responsibility in the form of redemption of paper money and the payment of back taxes. They committed to repeal the law suspending suits for debt collection and sought higher pay to attract a superior judiciary. They sought development of commerce and manufacturing, and, as public confirmation of this commitment, advocated an end to persecution of loyalist merchants in order to encourage their return to the state.[4] The antithesis of this perspective is less obvious because it existed in those who held counterviews but made no effort at this time to publicly define or proselytize these views. Chief among the farmers and debtors were Timothy Bloodworth, Thomas Person, Griffith Rutherford and Waightstill Avery. Yet another group was driven by their self-indulgent commitment to speculation; this included the Blount family, Abner Nash and Richard Caswell.[5] Martin is missing from all these groupings, and this may explain why he is sometimes assigned little political influence in this period. Walter Clark, however, concluded "that he [Martin] was the leading influence in North Carolina at that period [1782–1784] hardly admits of question: and the Legislature seems to have been enthusiastic in honoring him. ... The office of Governor was then magnified; and in his administration of Governor, Martin did not detract from its importance. His addresses to the Assembly were on a high plane and he pressed upon the Assembly the necessity of public education and advanced views in regard to government and public concern."

Alexander Martin viewed land speculation as disruptive to the already contentious frontier but he encouraged, within his family and friends, the future of the west. He was committed to greater fiscal discipline, but he recognized that the natural poverty on the frontier had absorbed a disproportionate burden in the economic devastation of the last years of the revolution and therefore needed temporary relief represented by paper money and relaxation from strict debt prosecution. He proclaimed the importance of the encouragement of commerce and manufacturing but saw no justification for forgiving loyalists in order to hasten economic recovery. It is also possible to see now Martin's overarching dedication to the interests of the state, but with the lawyers and merchants he did find an increasing kinship in acknowledging that greater nationalism was necessary to gain credibility and sovereignty.[6]

The Society of the Cincinnati, organized as a branch at Hillsborough the previous October, had its first convocation there concurrent with the spring assembly.[7] At the time of organization, the Society tendered an honorary membership to the governor. There were restrictive regulations for membership for commissioned officers of the 13 regiments of the Continental Line. To qualify, officers had to be on active duty or honorably discharged after three years of service. Honorary members were allowed, but could not represent, more than 25 percent of the chapter; such memberships were awarded for life and could not descend to heirs. For many, this organization was viewed as an attempt to introduce hereditary nobility to the Confederation. Governor Martin accepted his honorary membership in a "pantheon" with William Blount, Richard Caswell, William R. Davie, Benjamin Hawkins, John Sevier, Isaac Shelby, and Richard Dobbs Spaight.[8] Including Martin in this honors list is further evidence that the professional soldiers, who had themselves experienced the unprincipled, vindictive, and manufactured lies that circulated in the American army throughout the Revolution, did not accept the charges that had been made against Martin in 1778. Had the Society considered Martin a coward, not even the office he then held would have qualified him for honorary membership.[9]

The small village of Hillsborough, ill-equipped to handle a combined meeting of the assembly and the first meeting of the Cincinnati, became a rustic hubbub of activity. This assembly has been singled out as "remarkable for its ability" and its accomplishments as having "breadth and patriotism, a just conception of the needs of the day and zeal in perfecting legislation," well beyond any other assembly of that period.[10]

Delegates who had failed to attend the previously aborted sessions, leaving a fragile state government without continuity or direction, now found themselves offering excuses for their absences that could be accepted as plausible. The assembly was eager to perform, but many of these same men knew that their absence had contributed to and earlier lack of action. They hastily corrected one problem. By eliminating the spring session of the assembly and shifting to a fall election and winter term, they recognized that North Carolina was a state of small farmers in the majority, and spring was the time of planting when no one wanted to be away from home. Fall legislatures were the common practice in several other states and the next election was set for the third Friday in August with the assembly meeting the first Monday in October.

This change also affected the term of the governor and Council of State. The assembly did not call the election for these offices until later in the session. Alexander Martin was therefore not re-elected until the 3rd of May.[11] On this occasion, the election was only in form. Samuel Johnston, Richard Caswell and Alexander Martin were placed in nomination. Johnston declined immediately and Caswell, astutely coy, confided, "I shall do the same before the day of election."[12]

In his consideration of the pursuit of the office of governor, Richard Caswell anticipated that the salary of the office, as well as that of the comptroller of the state which he held, was about to be reduced by the assembly. Such knowledge was small comfort when there were others maneuvering for handsome rewards in the opening of western land. Caswell considered resignation so as to visit the west.

Alexander Martin defined the legislative priorities to the new assembly: "You are building for posterity. For centuries to come the infant annals of our times will be traced with eagerness by inquisitive posterity for precedents, for maxims to which the future government may still conform." He endorsed the "great wisdom displayed in connecting the states under one common sovereignty in Congress" and recommended that this was "the important moment to establish on your part the Continental Power on its finest basis, by which people of these states rose and are to be continued a nation." He intended to recommend to the assembly certain modifications to the Articles of Confederation that the congressional delegation had suggested.[13] He recognized that river navigation "requires your immediate interposition and patronage. It was necessary our rivers be rendered navigable, our roads opened and supported, by which the industrious planter may have his produce carried to market with more ease and convenience." Navigable waterways that could constitute avenues of commerce were essential as infrastructure for a rural state, to encourage investment and "new resources of industry," and to attract "merchants of opulence ... to settle in the State." The lawyers and merchants smiled in agreement but he was speaking in the equal interest of the farmers and debtors.[14]

The concern about education was appropriated as a cause of the elite, but Martin understood that it had to be an equal concern of all the society that had to develop "men of ability to direct our councils and support her government." To this end he urged "the education of our youth. May seminaries be revived and encouraged, where the understanding may be enlightened, the heart mended and genius cherished."[15] This early and sustained introduction of the importance of the establishment of educational institutions in North Carolina was a fateful contribution of Governor Martin. William R. Davie was in his first assembly and his talents eventually earned him credit as the father of the university, but by following the record of Alexander Martin on that issue there is an observable critical history of political support.

The governor's charge to the assembly initiated a debate on the specifics of the commitment of Article XLI of the state constitution to the public support of "a school or schools" to be "established by the Legislature, for the convenient Instruction of Youth." This article was the basis of public education in North Carolina and the debate initiated public consideration of higher education. The debate also challenged the rejection (by King George and the Board of Trade in London) of earlier attempts by the colonial assembly to establish Queen's College in Mecklenburg County.[16]

William Sharpe, a former delegate to the Continental Congress, introduced the legislation establishing "a University in this State."[17] Another bill, for an academy at Salisbury called Liberty Hall, was the result of lobbying efforts that included the Rev. Samuel Eusebius McCorkle, Dr. Ephraim Brevard, Dr. Alexander McWhorter, and Spruce MacCay, all Princeton men.[18] The academy bill passed but the university bill failed.

With Martin's encouragement for "one common sovereignty in Congress," the legislature approved giving Congress the power to levy import duties. The governor reported to the state's delegates that the assembly had approved "almost all the substance of every principal recommendation relative to Finance," that had been pressed on them by the Congress.[19]

The efforts of the lawyers and merchants of the east to repeal the confiscation of property of Tories and British citizens were emotionally debated. George Hooper, son-in-law of Alexander Maclaine and brother of William Hooper, who had been defeated for this legislature, was a loyalist whose property was confiscated. Henry Eustace McCulloch had fast friends in the assembly but they were powerless to restore the land granted his father by Lord Granville in 1736. Samuel Johnston, Willie Jones, and Benjamin Hawkins, as well as General Butler and Thomas Person, spoke with earnestness and honor for repeal, but Griffith Rutherford called them "Imps of Hell" and they were soundly overwhelmed.[20]

Martin was allied with Rutherford and most of the farmers and debtors on the issue of confiscation, as were William Blount and Abner Nash. Willie Jones and Thomas Person crossed over the other way, demonstrating the difficulty in establishing firm party affiliations. The supporters of repeal of the act accused their opponents of "fanning the passions of the common people," a peculiar criticism in a popular democracy.[21] Alexander Martin has been faulted for having acquired some of the confiscated land of Edmund Fanning and, by implication, having profited by another man's distress. The land was acquired in partnership with his brother-in-law, Thomas Henderson, but there is no indication that it was acquired as anything but an open business transaction.

Congress continued to press the issue of cession of the western lands, which Martin considered "their favorite object."[22] Consideration of cession divided the states that had western territory from states that did not and magnified the weakness of the Congress in the face of deep division. In North Carolina no issue consumed greater attention in the assembly or inspired more examination of self-interest.

The North Carolina congressional delegation began to shift toward support of cession as early as October 1783 when Williamson and Blount reported to Martin that the pro-cession interests in Congress were gaining strength. Rhode Island appeared as the gadfly refusing taxes, in the form of the 5 percent impost tax on trade, for raising federal revenue. As an alternative their delegates suggested use of the western lands of which they had none. The North Carolina delegates recognized the sham of this argument but states with western lands were in the minority. As Williamson advised the governor, the pressure for federal access to the western country had reached epidemic proportions and the envy of the small states threatened "to make us all of the Pigmy breed."[23] Martin's response was a reminder that "This business [the debate over cession] you will conduct according to your prudence, not being limited to any particular instructions more than the reservations in the act."[24] His reference was to the three conditions he had set for cession in January 1783: acceptance by the Congress of the earlier costs of Indian expeditions as part of the North Carolina quota of the federal debt; acceptance by all states of cession concurrent with the establishment of state-by-state debt quotas; and, should states be formed in the western lands, as surely would happen, assumption by these new states of their share of the debt.[25] By September, Williamson and Benjamin Hawkins suggested that the governor consider that North Carolina would gain from lands already ceded by New York and Virginia since sales of lands ceded by the states were to be included as part of the pay to the army and of other debts of the Confederation. The North Carolina position, in their view, was eroding, and pragmatically it would be better for the state to agree to cession before a vote of all the states forced them to concede. Williamson feigned embarrassment that North Carolina should benefit from the generosity of sister states; he cautioned, however, against quick cession which would deprive the delegates of considerable negotiating power.[26]

In December, when Governor Martin rejected the idea of cession, using his earlier analogy of the husbandman, he vigorously argued that the state had suffered disproportionately and that the burden of obligation and debt had to be linked to the ultimate distribution of western territory. Congress continued to press for commitment and the spring assembly debated bitterly. Over the stormy vocal protest of 37 members, the act of cession was approved. A reversionary clause was added to the legislation should the Congress fail to accept cession within 12 months and the state retained sovereignty over the territory until cession was enacted.[27] The legislation once again included the familiar reservations, somewhat more narrowly defined. The act did preempt the efforts of the small states to pressure cession by passage of per capita or land taxes to finance the Confederation. In effect, the North Carolina legislation agreed to cede subject to retirement of the North Carolina obligation to state veterans and a fair quota basis for debt reduction.

The citizens whose territory was to be ceded watched this governmental chess game at such a remote distance as to feel more pawn than participant. Even though many of the conditions added to the North Carolina cession act were designed to protect western interests, those very conditions gave the impression in the West that Congress was unlikely to accept the act.

Representatives of the western counties begged the assembly to give attention to a range of plights on the frontier.[28] According to their account of their experiences, they "were supplicating to be continued a part of the state." They claimed, however, that they were scorned with demeaning epithets that characterized them as "the offscourings of the Earth, fugitives from justice," which many in the assembly would delight in removing.[29] Sevier, who was not a delegate to the assembly, had a different version of the attitude in the assembly. His account claimed "that the Assembly of North Carolina deceived us, and were urging us on into total ruin, and laying a plan to destroy that part of her Citizens who she so often frankly confessed, saved the parent State from ruin."[30] The image of the innocent victims ill-used by schemers was advanced to justify the convention that would establish the state of Franklin.

Under the leadership of Sevier, Arthur Campbell and others, delegates of the western counties of Washington, Sullivan, and Greene (Davidson apparently did not elect delegates) met August 23 at Jonesboro in convention.[31] The first report placed before the convention sought to accept cession by North Carolina and petitioned Congress to accept. The second motion, carried 27 to 15, proposed "forming ourselves into a separate and distinct state, independent of the State of North Carolina, at this time."[32]

Hugh Williamson, on hearing that the Hillsborough assembly had agreed to cession, reversed his advocacy and cautioned delay. He was pursuing a very narrow line in Congress. The governor, cool to cession in 1783, had conversely heeded the urging of the congressional delegates and reluctantly advocated the approval of cession before the deeply divided assembly in 1784. That approach was not an example of the inability of the governor and his delegates in Congress to gee and haw in tandem. The governor and the delegates held a common purpose to protect adequately the reasonable interests of the state. Martin and Williamson functioned as sensitive antennae of a very delicate three-way negotiation conducted in the face of enormous communication barriers as the federal system sought to evolve.

Williamson did not take issue with the strict conditions set within the act of cession, but with the omission of a previous condition that Congress recognize the cost of the Indian expeditions when calculating the national debt. Williamson thought that the assembly might reconsider their action when they realized the important negotiating point they had overlooked and "they will at least suspend certain conditions in the Cession."[33]

Between the spring and fall sessions of the 1784 assembly, the citizens of the western counties prepared for statehood. The bill of rights that was added to the original state constitution of North Carolina had made provision for the possibility of another state to be formed in the western territory.[34] The delegates of the western counties had voted for cession and they arrived home from the legislature with details of the action of the assembly.

The dimension of the approval of an act of cession masked the maneuvers of the land speculators, but they were as intimate with the terms and timing of cession action as any modern-day lobbyist. No man ranged more widely or manipulated more adroitly on the political stage as a land speculator than William Blount. This "manipulator of men" could buy goods for his brother and state legislators for his land company.[35] In the historical metaphor, speculators of any kind are seldom heroes but something more akin to profiteers in wartime, and they may set the tempo for the age. The Blount family epitomized the heirs of the Scottish merchants of the colonial period. They mixed together a lingering fear of the Indians, a direct familiarity with the new state assemblies, penetrating business acumen, and a *soupçon* of human greed into a recipe that overshadowed the settlement of the old southwest. Alexander Martin was sometimes an ingredient of this concoction.

Martin had the sagacity to recognize that such men as William and John Gray Blount or their like would seize the economic moment—in fact, he depended on it. His friendship with John Frohock and Richard Henderson had been a foretaste of that. Martin also knew that men like John Sevier and John Donaldson would rip at the frontier curtain just as his friends Daniel Boone and Griffith Rutherford had done. Martin himself could be of this current but he could not be in the current. Not aloof, he was an evocative force in what was transpiring.

After the 1783 assembly had directed the negotiation to establish the boundary between the settlers and the Cherokee beyond the mountains, Martin wrote William Blount, from whom he ordered goods to be used in the negotiation, to "consider me as joint partner," with the Blount merchant house, "on the venture of the purchase of the goods for the Cherokee Indians." Chargeable for one half of the cost, he accepted "one half of the losses as may attend said goods," but he expected "to derive and share one half of the profits that may arise."[36] Later Blount secured a local monopoly in the eastern tar market and "engaged cargoes for Blount ships by offering Governor Martin 50 percent interest in the enterprise.[37] When the survey of the western acres that were reserved to satisfy military service warrants found the designated territory was infested with Cherokees and was generally inaccessible, the legislative committee headed by William Blount moved the lines of the reserve "to be bounded by lines drawn south from the Cumberland Gap and from the intersection of the Tennessee River and the Virginia line."[38] Along with other inducements placed in the legislation to gain approval of the resurvey action, the governor was granted 2,000 acres of the reserve. It could be argued that this grant was justified as compensation for Martin's service as a colonel of the Continental line and that he had not received such a grant earlier because his length of service did not qualify him. In fact, it is difficult to consider this grant as anything but largesse given to Martin as governor to encourage his support for the interests of the speculators.[39]

Governor Martin was not therefore a speculator in the style of his contemporaries. As governor he had the opportunity to amass unlimited holdings. Richard

Caswell certainly did, and Blount did, so much so that he ultimately became involved in fraud. It is the more remarkable that Martin profited so little either openly or surreptitiously in this land speculation. The act of 1783, approved with the governor's influence, placed his friend, Martin Armstrong, in charge of the newly opened land office at Nashville established to process the military warrants for land in the reserve. John Armstrong, Martin's brother, was placed in charge of a similar office in eastern Tennessee.[40] Through such appointments, Alexander Martin was positioned to make enormous profit from western land speculation. Many of his friends took advantage of the opportunity that the governor had assisted them in acquiring and ultimately would let greed lure them into fraud. In the summer of 1783, it would appear that Governor Martin had maneuvered himself into a position to follow the same course.

The containment of the Indian nations proceeded implacably. The Indians, as a people of the land, ever migrated to the best land nature offered. The speculator expected to warrant the choice lands. Governor Martin instructed that the commissioners he sent to negotiate with the Cherokee "agree upon a western land by which they and you shall be sacredly bounded, which confining and contracting their settlements, they will soon be circumscribed by white Inhabitants and their power reduced to the harmless and inoffensive situation of the Catawbas."[41] Martin had no qualms about the circumspection of the native people. His focus is not vindictive nor is it sympathetic. His priority was the white settlers and he held no overarching concept for native rights. His limited personal experience with Indians had provided little innate respect or compassion beyond his insistence on legal respect for treaty agreements. Indians ignored land ownership as unnatural, while Martin held land title as sacred to governance.

The influence of William Blount in North Carolina peaked in the assembly of 1783 and his shrewd eye was directed to his friends, his state, and to himself.[42] This *troika* of interests channeled his voting influence to the lawyers and conservatives in support of a stronger central government. His purpose was without subterfuge and he professed congressional ownership of the western land would not only reduce state debt burdens, but, more important, it would raise the land prices.[43]

Davie, in his freshman assembly, took every opportunity to gain attention and with dramatic public utterances worthy of the dash of a cavalry officer, he was soon the rising star of the lawyers and creditors. His technique made him easily quotable on issues in an age when the language of politics tended to the obscure and obtuse. Alexander Martin was a master of the political maneuver, in keeping with the regimental commander who moves foot soldier farmers in the unpredictable fogs of conflict. Davie's biographer has characterized the animosity of the relationship between the two men.[44] That relationship at this moment was less animosity than simply the tension that strong-willed individuals bring to the point of debate.

The issue of cession provided Davie with the opportunity to demonstrate his leadership style in the assembly. Concluding in the spring assembly of 1784 that there was a close division, he proposed that cession be tabled until the fall term. That maneuver failed by a single vote; when cession was approved, Davie prepared the written dissent for the 36 who voted no.[45] He restated as concerns many of the reservations that had been dealt with in the act, and reinforced Williamson's fear that the credit due the state on the war debt was needed to cover the expenses of the Indian expeditions. It was the focus on the debt that identified the lawyer group coalescing around fiscal issues. Davie also cautioned patience while neighbor states of Virginia and Georgia retained their large western territories. This was a specious issue for those who were expressing support of a stronger central government. If the new states were sucked into the debilitating whirlpool of self-serving actions on every intrastate issue, federalism would be snuffed out in its cradle. Cession by Virginia had in fact been accepted conditionally by Congress the previous September and the state had approved cession in March.[46]

When the assembly met in October, Iredell, Benjamin Hawkins and Hooper had been defeated, weakening the group of lawyers and merchants now led by Maclaine.[47] At the opening of the assembly the governor was saluted. "We cannot close this address to your Excellency without assuring you that in taking a review of your administration, which has continued nearly as long as the Constitution will allow of, we find every reason to be satisfied that you have constantly employed your best endeavors for the general good and welfare of the people over whom you have presided."[48] Martin thanked the assembly and added that "he considers it the most fortunate circumstance in his life, that the greatest event that ever took place in the new world, the Revolution of those States, was gloriously completed during his administration."[49]

The contest for the governor to succeed Martin was between two former governors: Richard Caswell and Abner Nash. Caswell won by 20 votes.[50] The governor had always taken over the office when elected at the spring term. Martin, however, having been elected May 3, 1784, did not go out of office until the following May, and Caswell, elected November 9, 1784, was not qualified as governor until May 13, 1785. Caswell was functioning as Speaker of the Senate and for a six-month period North Carolina had a governor and a governor-elect. Is it any wonder that these two men, who were now exchanging these two highest offices, virtually as a fiefdom, demonstrated a jealous guarding of their authority and job seekers and political functionaries were confused about who held authority or took advantage of this elongated transition for their own gain?

The assembly had news from their delegates that their cession act had reached Philadelphia in April, a day after the Congress had adjourned, and they also had those reservations to their act forwarded to them by Williamson. The group that had voted against cession, now led by Davie, Thomas Person, and Alexander Mebane, campaigned hard in the election to choose this assembly. They resorted to personal charges of bribery and corruption and they preyed on creditors' fears that their collateral was not secure. William and John Gray Blount were both elected to the assembly and William was chosen Speaker of the Commons. They were positioned strategically to protect their interests and those of their friends as speculators. The western counties had but a single elected delegate and members heard that on August 23 the Jonesboro convention had charged North Carolina with neglect and had petitioned Congress to accept the Cession Act.[51]

In this environment the debate on cession was renewed. Martin had been almost relieved in his notification to Commissioner of Indian Affairs Richard Beresford in June that "this state have [sic] ceded all the Territory west of the Appalachian Mountains to the Mississippi to Congress," and that Indian treaty questions would now be directed to Congress, "if the Cession is accepted."[52] In the new legislature, Martin faced the reversal of the previous act, thus placing those problems back in his lap.

Action came in the House on November 18 and by a vote of 37 to 22 and a day later by 19 to 11 in the Senate, the Act of Cession was repealed.[53] The act of repeal was justified because "cession, so intended was made in full confidence that the whole expense of the Indian expeditions, and the militia aids to the States of South Carolina and Georgia should pass to account in quota of the continental expenses in the late war; and also, that the other states, holding western territory, would make similar cessions, and that all states would unanimously grant imposts of five per cent as a common fund for the discharge of the federal debt; and, whereas, the States of Massachusetts and Connecticut, after accepting the cessions of New York and Virginia, have since put in their claims for the whole or a large part of that territory, and all the above expected measures for constituting a substantial common fund have been either frustrated or delayed."[54] North Carolina was deemed fickle by other states in a round-robin of contradictions that erupted out of the weaknesses of the Confederation.

In his notification to the delegates in Congress of the repeal of cession, Martin also confirmed that North Carolina was resuming its responsibility to treaty with the Indians.[55] Williamson responded from Trenton in December that Congress had been advised of the action of the state.[56] This exchange was significant because it was not a mere rejection of the act of cession but a resumption of sovereignty. Congress was also on notice that while it sought clarity, under defined circumstances, the state anticipated cession.

It was now up to the assembly and governor to clarify sovereignty over the western territory. Alexander Outlaw, the sole delegate of the western counties who had bothered to attend this session, put forward a resolution to create a separate state in the west that would pledge its land receipts as payment for the North Carolina war debt. The proposal was defeated. To appease some of the more reasonable complaints of the western counties, the assembly created a new judicial district and named David Campbell, an opponent of a separate state at the Jonesboro convention, as the judge. In a tactical move to destabilize the leadership in the west, the assembly named John Sevier as brigadier general for the new militia district.[57] Sevier was judged to be "ambitious of fame, character, distinction and achievement."[58] He was the most esteemed leader in the west but, on this passionate issue, he was led by expediency in lieu of resolute principles. He did not want to sacrifice his popularity to a losing cause.[59]

Martin remained in New Bern through the end of the session and into the first part of December, concurring on strategy with his Council of State. The assembly had elected a new council but, like the governor-elect, they were not qualified until the next May. The east was reasserting itself in structuring the council. Martin's last council contained from the west only a representative from Caswell and one from

Mecklenburg counties. The rest were all from the east and all members elected to serve with the new governor were from the east. The paradox was that the governor had to come east to meet with his council when the primary issue on the agenda concerned the western territory.

Martin left New Bern and arrived at "Danbury" by mid–December. From there he placed in action what he considered the intent of his assembly and council. He had dispatched his letter of commission to Sevier by way of the returning Alexander Outlaw, and it was Outlaw who would be the authority, when he reached home, on the actions and issues of the New Bern assembly. Martin's letter to Sevier was direct—here is your commission, here are your orders. The issue of cession or statehood was not mentioned. The governor said he had "received a Talk from the Cherokee nation" that was greatly concerned about the various excesses of the white settlers. He was satisfied that "keeping peace with the Indians [was] sufficiently impressed" on Sevier and that "the powers with which you are armed are sufficient to check the licentious and disobedient."[60] He advised that he intended to treaty with the Indians about the 25th of April at the Great Island.[61] Governor-elect Caswell and Colonel Blount were commissioned and Sevier would be expected to provide the military guard for the delegation.

The governor's response to the concerns of the Cherokee nation was directed to Old Tassel who had communicated his grievances through Colonel Joseph Martin. He apologized to his "brother" for his inability to "see you last spring, as I promised you, as our beloved men at Hillsborough had prevented me, by agreeing and counseling among themselves, that the Great Council of the thirteen American States, at Philadelphia, should transact all affairs belonging to the Red People." How Martin must have delighted in such stylish phrasing to rise above the bickering of his "beloved men at Hillsborough." He recognizes that during this period of neglect "our bad men living near your lands thought we had laid aside all government over them, and that they had a right to do as they pleased." All this was done "against the order of your elder brother," as Martin was greeted, and was not approved by "the good men of North Carolina." Understanding their complaints, he had taken action to repair them. He had made their friend, General Sevier, "our First Warrior for the western country," to whom he had sent "my particular directions to have these intruders moved off." Finally, he declared his intentions to meet with Old Tassel to treaty on April 25 at the Great Island of Holston.[62]

Governor Martin was a guest at Blount Hall on his return from New Bern and at that time he made the arrangements with John Gray Blount to provide the Indian goods to be presented at the treaty "sometime in April or [the] 1st part of May." He exhibited a clear familiarity with the specific preferences of the Cherokee people, ordering "that you will change the light colored Cloths for Blue, as that color will not be agreeable to the Indians, a few fine pieces of blue Cloth will be necessary for the chief Warriors."[63]

Martin did not use Outlaw as his messenger to the Cherokee: he turned instead to Major Samuel Henderson.[64] Well known on the frontier and as a respected warrior by the Indians, Samuel Henderson was the ideal member of the governor's inner family to be trusted as his emissary.[65] The precise direction of the governor to

Henderson was to proceed with dispatch to General Sevier with letters of instruction and that he expected answers in return.[66] He also encouraged Henderson to be an alert observer, to find out what was going on in the West, and to determine whether the acts of the Jonesboro convention were the posturing of a few ambitious individuals or, since the repeal of the Act of Cession, if they actually intended to pursue statehood. Henderson should get copies of everything: names, the constitution they propose, the boundaries they would include, and the laws they would enact to support such a government. As an astute politician, he asked Henderson to discover "whether a faction of a few leading men be at the head of this business, or whether it be a sense of a large majority of the people." He expressed individual concern for the attitude of the Indians, particularly in light of the case of Major John Hubbard, who was accused of killing an Indian.[67] Finally, Martin offered a blank request for "ever other information you think necessary to procure," but he warned Henderson to "conduct yourself with that prudence you are master of."[68] This was a delicate and critical mission.

The letter to Sevier reminded him that the late legislature had not only repealed the ill-conceived Act of Cession but also established the new court district and appointed a new militia commander and an assistant judge for the court district, thus redressing all the grievances put forward as justifications for separation.

In his letter to Old Tassel, Martin provided an official report of the transition that would soon happen in the state government and of the ongoing "talks together on the terms of the separation" of the western region from your "elder brothers in North Carolina." The governor was soon to become a "private brother"; however, "the good Talks that have passed between us will not be forgotten. I will deliver them carefully to my successor, Governor Caswell, who loves you, and wishes to Talk with you in the same manner I have."

The Henderson mission and the delivery of the General's commission mollified John Sevier for a time, and in speeches and letters the General sought to stall the tide of the Franklinites. He reassured Governor Martin from Washington Courthouse on March 22 that "no person here blames you for any past measures, but on the contrary believed you to be a friend of the Western Country."[69] Initially, he prevented delegate elections in two counties for a new convention, but he progressively met the rising current for separation and realized that his popularity was in jeopardy.[70] Reversing his conciliatory tone, "Nallachucky Jack" yielded to the political reality.[71] He attended the new convention and was chosen to preside. The convention framed a constitution and called an assembly that in its first session elected Sevier governor of the state of Franklin.

Martin was at Danbury when he received word of Sevier's public reversal in the form of an official notification signed by John Sevier, Landon Carter and John Cage as governor and speakers of the Senate and House of Commons respectively of the state of Franklin.[72] It was a declaration of independence that Martin, so near the end of his term that his congressional delegates were already sending documents needing urgent action to Caswell, must have considered opportunism. On April 7, Martin issued a circular to the members of the council asking them to meet him at Hillsborough on the 22nd. The summons advised them that the inhabitants of the western counties had declared they were independent and refused the sovereignty of North Carolina. He was convening the council at Hillsborough "then and there in your wisdom to deliberate and advise the measures necessary to be taken on this occasion."[73]

Martin and the council met as appointed and on examination of the letter from Sevier, the statement from the Franklin assembly, and a vast amount of information put together by Major Henderson, there was an explosion of rage. Some of the council wanted an immediate call out of the militia to march across the mountain, arrest the leaders and quell the revolt. They dispatched requests for military support to the governors of Georgia, South Carolina, Virginia, and Maryland. Only South Carolina agreed with the caveat, "Colonel John Sevier might be a fool in his political ventures but his riflemen didn't shoot like fools."[74] Ultimately, cooler heads produced a more diplomatic approach designed to appeal to reasonable caution and logic. On the third day, the council issued "A Manifesto" under the hand of "His Excellency Alexander Martin, Esquire, Governor, Captain-General and Commander-in-Chief of the State aforesaid—To the Inhabitants of the Counties of Washington, Sullivan and Greene." In language that was both conciliatory and respectful but earnest and unyielding, it offered no quarter. It spoke with contempt of "a restless ambition and a lawless thirst for power," coupled with "specious pretences and the acts of designing men," and finally of "the pageantry of a mock government without the essentials—the shadow without the substance—which always dazzles weak minds." It was a reminder that "far less causes have deluged states and kingdoms with blood." It reflected on the "laurels you have so gloriously won at King's Mountain" in contrast with "a black and traitorous revolt from that government in whose defense you have so copiously bled." Imagine the paradox of "seizing that by violence which, in time, no doubt, would have been obtained by consent." The government of North Carolina could never accept this kind of usurpation wherein "a precedent is formed for every district, and even every county of the state, to claim the right of separation and independency for any supposed grievance of the inhabitants."[75]

Copies of this manifesto, in manuscript, were delivered and read throughout the territory. The government of North Carolina would not accept this preemptive severing of the territory by opportunists. General Evan Shelby, who had succeeded Sevier as brigadier general of the militia; John Tipton, the colonel of Washington County; and Colonel James Martin, the Indian agent, all men of considerable influence, exerted sufficient energy to slow briefly the progress toward separation. The manifesto gave them a sound platform for debate but that only stalled the momentum of statehood.[76]

The governor and council recognized that this flashpoint over cession had come when the organization of state government was in transition and vulnerable, so they issued a call for a special session of the assembly to meet at New Bern on June 1 to debate the action of the western counties.[77] The summons mailed to each member of the assembly contained a copy of the manifesto.

There is recent research that asserts that had Martin remained longer as governor, "Franklin would have succeeded in gaining statehood."[78] This thesis views the manifesto as an acceleration of the rhetoric leading to open hostilities. As to rhetoric, it gave as good as it got, but the truth is that on neither side of the mountain were cousins prepared to fight. Martin had strong emissaries in Henderson, Joseph Martin, and General Evan Shelby, and the people of the western counties were by no means united in their desire to fight for statehood surrounded, as they knew themselves to be, by resentful Indians. They understood the wisdom of the observation that there was no need to try to seize by violence that "which, in time, no doubt, would have been obtained by consent." At the same time, Martin had no wish to appear to repeat the role Governor Tryon had taken in crushing the protests of the Regulators.

The act changing yearly sessions of the assembly to late fall had ruled that the new governor would be qualified in June 1785.[79] It appears that Martin wanted the new governor in place when the assembly met, and his final filing report of all land warrants granted by him specifies "during my administration as Governor of the State from the 22nd of April 1782 to May 5, 1785."[80] Richard Caswell was qualified as governor on May 13, 1785.[81]

10

Martin's Personal Life at Danbury

No gracious transfer of power occurred as Alexander Martin ended three and a half years as governor and Richard Caswell assumed the office. The change in the executive leadership had a destabilizing impact on the evolution of western cession that Martin made attempts to avoid but Caswell approached with indifference. There was no change in policy because progress toward cession was now beyond the point of significant alteration. Caswell was simply going to deal with cession in his own fashion. Immediately after he was qualified for office, Caswell received an official letter from Sevier, as governor of Franklin, that was in the form of a countermanifesto "inveighing strongly against Governor Martin."[1] Instead of exhibiting firm continuity with his predecessor, Caswell responded that "I have not seen Governor Martin's Manifesto."[2] If he in fact had not seen the document, he was perhaps the only elected state official east or west of the Appalachian Mountains who had not, and to feign ignorance of such an important declaration gave further appearance of the weak continuity brought about by the change in governors. As if warning off a bully, however, Caswell told Sevier not to assume that he was giving countenance to any action of the so-called state of Franklin. Were Martin and Caswell truly so estranged at this important moment in these negotiations?[3]

Caswell's attitude on the issue of the western lands had a somewhat different purpose to be served. The new governor was much more involved in land speculation in the west and that made him appear more sympathetic to the cessionists. In spite of his interest in western land, Martin attempted to appear even-handed as the governor of all the citizens. It was revealing of Sevier and Caswell that "in private correspondence the two governors, ostensibly bitter enemies, gave mutual assurances of continued business co-operation."[4]

On May 13, 1785, William Blount, serving his only term as speaker of the North Carolina House of Commons, invested his "friend and mentor" with the insignia of the office of governor.[5] At Caswell's direction, the ceremony was "not done in a corner."[6] There were speeches, proclamations, and artillery salutes. Martin apparently was not there and, on June 1, neither was a quorum in attendance at New Bern for the meeting of the assembly called to consider the issue of cession and the preemptive action of the western counties.

At 47, Alexander Martin was out of public office but he had no plans to retire as a farmer. He spent much of his time at Danbury where his mother reigned. While giving befitting deference to his mother, Alexander still was considered the leader of the Martin family and that circumstance was not diminished by the public recognition of his honored service to the state as governor.

This brief period without elective office allowed Martin to concentrate on rapidly breaking business opportunities connected with Guilford County. His brother-in-law, Thomas Henderson, operated a general store at Guilford Courthouse in partnership with Thomas Searcy, another relation.[7] Martin owned land adjoining the site of the courthouse as early as 1772; he and Henderson acquired an additional 350 acres of the confiscated estate of Edmund Fanning. On December 29, 1785, the assembly approved the establishment of a town on 100 acres belonging to Alexander Martin and Thomas Henderson at the site of Guilford Courthouse to be named Martinville. Martin and Henderson were awarded a lot each of their choosing in the plan of the town; a town common was to be laid off by William Dent, Esquire, and commissioners were chosen.[8] Alexander Martin was added as a commissioner a week later.

At the same time that Martin and Henderson were active in chartering the town of Martinville, they were cooperating with residents of the northern half of Guilford County in engineering its division. The southern third of Guilford County had become Randolph County in 1779. That division had left Guilford Courthouse in the southern half of the county. To the north, the transverse flow of the Dan and Haw Rivers encouraged complaints about inconvenience and separation. Danbury lay in this northern half of the county and Martinville had just been created on Martin's land in the south.

Thomas Henderson also was forced to make choices as the new county was created. He had been clerk of court for Guilford County since 1783. Recently he had been allowed to move a store building from James Buchanan's lot at Martinville to his own lot "for the purpose of keeping the Records & other papers belonging to the Clerks office of said County."[9] This image of a county town without a courthouse sufficient to hold the public papers indicates the primitive conditions in the Piedmont of North Carolina where a retired governor lived.

The particular timing of the division of Guilford County was surely the work of Alexander Martin and his family. Of the 12 justices listed for the new county of Rockingham, 4 were Martin's relatives, and Thomas Henderson resigned his clerkship in Guilford and accepted the same position in the new county. As clerk he had to reside in the county and so he and his family came to live at Danbury, very near the center of Rockingham. Martin was a bondsman for the new clerk and the coroner, Adam Tate.[10]

Martin kept his own residence at Martinville.[11] That maintained his base from which he was again elected to the North Carolina Senate for the fall term in 1785. He now had two counties directly under his patronage, and that was redundant unless he continued to aspire to statewide office. Within the confines of state government and electoral law, this power platform was not insignificant. At the seating of the fall assembly, James Coor of Craven County proposed Martin again as Speaker; the office had been vacant since the ascension of Caswell to governor, and Martin was elected unanimously.[12] Martin's statewide influence was considered to be unabated.[13]

The issue of cession had cooled since Martin's manifesto. Caswell had refused to promulgate that document, preferring instead to allow the western counties to grumble among themselves, and allowed the state of Franklin to founder. This approach was encouraged by his fellow speculators who did not want to be behind a threat that the state probably was unequal to pursue and that could only draw lines and make enemies. Prospects were too sweet to allow either law or policy to get in the way. Encroachment on Indian lands continued, and with it, the easing of fear of the power of the tribes to defend their treaty rights. The settlements farthest west seemed unenthusiastic about Franklin, sending no delegates to their meetings and continuing to elect delegates to the North Carolina assembly.

The assembly approved standards for export products and created copyright laws but Davie, who was not a delegate, pronounced the session "infamous" because of the issue of court reform and the open question of loyalist property. The lawyer elite chose this session to seek fundamental changes in the court system established under the 1777 constitution. The core of the system lay in the six district courts, each of which met twice a year. Three judges, elected by the legislature, served this court as a circuit but two of the serving judges, Samuel Ashe and Samuel Spencer, were regarded by the lawyers and conservatives as favoring the radicals and rural inhabitants. Only James Iredell could be considered a part of the lawyer party. The conservatives presented a bill establishing a superior court of appeals with six judges and a separate court of impeachment (this directed specifically as a threat against Ashe and Spencer). Both bills were defeated, the former not until it reached the senate, and the rural majority countered with legislation that extended the jurisdiction of the district courts to cover land suits. This placed in the hands of often untrained and prejudiced justices of the peace the sometimes complicated issue of confiscated property.[14]

Still sensitive to their neighbor Tories, whom they saw regaining support particularly with the lawyers and the elite, the rural majority also appropriated legal prerogatives that the Treaty of Paris clearly denied them by passing legislation denying public office to anyone who had been convicted of aiding the British. Another prerogative ratified all sales that had been made by the state commissioners on confiscated property and declared all such titles had passed to purchasers annulling all liability of the purchasers to legal action. The combined actions regarding court reform and loyalist rights manifested the preeminent position of the legislature over the judiciary, a condition that the elite could not allow to be perpetuated. It was a cohesive core issue around which party politics could coalesce. Martin was a senior classmate of Samuel Spencer at Princeton and they had come south at nearly the same time, with Spencer settling in Anson County. Although both were experienced lawyers, neither found a home in the lawyer faction forming around Alexander Maclaine, James Iredell, and William R. Davie.

Alexander Martin's views on the treatment of the loyalists after the Treaty of Paris reflected the intensity of the bitterness and demand for revenge of the frontier Whigs, but it also identified the palliative effect of reason and justice when exercised by enlightened leadership. What the elite class could never seem to understand was that the grasping, self-serving, intolerant attitude of the rural majority in North Carolina was produced by their general poverty and their generational experiences with religious and political persecution. When threatened by a distant political elite class or by armies on the march, these people could become heroic in defense of their home and family while at the same moment they could be intolerant and unreasonable, capable of unpardonable acts of brutality and revenge. These rooted qualities have made this majority an open platform for demagoguery, religious fundamentalism and political conservatism. When leadership, however, arose from within that was reasoned and reflective, that did not confront or demand immediate solution but developed essential change over time and as tolerable modifications, these people could become valiant guardians of personal rights and religious faith. They were, however, by nature, prejudiced and intolerant and it took a strong leader with sound ethical understanding to resist the opportunity for the demagogic and to attempt the high road of principled leadership. Alexander Martin was one of the first examples of such a man, not always successful in resisting the siren song of self, but generally committed to that principled leadership articulated early in his youth by Princeton President Samuel Davies to "cherish a publick spirit. Serve your Generation. Live not for yourselves, but the Publick. Be the Servants of the Church; the Servants of your Country; the Servants of all."[15]

The leadership that Martin gave to the issue of the treatment of the loyalists through this post-revolution decade illustrates his ability to mold a result that served the public trust. In the bitterness of the revolution, he spoke out and repeatedly counseled nonconformist churchmen who refused to take up arms. In 1779, he helped prepare the bill to enforce the 1777 Confiscation Act, but he sought to include a provision protecting indigent members of Tory families.[16] At the end of the war, as acting governor, he sought pardons for Tories who agreed to join the Continental Line. In 1783, armed with the provisional peace treaty, he sought to gain more humane treatment for Tories, but his own proclamation as governor led to confused actions. The Treaty of Paris represented an opportunity for normalized relations with Britain and Martin led those attempting to vote North Carolina into conformity, urging the assembly to "remove every obstacle to harmony."[17] He must have been personally pragmatic about the treaty, knowing he himself held confiscated land that had belonged to Edmund Fanning.[18] Picking out any of these actions from their context begs a conclusion that may not fairly evaluate Martin's aims. A comprehensive analysis of his actions demonstrates that on this issue he was firm but fair, committed to the protection of the weak, and willing to sacrifice personally for the public good.

Martin also became directly involved as an attorney in the administration of the Farley estate, the heirs of which were four minor Virginia girls bracketed with a major general in the British army and a London widow.[19] Under the continued sway of the controversy over loyalist property, James Parke Farley's widow married the Rev. Henry Dunbar, later to be identified as a true charlatan on the public stage.[20] Dunbar was the priest at the glebe church at Westover, the estate of the bride's late father. He now became trustee for the minor daughters and he retained Martin to act as his attorney in North Carolina in order to obtain appointment as administrator of the wills of the Farley men and guardian for the four little girls.[21] In all these actions, Alexander Martin functioned as attorney-in-fact for the Farley family, and Willie Jones was named surety for the Rev. Dunbar.[22] As administrator, Dunbar was employing prominent North Carolina lawyer-politicians to help him gloss over the connection that his part of the estate had to British citizens.

Alexander Martin's personal life became complicated in 1786. He was a bachelor, a fact that had little significance for a governor when there was no state capital or governor's mansion for a first lady. His siblings had all married and most had produced at least one son whom they had named Alexander. He was certainly an eligible bachelor, good looking, wealthy by the standards of the day, and socially and politically prominent.

Elizabeth Strong arrived in Rockingham County at least by September 1783 when she purchased, in her own right, 188 acres on Double Creek of Fisher Creek and north of the Dan River.[23] She had been born in Virginia about 1750, the daughter of Thomas and Ruth Baker Lewis. About 1769, she married Thomas Strong of Halifax County, Virginia. They located on Sandy River and had at least five sons.[24] Thomas became a "Long Hunter," a term used for men who in October each year left home, to go hunting over the mountains until April. It has been estimated that their profits in one season could exceed that of a farmer for a lifetime.[25] Thomas Strong disappeared during the early years of the Revolution. He may have died in battle, been killed by Indians, or just never returned home from one of the long hunts; the latter is a good possibility because Elizabeth was never identified as a "widow."[26] During the Revolution, Elizabeth's brother-in-law, John Strong, moved south across the border into Rockingham County, North Carolina, where she bought her property in 1783.[27] All those who settled in this neighborhood around Sharps Creek, were friends and relations from Virginia including James Holderness, Lewis Irion, William Langston Lewis (Elizabeth Lewis Strong's half-brother), Mary Fields, John Fields, Valentine Allen, John Pratt, Sarah DeGraffenreidt (widow of Baker DeGraffenreidt), and Turbefield Barnes.

Elizabeth Strong built a home on her property for her family and eventually met Governor Martin.[28] She was not his equal in education, but, on the frontier, such a difference tended to be unimportant.[29] Although he had more than enough social opportunities through which to choose a wife in eastern North Carolina plantation society or in Philadelphia, it would be difficult to find in such places a wife willing to come to "Hoop-hole Bottom." The attraction between Alexander and Elizabeth was obviously more than a physical dalliance but their relationship was never sanctified through marriage. The reason that may have been used by either party could blame the house full of children Elizabeth already had or the lack of proof that she did not have a husband somewhere. Sometime in October 1786, they conceived a child.

The assembly meeting of 1786 coincided with a scandal over actions of the commissioners appointed by the assembly under Governor Martin to liquidate the state's indebtedness to the officers and soldiers of the Continental Line.[30] A year after their appointment, rumors were rampant that fraudulent certificates, some given in blank, had been issued, forgeries had been circulated, and blank service records were claimed.[31] The former governor was not implicated in these illegal activities, but his close associates certainly were, and he was himself busy throughout the year representing others in obtaining and satisfying their claims. As the senior former Continental officer in his district, the former governor under whom the deferred compensation began to be honored, and as a lawyer, it was natural that his services would have been in demand.

Governor Caswell, in reaction to what was already a public outcry, requested a "minute inquiry" by the assembly focusing on the commissioners. Eventually, charges against John Macon were dropped. Benjamin McCulloch was expelled from the senate and Henry Montford, from the Commons, and both were brought to trial. Only McCulloch and a few lesser officers were convicted, fined and sent to prison. The mood throughout the state was one of suspicion and public embarrassment. Twenty-three people were arrested and twenty-eight others were forced to give evidence.[32] By expelling two of its members, the assembly appeared to be attempting to clear its own dirty hands. It is difficult for history to assign guilt over this matter because there was no contemporary standard of measurement for most of the activity. The weaknesses of the court system allowed so much latitude in the application of justice, and the lack of a sufficient appellate system resulted in such misapplication of the law that the entire system seemed farcical. It is difficult to make the point that any person elected to any public office, or appointed to any position associated with the distribution of the bounty warrants, successfully rose above the corruption that operated at this time throughout the state in connection with the bounty lands. Having made that broad accusation of guilt, it is incumbent to add that there is no contemporary public charge or example of corruption or misapplication of the law that has surfaced against Alexander Martin connecting him with any bounty land fraud or misdemeanor. He was paid for services, formally awarded bounty lands by the assembly, and made some modest purchases of his own. Perhaps the best measure of the opinion of his contemporaries as to his reputation at this point of rampant public corruption, is that he was chosen as a delegate to the Continental Congress in December, and, on the last day of the assembly, he was selected as a delegate to the Constitutional Convention at Philadelphia.[33] Within another year, he was elevated again to the highest office in the state.

11

The U.S. Constitutional Convention in Philadelphia

Four years of independence had allowed the functions and branches of state government in North Carolina to begin to harmonize. The jealousies and contentiousness of the former colonies, however, had fed into the vacuum created by the elimination of foreign control and often seemed destined to cause inexorable disunion. Many in Britain were gambling on just such a scenario. Attempts to abrogate these conflicts in Congress had so far proved inconclusive. The five-state Annapolis Convention in 1786 had ended in the summons of all states to meet in May of the following year in Philadelphia to entertain the possibility of a complete revision of the Articles of Confederation. James Madison thought that the problem was that those upon whom change depended were not well informed nor well disposed so that "we have both ignorance and iniquity to control, we must defeat the designs of the latter by humoring the prejudices of the former." William Grayson, a Virginia delegate to the Continental Congress but not to the convention, seemed to have a grasp of the dynamics that a convention might offer to solve the shortcomings of the Congress. "Affairs are not arrived at such a crisis as to ensure success to a reformation [of the Confederation] on proper principles; a partial reformation will be fatal; things had better remain as they are than not to probe them to the bottom. If particular States gain their own particular objects, it will place other grievances perhaps of equal importance at a greater distance: if all are brought forward at the same time one object will facilitate the passage of another & by a general compromise perhaps a good government may be procured."[1]

On the last day of the 1786 fall assembly, the delegates affixed a preamble to their election of delegates to the proposed convention.[2] Largely the work of James Iredell, it spoke more for the position of the lawyers and nationalists when it found

North Carolina "ready always to make concessions to the well being and happiness of the whole."[3] Meeting in joint session, the assembly nominated Governor Caswell, former governor Alexander Martin, Richard Dobbs Spaight, Hugh Williamson, William R. Davie, Willie Jones, and Samuel Johnston. By ballot they chose Caswell, Martin, Spaight, Davie and Jones. Historians have repeatedly attempted to analyze the political balance in this delegation. As chosen by an assembly with a rural majority, it appears that a range of viewpoints were represented and only Jones was an avowed opponent of change to the Confederation. He immediately resigned his election and Caswell appointed Hugh Williamson in his place. Caswell had allowed his nomination but realized that his poor health would make it difficult for him to attend. He also convinced himself that it would not be good for the state if the governor were absent for months in a row. As his replacement, he selected William Blount, a delegate to Congress who was willing to come over from New York to attend the convention. In its final form, as it related to the federal government, the delegation was weighted toward a stronger national government by the views of Spaight, Williamson, and Davie. Martin also favored strengthening the national government but he balanced that with an arbitrary interest in protecting the rights of the states. "It is doubtful whether any of the other twelve states witnessed [in their legislative consideration over the selection of their delegations] such a clear, thorough, and deliberate debate on the merits of state rights versus federal union."[4] Blount's view was more that of a skeptic who could not afford to be left out of what might be a transforming debate, however, as he confided early to Caswell, "I still think we shall ultimately and not many years hence be separated and distinct Governments perfectly independent of each other."[5]

Alexander Martin has been called a particularist by virtue of his concern for the rights of the states but that seems a less than adequate sobriquet. He firmly believed in the strengthening of the central government as a necessary counterbalance to the international intentions of Britain, Spain, and France. He "hated both the English and the sort of government at a distance that the English had imposed on America."[6] He defined to Caswell, however, the scope of his concerns: "It is no small task to bring to a conclusion the great objects of a United Government viewed in different points by thirteen Independent Sovereignties; United America must have one general Interest to be a Nation, at the same time preserving the particular Interest of the Individual States."[7] Within the five-man delegation, Martin came closest to being the bellwether of the popular mood within the state that would ultimately be required to approve any governmental form created in convention. As the former governor, he was the senior elected official in the delegation and he was, in spite of Blount's considerable dealings as a speculator, the only representative of the frontier farmer.

When Martin wrote the governor on April 1, he did not know that Caswell was planning to step aside as a delegate. He was concerned, as had been every member of the Congress, with the ability of the state to support the delegates to the convention. That concern may account in part for the fact that, although he had been elected already to be a member of the Continental Congress in session in New York, Martin had not made any move to take his seat.[8] The governor responded to Martin, suggesting that all delegates were concerned about the reported high cost of living in Philadelphia. "Mr. Spaight is in as disagreeable a situation with regard to Cash as myself."[9] Martin had apparently sent bills of exchange that Caswell had given to his son, Winston Caswell, to convert and thus the governor was able to return some cash that he would need. The delegates were to receive warrants in the value of £64 per month for expenses.[10] Although earlier Caswell and Martin had guessed that the convention would last three months, the governor sent four months' allowance at the recommendation of Spaight "least we should be stinted as he was at Congress & obliged to run in debt."[11] It was news to Martin that the date of the convention was now proposed as the second Monday in May, and Caswell thought that departure May 1 would be "time enough." This was the letter in which Caswell also advised that, because of his health, he was reconsidering the trip to Philadelphia and that he would meet with the council to make the decision. On the council was John Gray Blount, and the Craven representative advised that if the governor were unwilling to attend the convention, Blount's brother, William, would be able to serve. "To all Blounts at all times political power meant economic advantage and personal prestige" and they recognized the convention as an opportunity that the assembly had not chosen to offer to any of the Blounts.[12]

Caswell also sent Martin "testimonials under seal of the State to the papers relating to the estate of Messrs. Farley." This trip to Philadelphia was an expedient opportunity to carry forward some of the legal proceedings surrounding the Farley estate. The trip originated in late April in Martin's own carriage driven by Prince, his manservant.[13] The normal route would have been by way of Petersburg, which allowed a stop at Westover and a meeting with the Rev. and Mrs. Dunbar and the four Farley girls. Aside from the opportunity to make current matters concerning the Sauratown, this was a chance to recommend the governor to other family relations in Philadelphia upon whom he would be expected to make a call. There was the widow Byrd's brother, Thomas Willing—a partner of the financier Robert Morris—and certainly Martin would call on the Shippens, her mother's family.[14] Since two of her uncles had been classmates of Martin's at Princeton, it was a meeting he would have anticipated.[15]

By the 22nd of May, Martin reached Philadelphia and took rooms at the Indian Queen, which became the informal headquarters of the convention. Other locations like the City Tavern, the George, and the Black Horse were alternate locations for after-hours debates.[16] He was joined at the Indian Queen (at Fourth Street between Market and Chestnut) by Hugh Williamson, Richard Bassett of Delaware, Alexander Hamilton of New York, John Rutledge and Charles Pinckney of South Carolina, George Mason and James Madison of Virginia, and Cabel Strong, Nathaniel Gorham and Elbridge Gerry of Massachusetts.[17] In the course of the months of debate these delegates at the Indian Queen had a "hall or common room to themselves, where they could talk informally about convention issues that needed to be kept secret."[18] With many delegates privately quartered and others scattered about the city, the Indian Queen took on the roll of a gymnasium and debating society where arguments were tested and honed and where opinions were shaped and alliances achieved. "They could hold informal gatherings, pass around cigars, and circulate decanters of wine as they called over each day's events and prepared the strategies and surprises of tomorrow's."[19] The Indian Queen had 16 rooms on the second and third floors for guests and a fourth-floor garret for servants. The stable accommodated 50 to 60 horses with sheds for the carriages belonging to the guests. The five large public rooms on the first floor were furnished with plain, sturdy furniture, cheap engravings and maps. Guest rooms were furnished "with a rich field bed, bureau, table with drawers, a large looking glass, neat chairs, and other furniture."[20]

Those who took up lodging at the Indian Queen represented no particular political agenda or regional bias. Pinckney, for example, arrived with ideas for amending the Articles of Confederation and Hamilton was committed to centralism. It was Madison, however, who, by placing what came to be called the Virginia Plan on the floor first, set the rubric for the debate at an elevated perspective. The Virginia Plan took for granted that a substantial transfer of powers would have to be made from the states to the federal union, and a further critical feature of the plan introduced the still-undefined necessity of the separation of powers.[21]

James Monroe described the Philadelphia convention as "a body assembled under the particular direction of the States for a temporary purpose in whom the lust for power cannot be supposed to exist."[22] Philadelphia shared with the Annapolis convention the characteristics Monroe described, but Annapolis had been poorly attended and limited in scope. The Philadelphia convention added two ingredients absent at Annapolis: it was attended by not only more delegations but by more substantial delegates. The inclusion of General Washington on the Virginia delegation added stature and it was supposed that he would be called to the chair. In fact, Madison fretted that Washington's great prestige might be squandered if the convention were aborted.

The other consequential distinction introduced at the Philadelphia convention was the presence of delegates who came prepared to seize the initiative in defining the issues. James Madison's "own political career and influence rested, quite simply, on the recognition that a man who did his homework and thought through issues and alternatives before debate began, could often lead the lazier colleagues along the avenue he had selected." It has been concluded of Madison that his success in launching this convention in the direction that he envisioned was "a tribute to his preeminence at a certain style of elitist politics," and on the other hand it was "a measure of how little systematic thought the problems of the confederation had previously engendered."[23]

At informal gatherings at the Indian Queen, Alexander Martin was able to renew his relationship with James Madison. He had been influential 20 years earlier in persuading the senior James Madison to allow his heir to matriculate at Princeton. Now, there were nine graduates of that school at Philadelphia, more than double the number represented by any other school. Gunning Bedford of Connecticut, Madison's roommate as a student, was of exceeding physical size. Oliver Ellsworth, also representing Connecticut, was known broadly throughout the colonies and acted as a vigorous defender of the rights of the states. Luther Martin of Maryland spoke long and often as a legalist. William Paterson of New Jersey was the author, probably with Luther Martin, of the New Jersey Plan that demanded states have an equal vote in a unicameral legislature. As a group they tended toward the protection of states' rights. Paterson, along with Roger Sherman of Connecticut and John Dickinson of Delaware, led the local power faction that could often count on Alexander Martin's support.

Aside from his natural associations with fellow Princeton graduates, Martin already had respectable introductions into the often-elegant Philadelphia society, aroused as it was to singular anticipation by the arrival of George Washington. The general and his wife were already housed at Lemon Hill, the three-story brick mansion of Robert Morris, considered the grandest mansion in Philadelphia. They had arrived a week before Martin, in time to attend the second triennial of the General Society of Cincinnati. There were those who saw the members of this society, "panting for nobility and with the eagle dangling at their breast," as a developing American aristocracy.[24] Washington was cautiously sensitive to that criticism from the likes of Jefferson. The Cincinnati had adjourned on the 19th but their triennial had been a suspicious omen for those who feared a grand alliance to create a monarchy.[25] Dr. William Shippen had advised his son that much was expected of the delegates gathered but "Aristocracy is said to be the Idea of almost all of them—I shall not call it a Miracle if [General Washington] is seen living in Philadelphia as Emperor of America in a few years."[26] Martin was not being frivolous in giving Governor Caswell a hint of the work of the convention, after months of debate and before the actions were made public, when he confided, "they are not about to create a King."[27]

Alexander Martin enjoyed immediate access to the Philadelphia society through his friendship with the Byrd/Farley family at Westover. The widow of William Byrd III, Mary Willing Byrd, was the sister of Robert Morris' partner, Thomas Willing, and of Elizabeth Powell, wife of Samuel Powell. The Powells' niece, Anne, was married to William Bingham, a former British consul and commercial agent in the West Indies. The Morrises, Powells, and Binghams all had fine homes in a four-house compound, surrounded by a large formal garden that Washington noted in his diary included "lemon, orange, and citron trees, and many aloes and other exotics." Martin was a guest at many of the teas, country outings, and dinner parties where he might have noted how Elizabeth Powell enjoyed teasing Washington and how much he enjoyed her attention.[28]

He also had his own introduction at the homes of William Shippen, Jr., and his brother John, both his Princeton schoolmates.[29] William Shippen's wife was Alice Lee, daughter of Thomas Lee of Stratford Hall and sister of "Light Horse" Harry Lee. In 1791 their son, Thomas Lee Shippen, was to marry Elizabeth Carter Farley, the eldest of four minor Farley children. Dr. Shippen had been director general and chief physician of the American army at the beginning of the Revolution.[30] Martin was a welcome guest at Shippen House whenever he was in Philadelphia.

It is critical to appreciate the power of the powerless in order to explain the dynamics that made this convention unique among the world's assemblies. George Washington "embodied the ideal of limited power, restrained and checked, but with a dignified authority."[31] In a similar way Madison saw the convention in its unique form as "the transcendent and precious right of the people to 'abolish and alter their governments,'" and the Philadelphia Convention was thus "a body, irregular and powerless, outside both the constitution it replaced and the one it proposed; it defined its own role and then disappeared."[32]

Extending to the debate over the various powers of the executive, it was this same calm, dignified manner that gradually eased delegates' "commitment to the supremacy of the legislature and the evisceration of the executive."[33] Such extreme precautions against monarchial rule as a three-member executive were resisted. Then, reasonable limits on power such as legislative override of the presidential veto helped create a balance between the legislative and executive branches of government. In each of the state constitutions, the local legislature was supreme, "looked on as the voice of the people which could control a governor any day."[34] Alexander Martin's experience, as one of those present who had been a state governor and had been restricted in his actions at critical moments by an overcautious constitution, was critical to temporizing these fears and encouraging the creation of an executive with enough power to balance the jurisdiction of the legislature.

Alexander Martin already knew many people in other delegations and he has been recognized as one of the few political bosses at the convention.[35] It is, however, hard to see him as anything but the lone representative of the rural majority of his state. He was considered well-to-do, arriving in his own carriage replete with gold shoe buckles, sleeve buttons and a gold-headed cane, and his own manservant. He was one of only 16 members who owned "what we might call productive slaves."[36] Martin and Hugh Williamson were judged to be the antitheses within the North Carolina delegation. It has been asserted, "depending on whether Williamson's or Martin's point of view dominated, North Carolina could be lured into the Madisonian camp."[37] Although both held strongly to the interests of their state, Martin's view was molded more through state government and Williamson's evolved more through his service as a regular delegate to the national Congress. To that extent, it is possible to see Martin more as the advocate of states' rights and Williamson more as the nationalist, with the others falling on the spectrum in between.

North Carolina didn't even realize that it was the third most populist state in the union.[38] Since it did not have the commerce and budding industry or the grand plantations of the large states, it thought of itself as somehow small. The lawyers and merchants of the east could no longer control the new majority of the subsistence farmers who had no grand aspirations except to be free of great powers who ruled from afar. As the only delegate representing this modest majority, Alexander Martin found frequent sympathy for the interests of the small states or local-power faction. His friend William Paterson of New Jersey could assemble such a faction, often referred to as the Patersonians.[39] That did not preclude Martin's acceptance of the broad premise of the Madisonians in the Virginia Plan but the small state plan always represented a check against the perception of the juggernaut of nationalism. No matter how cosmopolitan Martin might be, or prone to the business potential of America in the larger world, it was the fears of bigness and growth and the remoteness of government that he and all the North Carolina delegation would have to assuage when they got home. Martin realized that he represented the "outsiders" in the union, the people who "wanted government to leave them completely alone and free." Charles Mee is wrong when he asserts, "the real outsiders were not represented at the convention at all."⁴⁰ Is his description of the outsiders not the epitome of the Scotch-Irish who were Martin's people? What has to be recognized in Martin is that he does represent these interests but not by exploiting their fears and uncertainties. Rather he knew their misgivings and spoke for them but he also recognized that they would never be great as long as they remained so narrow. So he was always leading them to do more, to be better, to break out of the paralysis of suspicion and look beyond their concerns. As William Pierce of Georgia noted, Martin was "not skilled in public debate" but he was "a man of sense and a good politician."⁴¹ In that conference room at the Indian Queen and at outings and social gatherings, Martin represented the outsider with equal vigor and fine impartiality. The rural majority in the North Carolina assembly in 1786, lukewarm to the entire prospect of a national convention, could have sent a delegation to firmly espouse the antinational sentiment in the state. In the original nomination, including Caswell and Jones along with Martin, that was their intent, but in the end they resorted to those who were willing to go and those for whom it was convenient. Martin was the closest thing that majority had to a standard bearer and he could have been a spoiler or a reactionary. There were such delegates. He has been criticized for speaking so seldom in the public debate and the assumption is that he had little impact on the convention or on the ultimate acceptance of the constitution. His debate, as it always was in the North Carolina legislature, was most effective off the floor where his opinions were heard because he represented so well the best interests of the people who sent him. His was the early example, in the purest form, of the politician as public servant and nowhere is that more evident than at this convention.

Philadelphia lay between the Delaware and Schuylkill Rivers and the humidity could be unbearable. By noon on a summer day the air was lifeless behind the windows that were shuttered to protect the privacy of the proceedings. The flies were intolerable.⁴² Southerners were fortunate in their dress, which accommodated the climate. Light camel coats and breeches provided comfort that the woolen-suited New Englanders coveted.

Philadelphia was considered the first city of America with a population of 43,000. It boasted a college of physicians that included Dr. Shippen on the faculty.⁴³ However, filth was thrown in the streets. Backyard privies contaminated wells; all the accompanying pestilence associated with typhoid fever, smallpox, bloody flux, and diphtheria ravaged society. Martin knew Philadelphia from his boyhood. This was the big city of his youth, the stopping place on his returns to Princeton or to see his family. He had known the city as a soldier and tried to protect it from capture early in the Revolution. Now he returned as the former governor of a sovereign state. When he was accorded the appellation of "Excellency" (that was the salutation given to the attending governors), he rose tall among equals.⁴⁴

It was almost a month after the opening session of the convention before Alexander Martin was recorded as part of any public action on the floor. On Saturday, June 23, he seconded Madison's motion that was directed at eliminating from the Federal Constitution a practice, found in some state laws, that allowed legislators to create positions to which they would have themselves appointed and from receiving benefit from a salary increase for an office if they were party to approving the increase.

Such practices had contributed to the erosion of public confidence in elected representatives. On that day North Carolina voted in the negative in spite of Martin's second. Ultimately the draft document contained the prohibition against double officeholding.[45]

A late arrival at the convention on June 6 was the self-styled champion of state rights, Luther Martin. "A wild, slovenly, heavy-drinking fellow," this Martin could harangue the delegates for as much as a day and a half in contrast to Alexander Martin's reluctance to rise to any public pronouncements.[46] The two Martins did have some shared similarities in their background. They were both born near the Raritan River in New Jersey. Both graduated from Princeton: Luther Martin was in the same class (1766) as Waightstill Avery, Hezekiah Balch, and Hezekiah James Balch, who all settled in North Carolina. They were at Princeton with Alexander's brother, Thomas.[47]

By the middle of June, when William Paterson placed the New Jersey Plan before the convention, the obstinate of the states' righters had made it in fact a makeover of the Articles of Confederation. A vote of seven states to three, with Maryland divided, rejected the New Jersey Plan and committed the convention to a total redesign of a new form of government. North Carolina voted with the majority.

The question now lay in the makeup of the legislative branch of the government. Even some of the states that had opposed the New Jersey Plan were unwilling to submit to a legislature based solely on proportional representation. Hints of compromise abounded. "On the floor and off it, over tea at Robert Morris's, Madeira at Mrs. House's, and brandy at the Indian Queen, the delegates moved toward a consensus on the structure and basis of the new government that could be recommended alike to the citizens" of the various states. The Madisonians had a "majority for their solution, but in this gathering, it was now quite plain, a simple majority would not be enough. Somehow a 'sense of the meeting' would have to be fashioned."[48]

On July 2, a grand committee was made up of rigid small-staters and adaptable large-staters and a few known compromisers thrown in—one member from each state delegation. Davie was appointed from North Carolina. The "Great" Compromise that this committee fashioned established the two branches of the legislature: one branch based on proportional representation and the second branch with each state holding an equal vote. All appropriation authority was vested in the former branch to appease the large states. During the days of debate on this compromise, North Carolina seemed to remain within the reach of both sides.

There was a critical debate within the overall consideration of the compromise, which had particular interest for the North Carolina delegation. The debate concerned the way the slave population was to be counted in calculating a state's population. Sometime on July 1 or 2, William Blount, William Pierce, and William Few, delegates to the convention and the Congress, received word that, if they would come to New York, Congress would have a quorum and could vote on the question of reasserting American claims to navigation rights on the Mississippi, an issue of great personal importance to the three southern speculators and critical to the ultimate value of western lands.[49]

There is a theory, developed by historian Staughton Lynd, that the departure of Blount, Few, and Pierce was the first step in the evolution of an intrigue over counting the slaves in allotting proportional state representation in the lower house of the proposed legislature. The speculators were still in New York when the original proposal, to count slaves on a three-fifths basis in the census of each state to calculate population, was defeated by the convention On July 11 Alexander Hamilton returned to the convention from the meeting of Congress. Arriving on the same day in Philadelphia was Manesseh Cutler, a Massachusetts clergyman; he was also the chief lobbyist of the Ohio Company and holder of a grant of six or seven million acres of the Northwest Territory.[50] Cutler's diary, which provides the best contemporary description of the setting at the Indian Queen that summer, lists Madison and Alexander Martin among the delegates to whom he was introduced on his arrival. He says that the delegates stayed up "until half after one," presumably with Cutler in attendance. He gives no details of the discussions nor does he suggest what other caucuses may have been held by Hamilton elsewhere in the city. However, at the opening of debate on the 12th, Gouverneur Morris of New York moved to add a clause to the compromise "that taxation shall be in proportion to Representation."[51] The clever maneuver was designed to dampen the appetite of delegates from slave states for pressing for higher populations. To this version of the three-fifths compromise, Staughton Lynd suggests a second national compromise. On the 13th, Congress in New York approved the Northwest Ordinance, which settled the question of slavery north of the Ohio River. Congress, with a Southern majority, made possible by the presence of Blount, Few, and Pierce, approved the exclusion of slavery from any future states in the Northwest Territory. If these separate votes did in fact represent a Quid Pro Quo, the North Carolina delegation was hip deep in the design and execution. Congress needed to sell land in the territory in order to pay its debts and the Ohio Company was offering to purchase a large piece and to organize it. Cutler could put tremendous pressure on Congress to sell using counterthreats to deal directly with the states. If he made such a settlement with New York, Massachusetts, and Connecticut, it would tame the factions in those states that had been so opposed to the actions of the Southern states with western lands—Virginia, North Carolina, and Georgia—in dealing with their own speculators.

On July 14, at 5:00 A.M., Manesseh Cutler left the Indian Queen with Alexander Martin, Caleb Strong, George Mason, and his son, Hugh Williamson, James Madison, John Rutledge, Alexander Hamilton, and some other friends. Riding in their carriages, the expedition crossed the Schuylkill River to visit the renowned botanical garden of John Bartram.[52] The early hour had been selected so as to be back in Philadelphia for the session at 11:00 A.M. Was this excursion just an outing in the country of all the principals, as the play approached the climactic act, or was it a necessary getaway from other delegates to finalize commitments?[53] That Saturday session on their return appeared to be a rounding out of last comments before fateful action. On Monday morning, as the session opened, the question on "the whole Report amended & including the equality of votes in the 2d.branch" was carried five states to four.[54] North Carolina voted with the small states (Spaight alone voting no), to make the majority that finally confirmed the grand committee report. Note that Caleb Strong, who had been on the Saturday outing across the river, voted yes and split the Massachusetts vote that otherwise would have been expected as a no; Alexander Martin and Hugh Williamson, who had been on the same outing, were joined by Davie to carry the North Carolina vote as "aye." In voting with the small states, North Carolina had voted to save the convention.

Reverend Cutler's diary of self-approbation is one of the few animated glimpses of the convention. The secrecy had been so heavily imposed on the delegates that it inhibited their literary inspiration, leaving the musings of the Rev. Cutler to capture the setting from Independence Hall. Cutler reported that on arrival at the Indian Queen, he had been met by a young Negro in ruffled shirt and powdered hair, who showed him to his room that looked out upon the river and the Jersey shore. He characterized the furniture as handsome and found two current issues of the latest London magazines.[55] On Cutler's first night, Caleb Strong had introduced him to Governor Alexander Martin. Cutler, an engaging, irresistible man of insatiable curiosity who lobbied for the prospects of the Ohio Company, must have approached Martin with informed knowledge of Richard Henderson, Daniel Boone, and Martin's manifesto on the state of Franklin.

Having settled the large-state/small-state controversy over proportional representation, the convention addressed a series of North-South compromises. There was an overriding feeling that, if this government were to succeed, "no faction could leave Philadelphia feeling it had got the short end of the bargain."[56]

Alexander Martin seconded one last motion on the convention floor on July 26. George Mason had proposed that the location to be chosen for the new federal government not be in a city already the seat of a state government. The prohibition had merit but it was agreed that it could be dealt with outside the Constitution and Mason withdrew the motion as an unnecessary obstacle to the work of the Committee on Detail that was, on that day, to begin 11 days of deliberation to work through the details and to put the resolutions already passed into order. The convention adjourned for these 11 days. Delegates had an opportunity to report to their governors and political allies in their states. Martin wrote Governor Caswell the next day, apologizing that the "Injunction on Secrecy" had prevented the full disclosure of the events of the deliberations that had been promised before the convention. He considered the ban to have been prudent "least unfavorable Representations might be made by imprudent printers of the many crude matters & things daily uttered & produced in this Body, which are unavoidable & which in their unfinished state might make an undue impression on the too credulous and unthinking Mobility."[57] The scrutiny of the press would have made impossible the work that this convention accomplished.

Martin had the opportunity to call on, and to attend the sailing of, Baron Johannes von Watteville and his wife, Countess Benigna, whom he had met on several occasions in visits to Salem, where, since October 1785, they had been Bishop and "General Eldress" of the *Unitas Fratrum*. They had come from Germany to make extended visits to Moravians in Pennsylvania and North Carolina and to missions among the Indians. They sailed from Philadelphia on their return, while Martin was at the convention, and he was the source of the news of their safe departure when he got back to Salem in September.[58]

By the Monday when the convention reconvened, William Blount was back in New York in Congress ready "to keep his mouth shut and eschew his usual rascality."[59] William R. Davie, on the other hand, had written Iredell and Governor Caswell that he now intended to return home. He was bored. He thought that matters would be drawn out into September but "all the general principle were already fixed," and he had pressing business. Davie departed on the 13th without signing or seeing the final draft document. Delegates like George Mason, who were not won over by the final document, began to lose patience with "the precipitate, and intemperate, not to say indecent manner, in which the business was conducted, during the last week of the convention, after the patrons of this new plan found they had a decided majority in their favor."[60]

Alexander Martin was diligent in his attendance as a delegate, both on the floor of the convention and in the extended debate. He was not a frequent speaker nor was he inclined to take center stage. He was, as were all members of the state delegation, aware that the Constitutional Convention was "a Circumstance that has not Occurred in the History of men," and thus he accepted his office as a high trust. He had departed for Philadelphia as the member of his delegation most closely representing the rural majority, therefore, by assumption, most skeptical of Federalism. He returned as an energetic advocate of a revolutionary concept of government of the people in union. He would have to convince his constituency that, as such an advocate, he was not a traitor to their trust.

It was during the 11 days of recess—called so that the Committee on Details could work out the Great Compromise—that Martin was notified of the birth of his son, Alexander Strong, on July 8. It was news he appears not to have shared. Perhaps something of his mysterious ambiguity may be alluded to in Hugh Williamson's remark to Iredell that he was "inclined to think that the great exertions of political wisdom in our late governor [Martin], while he sat at the helm of our state, have so exhausted his funds, that time will be required to enable him again to exert his abilities to the advantage of the nation."[61]

Alexander Martin left Philadelphia two weeks after Davie, having given the governor advance warning and in the belief that he could more easily leave the convention at this point, because "the Deputations from the State of North Carolina have generally been unanimous on all great questions, and I flatter myself will continue so until the Objects of their mission be finished."[62] Williamson was not convinced that he too could be spared since North Carolina was now "reduced to a mere representation," and only one of the delegates originally appointed by the legislature remained. Then in a competitive jibe that could only elevate his own rectitude, he assured Caswell that he and Blount could be depended upon "for we would not have it alleged that Gentlemen whom you had been pleased to honor with the Public trust have failed in a single Iota of their duty to the Public."[63] Obviously Martin's priority had shifted from hearing out the final details of debate to attending to the pressing business of convincing an electorate of the wisdom in that document. He advised Governor Caswell that he was "obliged to be at Salisbury Court in Sept. next," which he viewed as more critical than the honor of his signature on the seminal document of his age.

12

Debate over Ratification of the Constitution

The trip from Philadelphia took ten days, putting Martin in North Carolina on about the 6th of September. The August election for the assembly was engaged in "a curious mixture of expectancy and passivity" with old virulent fears unattended by any details from Philadelphia.[1] On his arrival in Guilford and Rockingham counties, Martin delivered his personal evaluation of a constitution that even he had not seen. His paradoxical situation allowed him the first word on the new government so he could put the best spin on the contents that he thought would not be betrayed when the published document arrived in a few weeks. He could not be seen as having deceived his friends, but he wanted to avoid, as best he could, taking on all the anger he anticipated from these enemies of central authority. In the August election to the assembly, he had already been chosen as one of their senators. How quickly might they turn on him? Of the five delegates from North Carolina, he was the one who risked the greatest backlash as a politician for his steadfast participation in the debate and the action of the Philadelphia convention. Some detractors have insinuated that Martin's failure to sign the Constitution was his effort to mask his involvement or his support of the procedures. The contradiction of this theory lies in Martin's actions in the next 12 months.

An examination of the Salisbury District Court Minutes of 1787 offers no clue to any pressing business that required Martin's urgent attention but the birth of his son did. Ten days after Martin sent the notice to Caswell of his intent to leave the convention, Elizabeth Strong deeded her property on Fishing Creek to James Rhodes for £50.[2] Elizabeth and the baby were at Danbury. They remained there at least through 1790 under the watchful eye and stern observation of Grandmother Jane Hunter Martin.[3] On February 23, 1788, Elizabeth purchased 50 acres on the north side of Dan River from Danbury for £40; the sale was witnessed by her son John. A residence was constructed there for Elizabeth's older children.

By September 27, Martin was again in Salem with several other gentlemen, probably lawyers, on the way to Salisbury court.[4] He provided the Moravians with his report on the work of the Federal Convention and delivered letters and *nachrichten* from their Pennsylvania brethren. By October 18, the Moravians had a copy of the new Constitution "prepared by the Convention in Philadelphia for the future government of the United States" and, as was their practice with such public enactments, they studied and thoroughly debated the probable impact of the new Constitution on their congregation.[5]

The campaign for ratification began throughout the state in churches and at court sessions. A look at the results of the August election showed that a clear majority of delegates would continue to be cool toward central authority. In defining the sides in relation to ratification of the Constitution, it became convenient for historians, even in North Carolina, to use the terms federalist and anti-federalist although those labels did not yet refer to formal political parties.[6] In Surry, Joseph Winston, one of the senators, called a county meeting at Richmond Courthouse for November 3. The Moravians sent brothers Stotz and Reuz as their representatives. They reported that they found "nearly all were in favor of it [the Constitution]."[7] This initial support of the work of the convention may reflect the interpretation of the document provided by Alexander Martin at the Superior Court. In the Piedmont counties there was customarily strong Whig enthusiasm for anything that appeared to be part of the evolution of independence. The Scotch-Irish were emboldened by independence that had confirmed to them their Jerusalem. The Moravians, and most of the dissenters, saw stable government as their security from marauders and horse thieves and as a guarantee of economic security. Initial harmonies, however, gave way quickly to their natural particularism.

At each of the county courts, at Surry, followed later in November at Martinville in Guilford, and at Rockingham Courthouse, then in December at Randolph Courthouse, Alexander Martin faced an opposition mustering against the Philadelphia convention.[8] He was, at each venue, the authority on what had happened at Philadelphia. This campaign progressed from the courthouses to the legislature when that body met on November 19 at Tarboro. On the first day, the senator from Guilford County was elected once more as Speaker. He was also the only senator who had been a delegate to the Constitutional Convention, although Davie and Spaight were elected to the Commons. These were the three men who had been in the delegation and who actually had been chosen as delegates by action of the previous assembly. Informally, therefore, they were in the position of reporting to their peers. It was the task of formulating plans for the North Carolina ratification convention that occupied much of the attention of the delegates to this legislature. Two days into the session, they set Wednesday, December 5, as the date at which they would "enter on the important business of the Federal Convention."[9] This schedule allowed precisely two weeks for the usual agenda on the Senate floor and for the informal debates in upper rooms and private homes where delegates were lodging.

When the legislative debate eventually opened on the design of the ratification convention, it was agreed that the two houses would meet in joint conference. The debate quickly reflected the mounting opposition to ratification. Thomas Person rose to object to the joint session. When his energetic opposition exceeded Senate rules, Speaker Martin held him out of order and the majority had heard enough of Person.[10] The two bodies then formed themselves into a committee of the whole and placed Elisha Battle, an anti-federalist, in the chair.

The ratification convention that this assembly anticipated was to be as broad a democratic assemblage as had yet been attempted in the state. Citizens eligible to vote for the lower house of the legislature were directed to gather at the designated voting places in their counties on the last Friday and Saturday of March. There they would elect five delegates from each county and one from each borough town.[11] Any freeholder of the state was eligible to election as a delegate to the convention that would meet July 3. Hillsborough was chosen as the site of the convention where delegates were "to take into Consideration the Federal Constitution, and if approved of by them to confirm and ratify the same."[12] Alexander Martin, from his chair, observed this debate as a murky reflection of the Philadelphia deliberations. General moods of hostility were on the rise. An effort to anticipate proposals from the convention to modify the Constitution was defeated but it was clear there would be such proposals. The anti-Federalists were described as a "blind, stupid set that wish Damnation on their country."[13] It would be a divisive campaign and the ratification of the Constitution, an end to which Alexander Martin had become ardently committed, was in no way certain.

The assembly, having returned to more routine business in December, sought to elect a governor to replace Caswell, who was at the end of his third one-year term. The Commons nominated Samuel Johnston, William R. Davie, Judge John Williams, and William Blount; the Senate nominated Alexander Martin and Richard Dobbs Spaight. Blount and Davie quickly withdrew their nominations; Blount felt that the position was too powerless.[14] Martin's nomination raised immediate objections from the Commons on a technical interpretation of the state constitutional limit that a governor was not to be "eligible to that office longer than three years, in six successive years."[15] Martin's friends questioned the point at which the three in six year measure began and the Senate rejected the Commons' effort. Martin was shrewd enough to see that in this critical year he had little likelihood of gaining from a debate on a technicality however it was interpreted. He could easily understand that this limitation on eligibility reflected the popular fear of executive power and he could not gain by becoming the face on that fear. He withdrew his nomination and three days later Samuel Johnston was elected in "one of those strange inconsistencies in political history."[16] Although Johnston was considered aristocratic, conservative, and Federalist, he was also a man of absolute integrity.[17] The conservatives greeted the new governor with great ostentation partly in order to embarrass Governor Caswell.[18]

Obscured by the concentration on setting up the convention was the approval by the assembly of the Treaty of Paris. It had been five years since Martin, as governor, had first laid before the assembly a negotiated end to the war by espousing its importance, and making that optimistic prediction about nothing remaining but "to enjoy the fruits of Uninterrupted Constitutional Freedom." He must have reflected on those words during this final debate on ratification of the treaty. Constitutional freedom was a difficult commodity, demanding a level of public sagacity that was difficult to sustain.

This assembly also revisited the contentious subject of the western counties three years after Martin's manifesto had, in the opinion of some, brought North Carolina to the brink of civil war. The state of Franklin was a shadow of government, and, under the circumstances of constitutional debate, there was little federal encouragement for its continuation. Moderates had broken with Sevier. Washington and Sullivan counties had elected full delegations to the North Carolina legislature. In a spirit of reconciliation, the assembly approved an act to pardon the offenses and misconduct "of Certain Persons in the counties of Washington, Sullivan, Green and Hawkins," necessary to the restoration of those counties under the law of North Carolina.

These two actions of the 1787 assembly characterized the mood of North Carolina. A legislature with an anti-Federalist majority, gained in a vicious campaign, selected a classic conservative Federalist as governor. At the same time, preparing a siege against ratification of the Constitution, that same body put aside issues of previous bitterness by ratifying a peace treaty and pardoning a determined civil disobedience. It was the attitude of a people jealous of their liberty, nationally unassertive, and traditionally suspicious of crowns and executives. It was clear, even at this stage, that ultimately North Carolina would ratify the Federal Constitution. In the two years of debate preceding that ratification, the state confirmed what could be called its identity. North Carolina by character had been slower and more deliberate in defining its course and articulating a political position within the newborn union. Its slowness to speak may have been interpreted by some as indifference or indolence but the other states were now to observe how these people processed the debate. It was asserted at the time that the differences among the American republics were greater than those between European nations. That fact is often overlooked when historians lump the position of North Carolina with that of Virginia in an analysis of the Constitutional Convention. A compatible neighbor, North Carolina was never a vassal state.

David Hackett Fischer identified four dominant regions of the new nation and claimed that the overarching task of the Constitutional Convention had been to "reconcile the different political cultures in the four regions."[19] He also asserted that one region, the backcountry, was largely unrepresented at the convention, a conclusion already discussed in relation to Martin. Repeatedly, throughout the history of the state, these citizens had come late into the field but in the end made the greatest sacrifice.

If Martin sat in the speaker's chair, confident that North Carolina would eventually be persuaded to enter the union, he also knew that the debate would be long, tedious, and bitter. The position of Senate Speaker placed him in strategic political power outside the flashpoints of debate. He recognized before him Thomas Person, James Gallaway, and Allen Jones in aggressive control of the discussion. Federalists considered anti-Federalists to be "a nest of hornets with Tom Person at their head."[20] Martin remained elevated, just above the debate, as Washington had defined himself at Philadelphia. To some partisans, warmed by their visceral fire, that apparent aloofness inspired jealousy and resentment but, as long as Martin survived, that status made no man his enemy.

The end of the session on January 6 disbursed the debate across the state. The legislature had ordered 1,500 copies of the Constitution to be distributed, along with copies of the action calling for the election and the state convention. In Alexander Martin's district, the antithesis of the measured, pragmatic debate of the Moravians on the subject of the Constitution was the Buffalo Presbyterian Church pulpit of David Caldwell.[21] Although there is no surviving record of Martin's membership, Buffalo was surely the church that he attended. The relationship between these two men was lifelong and represented a deep mutual respect and friendship.[22] The Rev. Caldwell was the most influential leader among the Scotch-Irish Presbyterians in the northern Piedmont. There was no home in the backcountry where the work of Philadelphia was debated with more vigor than at Caldwell's. Nowhere could Martin have found a friend who would hear and respond with greater agitation or more partisanship than there.

At Martinville he had other neighbors who would also press him for details of the convention—Francis McNairy, McNairy's son John, and the son's friend, Andrew Jackson, who was often at the McNairy house. Jackson and the younger McNairy had studied law together in Salisbury under Spruce Macay and had begun riding the Salisbury court circuit. Andrew Jackson lived with Thomas Henderson and Thomas Searcy at their Martinville store and he helped as a clerk.[23] It was through connections with Martin and other political leaders, that young John McNairy in December was named judge of the newly created judicial district of Mero, in the western district stretching to the Mississippi. Martin could regale these eager young men with reflection on his conversations with the Rev. Cutler at the Indian Queen and the contacts that he had in the western district certainly enhanced their prospects in the west. McNairy enticed Jackson to accompany him west by appointing him prosecuting attorney for the Mero district. A third man left with McNairy and Jackson: Thomas Searcy, nephew of Alexander Martin, who received the appointment as clerk of court for Mero and was the only one of the three men with "a particle of actual experience."[24] The Mero district offices were critical political and financial stepping-stones for both young men.[25]

The early months of 1788 were fired with the rhetoric of suspicion and its by-product, fear. Martin's friends and legal associates, Judge Samuel Spencer and Willie Jones, raised the specter of the all-powerful, credit-minded judiciary. Thomas Person and Timothy Bloodworth pictured a hoard of tax collectors. Caldwell and James Tate deplored the complete absence of a bill of rights. The speculators remained quiet. On the other side, Hooper and Maclaine were sharp-tongued in their attacks on personalities. Iredell, Spaight and Williamson wrote on the virtues of the conservative government.[26]

To the east the old-fashioned radical-conservative rivalries inspired the form on which the campaign for ratification was managed. In the backcountry, the campaign was less consummate. It was, however, this debate that gave voice to the political temperament of the region. By designating the eligibility of five delegates per county elected by the broadest possible base of voters, the legislature had guaranteed new voices would be heard at this convention, but could they be contained? Had the debate unleashed the whirlwind? In taverns across the state, in muster grounds, even in churchyards, flying fists often followed heated words. Editors and tract writers came forward with warnings and polished theses of logic appeared over the signature of "Marcus," "Publicola," or "Sylvius."[27]

Martin and several judges, including John Williams of Granville, made a detour through Salem to Hillsborough on their way back from general court at Salisbury. They were on the campaign trail speaking in favor of ratification. Salem was one of the infrequent locations where they captured popular favor. The next day the Moravians sent their delegates to the election at Surry court with directions to vote for Federalist candidates. They were outnumbered. Surry, Guilford, Rockingham, Rowan, Mecklenburg, Randolph, Orange, Caswell, and Wilkes all chose delegations that were anti-Federalist. The most dramatic result of the election was the defeat of Alexander Martin. Thirty framers of the Federal Constitution were elected as delegates to their state ratifying conventions. Only one framer, Alexander Martin of North Carolina, actively sought election and was defeated.[28] This result alone would be proof that Martin had risked the most as the price of his resolute support of the Constitution. The breadth of this denial was that his victorious opponent was the Rev. David Caldwell. In one of the most peculiar results of any early election in North Carolina, Guilford County elected Caldwell and four members of his Buffalo Presbyterian congregation as their entire delegation—people that in all other elections Martin had been able to count as his core supporters. Martin's traveling companion at Salem, Judge Williams; William Hooper of Orange, a signer of the Declaration of Independence; former Governor Richard Caswell; General Allen Jones of Northampton; even William Blount, were all defeated.[29] The power of the east as well as the landed control of state government was defeated.

The convention assembled on July 21 at the Presbyterian Church in Hillsborough. The goal of the most extreme of the anti-Federalists (to defeat the Constitution), was itself made moot by the ratification of ten of the states before the North Carolina convention met; news was received, during the deliberations, that an eleventh had been approved. The lopsided majority, therefore, were assembled in hollow defense of a cause. The Rev. Caldwell took issue with the first assumption of the Constitution. He found that "We the People" was in fact a contradiction since it was not the people but representatives of the legislatures of the various states who had drawn the Constitution.[30] It was a contradiction of the will of the people which he felt was expressed effectively only in the state governments. This phrase used for two centuries by populists, reactionaries and patriots as the clarion cry of the American Constitution, as the perfect act of the people, was interpreted by Caldwell as the popular political spin placed on the acts of a few.

Willie Jones, who was considered the most powerful delegate at the convention, suggested a straight up or down vote on the first day so the delegates could confirm what was already foreordained and could then go home and not waste public funds. Others on both sides saw more to be done at Hillsborough than the casting of a hollow vote of protest. Their unanimous choice of Governor Samuel Johnston as president of the convention was a courteous bow to order and decorum. With all the salient documents laid before them—the proposed Constitution, the bill of rights and constitution of North Carolina, the Articles of Confederation, the resolves that had called the Philadelphia convention, and accounts of the ratification conventions of Massachusetts and South Carolina—the convention resolved itself into a committee of the whole to deliberate. A week later they emerged with a bill of rights containing 20 parts and 26 amendments to the proposed Constitution.

Willie Jones read before the convention a letter to James Madison from Thomas Jefferson in which the latter suggested the hope that nine states might ratify and four demur. That would then precipitate the guarantee of human rights in the form of amendments. A few days later, the report of the committee of the whole proposed just that position for North Carolina. It had not been necessary for the debates of the Virginia convention to be laid before this gathering because the delegates well knew the details of those debates. Had Jefferson's letter been read at the Virginia assembly, Madison probably could not have carried ratification. Now, with ratification ultimately assured, it served Madison's purpose, and the purpose of many others in Virginia, to begin to maneuver into place the debate over the bill of rights that had been unattainable at Philadelphia. North Carolina again appeared as the tool of Virginia's purpose, which in this occasion, it surely was. The action also served Jones and other anti-Federalists since it provided a substance for their efforts. Judge Spencer rationalized that the rejection of the Constitution by North Carolina would be a "modest" stand that could demonstrate the independent public opinion of the majority. Sarcastically, Davie compared such action to "a beggarly bankrupt addressing an opulent company of merchants, and arrogantly telling them, 'I wish to be in co partnership with you but the terms must be such as I please.'"[31]

On Saturday, August 2, the debated bill of rights and amendments were approved by a vote of 184 to 83 with the stipulation that North Carolina would withhold ratification until another federal convention should be held "for their consideration." On Monday, the convention ended.

The debate during this convention, concerning religious toleration, is an example of the deep philosophical differences on some issues held by David Caldwell and Alexander Martin. Expressing rigidity typical of the Scotch-Irish, Caldwell decried the lack of a religious test for officeholders in the Constitution. Without shame, he expressed the fear that "there was an invitation for Jews and Pagans of every kind, to come among us." Claiming further that "all those who have any religion are against the emigration of those people from the eastern hemisphere," he argued that "even those who do not regard religion, acknowledge that the Christian religion is best calculated of all religions to make good members of society."[32] These expressions of unbridled bigotry offer no middle ground with Martin's principle of religious and political toleration of dissenters. We can be certain these men had this debate more than once. Unfortunately, no record of such a debate survived.

Without ratification, North Carolina would not be part of the new government of the United States, but instead would be a sovereign state presuming independence. At the end of the convention Willie Jones and James Gallaway promoted passage of resolutions matching the state's impost laws with those of Congress, even appropriating "the money arising there from to the use of Congress," and redeeming paper currency as quickly as possible. The convention resolved to send copies of all their actions to all the state executives, demonstrating their felicity.

It is difficult to establish any losers out of the Hillsborough convention. The federalists had been heard and eventual ratification appeared probable. Iredell, assisted by Davie, Johnston, and Williamson, had defined the value of a strong government and the wisdom of Philadelphia. The anti-federalists had been denied the impact of their rejection of the Constitution, not by their own failures but by the eagerness of other state conventions. In the course of the Hillsborough convention, however, they had roundly assumed the role of champions of individual rights, had articulated their position in a bill of rights and accompanying amendments, and had reinforced their position with the limited leverage of withholding ratification.

Alexander Martin individually had won as well. Had he been an elected member of the convention, his vote would have to be recorded with one side or the other; in fact, what both sides won bridged Martin's position in exactly the same way as the suggestions in the Madison/Jefferson letter had bridged the positions of both those men.

Two weeks after the end of the Hillsborough convention, the elections for the next assembly were inevitably linked to the ratification question. This debate had created such a statewide urgency that news was traveling with unprecedented speed. The Federalists began the most intensive campaign of political education in the history of the state, an extension of all the national debates. Petitions were circulated in most counties, beginning the call for a new convention. Reservations about details of the Constitution were receding in importance. For the backcountry, nuances of the debate were subverted by the obvious—the Constitution had already been approved by 11 states. The new nation was going to be created. In Surry, "many people have changed their minds and most of them now want it [the vote on ratification] altered."[33] None of that county's delegates to the Hillsborough convention were elected to the assembly. In Guilford, Martin was returned to the Senate along with two of the Hillsborough delegates elected to the Commons.[34]

In many ways the 1788 assembly was the link between the two conventions. This was not a secessionist legislature. It operated awkwardly in the role of protest and seemed cautious in everything, in order to be in step with Congress. The state attitude in this public assembly shifted from bravado to a form of contrition. Only a few months before, the mood of the majority was to relish the exhilaration of independence in terms of license and they had given to the anti-federalists their dramatic majority. Now, as the legislature assembled, the reality of responsibility returned, and the risk that their refusal to ratify might somehow deny the state the blessings of this new nation gave them pause. Alexander Martin, however, in the guise of neutrality that his absence from Hillsborough gave him and his pivotal position as speaker, could espouse the pragmatic reality at the pivotal moment. He could provide the waiverers a course of action that need not compromise any position that they had previously held.

The new assembly met at Fayetteville on November 3, and, on the nomination of Richard Caswell, Martin was re-elected Speaker. His sometime private secretary, Pleasant Henderson, was chosen as one of the three Senate clerks.[35] The Federalists had regained control of the Senate, while the anti-Federalists retained a slim majority in the Commons. The assembly made manifest the inevitable paralysis that would overshadow North Carolina if the state remained outside the federal government. The concern was justified that the state had been used again by Virginia and now was left to dangle in embarrassment beside the "pigmy state" of Rhode Island. At least that state surrounded a major port, and commerce gave it some clout with its neighbors. Only the greater value of an interlocking chain of federated states assured North Carolina of being wanted in the United States.

When the legislature convened, most of the bills and petitions concerned local issues and individuals and the overarching spotlight fell on the time, place, and circumstances of a second ratification convention. Caswell introduced the motion for a second convention. Jones countered. Noting the many petitions on convention, he suggested a joint session on the issue. With the two houses led by different majorities, he hoped that this would produce stalemate. The anti-Federalist Commons inexplicably voted against the resolution.[36] It was an example of either political ineptitude or paranoia when majorities in each house cancelled each other by misreading the intent of their leadership.[37] The momentum of the inevitable now supported the Federalists.

The two houses maneuvered on details to create some political advantage. Eventually, the anti-Federalists succeeded in delaying the convention until November and in keeping the delegate size at five per county. In keeping the convention as large and inclusive as possible, they hoped populism would override the established leadership of eastern conservatives.

William Blount manipulated his special agenda in this legislature against a strong countering opposition. The delegations from the western counties, led by the Robertsons and John Tipton, were known to be closely associated with Blount in business and he was even arranging further land purchases from Elijah Robertson while the assembly was in session.[38]

The Act of Pardon and Oblivion passed by this assembly sought to define the end of Franklin state and the return of the western counties to full citizenship within the state. John Sevier, however, had led his close followers beyond the law and his action against the Indians, in warlike defense of white squatters, threatened to create open conflict for which the state was ill-prepared.[39] Martin must have viewed this sorry end of the attempt at secession and of any honorable relationship with the Indians as evidence of how impossible it would be for North Carolina to function long as an independent state and how necessary it was to have a stronger union.

At this moment, Blount found an unlikely ally in Willie Jones, when this constant particularist struck out on a course of neo-federalism that must have startled his friends. He introduced the measure to grant pardons to the former Franklinites, then moved to cede the western counties to the national government.[40] In spite of this odd mixture of advocates, the Cession Bill was tabled until the next assembly, in part because delegates were confused and could not comprehend the logic of ceding half the state to a government with whom the state had refused affiliation.

There was a growing, formidable animosity in the assembly against William

Blount led by the two Joseph McDowells of Burke and James Gallaway of Rockingham. These anti-federalist lieutenants of Willie Jones were ascribed by Blount as out for "the Ruin of Caswell, you [John Gray Blount] and myself and with us our friends."[41] As Blount's tactics showed themselves in greater self-serving transparency, more of his political friendships cooled. His detractors in the Senate arranged to embarrass him toward the end of the session when he asked for the deferral of an unsettled account with the state that he accrued over the course of his agency in Indian treaty negotiations. Instead, immediate settlement was demanded and legal action was threatened to recover the balance.[42] In contrast the members resolved to defer until the next session an account that Speaker Martin had with the state that he acknowledged.[43]

James Gallaway was approaching the zenith of his influence as an anti-federalist politician. With his brother, Robert, and uncle, Charles Gallaway, he had built Gallaway & Company into a large merchant house and real estate agency on the frontier. Their connection to commerce was not through eastern Carolina but through Virginia and from there through the merchant houses of Scotland. The Gallaways had each come out to the colonies from Scotland before the Revolutionary War ruined the colonial trade that had so successfully functioned in contravention of the British system by the Scots and their frontier branches. The Gallaway Company begs further study but it certainly represented one rivalry to the Blounts.[44] Martin was a natural ally of the Gallaways and James, as a force in the anti-Federalist majority in Rockingham County, was his close associate.

Although he eventually withdrew his nomination, James Gallaway was advanced as a delegate for the federal convention that the Fayetteville ratification convention had envisioned as necessary after North Carolina demanded a bill of rights.[45] In North Carolina that expectation may have been a high point of public gullibility. The state had been an unknowing pawn, played by that portion of the anti-Federalist leadership led by Madison, who intended to include civil rights within the Constitution. If there was to be another Constitutional Convention, the North Carolina anti-Federalists were determined to appoint a majority for their views. Not one of those who had served at Philadelphia was to be elected. Continuity did not matter. Those leaders had their chance. Timothy Bloodworth, Joseph McDowell, Thomas Person, and Matthew Locke, all anti-Federalist, were elected and, after several more ballots, James Iredell was added to the delegation to a federal convention that never materialized.

Willie Jones, in harmony with the old elite class of lawyers and merchants, sought to enable the second ratification convention to consider modifications to the state constitution that would link representation in the legislature to tax revenue rather than population. It was a measure to protect merchants in the east, the wealthy counties, and the moneyed interests that decried those frontier counties that were lax in their tax collection. Gallaway joined Blount to support Jones' resolution but Martin broke the final tie, opposing the measure and finding the cure to exceed the ill. Gallaway's frustration on this continuing problem for the state's merchants was assuaged by passage of a law he introduced, requesting that all tax collectors, authorized by any county clerk, give sufficient bond. If not, the clerk would be liable for the claims that accrued against the collector.[46] This legislation was inspired by the frustrations of James Hunter, former sheriff of Guilford County and Martin's cousin, who had been faced with the recovery of taxes collected and not reported by a tax collector who was not properly bonded.[47]

Martin joined the other lawyers in efforts to clarify land title, particularly in the west where grant and deed conveyances were often recorded late or not at all in a lax system carelessly applied. The assembly gave a two-year period of grace during which such titles could be registered, extending it even to the grants of the old Granville Land Office. In tandem the assembly ruled that each year, at the time of the listing of taxable property, citizens must also list all land that they claimed such as military grants and land entries in the west. These title laws were critical in the west where the acquisitiveness of the landless poor had produced squatters and casual land claims. The grant process was often half completed, deeds were unrecorded because the courthouse was too distant, and land was bought and sold without a title search. Martin, in his role as a circuit attorney, operated with the chaos of clouded titles and thus had a direct interest in greater title clarity.[48]

13

Elected Governor Again

In March 1789, the first United States Congress assembled and in April General Washington was sworn in as president in New York. A month later, the States-General assembled at Versailles and Mirabeau began the work of humbling Louis XVI, whose support of the colonies in the course of their Revolution had helped create the public tax burden on his people that now brought his monarchy down. The blood and confusion had just begun as the masses asserted themselves. The French-American counterpoint on revolution was not lost on any American politician. It was said of Washington, "perhaps no other man could have been so circumspect and regardful of the future."[1]

The weight of events was more than a subtle influence on public opinion in the state and the Federalists savored a perceptible rising tide in their favor. James Madison in Congress proposed his own amendments to the Constitution; this action immediately silenced the most ardent argument to their ratification—that such amendments, if not made prior to ratification, would not be possible later. They lost their most effective issue in reasoned debate.[2]

Davie recorded with satisfaction that, in the east, people were "all determined Federalists," and that he understood that in the backcountry there was "an alteration in the sentiments of the people, who, it seems, from rank Anti's are now become perfect fed's; so fully are they convinced of the ill policy of separating themselves from the Union, and of the excellency of our Constitution."[3] Davie's high tone and imperial prerogative of "our Constitution" was the kind of overbearing bravado that earned him the characterization of "an impetuous and impecunious bootlicker" at the time of the debate on ratification.[4]

Even Willie Jones, ordinarily immune to the shifting of political winds, attempted to modify his rigid opposition to the Constitution. His motives, however, were too self-serving for most. One critic, more sarcastic than others, reported, "I hear that even Wiley Jones has Apostatized from Anti-federalism, another St. Paul's Conversion, if it is really so, tho I confess I have as little faith as St. Paul had."[5]

Martin, with his modest ability as a public speaker, was out-shouted at debate where his florid style, once admired, was sometimes ridiculed. His own particularism had encouraged the rise of the Anti-Federalist strength. Martin again navigated through this campaign, uninterested in being part of the convention. When the freeholders went to the courthouse to vote in August, they were called on to ballot for five convention delegates, a senator, and two Commons members, all of whom would be attending two meetings at the same place and time. It was predictable that from the five delegates might emerge the senator and Commons members as a natural economy, and so it happened in most counties. Of the 180 members of the legislature elected, 148 were also members of the second ratification convention. Alexander Martin was elected to neither, nor was General Griffith Rutherford or Willie Jones, who was never elected to state office again.

It was not possible to contain personal affairs in a political atmosphere, a fact that came to be established in the two centuries of this evolving democracy. What Martin next went through was prophetic of public exposure in a democracy. His brother, Robert Martin, was clerk of the Salisbury District Court from September 1782 until March 1788.[6] The Constitution of the United States was finally ratified in November 1789 and Alexander Martin was elected governor the same month. Strangely, the minutes of that important Salisbury District Court are missing for 1789. When they resumed, it was with a case in the February 1790 court against John Hunter for neglect. Next, it was James Taylor, the governor's most active agent in securing his election as governor and the secretary of the ratification convention, who petitioned to quash the grand jury indictment of Elizabeth Gunn in the last court for having an illegitimate child. Elizabeth Gunn appears to have been Elizabeth Strong.[7] In the May term, John Odeneal was charged with destroying the court minutes.[8] In the 1791 term, James Hunter was foreman of the jury, that non-suited a charge of slander against John Odeneal by Benjamin Parrott, that found Odeneal guilty of a misdemeanor against the state and, on motion of another of the governor's friends, Judge John Williams then suspended judgment against Odeneal. It was within the clear purview of Alexander Martin, as governor of the state, that his well-placed friends and family could suppress a charge against Elizabeth Strong of having an illegitimate child by the governor, a charge brought by a political enemy. A case of "dirty tricks," this charge of illegitimacy would routinely have been handled by a justice of the peace in the county in which the case is brought, since the aim of such a case was to protect the child under the care of the court, as a ward, apprentice, etc. To bring such a case to this higher level of court would not be to simply secure the rights of the child, but would imply some sort of complication as in an attempt, perhaps by an enemy, to embarrass a politician at the time seeking to be elected governor of the state.[9] In 1789, illegitimacy on the frontier was so common that the laws were not directed at a moral judgment but at protecting children from abandonment. In this whole series of actions unwinding in the Salisbury District Court can be observed a contemporary example of backwoods character assassination.

Bastardy laws of the time allowed routine processing before a single justice of the peace, where a fee or fine for support of the child could be set. The fact that the Elizabeth Strong/Gunn case reached the District Court, and that a year's worth of crucial public records appear to have been destroyed under the influence of a prominent citizen, points to a contentious litigation. Martin succeeded in confounding his enemies. His surrogates contained the damage albeit with extralegal methods. In the census of 1790 the governor's household listed his son as one child under 16, and three adult women, apparently including the governor's mother and Elizabeth Strong.

The legislature had assembled on the 2nd of November at Fayetteville in the midst of a local epidemic.[10] With Martin absent, the legislature turned to former Governor Caswell, who had a year earlier advanced Martin, and selected him as Senate Speaker. On the third day, Caswell was stricken with paralysis while in the chair. He had often complained of his poor health, evidently caused by high blood pressure. The stroke left him unable to speak and he died on the 10th of November.[11] The assembly was deeply grieved and the news of his death spread quickly across the state. His state funeral was an elaborate show of public grief made possible because the legislature was in session.[12]

The Federalists in control of both branches of the legislature re-elected Samuel Johnston as governor, selected Charles Johnson to succeed Caswell and Stephen Cabarrus as Speaker of the Commons. On November 16, having made sufficient headway in organization, the legislature adjourned to allow the formation of the second ratification convention. On the opening day Governor Samuel Johnston was placed in the chair as he had been at Hillsborough. James Taylor, Martin's key supporter and his stand-in at Salisbury District Court, was appointed one of the secretaries of the convention. Hugh Williamson put forth the question on ratification, seconded by William Blount. That action was countered by objections from the Anti-Federalists and the entire convention resolved into a committee of the whole. Without the leadership of Willie Jones, it was James Gallaway who assumed that role for the opponents of ratification. The debate had virtually nothing to do with ratification, which was foregone. Even the issue of the civil rights amendments had been blunted by Madison's actions in Congress. Gallaway, pleading "union with our sister states is our most earnest wish and desire," advanced five amendments that were significant in that they represented the core of the particularist's concerns for North Carolina. They were not directed at civil rights but at imagined excessive federal power. Twice Gallaway's amendments were rejected. The eight amendments that were reported included two of Gallaway's limits on federal control. The amendments were approved unanimously after the Constitution was ratified by a vote of 195 to 77. It was as if the entire body, confused by the sound and fury of the duel convention, uncertain in the end of what point they had made or intended to make, sought to agree among themselves on a few good issues that might impress their sister states in union.[13] At the end of this legislative session, James Gallaway went back to Rockingham County to mind his business interests and never again attained public office. The Rev. David Caldwell went back to his pulpit.

A week after the convention ended, the legislature took up the matter of choosing two senators for the state to send to Congress. The formality of qualifying Johnston to his third term as governor had been judiciously delayed and he, Benjamin Hawkins, James White, Joseph McDowell, Timothy Bloodworth, Thomas Person, William Blount, the Honorable John Williams, William Lenoir, John Stokes, Richard Dobbs Spaight, and William Polk were nominated for the two Senate seats by the Commons, and the Senate accepted the list.[14] McDowell, Bloodworth, Person, and Lenoir were Anti-Federalists. The other eight supported the Constitution. Spaight and White withdrew before the vote and a large majority selected Samuel Johnston on the first ballot. Consequently, the office of governor was vacant and the Senate nominated Judge Williams, Charles Johnson, and Alexander Martin to succeed Johnston. They carried forward in nomination for the remaining Senate seat, Lenoir, Blount, and Hawkins and, as an afterthought, added Bloodworth. Fayetteville was electric with the maneuvering of the various nominees for the two offices and the Commons declined the invitation to ballot the next day, choosing instead to end the week and to hold the vote the following Wednesday. In the strident, uncivil nature of the political struggle that consumed Fayetteville, no attack was beyond propriety. It may have been at this moment that Martin, who was not present, was fettered with having been so long restricted to the splendid isolation of his backcountry plantation that he "had begun doing things with his slaves that made even rednecks blush."[15] This aspersion may be a sly extension of the insinuations of the Salisbury District Court case. Mudslinging was well developed by the end of the 18th century.

In this atmosphere no winner was found in the Wednesday balloting or in ballots the next two evenings. On Saturday, however, Alexander Martin was elected governor. His victory was not announced in the Commons until Monday and a letter was dispatched, informing him of his election and requesting that he come immediately to the assembly to be qualified as governor of the state. His lieutenants had been efficient on his behalf. No record names his supporters but we can suggest James Taylor, who had been a convention secretary; William Gowdy, a good friend from Guilford; James Gallaway in the Senate; and General Abram Phillips in the Commons from Rockingham. His opponent, Charles Johnson, was a state senator whose base was limited to the Federalist east and recently he had been ill during a local epidemic, which prevented him from attending the Senate.[16] Judge Williams, whom Martin knew well, might have taken votes from him but Williams was a judge and his campaign suffered from the bad blood that had existed between the legislature and the courts since 1782.

No sooner had Martin's election been announced than a letter was sent from the Senate to the Commons over the signature of Charles Johnson as speaker, "thinking it proper to withhold their concurrence to the report from the late balloting for Governor, from a suggestion that the Gentleman elected to that office is not eligible to that office."[17] Johnson had set his name to what obviously had been his chief political charge against Martin's election.

The issue that had been raised about Martin's eligibility in the election in 1787 was over consecutive years in office, because the Constitution allowed individuals to serve no more than three out of every six years.[18] That issue was now moot. It had been almost five years since Martin had last held the governor's office. There was, however, the question raised at the end of the previous legislature concerning an open account that Martin had with the state. Having acknowledged the indebtedness, the Senate had allowed it to be laid over. Included with the notification to the Senate of Martin's election as governor was a letter from James Taylor that apparently dealt with this debt.[19] The answer anticipated the action of Martin's opponent and attempted to make this a non-issue. The Commons proposed an immediate dispatch of a letter from the two speakers notifying Martin of his election. A week later the notification had not reached Martin so the Senate dispatched Thomas Brown of Bladen and James Gallaway, and the Commons added John Gray Blount and Thomas Person "to wait on and give Martin this information."[20] On December 17, Brown, Gallaway, Person, and John Stokes conducted Martin into the Commons chamber where, before the two houses, he was qualified for the fourth time as governor of North Carolina and he took the oath.

Alexander Martin's return to the office of governor had noticeable parallels to the historical moment at which he had first assumed that post. In 1781, the battles were essentially over. The task before the assembly was to bring order, to begin the process of independent government and to heal the animosities. In 1789, North Carolina ratified the Constitution of the United States and became part of an emerging nation and many of the same coalescing needs were present in a marginally different form. At that moment two issues were fulfilled in which Martin previously had been a significant influence. The western lands were ceded to the national government and the University of North Carolina became a reality.

With the passage of time, cession had become the object of most political and economic interests in the new nation. In North Carolina the issue was not when would cession happen but how would it be implemented? It was not to happen with propriety. John Sevier, whom the previous legislature had exempted from the act of pardon given to the Franklinites for their civil disobedience, exacted his revenge on his enemies. In February 1789, Joseph Martin, the representative of North Carolina and Virginia for more than a decade as commissioner to the Indians, wrote to Governor Johnston. Having successfully convinced the Indians in conference at Long Island that "the wish of North Carolina was to live in peace & friendship with them," his credibility was destroyed when "Col. Sevier with a party of men went into one of their Towns, the men all but one were out hunting, and brought off 29 of their women and children with them, with one of their traders who had a license for that purpose & plundered the Town."[21]

Far more gratifying to the new governor than this sorry treatment of a trusted friend and emissary was the action of the legislature toward finally creating the state university. A hundred years later, Judge Walter Clark said Alexander Martin, who had ever been a promoter of education, should be gratefully remembered by posterity for his warm interest in the university.[22]

Davie had drafted the legislation that established the university. The Princeton connection with the beginnings of this institution continued. The emphasis that Martin placed earlier on establishing colleges was a lower order of priority for the ensuing governors, Caswell and Johnston, so that when Martin returned to office, it was propitious for the birth of the university that had just been established in law.

Equally fortuitous was the gift to the state of 20,000 acres of western land by Colonel Benjamin Smith for the benefit of the university.[23] The law, the will, and the means came together.

North Carolina partisans have frequently claimed that the rejection of ratification in the first state ratification convention resulted in the inclusion of the Bill of Rights as part of the American Constitution. The claim for such credit is unbecoming. R. D. W. Conners saw "two acts of supreme statesmanship" in the ratification convention and in the legislation of the 1789 legislature that "had established and endowed the University of North Carolina."[24] Greater evidence supports the credibility of the latter than the boast of the former. In the issue of ratification, North Carolina performed a role closer to dupe or lackey, but, in the creation of the university, the state stepped forward to perform for its people a truly imaginative and provocative act of leadership.

The charter for the university was dated December 11, a week before Martin arrived at Fayetteville. The proceedings that surrounded the endowment bill for the university and the funding for the erection of the buildings, were being debated when he arrived.[25] The first informal and unofficial meeting of the trustees was December 18 when Benjamin Smith presented patents for the acreage in Obion County in the extreme northwest portion of Tennessee.[26] Governor Martin then initiated the search for all other sources of funds and support to give the university "a more essential [form] than a paper being."[27]

The Masons were to be an important force in the founding of the university and Alexander Martin "received his Master Mason degree in a 'special lodge' held under a dispensation of the Grand Lodge," in 1789. At DeKeyser's Tavern in Fayetteville on December 23, 1790, he received the Mark Master and Past Master degrees. He remained active as a Mason for the rest of his life as a member of the Grand Lodge.[28] It is worth noting that all the field officers of the 2nd North Carolina Regiment later were Masons.

In the selection of the new Council of State there was a shift away from the eastern power base. Still lacking a permanent capital, the state government continued to be obliged to travel with the source of power. During the yearly sessions of the legislature, the records of the state were literally carted to each meeting place. During the remainder of the year, the governor and clerk held the offices that represented the continuity of power, so many records went with the governor. His clerk had to be handy and the council had to be close enough that dispatch riders could easily notify them if a meeting was necessary. The men that the Senate nominated as councilmembers reflected the wishes and influence of Martin, those from the House somewhat less so. Most were particularists, friends, neighbors, or, in one case, a relative. John Hamilton and Charles Bruce were Martin's neighbors in Guilford. Maxwell Chambers and Spruce Maccay were friends from Salisbury days, the latter credited as the author of the first (1784) university bill.[29] Nathaniel Macon was a rising Anti-Federalist leader, and he and Wyatt Hawkins of Warren incorporated the influence of Willie Jones. The three Jameses from Rockingham County—Taylor, Gallaway, and Hunter—all lived close to Danbury. Memucan Hunt was from Surry; Joseph Winston, and Traugott Bagge, were from Stokes. Bagge was a prominent Moravian who represented the changing attitude of his community about involvement in government and business.

The legislature elected Hamilton, James Gillespie of Duplin, Taylor, Bruce, Hawkins, and Jesse Franklin. On a later ballot they added General Griffith Rutherford. All of these men were considered Anti-Federalists. This fact alone speaks unequivocally about Martin's political views at this point since, if the legislature had been able to dictate the council composition, it obviously would have chosen from its Federalist majority. At least two councilors, Gillespie and Rutherford, were born Irishmen and Bruce was probably a native Scot reflective of Martin's ancestry. Hamilton, Hawkins and Rutherford had voted in the convention against ratification. Wyatt Hawkins was selected president of the council. Thomas Henderson, the governor's brother-in-law, business partner at Martinville, and clerk of court in Rockingham, was the clerk of the council.[30]

North Carolina was now prepared to be part of the United States but the commitment to nationalism was not present. Nowhere was there a North Carolina politician who campaigned for a national office or who had a national agenda. Marginal exceptions might be suggested for John Steele, Davie and Iredell.

Alexander Martin had survived the political passage through ratification without becoming a victim. Whatever his genuine reason for leaving the Philadelphia convention, the fact remained that he did leave. He had not signed the Constitution, which had removed him from the role of responsible advocate for that document. It seems unreasonable to believe that the secure and broad base of his regional support could not have elected him to at least one of the two state ratification conventions, among all the Anti-Federalists that were selected, had he really wanted such election. He was not sent, and therein avoided the role of opponent of the Constitution. Now, within days of the reality of ratification, he was summoned by his friends to Fayetteville to assume the leadership of the state with the Federalist governor moved to national office as senator. There is more design evident in that scenario than fate or coincidence. Martin's service as governor in the next three years set the state on a course of particularism for which it has been characterized to this day. He was not the creator of this public attitude, rooted in deep suspicion of government in general and distant government in particular, but he was among the first politicians to realize that it was present in the majority. His particularism, however, was set within his abiding support of the union of states and a Presbyterian ethic of representative government that gave to the elected members authority to make choices on behalf of the electorate, as opposed to being ciphers for the electorate.

As the legislative session ended on December 22, it received a message "from His Excellency the Governor" that defined Martin's grasp of his role as first governor of North Carolina in the United States and the individual roles each man present at Fayetteville would have when each returned home as a citizen. This message, more than any other he ever delivered, interprets Alexander Martin's republican political philosophy.

> As the session is drawing near to a close, and you about to return to your respective Counties where your constituents will no doubt be anxious to

receive such public information you will please to communicate, who reposing confidence in you, will be influenced with your sentiments of political measures more or less, as you yourselves appear to be actuated with; and as a great event hath turned up during your Session not only interesting to them but the Citizens of the United States, the adoption of the Federal Constitution by the Convention of this State, I beg leave to draw your attention a moment to this subject, and impress on your minds a few observations.

That this event must be the subject of great joy to our sister States, as well as to our friends and allies in Europe, on hearing that one important link broken in the American Union is again restored; That unanimity, the great Basis of all Civil Government is about again to pervade the whole of our Councils, and we become again a member of this Federal body. [North Carolina, he said, was back in the union where there would be] advantages arising therefrom, [and disadvantages but in the end,] trying time must determine the question. [Then, in an affirmation, he declared,] at this early dawn of the new Government fair prospects seem to brighten and promise a propitious day.

[Martin lamented that some] great establishments have been formed on which it is to be wished this state had borne her part at an early period, [a recognition that the state had missed the startup of the union. He rationalized,] perhaps it is all for the best, [since it may not have been] precipitate in Ratifying a form of Government intended to last for ages, without maturely deliberating how far the lives, liberties and properties of her Citizens were to be protected and secured by it. A jealousy of their ruler ought to subsist in all free Governments as the grand check that freedom hath over tyranny.

[Martin followed with credit given to the spirit of the British government,] the most perfect Model of a free Government under Heaven, [which] required a thousand years to shape ... in its present beautiful, tho' vitiated form.

Let us remember that we embarked with our Sister States in one bottom making one common cause, which by the effusion of kindred and united Blood spent in its support hath cemented our mutual interests in one great family that hath gained a rank among the nations as an independent Sovereignty. That purchased at so dear a price the American Government was too precious a prize to ever become the sport & prey of restless faction, or enterprising ambition, without affording it the necessary means for its own security and the protection of its Citizens. To arm it with additional powers for this great end was the object of the Federal Constitution, which hath been ratified by the convention of this State as the future form of Government of the United States.

As you, Gentlemen, composed a great part of that respectable body, it is greatly incumbent in you whether as officers or private persons you return to the citizens you represent, to reconcile those jarring sentiments, if any remain, that seemed unfortunately to prevail in different parts of the State. Although the public peace hath not been immediately disturbed, yet invidious distinctions have arisen that tended to that end. Let hereafter the Federal and antefederal name be no more heard as a reproach. Let the people be told that the Government of the United States is still in the power of their Citizens, and so must remain while composed of its present materials. That the President with all of his supposed prerogatives of royalty, the Senators with their pretended aristocratic authority, and the Members of the House of Representatives after the several periods of their political existence limited by the Constitution have expired, must all return to the Class of fellow Citizens, be amenable for their conduct and feel with them, the effects of that Government they have administered.

Let our citizens be led to embrace again their Northern and Southern brethren, with former affection and cordiality in the adoption of this new system of Government, that be the same perfect or imperfect, tho' at present the most perfect to be obtained, the same they are determined to stand or fall together in its support, and as they with the other citizens of the United States under the old, notwithstanding its feeble powers, performed wonders in its defense, and have therefore been called a glorious **Band of Brothers** [emphasis added], let the name still inspire them to enter the new Union now fixed on firmer Ground with joy, and with united efforts maintain and defend it against all its enemies and opposers wherever to be found. Lastly let them rest assured that while we all pursue the practice of the great national as well as private virtues, we shall meet the countenance of Heaven, and that the God of virtue and of liberty who hath so remarkably led those States to Sovereignty and Independence will not forsake them, and suffer them to fall a prey to foreign or domestic tyranny, but will preserve them in his holy keeping.[31]

This message was intended to define a responsible and sovereign state, proud of its actions and committed to union. Martin, in this speech and through these representatives, sought to make clear to people, who were still trying to deal with liberty, their role of citizenship. In the process, he also defined his perception of public service as a risk matching that taken by those who fought a revolution.

14

The Development of the First State University

After 1790 it is possible to delineate political parties as an emerging reality. North Carolina had functioned politically with factions that had waxed and waned around personalities. None held together long and even the emerging leaders seem not to have been sensitive to the tactful maneuvers that would keep others committed to an issue. Many, like John Steele, still naively looked for government to be the product of consensus that "would unite all parties, give general satisfaction, and destroy those invidious party distinctions that have heretofore subsisted."[1]

Pro-federal leaders interpreted the 1789 legislature as moderate because it set such a broad perspective dealing with ratification, founding and funding the university, and agreeing to the cession of the western counties. It also had selected clear Federalists for both the Senate seats and four of the five seats in the lower house of Congress. The power, however, of the Federalists in that legislature did not come from a value change in the attitude of the majority in North Carolina. The momentum that had driven the pendulum of opinion to swing toward ratification so completely came from the fear of being left out of something important. The state did not seek independence but it was also not keen on interdependence either, except in its most benign form. The Federalists had succeeded in gaining ratification and then in controlling the federal elective offices that were created by ratification. They did not seem to recognize that most of the Anti-Federalists at this moment did not covet these government seats so far away from home. Conversely, the Federalists were less combative and allowed the Anti-Federalists to capture the governor's office and all the council seats because they saw those offices as less significant. What the Federalists failed to see was the ultimate power of particularism. The year 1790 defined that distinction.

Governor Martin returned home at the end of the Fayetteville legislature for the rest of the winter. He was now spending more time at Danbury making it a kind of family compound; the federal census of 1790 identified it as his official residence. "Alexander Martin, Go'" is one of three males over 16 along with one under 16 at Danbury. His brother, Robert Martin, had acreage to the east of Danbury. His sister, Martha, spent much time at Danbury. She would be widowed in three years but her home was in Stokes with the large Rogers family.

Brother James Martin had moved to Surry at the end of the Revolution and by his first wife, Ruth Rogers, he had ten children. James acquired a considerable estate on Snow Creek where he operated a lime kiln that sold its production to a wide area.[2] As a militia officer, then as sheriff of Surry County, James was a political leader, who served in the Commons from 1783 to 1786 as a representative for Surry, and after the county was divided, for Stokes from 1792 to 1793.[3]

His brother, Samuel Martin, in Mecklenburg County, had been a leader at the time of the Revolution but had made bad management decisions in peace time. He was insolvent when he died in 1789.[4] His daughter came to Danbury, until she was married, to function as her grandmother's companion.[5]

Sister Jane and her husband, Thomas Henderson, lived adjoining the governor's home. Along with his elective office as clerk of Rockingham County, Thomas became secretary of the Council of State.[6] That meant that, between meetings of the legislature, the government of North Carolina essentially existed on the banks of Dan River, remote from the few population centers of the state.

Several members of the Hunter family—brothers, sisters, and cousins of Jane Martin—were located along the Dan River on either side of Danbury. The most notable was James Hunter who had been sheriff in Guilford County. The image of Danbury as the center of this Martin clan with its allied families, and the image of Alexander Martin as clan chief, seemed somehow a more familiar example of old-world history than a model for the expansive, adventurous century that was about to dawn on America. Martin was operating in both those worlds and it is not difficult to see that his enemies could use this dichotomy to his discredit.

Alexander Martin had asked, as he accepted his election, that "the people be told that the government of the United States is still in the power of their citizens." Before January was run, he had reason to wonder if such thoughts were premature. On January 14, Alexander Hamilton presented to Congress his plan for support of public credit. The first of the reports of the secretary of the treasury, taken together with major and minor reports that were to swiftly follow, constituted the seven-point legislative program of Washington's first term. No new emerging nation since, nor any new administration of the United States since 1790, has placed such intense, politically painful emphasis on financial policy, or been more comprehensive and far-reaching, in establishing public credit at its beginning.[7]

In North Carolina the odious nature of the Hamilton Plan centered on the section that called for assumption of state debts. Hamilton argued that, since the states and the national government had issued paper money to cover their wartime obligations, it would be wrong to distinguish between local and national currencies. The new government should assume the varying state debts and substitute its own obligation with creditors. A windfall for creditors and speculators, assumption was a disaster for North Carolina, overburdened as it was with paper money and careless as it had been in its financial administration.[8] The state had already levied taxes to meet its Revolutionary War debt. To be drawn into the assumption of delinquent debts in other states seemed an inequitable solution for poor Carolina farmers. Even more detrimental was that the Hamilton Plan assumed all paper and security at face value. In North Carolina it was considered better to pay the state debts as best the state could with her depreciated paper than to have to make a businesslike settlement that would surely involve "the services of the much-dreaded federal taxgatherers."[9]

Historians are divided, but some purport advantage to North Carolina on debt assumption. Flexner contended that the state had really done little to settle its extensive war debt so that it gained by transferring the collection problems to the central government. He argued that they "were enchanted to hand over their debts."[10] This interpretation is more deduction than a reflection of reality. Public perception in North Carolina saw assumption as the first manifestation of what had always been feared from a strong central government, and even though the state was relieved of some thorny fiscal responsibilities, citizens felt preempted. One of the amendments James Gallaway succeeded in passing at the second ratification convention was to deny Congress control of the redemption of state money and security.[11]

The demonstration of the worth of the federal plan to establish public credit was made evident when a swarm of speculators raced in to buy up the Carolina debt that was "widely scattered among many smallholders." There was the report of Senator William Maclay of Pennsylvania that a man coming from North Carolina had "passed two expresses with very large sums of money on their way to North Carolina for purposes of speculating in certificates."[12]

This was an international speculation that involved the most sophisticated financial interests in the new country and several foreign countries "trading on ignorance" in the backcountry.[13] It may have been perpetrated in the backcountry of the Carolinas, but it was negotiated in silk salons and the plan could not have been executed without the imprint of the secretary of the treasury. Hamilton's monetary plan created the international financial stability that placed the United States in the company of nations. It is certain, however, that the bitterness engendered in the cavalier attitude of assumption and security redemption helped galvanize anti-federalism in the state.

The most complicated design for speculation involved William Duer, Hamilton's assistant secretary of the treasury (the man on the inside), and William Constable, a wealthy New York friend of Hamilton's (the money man). They contrived to purchase continental securities on time and invest the proceeds in North and South Carolina debts. Duer had agents in the Carolinas for months, operating under the cover story that they were purchasing land rights, who were buying the widely scattered revolutionary debt claims at huge discounts on par. They planned to purchase one million dollars in Carolina debt at two shillings on the pound ($100,000) and float it over several years, until Hamilton had succeeded in passing his assumption and funding plan, in which case the certificates would be valued at par.[14]

Elbridge Gerry called the proposed treasury system an almost perfect plan to promote "speculation and peculation in the public funds."[15] More succinct was the characterization of assumption as the "bastard of eastern speculators."[16] The *State Gazette* of North Carolina complained that, if the "paper nobility" of Philadelphia succeeded in gaining control of the certificates of the southern states, one section of the country would be paying taxes to support the favored class of another.[17]

Governor Martin asked of Hugh Williamson the following question: "What have Congress to do with our Contracts made with our citizens, where they are satisfied with the mode of payment, why compel them to receive twenty shillings on the pound when they are content with four? Where will such a Precedent lead—will not the General Government quickly bear down the State Government, not even our civil list, or any pecuniary state transaction will escape their intrusion or interference."[18]

Martin used a peculiar line of logic to demonstrate his opposition to assumption. At this time his particularist focus was on retaining the state control over redemption and as much of its financial independence as he could defend. Thus, while an international syndicate prepared to exploit inside information to pyramid into thousands of dollars in profit, the governor, remote in his residence, without a state capital and with access to only state news from outdated national newspapers, complained that the state was being denied opportunity to make a cheap redemption of its obligations.

There is a nuance to be observed here between opportunity and design when applied to speculation. On the frontier, a public official who was presented the opportunity to speculate on land or state securities, tended to be forgiven by the electorate, who was either similarly involved or hoping to have such an opportunity. This tendency helps to explain flagrant, repeated speculation with the public trust by men like William Blount and John Sevier that never appears to have diminished their electoral support. Designed plans of speculation as elaborate as the Duer-Constable scheme, however, were beyond the comprehension of uninformed citizens, removed as they were from the seat of power. These conspiracies naturally were adapted into their suspicion of executive authority.

Martin was consistent in his defense of state government as citizen government. He was less certain that the federal government could be made a citizen government but he always pressed those issues that would make it so. He was not above a certain amount of land and commodity speculation that he treated liberally as accruals of office. His kind of speculation seemed to have a justifiable measure of public risk-taking and he fought to open government so there could be public accountability.

The Federalist delegation from North Carolina, finally seated in Congress, discovered that the program of national Federalism was little to their taste. Their correspondence with the governor and others in North Carolina made particularists of them all. As representatives of one of the largest, most populated, and poorest states, they were impaled on both horns of the dilemma. Any national legislation reflective of size or population made them a major player but, when the pro-rata cost factor was applied to legislation, they were least able to find adequate state resources. When an excise tax was part of the Hamilton Plan, it fell heaviest on the distilleries of the west that already had precious little local industry.[19] The legislature instructed their delegation to oppose the tax. Their two senators refused, but the House delegation voted solidly against the measure. In the end the opposition was so strong that the act was amended, exempting small distilleries entirely.[20]

Hugh Williamson appeared most politically befuddled. He penned long reports to the governor, casting himself as the perfect particularist. "I promise you formally," he claimed, "that while serving in Congress I should not lose sight of the State's accounts." Arriving in New York, he set about framing the position of North Carolina in opposition to the Hamilton Plan. Grandly boastful at first, he quickly became aware that some sort of federal plan would prevail. He pressed the governor to exert every executive energy to accumulate proof of the widely scattered revolutionary claims that were still outstanding to the state. If debts were to be assumed and obligations to be fully satisfied, it behooved North Carolina, nearly bled dry as it was by that conflict, to step forward at this point of reconciliation. As Williamson put it, the task would be "painful business, but the play will be worth the candle."[21] Martin made efforts to screen for vouchers among the hopelessly scattered state records and made contacts with former officers who had service vouchers.

The arrival of the North Carolina congressional delegation appeared to create an April majority in New York against assumption in the House, which was victoriously reported to the governor as a defeat of the issue. Martin responded to Senator Johnston that the rejection "seems to give general approval to our citizens, the more especially when they are told it was affected by means of the Senators and Representatives of this State in Congress."[22] The state sadly discovered, however, the efficiency of Hamilton when the assumption bill was introduced again and passed— "a bitter drought for North Carolina."[23]

Public resentment decried the "reptile speculators" invading the state and the six million dollars in North Carolina Continental securities already in the hands of Dutch investors, but the focus of the ire was directed at the congressional delegates. Unrealistically, they were viewed as having been sent to Congress with the charge to protect the state's interests and to convert others to opposition to assumption. Having been the object of Hugh Williamson's deprecatory evaluation of his performance at the Constitutional Convention in Philadelphia, Governor Martin must have been at least privately amused when Alexander Maclaine spoke in similar terms now about Williamson, asking, "Is the all-knowing Doctor Williamson instead of being on the road to attend his duty as a representative of the United States, torturing his ingenuity how to evade the laws of that body of which he has the undeserved honor to be a member? He would have made a good pettifogging attorney; but nature never intended him for a legislator."[24]

Martin continued to have his critics among the Federalists. John Steele received a letter from Wallace Alexander, decrying the appointment of Montford Stokes as clerk of the Superior Court in the Salisbury District.[25] Matter-of-factly, Alexander observed that for the appointment Stokes had given the governor "the present docket profits & three Negroes."[26] There is no corroboration for this accusation but it sounds specific and credible. This is the same court term at Salisbury where James Taylor was quashing the case against Elizabeth Gunn for bastardy.

The issue of the separation of the Tremontaine had always been a product of time and circumstance. North Carolina and her western counties were never enemies. They were blood brothers who shared a common ancestry. On September 1, the governor signed a proclamation that announced receipt of the certified act of the United States Congress accepting the cession of the western counties. It was recognized that "North Carolina had been for years anxious to convey, on proper terms, this portion of her soil, so that it might become another star in the galaxy of States."[27]

The Council of State was summoned by the governor to meet at Rockingham Springs on June 24, 1790, in preparation for the meeting of the legislature. Martin also intended to outline the assimilation of the state into the federal system. A letter was sent on the first day of the month to each member elected officially on December 18 of the previous year. It was a reminder notice and at this meeting they would be qualified to the office. This council, dramatically more western and anti-federalist, was in a position to plan to undo all the actions of the previous session and thereby destroy the foundation of good feeling set the previous year. Instead, they joined with the governor in preparing a message for President Washington:

> To the President of the United States.
> Sir,
> The governor and council of the State of North Carolina embrace the earliest opportunity afforded them since the accession of this State to the constitution, and the completion of the union by all the states, of congratulating you upon this most auspicious event, by which all causes of future dissention among the states will be obviated—the impost, that great branch of revenue and support of public credit, collected with more facility, and our finances more properly arranged.
> We congratulate ourselves with equal sincerity on beholding you, sir, in the highest departments, which your virtues merited, and to which your country unanimously and gratefully appointed you.
> The importance of your situation receives additional dignity by the veneration your country possesses for your character, and from a confidence that every power vested in you by the constitution, will be exerted for the happiness and prosperity of your country, by giving efficacy to such a system as will ensure and conciliate the public mind—a confidence felt by all—by none more powerfully than the citizens of this State.[28]

This letter was pure Martin prose and was approved unanimously on the 26th, signed by the governor and Wyatt Hawkins, president of the council. Congratulatory as it was intended to sound, this letter represents a statement of the particularist platform at the outset of statehood and it is an important exposition of the political convictions of Alexander Martin. It succinctly limits federal powers to adjudication of dissention between states and to the collection and application of all impost revenue. Beyond that, the person of Washington as president, acting within the powers vested by the Constitution, was presumed to give efficacy and to conciliate the public mind. Washington's response was a letter of thanks in which he chose not to take exception to the description of a very limited federal prerogative.

This meeting of the council took place at Rockingham Springs, a place of rustic merriment and affectation on the raucous American frontier. There are descriptions of coastal towns and such bustling interior towns as Charlotte, Salisbury and Salem around 1790. Rockingham Springs was more typical of some bawdy Hogarth-like portrait of the American frontier that had made a revolution.[29]

Governor Martin relocated in September to Fayetteville, where the assembly would meet in December. Some of the pomp that on occasion surrounded the person of the governor greeted him on his arrival from Danbury. He was met by Captain Dudley's troop of Light Horse and he received the salute of Captain Winslow's company of artillery on the State House Square.[30]

The governor's message to this legislature, on the 2nd day of November, was that of a trustee reporting to a board. Cession of the western territory was complete. Only the reapportioning of the congressional districts would be required of this assembly. Assumption had been legislated, against the majority opinion in this state, and that action "seems to exhibit, at an early period, a new and unexpected precedent of legislation in the federal government." Martin avoided confrontation on the issue of assumption by characterizing it as an "extraordinary measure" that still seemed beyond the "principles of pure and equal justice" that he expected from Congress. He advised his listeners to live with it because, as the result of this act, "our public accounts are to wear a new dress." His advice was not to fight the inevitable but to learn to adapt the new process to the best advantage of the state and so he advised Williamson to gather all the state's many-faceted war claims so they could be included in redemption.[31]

The university, he pointed out, was still "a paper thing" that would need the further support of the new assembly. Funds allotted by the previous assembly were slow in coming and he asked that the session consider a loan, secured by the existing funds, so that building could be started.

On only one national issue did he suggest that the legislature might send to "our Senators in Congress ... your particular instruction." He found the allocating of the only post road in the state through the seaboard towns as unsatisfactory "in consequence of the great bulk of the people of the interior country [who are] deprived of them." Even cross posts, that might have been connected with the present post-stages, would have been a help but even they had been rejected by Congress.[32]

This address to the legislature was not as broad as might have been expected nor as inclusive of issues. The executive branch did advance four areas that the legislature followed with agreeable action—financial reform, court reform, support of the university and instruction. The tone avoided coercion that these delegates resented in any man or government. It led with guidance as in the case of the university, appealing to pride and the future standing of the people who were generally poor but honorable. It also did not cast citizens against citizens or state government against federal government; that as a political style won elections but rarely governed effectively.

In this formative stage of public policy and government in the United States, had there been an Alexander Hamilton in every state, the civil experience of a federal union would probably have been stillborn. Had there not been a Hamilton in Washington's cabinet, conversely, the union might have been the result of a very long gestation. The presence of Alexander Martin in North Carolina facilitated the expression of the frustrated and less privileged, but it also extended the horizons of very provincial people, allowing them to envision something beyond their immediate covetousness. In the example of education, it allowed them a preeminent position among the states of the union.

The name of Alexander Martin was conspicuously absent from both the list of trustees included in Davie's university bill in 1789 and from the subsequent university charter dated December 11 of that year. That charter came four days after Martin, the first governor to advance the idea of such a university, had been elected again as governor. Davie quickly had reason to regret the oversight. Though he was not a member of the new assembly, he wrote to Martin from Halifax as the session began, "You will I am certain give the University every assistance in your power, as a man who knows the importance of education in a country just forming its manners and its government."[33] The governor knew full well the importance of the university and he didn't need the prodding of Davie the day after he had delivered his own message to the legislature.

The trustees were prescribed by the charter to "meet at Fayetteville on the third Monday in the session of the next General Assembly."[34] That meeting, on November 15, recognized that this was a state-chartered university whose nurture depended on its close proximity to its source. The acorn did not grow very far from the tree. Having chosen William Lenoir as president protem, the trustees elected James Taylor as secretary protem. Then, to replace John Stokes and Robert Dickson, who had died, and William Blount, who had left the state, they elected Alexander Martin, General James Kenan, and James Glasgow to the board. These trustees met at various times, when the assembly was not seated, until the 27th. This group represented an overwhelming potential power in the assembly that characteristically resented power. The very existence of the trustees constituted an elected elite among the legislators. There was a delicate balance that recognized those conditions and could control the natural resentment while appealing to those same delegates for funds to support a nonexistent university in a state under extreme financial pressure. It may have been fortunate that at this moment Davie was absent from the legislature and that Anti-Federalists like Lenoir, Martin, James Taylor, Person, Alexander, and McDowell were among those who led the solicitation for funding to build the university. Party politics could easily have been transferred to the chartering of the university if the institution could be associated with privilege. It should not go unnoticed that five of these new trustees had attended the first convention and opposed ratification but had approved ratification at the second convention. They were thus open-minded swing voters on the issue of federalism. The suspicion of privilege surfaced when David Caldwell of Iredell offered a bill declaring it "Impolitic and Dangerous to the privileges of the Citizens" for trustees to be members of the general assembly. Six members of the first meeting board were members of the assembly. The bill failed on first reading.[35]

Governor Martin attended each of the trustee meetings. The acceptance of the valuable gift of land from Benjamin Smith provided a substantial asset that could be parlayed politically into justification for the funding legislation that was drawn by a committee of the trustees and introduced on the 27th by a letter from Martin, not as governor of North Carolina, but as president of the board of trustees of the university.[36] He served in that capacity until 1793. With his close political associate, James Taylor, serving as secretary of the board, there is further indication that Martin was the pivotal leader in these years when the university evolved.

On December 3, the House of Commons, presented with the university loan legislation on a second reading, voted 66 to 16 to table the bill until the next session. Even trustee William Porter and the secretary of the trustees, James Taylor, voted to table the loan bill.[37] Wyatt Hawkins, James Taylor, and Jesse Franklin had all resigned November 12 from the council a few days before their terms were to end. The size of the vote to table the loan was not a simple rejection of the university but a temporary stay on public financial commitments when the state's financial position was so inherently weak. The assembly had committed the collected arrearages due the state and all escheated land toward funding the university. They knew of the bequest of General Smith, which at that point appeared to have a grand prospect of a handsome sum.[38] Natural cautiousness was a reasonable prospect for the legislators.

James Taylor appears at Fayetteville as a major ally of Governor Martin. Taylor was living at Sauratown, the Farley estate near Danbury, as the agent for the family.[39] It appears that he was the brother of John Louis Taylor, who became chief justice of North Carolina in 1818.[40] In this session of the legislature, Taylor took a very high profile as an Anti-Federalist delegate, often operating in reflection of the governor's state-of-the-state speech. He introduced the bill appointing a committee to work on financial reform, joined with Nathaniel Macon in proposing a Committee of the Whole to define instruction of the senators, and introduced the bill to enjoin double officeholding. He signed protest reports of actions taken by the legislature that were in the form of minority reports, protesting the ill-advised elimination of the tobacco grading system; he also protested a bill that disallowed an individual owner's right to emancipate a slave, which he found "tyranic and Unconstitutional" and he argued against the increase by the assembly of members' salaries. Taylor was chosen one of the legislators to deliver to the governor, at the end of his first term, the thanks of the assembly "for the many and uniform marks strongly evinced in the discharge of the office you now fill." He reported to the House the results of the ballot that re-elected Martin and he introduced the petition for relief on an individual matter of the governor's brother, Robert.[41] These activities of James Taylor in this legislature confirm his close association with the governor. Finally, it was Taylor who was appointed agent of North Carolina in settling the state's financial accounts with Congress when Williamson was stripped of that job in 1790 by passage of the law limiting elected officials to a single public office.

The first public action of this assembly was to open the Dismal Swamp canal, which ran from the Pasquotank River in North Carolina to the Elizabeth River in Virginia. This comprehensive action placed North Carolina ahead of her sister state in the actions necessary to develop the canal. Chartered first in 1764 in Virginia, the original land company included George Washington and Francis Farley; the latter invested his sugar dollars in this public work and in the purchase of Sauratown. In 1786, Captain John Stokes and James Gallaway represented North Carolina on the joint commission to design the canal that was enabled by this legislature. The involvement of the Farleys and Gallaway in the thirty-year development of the Dismal Swamp canal plan is the link to the support of Governor Alexander Martin.[42]

The issue of instruction as laid before the assembly by Martin could focus the general frustration of citizens and legislators on a principle of representative democracy. The legislature was so thoroughly disgruntled with federalism that it voted 55 to 26 against the oath of allegiance to the United States. Far away from North Carolina, the same political leadership was meeting behind closed doors, debating issues affecting the people, and making decisions with apparently as much arbitrary insensitivity as the colonists had previously experienced at the hands of the British Parliament. When the resolution on instruction was approved by a Committee of the Whole in the assembly, it included a clause directing their senators to "use their constant and unremitted exertions until they effect having the doors of the Senate of the United States kept open, that the public may have access to hear the debates of the Senate."[43]

Alexander Martin's birthright as a Presbyterian and his education at Princeton made him a curious advocate of instruction. His tradition held to a system of congregational (popular) election of Presbyters, called to office by the Holy Spirit, who, meeting together in a court, acted as they interpreted the will of the Spirit, not in any manner beholden to the will of their congregational majority. Transferred to the political system, such a structure was analogous to elitism. Reinforced by the fear of monarchy, setting the elect apart to a task raised the suspicion of the electorate and was ever at the root of populism. Instruction of legislators, as it developed in the 19th century, derived from the purpose of making the legislators voters of the popular will, not independent interpreters of the public interest. Martin was to prove consistent in his advocacy of open government in his later actions as a senator, but he never saw instruction as the removal from the elected senator of the right to independent, informed judgment.

15

Washington's Southern Tour and the Establishment of a State Capital

George Washington applied his very sensitive grasp of image in determining to make his tour of the union of states. There was for him the ancient precedent of a royal progress used with varying effectiveness by crowned heads to show them as the national symbol. Washington determined that he would travel, not as a royal, but as a citizen head of state. Since these citizens had known of only the former, it was to be in his person and actions that Washington created, before their eyes, the reality of the presidency.

In his tour of the North in 1790, he refined the image. In the first state, Massachusetts, he stood aloof from the strong state supremacy advocate, in the person of Governor John Hancock, refusing to visit him at the statehouse but giving audience to the governor in a public house that, by Washington's presence, was temporarily the place of executive power.[1] Breaking with the royal image, he refused to accept any private largess, never knowingly staying in a private home or accepting a meal there. Thus, he maintained public accessibility without the obligation of favoritism.

The southern leg of his tour was deferred in anticipation of the final approval of the Federal Constitution by North Carolina. A trip prior to that action could not have been overland for fear of calling attention to this gap in the union. Once the Fayetteville convention approved ratification, the president looked forward to moving through the South.[2]

By fall, Martin had been advised that Washington would soon begin the southern tour. He asked William Blount, who was going to Mt. Vernon to thank Washington personally for appointing him governor of the territory south of the Ohio, to confirm the president's intent. Blount, struck by the dignity of his host, commented, "I verily believe he is as awful as a God." He heard the great man lay out a route along the east from Norfolk to Edenton, Washington, New Bern, Wilmington, Charleston, Savannah and Augusta. His return was planned through Columbia, Camden, Charlotte, and Salisbury to Richmond. Blount advised Governor Martin and wrote his brother, "I have given this information to Gov. Martin so that you may shortly expect to hear of pompous orders for equipping and training the Cavalry."[3]

Archibald Henderson seemed to have thought that Blount was making a joke at the governor's expense; Blount, however, went on to qualify the expectations that Washington had about his reception in the South. "If the very greatest attention and respect is not paid to him, he will be greatly disappointed and mortified," because it was being said in the North that his native South would not be able to receive him with as much attention as he had already received from them. Blount went on to detail a part of Washington's progress from Boston with 400 cavalry to the New Hampshire line where the president was met by the governor at the head of a military company of 700 soldiers.[4] So William Blount had placed North Carolina on notice that the president was expecting to be received and entertained in grand style; hence no one could be fairly criticized for too much pretension.

Without a seat of government, North Carolina had no official place to welcome the president. He entered the state in mid-April 1791, stopping first at Halifax. Though he found that place "in decline," two men who lived there, Willie Jones and William R. Davie, represented the range of current opinion concerning federalism. Davie had championed ratification as the perfect Federalist while Jones, who had refused his appointment to the Constitutional Convention at Philadelphia, is said to have declared when told of Washington's visit, "I shall be glad to greet General Washington as soldier and man; but I am unwilling to greet him in his official capacity as President of the United States."[5] In point of fact, Washington's greeting in North Carolina often was more as soldier or as a Mason, than as president. Each town in succession made its greeting and offered their best entertainment. Governor Martin did not appear at any of these eastern stops, even at the melancholy reception in New Bern at the threadbare palace of the former royal governor that was, "hastening to Ruin."[6] The eastern merchants did not need the governor to add dignity to their reception. There is no indication that he was even invited to attend.

When Washington re-entered the state on his return leg to Mt. Vernon at the end of May, he was interested in measuring the mood of the backcountry. His major concern was a report that the backcountry was in a very hostile frame of mind concerning the federal excise tax to be levied on homemade spirits. On this part of his trip, Washington was confronted by people he could not understand. He convinced himself that the public worship of his person translated into a grudging increase in support of the government. When he saw or heard of public criticism of federalism, he was satisfied to dismiss it as the rantings of "demagogues." In Charlotte and Salisbury, he experienced the difference in leadership in North Carolina between the merchant east and the small farmer west. A hornet's nest for Cornwallis could be equally hostile to what those people perceived as an intrusive, federal, civil government.[7]

At Salem he rested at an oasis of reason and industry. The Moravians received him with dignity and simplicity. There were no dignitaries beyond the leadership of the community and they demonstrated their willingness to assimilate citizenship in the new nation into their independent communal life.[8] With satisfaction, Washington attended their worship, enjoyed their music, and strolled their neat streets, visiting merchants and craftsmen. At Salem Tavern, he was accommodated in probably the best public house he found on his southern tour.

He learned that Governor Martin intended to arrive the next day and the president readily delayed his departure.[9] Martin's choice to wait upon the president at Salem reflected the lack of a capital or governor's house for entertainment. In New Bern or Wilmington, Martin would have been as much a guest as was the president, and, with all the attention on Washington, the governor would have been totally pre-empted. Salem was a setting where Martin was much respected and appreciated. After hearing the discontent of the backcountry, the president was seeing at Salem the best the frontier could offer to be. It was a shrewd choice for the official meeting of governor and president. Unlike John Hancock, Martin would wait on the president in the most wholesome and friendly locality in North Carolina. Martin would not use the meeting to enhance his own office but to defer to the man and to the office that he had served under in war and had watched preside in the creation of a constitutional government.

On the afternoon of June 1, the governor arrived as expected. That evening the president and governor attended a singing service and were entertained later with music at the tavern.[10] In conversations that included Moravian town authorities, they spoke in French as a common language all could manage.[11] The occasions when these men met were each critical moments in the national life. Meeting at the end of the Southern tour gave Washington the opportunity to exchange with the governor the impressions he had absorbed and the opinions he had heard expressed. Martin was a reasonable spokesman for the rights of states but his experience at Philadelphia, and through his years of public service, also gave him an appreciation of the wisdom of a strengthened nation. For him it could not be either-or and that was the pragmatism with which he faced the resolute views of a commander-in-chief.

The symbolism intended in the two tours did much to confirm the national adoration of Washington. It created a level of respect for the office of president that was sustained for almost 200 years and did much to create the balance between the legislative and executive branches of the new government. At one point, when greeted roundly by the Moravian crowd, Washington responded, "after all good people, I am but a citizen of our free country, like you all; I thank you for the honor shown me."[12]

Governor Martin confirmed his own deep respect for Washington that many subsequent historians have read as proof that he was a Federalist. They have read reverence for the man as commitment to that man's political views. Accepting that hypothesis makes inevitable the assumption that Martin's later opinions and votes were erratic and vacillating.

At 4:00 the next morning, the president and governor and their respective entourages, left Salem, had breakfast with one Dodson, and arrived before noon at the battle site at Guilford Courthouse.[13] The president observed the ground as a trained commander. He had complete confidence in the performance of General Nathaniel Greene. Had Washington commanded, however, he might have applied his militia troops as reserves instead of as first-line shock troops. It was a point of battle strategy upon which those two commanders, Washington and Greene, always disagreed.[14] Martin's brother, James, had commanded the Guilford militia that was specifically criticized by Greene for their rapid retreat in the face of the British. James Martin always held that his orders had not been to stand but to get off two good rounds and fall back. In his opinion, the fusillade was well directed and the retreat was spirited.[15] Such points of tactics were no doubt part of the conversation that day on the battlefield between the president; his aide, Major Jackson; and the governor and his private secretary, Thomas Rogers.

Washington may have been entertained at the governor's residence in Martinville, the tiny village at the courthouse.[16] It had been his earlier plan to stay several nights at Guilford but that stay was shortened by the extra night at Salem. Washington has no comment on where he stayed the night at Guilford nor on how he was entertained, raising the assumption that neither was remarkable. During that time he discussed "the State of Politics in No. Carolina" with Martin. He was reassured that "the discontent of the people were subsiding fast." The president did hear Martin attack the speculators, however, singling out the speculators in land "and the purchases from the State of Georgia."[17] This reference was to the Yazoo Land Companies that included such speculators as Patrick Henry, John Sevier, and William Blount. The fear that this scheme "must involve the Country in trouble—perhaps in blood," grew out of the Yazoo involvement with Indian treaty lands. Both men could have recognized the new value of a federal settlement to such controversy.

At this point the tour ended. Although Martin intended to accompany the president to the Virginia border and had called up a unit of cavalry to provide proper escort, it was Washington's insistent wish to proceed alone. He clearly intended no insult. Washington wanted a public reception on the Southern tour that outdid the one he had experienced in the North but he repeatedly refused to allow people to be inconvenienced by his presence. At Guilford he departed for home. Receptions were over. Continuing this escort to the border would only be gratification to his ego and a hardship to the governor. It was in Washington's character to bid goodbye here and just be on his way. It is an example of what he saw as the subtle difference between a royal progress and the tour of the states by a citizen president.

In July, the university trustees met in Hillsborough with Martin in the chair. The focus of the meeting was the collection of arrearages on public taxes that had been pledged to the university. The board appointed men of prominence in each district in the anticipation that such men might have weight in collecting these past-due accounts. Although they obviously talked about their strategy for the next assembly, they recorded no planned action but agreed to meet next at New Bern on the third Monday in December while the legislature was in session.[18]

When Martin prepared his message for the next assembly, he concluded it with another committed plea on behalf of the university. "Once more let me hold up to your notice the university late created by your authority, which claims your further patronage and support." He asserted that the people had placed a duty upon that body to find "some productive revenue to give it [the university] effectual existence." He asked that "our native youth [be] fitted in time to assist our councils and conduct our government, ... to adorn society with polished manners or profit it by the discharge of private or professional duties ... to give greater dignity to the state." This attention to the need of the university, which took up one-third of his annual speech to the assembly, paralleled Martin's personal priority for education. Now he perceived a nation realizing the "full fruition of national happiness [while] internal commotions have shaken mighty governments abroad [and] pride and war have ravaged the half of Europe." It was thus an opportunity "to open new sources of industry [to insure that] agriculture, manufacturers commerce [are] properly encouraged at home." His attention was directed to only two actions: the "nurture of our youth" through the opening of the university and the encouragement of internal navigation. He set out no creative panoply of ideas. It was time to build a permanent future one essential step at a time.[19]

The copies of the Acts of Congress that Martin had expected at the time of his meeting with Washington came after that visit. Among the actions necessary to establish the state government as part of the federal system, the assembly was required to approve a new Oath of Allegiance for officeholders to the Constitution of the United States.[20] In compliance with the treaty obligations of the nations, the assembly confirmed the right of British citizens to their property previously attached under the Acts of Confiscation. Rebels, who were to lose land they had purchased under the confiscation, would be reimbursed. An acrimonious issue for many years in the state was finally put to rest.[21]

The shadow of parochial politics that had neutralized the attempts of each previous assembly to establish a state capital shifted once again. The western counties had been ceded. The support of Fayetteville, because it was the established marketplace for the backcountry, was no longer as powerful. Ignoring the previous debate between the established towns of the state, this assembly focused on the impartial logic of a location in the center of the state in Wake County. Site selection had been contested for so long that the final selection became a symbol of the maturity of statehood. The assembly appointed a commission of ten members—one from each congressional district—to meet in the spring to finalize the site and lay plans for a capital city. North Carolina was to have a new governmental city, as the nation was to have a new federal city.[22]

The university loan bill, tabled in the last assembly, was reintroduced with the full support of Martin as governor and president of the board of trustees. Davie was back in the assembly, having decided to return to the public arena that he had disdained in the last term, and took credit for the successful piloting of the funding legislation. He was confirmed in this praise, "his eloquent appeal to the assembly was long remembered," by subsequent historians ignoring the contribution made by the governor who, instead of rallying support of the backcountry to this investment in the future, could have adopted the roll of the demigod and doomed it to defeat as an elitist's plaything.[23] Eloquence didn't save the university funding legislation— pragmatic good sense did. James Iredell gave credit to Davie and vague praise to

Martin saying, "this wise and beneficent measure was chiefly due to the exertions of Col. Davie, aided by the exterior influence of the Executive."[24]

A loan of $10,000 was authorized from the state treasury for the university; this was approved by a four-vote margin in the Commons and by seven votes in the Senate. The governor had risked the loss of his core political support through his commitment to the university loan bill. When the act was submitted by the governor on Christmas Eve, it was ordered to "lie on the table" during the adjournment for the holiday. On the 29th, the narrow approving majority in the Commons did include the governor's brother but not the votes of such associates as Jesse Franklin, Wyatt Hawkins, Bostick of Stokes, Hamilton of Guilford, or Henry Scales of Rockingham. The Senate majority for approval did not include Joseph Winston or Charles Gallaway.[25]

In 1792, sites were selected for both the new university and for the capital city. At the end of March, six of the ten commissioners met to choose the capital site near the Wake County Courthouse. Based on their selection, 1,000 acres owned by Joel Lane was conveyed to "Alexander Martin, Esquire, Governor for the time being."[26] A city plan was laid out on this tract, designed in a classic form, with five public squares. The central, Union Square, was to contain the capitol. Three of the four quadrant squares were to be named for Martin's three, now deceased, predecessors, Richard Caswell, Abner Nash, and Thomas Burke. One of the streets recognized both Governor Martin and his brother, James, who was one of the commissioners. It was James who was reputed to have first suggested the name Raleigh for the capital city.[27] A public auction was held for the sale of the lots and many interested citizens, including the governor, purchased one. As he had used the Hendersons and Joseph Martin to carry out cession in the west, the governor now used his brother to influence the plan and realization of the state capital. Governor Martin had experienced the frustration of a government on wheels more than most, since he first came to the office of governor in 1783. He had dealt with the anticipation of reaching quorum and with the frustration when failure to do so meant no assembly and the standstill of legislative administration.

The issue of the location of the capital had raged for a decade swathed in regional jealousy. The institution of the university struggled unfulfilled through the same decade, not because of regional jealousy, but because a state of small subsistence farmers had to be led by the most expansive, progressive, trusting motives they possessed to commit to higher education, particularly when they could not conceive of themselves or their kin as ever being able to participate. However, like the capital, once financing of the university was approved, progress on its physical structure moved swiftly. Chaired by the governor, 25 of the trustees met in Hillsborough in August 1792, and advanced seven locations, ranging from Charlotte to Smithfield, as general locations for the university. They agreed on a place called Cipritz Bridge on New Hope Creek in Orange County.[28] In November, the site committee selected New Hope in Chapel Hill and that same day deeds to eight parcels totaling 953 acres were made to the trustees. In less than two years, the university had 41 students and was literally the first state university.

Although most of North Carolina's concern about the encroachment of whites on treaty lands of the Indians had been ceded with the western counties, there was still a substantial area of Cherokee treaty land in the western corner of the state. White settlers were laying claims through the Armstrong land office, using "warrants called supernumeraries" on land entries said to be lost. There was the implication that Armstrong's office was overwhelmed but so far the confusion had not reached the level of fraud. Martin was unequivocal in issuing a proclamation that all "such grants obtained as aforesaid are declared to be utterly VOID" and any violator was subject to a fine of £50. The action insisted that the treaty lands would not be breached. The state could initiate this action on its own because it applied only to land within its borders.[29] William Blount, empowered by his new post as governor of the territory south of the Ohio, complained that Martin was continuing to issue grants in the western counties. Martin's explanation, communicated to Secretary of State Jefferson, was that, under terms of the Act of Cession, he was issuing grants only to people whose claims had already been taken by someone else. In other words, he was only confirming title to tracts, not initiating title.[30]

In Martin's last term as governor, the Federal Constitution proved its resilience against the first conflict of political extremes and confirmed itself capable of encompassing the limits of conflict within the latitude of law. Political parties took form as institutions that could represent a wide scope of individuals around extremes of opinion. This was less the design of the founders than the miracle of the system. It was to prove in two centuries that, as long as political parties debated, even battled, over the issues, the democracy was served. When the parties turned on the system, they would come very near to self-destruction. In 1792, Washington's agreement to run for re-election, and his success, assuaged the Federalists, even to the fringes of the so-called monarchists; while the assumption of control of the Congress by the Republicans, encompassing all shades of particularists and state firsters, pacified the Anti-Federalist majority.

The opposition to the Federalist Party had coalesced finally into the Anti-Federalists beginning with the contest for vice president between Adams and Clinton. Although Adams retained the office, the 54 electoral votes that Clinton received represented the political support of Virginia, North Carolina, New York, and Georgia.[31] This support already constituted a national voting block around which a party could be built. Thomas Jefferson emerged as the leader of this party in the public mind just as Hamilton had become the spokesman for the Federalist Party through his concept of centralized government.

By the time the assembly came together again in New Bern, Martin was completing his second three-year term as governor and, prohibited from succession, faced retirement from the public stage. He was as popular as he had ever been and, now that Richard Caswell was dead, he was unrivaled as the state's most durable political figure. Samuel Johnston's short term as one of North Carolina's first senators was soon to expire. Johnston's venerated status among state leaders had suffered since his elevation to the Senate. The tension inherent between federal officeholders of high reputation and the state legislators, to whom they were beholden for their office but who considered them to be little more than ciphers within the federal system, was to continue as a thankless formula for a politician. The issue of instruction kept all states at odds with their senators. Johnston was frustrated and recognized that he would very likely not be re-elected. If he were, he reasoned that he would only be more tarnished in another term.

Aware as he certainly was of the encumbrance of instruction that went with the office of United States senator, Martin had few options for advanced political office. He could reason that his years in the top positions of state government, executive and legislative, made him more sensitive to the attitudes of the legislature and offered him a reservoir of political goodwill that might offset the carping. His political savvy, however, must have filled him with reservations.

By the time a quorum was declared to open the new assembly, Martin's forces were in position and, with Johnston out of the way, the governor was fully committed to a run for the Senate. The Federalists, with the closest thing to a national strategy, put forward a young legislator from Salisbury, John Steele, who had the particular support of Davie. Steele had served in the first two Congresses but had been replaced in the third by Matthew Locke.[32] Well educated and attractive, he had made associations with the national government, including Hamilton, that promised to make him the first fast-track politician within the party in North Carolina. He also had a claim to the western vote as a resident of Salisbury.

John Leigh first appeared in North Carolina in 1787, was soon elected to the assembly from Tarboro, and had been Speaker of the Commons in the last two sessions. He gained a promising reputation within the legislature but was not broadly known throughout the state. His wife was Mary Baker, whose sister was married to another prospective candidate, General Thomas Blount.[33]

General Blount shared the support within eastern counties with Leigh and he was backed by some of the remaining members of the speculator coalition. Politically, his brother, William Blount, had always overshadowed him although he eventually did serve in Congress. He was active in all the Blount enterprises and a major general in the North Carolina militia: such associations could convert into political clout.[34] Blount's candidacy is curious in light of a letter that his brother wrote from his new post in Knoxville on November 8 to John Steele. He suggested "a Coalition of Eastern and Western interests between you and Colonel Spaight[,] one for governor and the other for Senator." He went on to caution, "beware of a Coalition between Charles Johnson and Lenoir, and between Charles Johnson and Governor Martin."[35]

It is illusive to place party labels on any of the four contestants for the Senate except Steele. On the first ballots, the Federalist association gave him the establishment position and made him a target. It was the Martin forces, led by James Taylor, which voiced the vulnerability of Steele. Electioneering loosed the ban on libel and slander. There was some residual bad blood between Steele and Montford Stokes of Rowan. It was Stokes who had been the object of that accusation in 1790, in a letter to Steele, that he owed his election as clerk of the Rowan Superior Court to a pledge of profits to Governor Martin.[36] A year later, James Taylor, whom Stokes characterized as "a damned scoundrel," borrowed some money from him at Salisbury court and failed to repay Stokes as promised. Stokes proceeded to dun Taylor through the sheriff of Rockingham County.

In the course of the electioneering, Stokes made the public assertion that he did not think Steele had "authorized" anyone to place his name in nomination for the Senate. He went on to support Governor Martin, as did Taylor, "from a principal [sic] of Gratitude." As balloting continued to be inconclusive, the pressure rose and Stokes was reported to Steele to have said things to injure his election. The specific disclosure was that Stokes "has asserted that you [Steele] had written two letters to two different men containing two different principles and contrary assertions." It was James Taylor, with the aid of William Faulkner, whom Stokes consigned as the wretches from whom there is no escape "and authors of this claim." Stokes avowed to Steele "the malice of Taylor with his vile accessory, the miserable vender [sic] of games, heretofore the scourge of our unfortunate and credulous countrymen—what might not the combination of two such imposters effect—Just God! Thou hast sent scorpions to vex us for our iniquities." Stokes claimed to have publicly confronted Taylor and to have denied authoring such contradictory letters to which Taylor had replied, "it is a damned lye, and you are a damned lyar."[37] Politics does indeed make strange combinations and, in spite of his vote for Governor Martin, Stokes disingenuously asserted after the fact, to comfort Steele, that "the friends of Mr. Martin or of Mr. Blount ... could do nothing to carry their points by saying things prejudicial to your character."

The sanctimonious Davie, employing "some of his most exquisite invective," found "nothing could equal the activity and scandalous behavior of several of Martin's friends."[38] He deplored Stokes' actions and accepted the charge of duplicity in the election debate as true and characteristic of that politician. Davie saw Stokes and Taylor as playing some sort of charade at Steele's expense.

Martin did not leave all the political debate to surrogates. He characterized Steele's political views as "all aristocratic, nay that you were the devoted—of Mr. Hamilton," adding epithets of "vain, pompous, arrogant."[39] These descriptions were aimed at the point where Federalists were most vulnerable. In the case of Steele and Davie, it was impossible to disclaim.[40] Davie made his summation of the tactics that delivered the Senate seat to Martin. "So completely had the wretch [Martin] poisoned the minds of the Edenton members," that they would not consider any rebuttal defending Steele and the Cape Fear men joined the westerners to elect Martin. "Damnably mortified [by] that despicable creature," Davie railed, "I am strongly inclined to fatalism of late, and have believed for some time that God almighty made that man on purpose to disgrace this country."[41]

On the fifth ballot, Martin was elected, his campaign succeeding so far in the end as to place Steele last in the field.[42] The celebrants saw Martin's election as the defeat of Federalism in the Hamilton style. As he had succeeded Samuel Johnston as governor in 1789, he now took the place of the Federalist as senator. His election was accepted as a Federalist defeat but not quite so clearly as an Anti-Federalist victory. The excesses of his lieutenants left scars that would be remembered. In his message to the assembly accepting his election, he restated his political perspective: "While my endeavors shall be exerted in promoting the general good of the nation, the individuality and internal sovereignty of the state shall be my principal care to preserve inviolate."[43]

Martin had been effective at this visceral campaign process. The North Carolina general assembly in 1792, however, contrasted dramatically with the decorum of Philadelphia in 1787 when the framework of this innovative government had been debated. That sense of a noble work had evolved now to a practical reality. In the campaign for ratification, Martin had retained his political viability by remaining aloof from the vortex of debate. In 1792, he had been embroiled in debate. He may have mused about Philadelphia on November 26 when he made out the bill to submit to the state to redeem warrants of £384 for travel and expenses to and from the Constitutional Convention.[44]

In discussing the 1792 assembly and the election of Alexander Martin to succeed Samuel Johnston, one of North Carolina's earlier historians printed a priggish judgment of Governor Martin's character that is one of the sources of later criticism. He argued, "Martin was not equal to him [Johnston] in solidity of character and attainments, but he was of such superior excellence that his appointment was likewise highly creditable to the State."[45]

16

Martin as United States Senator

As Martin savored his election as United States senator, the assembly passed a resolution of appreciation for his service to the state as governor. Federalist Richard Dobbs Spaight succeeded him. Martin left the governor's office with the certain knowledge that within a year the assembly would be meeting in the capital and a year later students would be attending a university. In response to their resolution of congratulations, the new senator's declaration reversed the position of the state's first two senators, who had defended their refusal to be instructed by the legislature by describing themselves to Martin as bound to act in accordance "with the general interests of the Union," acknowledging no overriding accountability to the state.[1] The legislature had now selected, out of its own leadership, a representative of its commitment to particularism.

Martin spent most of 1793 preparing for the convening of the Senate. For the next six years he could expect at least yearly trips to Philadelphia where he would spend four to six months in sessions. The first two Congresses had not established a fixed date of meeting, although the pattern of assembling at the end of the year and adjourning before mid-year was common. For a rural population this schedule meant winter crops were planted and senators might be home for spring planting. In North Carolina it was possible, on most occasions, for senators to prepare a report for the assembly of the acts of Congress and to know the sense of the new assembly before departing again for Philadelphia. Between meetings, correspondence with the governor and Council of State kept the national and state officials advised of issues, actions, and majority opinions. Martin had functioned within the dynamic of that political order. As he moved now to the third panel of the triptych of government, he possessed unarguably the most complete grasp of the public consensus in the state.

Martin was elected senator in November to a body whose term began the following March but that did not assemble in Congress until December. Arrangements

Martin's claim for travel and services. Not until he was preparing to go to Philadelphia as a United States senator did Martin render his expense report to the state for attending the "federal Convention." (Courtesy of Raeford Cates.)

that he made during that year of anticipation included contracts with overseers and plans for the care of his household, particularly his mother.[2] His brother-in-law, Samuel Rogers, died during the year. Samuel's son, Thomas, was also married in 1793 to his double first cousin, Mary "Polly" Martin.[3] For several years Thomas had been the private secretary for Governor Martin and secretary of the trustees of the university and was a great favorite of his uncle. In order to help the young couple establish themselves in Stokes County, where they intended to settle, Martin offered to sign over the warrant to the 640 acres on the Dan River he had held since 1778 but that he had not surveyed for a grant. It would prove to be a somewhat clouded gift in a few years.[4]

By virtue of the precedent set in the case of Governor Martin, the election of Governor Spaight should have carried with it the elevation of the new governor as president of the board of trustees of the university. When the trustees met on December 3, 1792, Martin presided. He signed the board minutes through their adjournment on December 14. When Spaight was elected on the 11th, he should have succeeded to the chair but Martin neither resigned nor executed a letter of resignation. A year later, when the trustees met on December 9, they could only elect Spaight as president pro tem and they unanimously promoted him when they received Martin's tardy letter of resignation on the 18th.[5]

On October 12, 1793, when the cornerstone of Old East, the first building at the university, was laid with elaborate Masonic rites, Martin technically was still president of the trustees. He was not present, however, leaving Davie another opportunity to shine before history. Martin was not at Chapel Hill at this historic moment because he was already on his way north to receive the singular distinction of an honorary Doctorate of Laws bestowed on him by his alma mater.

Graduation at Princeton was held in late September. When Martin had been a student, the ceremony had been held in the Prayer Hall of Nassau Hall, but since 1763 it was held in the Presbyterian Church. "Every house in the village was filled to overflowing with handsomely gowned women and men looking quite stiff and formal in white wigs, velvet coats, colored stockings, and shoes set off with silver buckles."[6] The academic procession began at the president's house. The Rev. John Witherspoon had also been a delegate to the Constitutional Convention in 1787 with that large class of Princetonians. He soon after became blind. Now ailing, this was his last graduation and he died suddenly on November 15, 1794. Witherspoon was certainly pivotal to the recognition that Princeton conferred on Alexander Martin. With few national newspapers to carry the story, there was no recognition picked up in North Carolina of this honor bestowed on the former governor but there was a great deal of personal satisfaction that he later could share in his family circle.

The year 1793 had been the year when a devastating yellow fever epidemic came to Philadelphia, corresponding with the influx of penniless survivors of the slave uprising against the French colonials in Santo Domingo. More than 4,000 citizens lost their lives and the national psyche was repeatedly tested by public fear. Benjamin Rush was considered a popular hero of the epidemic although his "discovered" prescription of extensive bleeding and doses of mercury as a purge are now thought to have contributed more to the death rate than the cure.[7] Martin was approaching his senate term as Philadelphia was gripped in this disaster. The government had fled along with most of the society that was able to depart. There was no certainty how either civil society or government would proceed. At Princeton, Martin heard the stories of the epidemic from many who had fled there from Philadelphia. Like them he would not approach the city until the cooler weather of late October gradually broke the epidemic. Washington considered alternative locations for the government since, even in December with Congress due to convene, there were questions about which houses in the city were safe to re-enter. In the end Philadelphia recovered but yellow fever was a recurring scourge in 1794, 1796, 1797, and 1798.[8]

Philadelphia had changed physically since Martin had last been there at the convention. On that occasion he had left the convention early. This time he arrived committed to remain perhaps for half a year in the Senate. He arrived in his own chariot with his manservant.[9] His ultimate accommodations again may have been at the Indian Queen Hotel, now located at 15 South Fourth Street. (James Thompson was proprietor and had been since the location was moved in 1790.) Philadelphia, after the population had returned, was a city of 65,000, "the center of all that was elegant and civilized and agreeable in American society."[10]

The decade of the 1790s, during which Alexander Martin served in the United States Senate, is considered by some the most critical and consequential in American history. "The Politics of the 1790s was a truly cacophonous affair. Previous historians have labeled it 'the Age of Passion' for good reason, for in terms of shrill accusatory rhetoric, flamboyant displays of ideological intransigence, intense personal rivalries, and hyperbolic claims of imminent catastrophe, it has no equal in American history."[11] This is hardly the description of an atmosphere in which Martin would have been naturally comfortable. Martin could never have been happy in "a decade-long shouting match." He was, however, a significant member of the revolutionary generation that was now hammering out the themes on which their nation would function. In most revolutions there was a victorious side that dictated the character of the surviving government. In the American Revolution, "the shape and character of the political institutions were determined by a relatively small number of leaders who knew each other." They were, for all purposes, "America's first and only natural aristocracy."[12] That is perhaps more evident in a review of Washington's cabinet members where names like Jay, Hamilton, Knox, Randolph, Pickering, and Lee all harkened to the era of war. In the legislature, fewer names jump out from the higher ranks of the army but among those Alexander Martin is one of the most prominent.

Martin arrived at a time when the United States was entangled in its first international crisis and that had eased the focus of the popular outcries against assumption. Many Americans had viewed the overthrow of Louis XVI with a degree of satisfaction as confirmation of their own revolution. Washington was more circumspect, remembering the risk that Louis had taken as an ally in that revolution. Early in 1794, a French declaration of a "war of all peoples against all kings" was news in America and popular enthusiasm had grown in some places to near hysteria. In April, as tensions between the two great European naval powers threatened to draw the United States into a widening European war, Washington declared national neutrality. Citizen Edmond Genet arrived in Charleston as the representative of the French Republic and, treating protocol as if it were a victim of revolution, proceeded to mount a public relations campaign on the side of the pro-French Republicans. The excesses of popular revolution unfolding in France were stirring the worst fears of educated Americans like Washington and Martin. The public utterances of Genet were transporting to the western hemisphere the unsettling mystique of the masses. Those excesses had obviously instigated the revolt in Santo Domingo that showed every indication of spreading throughout the Caribbean where slaves outnumbered their masters. For some in America, the French Revolution was a clear choice between monarchy and republicanism, just as their own revolution had been a battle between tyranny and liberty. Those views reinforced the Republicans. Federalists saw France as another manifestation of an eternal battle "between anarchy and order, atheism and religion, poverty and prosperity."[13]

Assumption was the issue, born so stridently by Hamilton and opposed with subtle intensity by those who gravitated to the opposition views of Jefferson through Madison that became the capstone of political difference in the new republic. In the latter stages of the Continental Congress and then in the first years of the Constitution, opinions were shaped by a series of natural opposing viewpoints, each claiming to have inherited the revolution. It is possible to measure "sectional versus national allegiances; agrarian versus commercial economic priorities; diffusion versus consolidation as social ideals; an impotent versus a potent federal government," as flashpoints of opinion and historians have attempted to project these into political philosophies, even into the embryo of the formation of political parties. Alexander

Martin, typical among the revolutionary generation, waffled between these social, economic and political persuasions in the belief that all opinions had to be respected and this republic could function by reasonable consensus in the forum. That is why, up to this point in examining his career, this writer has preferred to characterize Martin as a particularist, but it is obvious that even I have found that term inadequate. Out of the debate on assumption, however, the position differences were "eventually institutionalized and rendered safe by the creation of political parties."[14] With Washington above the fray, ennobled, Hamilton was the fulcrum on which the Federalists depended, and Jefferson the opposite fulcrum on which the Republicans depended. Generally, democratic New England, led by its heavy reliance on the economic health of its seaports, favored the pro–English Federalist position. The landed interests, particularly those with substantial slave property, became enthusiastic Francophiles and Republicans. The Hamiltonian Federalists carried the day on assumption of the state debts by a secret quid pro quo concluded with the Republicans, which located the capital of the republic at Philadelphia for the decade of the 1790s and then placed it permanently on the banks of the Potomac. It is in his term in the Senate where we can observe Martin's metamorphosis into a Republican, albeit one who never was completely comfortable with the fit.

Appropriate here is an examination of Martin's national career vis-à-vis the prodigious weight of Virginia leadership in the federal government. Observed against that Virginian dominance, Alexander Martin played well on the national stage, better than any other contemporary North Carolinian, but he had no aspirations within either political party. It might reasonably be asserted that had he served more than one term in the Senate, he likely would have been a force in the Jefferson administration but that suggests he was just a late bloomer, which he was not.[15] The other hypothesis could be that Martin was another Carolina cipher for Virginia political strategy, but though he idealized Washington in most respects, his record shows only independence and intense loyalty to the interests of his state. As an example of his detachment from the Virginia leadership, there is the coolness that continued in what had once been a warm lifelong relationship to James Madison, now the political strategist of the Republican Party.

In 1793, Eli Whitney made public his invention of the cotton gin, which so rapidly transformed the social and economic fabric of the South. In his remaining years, Martin did not see the impact of this agricultural advancement mature but he was in on the unsettling beginning. At this stage, the French Revolution, by emphasizing "Liberté, Egalité, Fraternité," was placing slavery out of favor. Most southern states were outlawing the importation of slaves.[16] There was strong sentiment for outlawing the entire slave system in light of the slave uprisings in the West Indies. Martin's 80 slaves represented a substantial proportion of his wealth, but until the advent of the cotton boom, there were few economically viable cash crops and most slaves did not produce much more than their family's share of subsistence within the plantation system. In Rockingham County the cash crop was tobacco, offered for sale in markets in Petersburg and Fayetteville. Martin became a tobacco and cotton farmer before his death and it was the lure of cotton wealth that would subsequently scatter his kin across the Deep South. The next legislature passed a very stringent act prohibiting any one from bringing into the state any slaves or indentured servants of color. At the same session, "owners were prohibited from allowing slaves to have their own time, and meetings of Negroes were prohibited."[17] Martin carried this background to Philadelphia where the issue of slavery had entered into the national "shouting match." The Declaration of Independence was becoming an unambiguous tract for abolition and it had been Martin's action as governor that encouraged the first celebration of the 4th of July as a national holiday. Conversely, he had served as a delegate to the convention that produced the Constitution, a document that would not have been possible had it not remained silent on the resolution of the issue of slavery. On this issue, the national tragedy, his personal experience very closely followed the molding of the conflict, and what had become clear before he finished his term in Philadelphia, was that "the larger the enslaved population grew, the more financially and politically impractical any emancipation scheme became."[18]

The first session of the Third United States Congress convened December 2, 1793. The credentials of the "Honorable Alexander Martin Esquire of our County of Rockingham" were presented by the new senator from North Carolina.[19] Martin's Republican approach to this legislative branch of government had a double taproot. He had been party to the design of the United States Senate and so had an opinion, more credible than most, of its purpose and limits. He had also been governor of one of the largest and most populated states represented in that body, and the majority of the citizens of that state were deeply fearful of the Senate as a model of privilege, in contrast to the popular will. He was not, therefore, skeptical of the Senate, as some Republicans were, nor did he intend to impede the actions of the Senate. As he had advised his North Carolina legislature, however, he was in Philadelphia to represent the will of the state and the sovereignty of the people.

As early as 1790, the North Carolina Senate had directed their senators to do everything in their power to open the doors of the United States Senate to the observation of the public.[20] Senator Martin made it his mission to consummate that directive. He introduced a bill on January 16 that would require the doors of the Senate to be open during public debate. The Senate model had been the English House of Lords where the privileged debated public law behind the privacy of locked doors.

Declaring his conviction "that in all representative governments the representatives are responsible for their conduct to their constituents who are entitled to such information that a discrimination and just estimate be made thereof," he added his resolves:

> That, the Senate of the United States, being the Representative of the sovereignties of the individual states, whose basis is the people, owe equal responsibility to the Powers by which they are appointed, as if that body were derived immediately from the people, and that all questions and debates, arising there upon ought to be public. ...
> Resolved, therefore that it be a standing rule that the doors of the Senate remain open while the Senate shall be sitting in a Legislative and Judiciary capacity, except on such occasions as in the judgment may require secrecy.[21]

In constructing this act, Alexander Martin gave voice to his political philosophy for this republic. Attributing all power to the people, a representative system governs in the states and, through the state legislatures, by representatives in federal branches. To the Senate, where the weight of the states was equal, went a special trust of defending or representing the individual, sovereign state interests. The implication is that he viewed this as a special, not necessarily exclusive, trust. That peculiar duty did not elevate the Senate beyond its "equal responsibility to the Powers by which they are appointed."

The debate over open access in the Senate was vigorous and philosophic and lasted until passage on February 20 of the amendment that "provided for" the gallery to be built for the Senate. In the end the approval was two to one in favor. A day later Martin advised Governor Spaight that this "tremendous bugbear" would now be removed after a four-year struggle.[22] Senator Pierce Butler of South Carolina confided to Iredell that "Martin behaves steadily well and with credit to his state."[23] A year later, the senate visitor's gallery was opened to the public.[24]

Focusing on the needs of North Carolina, Senator Martin next reported a bill to erect a lighthouse "on the head land, and Cape of Hatteras and another to erect a beacon on Occacock [sic] Island" in North Carolina.[25] As he had been in most of the addresses he had delivered to the legislature as governor, Martin was committed to opening the rivers of North Carolina and her treacherous coast to commercial traffic.

During his southern tour in 1791, President Washington had discussed with Governor Martin his fear that the backcountry would be brought into open rebellion by the imposition of the excise tax on manufactured whiskey promulgated by Hamilton. For a time his concern seemed to be overblown. At the end of his tour he had visited briefly western Pennsylvania where he was assured, as he seems to have been assured by Martin, that the antagonism would subside. There are conflicting opinions why this simmering tempest suddenly erupted in the spring of 1794 into the Whiskey Rebellion, including the assertion that Hamilton himself exacerbated the situation "for his own evil purposes."[26] It was 23 years since Alexander Martin had been among the objects of the rage of the Regulator mob and then a conciliator between the government and the insurgents. There were some obvious parallels with the Whiskey Rebellion. President Washington reflected on the experience of Shay's Rebellion in Massachusetts in 1786 when that backcountry conflict had helped prove the ineptitude of the Confederation. Washington recognized that he would have to depend on the loyalty of individual state militia armies to restore order in the face of a public insurrection and there was no guarantee that states would respond when solicited. The legislature could but watch as Washington, coaxed by Hamilton's shadow over a stretch of months, established the ultimate standard of the commander-in-chief with decisive organization and execution and thereby confirmed the viability of the new federal system.[27] During the summer legislative recess, the government mobilized and in October moved against the insurrection. General Washington noted that by "an unlucky measure" Herman Husband had been among some insurgents who were arrested in the latter stages of the uprising. Husband was the Regulator pamphleteer who had fled to Pennsylvania in 1771 after Governor Tyron's victory at Alamance.[28] When Alexander Martin returned to Philadelphia for the second session of the Third U.S. Congress on November 3,[29] his good friend and protagonist, the Rev. David Caldwell, may have accompanied him.[30] Martin and Caldwell had both known Dr. Benjamin Rush as students at the College of New Jersey and these three men prevailed upon the federal authorities to "release the aged agitator [Husband]."[31]

The Rev. David Caldwell was sympathetic to the view of Benjamin Rush "that the Revolution would bring about a regeneration of American society—a return to a past age of purity and piety." Rush expected "the exigencies of the Revolution to stimulate a behavioral reformation among Americans" but by the end of the war he knew that the adversities had not brought the extensive reformation that he had wished. He would lament, "we knocked up the substance of royalty, but now and then we worship the shadow."[32] Caldwell, in North Carolina, and Rush, in Philadelphia, could both be described as a "permanently incandescent revolutionary," and they represented the ever-present pressure on Martin to be a more radical Republican.[33]

The perspective of most senators was provincial as they watched Washington define and confirm executive leadership. Concurrently, in that year, the states found themselves inexorably influenced by broader world events. Martin had allowed himself to be elevated from state to federal office, believing that he was being called to guarantee provincial sensibilities, only to be faced squarely with the aggressive effort of the European naval powers to draw the untested republic into their war. Whipped by an increasingly strident press, a phenomenon few Americans understood, the nation took sides. Resisting this new pressure to flex muscle and defend pride, Martin's initial efforts had been to fine-tune democratic government, protect the commerce of his state, and to observe the machinations of the Whiskey Rebellion. It was the issue of Jay's Treaty that elevated his perspective on the scope of his new job from state to federal to international politics.

As part of the president's overall endeavors to maintain neutrality in the face of European conflict, John Jay was appointed a special emissary to London to attempt to negotiate an understanding on American rights. Although Jay's appointment was confirmed in the Senate, both Alexander Martin and Benjamin Hawkins opposed it.[34] Once Martin was convinced that European governments intended to draw the United States into their conflict through her commerce, his support went to France by default because he did not trust the British. He wished to "strike a blow that may wound the British heart ... through its commerce."[35]

Much of England still viewed the existence of the United States as a temporary illusion bound to collapse with time, and at this particular time England appeared close to victory in her European war. It was an unpropitious moment for Jay to exact rights. James Monroe had simultaneously been named minister to France, where he openly flattered the French national ego. Americans, whose nation had been created out of revolution, could not observe, without partiality, a social revolution ten years later in France, particularly since France was the European power that first had sanctioned their "unalienable" rights.

Most authorities agree that Jay probably negotiated the best terms open to him under these circumstances. When Washington was advised of the terms that materialized, he understood that they would be unpopular and his government made the error of attempting to keep those terms secret. Jay did secure the evacuation of the British forts south of the Great Lakes, an issue left open by the Treaty of Paris, and gained commercial privileges in British colonies in the Far East, a lasting future value. He failed to gain similar privileges in the British West Indies. His failure to establish American rights left to the British the definition of blockades, contraband, and the terms of neutral trade. The most controversial clause was an American promise not to levy discriminatory customs or duties against British ships for a period of ten years. It was an embarrassing acknowledgement of the reality of the British dominance in the waters of the hemisphere.[36]

Instead of presenting the treaty as the best that could be gotten, the government dithered in uncertainty for weeks and finally decided to release the terms to the Senate. The Senate decided to debate behind closed doors, preserving Washington's public secrecy. A solid ten-vote opposition took issue with terms of the treaty. Martin and Bloodworth joined Steven Mason and Henry Tazewell of Virginia, John Brown of Kentucky, Pierce Butler of South Carolina, James Jackson of Georgia, Aaron Burr of New York, Moses Robinson of Vermont and John Langdon of New Hampshire in a stormy debate winning an occasional convert on a specific provision.[37] At one point in the debate Aaron Burr attempted to rescind the secrecy of debate, at least as far as it deprived members of the ability to consult with outsiders on technical points. Martin broke with the Republicans and vigorously opposed the motion that was defeated 9 to 20.[38] Martin was taking the position that no reasonable resolution could be made of the Jay Treaty if it was to be debated in the partisanship of the press. This is an important distinction that Martin was making, obviously influenced by his experience in the debate at the Constitutional Convention—that there were circumstances where the Senate had to debate in secrecy. He was the leader in demanding open debate before the governed but on some issues that would be filtered through the politically partial press open debate would be so distorted as to skew any hope of judicious deliberation. Martin was again attempting to bridge the debate while the political interests attempted to define secrecy as an up or down issue.

The individual articles were debated with candor, members feeling free to voice their opinions. Governor Martin found the restrictions placed on American trade with the West Indies to be "truly humiliating."[39] As the debate progressed, the press dubbed the Senate "the secret lodge at Philadelphia." If the Senate could act "without consulting popular opinion, then that body, not the people, was sovereign."[40] The final 20 to 10 vote on the treaty precisely constituted the two-thirds majority necessary to approve a treaty and the Senate gave its advice and consent to the president. The Senate had maintained the secrecy of its debate. With approval of the treaty, however, Washington determined it was time to open the public debate. In reporting the approval of the treaty, the *Aurora* noted, "this imp of darkness, illegitimately begotten, commanded but the bare constitutional number required for ratification."[41] The issue of the Jay Treaty confirmed the power of the opposition press in the fourth estate. Newspapers across the states began to praise the "honorable ten" who had opposed ratification and picture the senators who had supported the treaty as "returning homeward from Philadelphia with hangdog looks and a furtive air."[42]

In Virginia the assembly approved a resolution commending the opposition of their senators, Tazewell and Mason, to the Jay Treaty. The treaty did not elicit the same partisan reaction in North Carolina except for a couple of meetings in New Bern and Edenton. Unlike the many planters deeply in debt to British creditors who would be threatened with ruin by the treaty, North Carolina's small farmers had little to fear from the British. There was some apprehension that the treaty might enable Lord Granville's heirs to successfully reclaim their extensive interests in North Carolina.[43] Martin communicated his fear that if Englishmen could own and sell property in the United States, the university might lose the funding the legislature had hoped to direct its way by making it the legatee of escheated land in Tennessee.[44] Martin and Bloodworth may not have received the adulation Virginia gave her two senators for their vote opposing the Jay Treaty, but the eastern Federalists were severely weakened by their support of the treaty.

At home during the summer of 1795, his friends at Salem accorded Martin a singular honor. The Moravians set aside several of the first copies of their newly translated *History of Missions among the Indians* to give to their special friends outside the Society. Martin, "who more than any other is acquainted with our matters," was the only one that they noted specifically in the *Salem Journal* as receiving a "copy of the Indian mission history and the letter of thanks which Br. Ettwein wrote to him." In the previous Congress he had guided through a grant of 12,000 acres of land on the Muskingum River in the Ohio Territory near the Moravian settlement at Gnadenhutten that had significantly expanded the community. When he stopped by Salem in September on his way to court he attended the evening liturgy and received their gift.[45]

Thomas Shippen and his wife, Betsy Farley, had been at Sauratown in the early summer of 1795 while the senator was at Danbury but a few miles away. Ordinary courtesy would have brought him to the uncompleted home called Bellview that Betsy's parents had located above the Dan River.[46] Sauratown was often the subject when Alexander Martin visited Shippen House on Locust Street in Philadelphia.[47] At other times, memories of their days at the log colleges of southeast Pennsylvania or later at Princeton engaged Dr. William Shippen and Governor Martin with Dr. Benjamin Rush, the family doctor, or the Rev. Samuel Blair, the Presbyterian minister at Germantown.[48] Often times Martin, always referred to as "Governor" in Philadelphia, would join Dr. Shippen in a drive out to Farley, Tommy and Betsy Shippen's just completed estate seventeen miles west of Philadelphia in Bucks County. Such outings broke the monotony of the city. Through the Shippens, Martin came into the social circle of Philadelphia that included the Livingstons and Blairs. As his term as senator progressed, Martin became more of a fixture as a political Republican, which made him welcome into yet another social context. Never comfortable as a partisan, Martin was drawn to good conversation and the excitement of enlightenment. He could debate with vigor without discrediting an opponent. He sought to be in Philadelphia what he had always tried to be in North Carolina—a bridge between extremes. His near worship of Washington was balanced by his dislike of Hamilton, which dated from the issue of assumption.

Immediately after the Senate reconvened, on December 9, Martin made the motion that the newly installed Senate gallery be opened to the public. The odious secret deliberation over the Jay Treaty and the subsequent outcry in the Republican press, established the atmosphere that opened this bastion of secrecy. Martin's leadership in defining popular government as it would be structured in America positioned him on the spectrum between the extremes of Federalism and Republicanism. He viewed a federal system as necessary to create a nation that could ultimately rival the great world maritime powers, but in that government the people had to be sovereign.

Those days of healthy bipartisan tension, that had seen Hamilton and Jefferson functioning in the same cabinet, were gone. In a letter to Filippo Mazzei, Jefferson made his cryptic characterization of Washington's late cabinet as "men who were Samsons in the field and Solomons in the Council, shorn by the harlot England."[49] Jefferson was convinced that the French Revolution was a natural progression of the revolutionary spirit of 1776. In the Jay Treaty, the Washington administration "bet, in effect, on England rather than France as the hegemonic European power of the future, which proved prophetic."[50]

Martin no longer held Washington in unassailable esteem. He voted not to send a letter of congratulations to the president for the success of his foreign policy.[51] During the summer recess, Washington appointed John Steele, the North Carolina Federalist who had been defeated for a seat in the Senate, first by Martin and later by Bloodworth, as comptroller general of the United States. This, with the earlier appointment of Iredell to the judiciary, was the only occasions when the Federalist administrations turned to North Carolina for leadership—a precise confirmation that the state was counted as Republican.

In the course of the debate in this session, in the press and in social circles, it was well known that Washington did not intend to stand for another term. This decision effectively ended the annoying fear about the establishment of a monarchy and confirmed the president's commitment to popular sovereignty. Joseph Ellis points out that "the departure of America's only American king necessitated the creation of centering forces institutionalized at the federal level to maintain the focusing functions he had performed personally."[52] Washington had exercised, with remarkable sensitivity, the absolute trust that his personality and patriotism held over 13 colonies until the mechanism of constitutional government was in place and reliably functioning. In political parlance it was a constitutional monarchy. When Washington delivered his farewell address to Congress in September 1796, he was aware that he had wrought a nation and he intended the address as the precedent and the vision for posterity. The political leadership in Philadelphia and in each state almost immediately recognized the address as the seminal guide on which constitutional government evolved. The sealing act of Washington's administration and the dedication of his vision was the presidential election of 1796. Executive power was effectively transferred, legislative power came into its own and judicial authority, although not yet in balance, was positioned.

The Federalists advanced John Adams and Thomas Pinckney; the Republicans, Jefferson and Aaron Burr. In the election in North Carolina, Jefferson received all the electoral votes for president save the one Federalist elector who voted for Adams. The votes in most states for vice president were scattered among the four candidates. The votes tabulated made Adams the president by three votes and Jefferson, vice president. At the summit of executive power, John Adams and Thomas Jefferson now gave specific definition to the Federalist and Republican parties. Within the framework of the Constitution and under the precedent defined by Washington in his farewell address, the two views of government conceived by American independence began their mutation.

17

Martin Becomes "Wonderfully Federal"

On July 21, 1797, which was 11 days after the end of the congressional session, Senator Alexander Martin was made a member of the American Philosophical Society.[1] It was a grand moment in the definition of Martin's career. Military cowards, political nonentities, and mental irresolutes were not invited into membership.

The American Philosophical Society was instituted in 1744 principally under the influence of Benjamin Franklin. Franklin envisioned a society of American intellectuals who shared the best aspirations of an adventurous people. He anticipated this group to be linked to the Royal Society in England and the Dublin Society.[2] He added to membership his French and English friends as a courtesy and in an attempt to give the society international credentials.[3] The society loftily claimed its purpose to be "for promoting useful knowledge ... advancing the Interest of the Society by associating to themselves Men of distinguished Eminence, and of conferring Marks of their Esteem upon Persons of literary Merit ... Rights of Fellowship, with all Liberties and Privileges thereunto belonging."[4]

The character of the society took on a more nation-centered flavor after Franklin's death. In 1783, James Madison, Tom Paine, and William Bradford were elected as members. Thomas Jefferson was elected and some authors conclude that the society was the nucleus around which the Republican Party evolved. The inclusion of Benjamin Franklin Bache and several other editors of the opposition press as members reinforced that view.[5] At the time of Martin's election, Jefferson was chosen president of the society. His opinion of the society was that it "comprehended whatever distinction in science and philosophy the Republic had." He described his election to the presidency of the body "as the 'most flattering incident' of his life." He remained its president until he was "six years into retirement at Monticello."[6]

In 1791, Jefferson, then secretary of state, passed on the name of Alexander Hamilton, then secretary of the treasury, for membership.[7] Two years later John Adams "was quite pleased to have been invited to join" and honored when Jefferson came to escort him to the Hall.[8] In North Carolina, Hugh Williamson touted his membership in the Philosophical Society equally with his membership in the Holland Society of Science and the Society of Arts and Sciences in Utrecht.[9]

From its organization, the society was headquartered in Philadelphia—the Athens of America. It was natural that, in the period when the federal government was centered in Philadelphia, many of the inductees had a political background. Also, most members lived in Philadelphia.[10] The standard of membership in the society was philosophical work or more broadly, work in science, literature, or the arts. Governor Martin first attended a meeting of the society on March 10, 1797, as a guest, probably of Hugh Williamson.[11] He was elected to membership on July 21 after Congress had adjourned.[12] He was not aware of his selection until his return for the second session of Congress in November when he addressed his thanks to Jonathan Williams, Esquire.[13] He became immediately active in attendance, having promised to do so when he was in town. He introduced a paper on "poisonous honey in N. Carolina" and later a paper by Governor Spaight "on Peach trees" and he became involved in the analysis of "two ancient Walls, lately discovered in N. Carolina."[14] Martin's election to membership in this society can be viewed as a measure of his acceptance into the inner circle of national leadership. Committed as he had been throughout his adult years to the rustic life of the Carolina frontier, it had only been in his visits at Salem; his conversations with Dr. David Caldwell, and less frequently, with his other Princeton brothers in Carolina; and at meetings of the state legislature, that he had found intellectual stimulation outside his family circle. His attendance at the Constitutional Convention had brought him briefly back to the lifestyle that he had left to go to Carolina and had placed him among that common brotherhood that had forged a revolution. On the frontier, people just wanted to be left alone with family and fields. In Philadelphia, his friends and political associates were aware that they were cultivating a new government form after having prosecuted the first successful revolution against colonial rule. These men knew they were making history.[15]

To Martin, membership in the American Philosophical Society was an exhilarating recognition of his leadership and of his creativity. His support for the establishment of the university was a measure that he had very early appreciated the special place his generation had in history. For the university he had extracted letters from Lt. Governor Alexander Spotswood's official letter book concerning the boundary of Virginia with North Carolina, Cary's rebellion and the Tuscarora War, "for some future historians."[16] While a senator, he presumably procured "a microscope and acromatic telescope 3½ feet long, magnifying 70 times for land objects and 80 times for astronomical purposes," that he donated to the university. He also presented the university copies of his "A New Science" in the pamphlet form.[17]

The earliest example of Alexander Martin, the poet, was a dirge composed in 1777 on the death of General Francis Nash. Another "languid production," named "On the Death of Governor Caswell," was dated to 1789. Dr. Richard Walser has classified Martin's poetry "as not much better, and certainly not much worse, than many other late-eighteenth-century American poets for whom writing verse was a pleasant adjunct to their politically active affairs."[18]

Martin's kinsman, Robert Martin Douglas, in an otherwise glowing tribute to his great uncle in 1898, concluded "even the greatest men generally prided themselves upon the particular qualities which they did not happen to possess." Then he added satirically, "his admiring kinsmen console themselves with the idea that his best poems must have been lost."[19]

In December 1797, just after he heard that he had been voted into membership in the society, a poem entitled "A New Scene Interesting to the Citizens of the United States of America, Additional to the Historical Play of Columbus," by Senator Alexander Martin, was added to the performance of *Columbus: or, A World Discovered*, a play by the English dramatist Thomas Morton that had been playing in Philadelphia since January. The poem was a dialogue between Columbus and the Genius of America, consisting of 226 iambic pentameter lines. Stage directions say "an older discouraged Columbus is greeted by The Genius of America, who 'descends in a Purple Robe, on his head a Roman Cap, encircled with a Crimson Tiara, adorned with Sixteen Stars, and crested with the American Eagle; holding in his Right Hand a Spear.'" He speaks to Columbus:

> To soothe thy anxious breast, and steel thy nerves
> Against black treason, and ambitious crimes,
> And more, the base ingratitude of Kings,
> Which thou wilt guiltless feel with heavy hands;
> I come permitted from above, Columbus.
> T' unfold to thee the future page of fate,
> Which blazons forth a train of great events,
> That wait successive on thy vast emprize.[20]

The poem was popularly received and was printed in two different publications the next year. The first was in 12 pages printed by his friend in the philosophical society, the Republican printer, Benjamin Franklin Bache. In the second publication, the poem was attested as "Supposed to be written by Alexander Martin, LL.D., late Governor of the state of North Carolina, and now Senator of the United States therefrom."[21] The dedication was a rare contemporary acknowledgement of Martin's honorary degree from Princeton and indicates that his friends in the society respected this academic recognition.[22]

Martin did not limit his literary contributions to poetry. Jedidiah Morse had published his *American Universal Geography* that was unfavorable to North Carolina. William Barry Grove felt that much of Morse's misrepresentation of the state had been provided him by Dr. Hugh Williamson, who had retired to write a history of the state. Grove anticipated that publication also would be a poor product because "he is a man of such prejudices that I fear all that time which he has acted so conspicuous a part in the state—which is from his coming into it, that the book will not be prized."[23] Another similar geography was to be published by Carey, and Grove said, "I have got him to expunge all Morse's libels," and added that "Gov. Martin has written several little additions to the acct. of the State, that in some measure may commence a refutation of that illiberal and ignorant author's [Morse's] Book."[24]

John Adams was inaugurated March 4, 1797. Washington's attendance, and the impact of this orderly transfer of power, outshone the president-elect, but in a few days the general had departed for Mt. Vernon, leaving his entire cabinet in place for the new Federalist administration.[25] At noon on the 4th, Congress adjourned and members and government officials made a congratulatory call, first on President Adams and then on his wife, Abigail. A tension may have been perceived by some since the president the day before had delivered to the Congress the copy of an incriminating letter that promised a major test in the authority of the legislature.[26]

When Tennessee was recognized as the sixteenth state, the quintessential speculator William Blount and John Cocke were elected its first senators. They arrived in Philadelphia in early May 1796 to present their credentials but the credibility of their election was at issue. On June 1, by a vote of 11 to 10, Martin voting in the majority, the Senate refused them seats.[27] A second election in Tennessee returned Blount and Cocke to the December session and, this time, they were seated. Blount and Martin were frequently correspondents in business, knew each other in the state government, and were delegates to the Constitutional Convention but they could only be called contemporaries who often accommodated each other. Until 1792, Blount had been a Federalist and he had worked shamelessly to gain the support of Washington to his appointment as governor of the territory west of the mountains. Now Blount was a Republican reflecting the predominant views of his state.[28]

When Blount arrived in Philadelphia, his profusion of land speculation projects stood as a house of cards. He had exhausted himself in the evolution of statehood for Tennessee, although the process had made him popular and powerful on the frontier. His shift of party, however, had made him an enemy to Adams' administration and he became a particular target for such shameful treatment that it "reduced him to rare tears."[29] His expansive land dealings had been based upon seizing opportunities in a boom market but the increasing appeal of the west depended on the accessibility of the Mississippi as an avenue to commercial markets. Pinckney's treaty with Spain had appeared to confirm access to Americans on the river but now a weakened Spain found itself at war with England. It was probable that if Spain were to succeed in drawing France into the conflict as an ally, the cost might be western Florida and Louisiana. France then would be solidly placed in predominant control in Canada and Louisiana, thus constituting an obstacle to western advancement and economic welfare. In control of millions of acres of land, that he either owned or pledged to buy on credit, Blount saw western land prices plummet. His creditors hounded him at every turn and apparently secure partners were dropping into bankruptcy.

Faced with financial catastrophe, Blount, with the confidence his family had always exhibited in such crises, became entangled in a scheme that sought to block French expansion. Sadly for him, a revealing letter that he wrote to a partner conspirator fell into the hands of two of Adams' cabinet members and he was clearly compromised. The attorney general was of the opinion "that Blount's actions constituted a crime subject to impeachment."[30]

On July 3, Adams delivered to the Senate the incriminating letter and the members immediately directed that it be read aloud. As the content became clear the chamber "exploded into an uproar." Soon after Blount strode, unaware, into the chamber and every head turned to him. Then, on a quick motion to re-read, he heard the clerk repeat to the Senate his letter to James Carey of April 21.[31] On the mission to involve the British in a preemptive takeover of Florida and Louisiana, Blount wrote he would "have a hand in the business, and probably shall be at the head of the business on the part of the British." His letter went on to detail a further conspiracy against Benjamin Hawkins, Blount's successor as Indian superintendent and he involved Washington to cover his proposed actions saying, "this sort of talk will be throwing all the blame off me upon the late President, and as he is now out of office, it will be of no consequence how much the Indians blame him."[32] The letter exposed Blount as a man without honor, open to involvement in any activity that would advance his ends. There were obviously other opportunists in government but, as a senator, Blount was acting on behalf of a foreign power. Vice President Jefferson, in the chair, demanded to know if indeed this was his letter. Blount demurred, asking for a day to examine his papers.[33]

The Federalist press began a withering campaign that would last well beyond the short session. Abigail Adams lamented, "When shall we cease to have Judases," and regretted the absence in Pennsylvania of a guillotine, no doubt a worthy punishment for a Republican.[34] Blount vacillated between defiant defense and open flight. At one point he attempted, in a disguise, to take a boat to Carolina. When peace officers arrived and seized the boat, he fled back to the city. A senatorial committee then took possession of his trunks, clothes and all his papers. The House of Representatives passed the impeachment charges by a vote of 41 to 30 and determined a trial at a future date. Bond was set by the Senate on Blount at $20,000 and on his sureties at $15,000 each.

On July 8, Senator Alexander Martin and William Cocke, the two senators who knew him best, were asked to identify Blount's handwriting in that fatal letter, which they did.[35] The Senate committee that had been investigating the case reported that "the matter was not fully sifted," but, on the evidence of the letter to Carey alone, Blount was guilty of various abuses of the public trust and of high misdemeanors. It announced Blount's expulsion from the Senate.

Attempts to delay the vote were defeated and Blount sat to hear the roll called. One by one, the senators, including his fellow senator, William Cocke, and the North Carolina senators, Bloodworth and Martin, condemned him. By a final vote of 25 to 1, he became the first member expelled from the United States Senate.[36] His bond for his impeachment trial was reduced to $100, which on the 10th he filed and fled. Before authorities were aware, "the fallen statesman was pushing his horse down the valley road."[37]

Blount's stratagems of deceit were reborn when he eventually reached Tennessee, spreading still wider the net of conspirators. Present in Philadelphia in 1795 was Andrew Jackson, Martin's young friend from Martinville, who was attempting to sell 50,000 acres of land in Tennessee and, in the process, very nearly ended in prison. His biographer has called this a strange period in Jackson's life and his efforts as a speculator in land anticipated the contribution he was about to make in the scandals surrounding speculation.[38] He was subsequently chosen, with William Blount's support, as the first congressman from the new state of Tennessee. When Blount was expelled, almost concurrently with the end of Cocke's abbreviated first term, Jackson was elected senator.

When he appeared on December 6, to take his seat, he confided to his friend, Alexander Martin, another astonishing tale of intrigue.[39] On the way to Philadelphia, he had met John Love, who said that, in his room at a lodging house in Nashville, he eavesdropped while his landlord, William Tyrell, and Tyrell's nephew, William Tyrell Lewis, pressed liquor on some former officers of the North Carolina Continental Line until they signed fraudulent certificates of military service. These certificates could then be used for procuring land warrants from the office of the North Carolina secretary of state. Senator Martin asked Jackson if he would sign a letter to these facts and he agreed saying that he would ask Love to do the same. Martin then forwarded the letter directly to Governor Samuel Ashe who, without the confirming letter from Love, seems to have immediately grasped the extent of this fraud. His comment was "it seems to have been a case of everyone being shocked but no one surprised."[40] Seeing that the fraud extended to the long-time secretary of state, James Glasgow, Ashe remarked with resignation, "an angel has fallen."[41]

When the North Carolina Legislature received the report from the committee assigned to investigate, it was known that four million acres in Tennessee was included in the fraud. Jackson was described as "shocked and dismayed" to find his own brother-in-law, Stokely Donaldson, implicated.[42] That shock appears disingenuous since Donaldson was also the son-in-law of James Glasgow.[43] Martin could have feigned equal surprise to find the Armstrong brothers, John and Martin, deeply implicated. No one, however, could have been surprised to find Blount and John Sevier involved. The nadir of the entire so-called Glasgow Fraud was reached when a committee of the conspirators met in Blount's house and plotted to break into the office of the secretary of state in the new statehouse in Raleigh, remove the files that were under subpoena investigation, and burn the statehouse. They succeeded in the break-in but were stopped before they could start the fire.[44]

Alexander Martin had been associated since 1783 in honoring the state's obligation to its Revolutionary War soldiers by using the western land warrants as payment. He was politically involved with a host of prominent land speculators. Martin owned land in Tennessee by warrant and land purchase but, significantly, he did not come into involvement in this sea of public scandal. His actions in the ejection of Senator Blount and the immediacy with which he forwarded to Governor Ashe the letter that exposed the Glasgow Land Fraud, provide *prima facie* evidence that he was above the fraud that had brought down so many of his contemporaries. Speculation in land did not carry with it the presumptive of fraud. After all, it was the willingness of land companies to risk speculation in North America that had brought most of the early settlement to America. By the 1790s a breed of land gamblers, however, some at the highest level of government, were willing to risk ethics, engage in rampant fraud of neighbors, and even to jeopardize their country's welfare, in order to become rich on land. Many of these men were members in good standing of the band of brothers that had made the Revolution and friends or close associates of Governor Martin. So far as it can be documented, all his acquisitions were well within the laws that then existed.[45] That is perhaps remarkably to his credit when considered against the extent of those frauds and misdemeanors of his place and time.

The published compilation of the land grants in Tennessee between 1778 and 1791 shows Martin to have received 2,314 acres on Big Harpeth River as colonel of the 2nd North Carolina Regiment. This is the land granted to him by the legislature while he was governor. There was a 1,114-acre grant to his brother, James, on West Harpeth River due him as a captain. There was a 640-acre grant to his cousin, James Hunter, and a 640-acre grant to Pleasant Henderson. These are the only family members connected with this list.[46]

The second session of the 5th United States Congress lasted for eight months, far and away the longest session in Martin's tenure. It was set to assemble three weeks earlier than was usual on November 13; Martin and Bloodworth were present. It did not reach quorum, however, until the 22nd. On the opening day, President Adams pointed out to Congress that, beginning in July, he had dispatched Charles Cotesworth Pinckney, John Marshall, and Elbridge Gerry as envoys extraordinary to the French Republic to ease the rising friction between the two nations, particularly that occasioned by the capture of American vessels by "French cruizers." Tension had continued to mount since the approval of the Jay Treaty and the Congress needed to act in the face of the threat. Federalists had a clear majority in the Senate but Jefferson was in the chair. In order to placate the power of the Hamilton faction, Adams, at the start of his term, had retained the Washington cabinet. Now the president, heir of a clearly weakened inheritance, faced the accumulating force of war.

The first months of the session proceeded in a low gear, in anticipation, as periodic reports from France and the high seas built public anxiety.[47] In February the consideration of the Articles of Impeachment against William Blount, received from the House of Representatives, was a parliamentary diversion. Martin voted with the majority, Bloodworth in the minority, to summon Blount to trial.[48] The continuation of the prosecution of Blount had become an embarrassment to some Federalists but to others the anticipation of the trial allowed them to isolate, by association, the Republicans as lawbreakers.

After March 19, Martin and the legislators who had made the Revolution, created a constitution, and organized the government of the first modern-day republic from a diverse association of states, faced a real threat of war. Most had anticipated for some years that their political experiment would be challenged from the outside, but because there was again no precedent, they brought to the menace of war their individual image of the threat and concept of national strategy. Martin was considered part of the Republican minority, but in four months in early 1798 he made as clear a declaration of national interest above party affiliation as any American in a position of political influence. While a corps of four to seven Republicans voted in opposition to the government, Alexander Martin voted with the majority to establish a Navy department in the executive branch, which would protect commerce, suspend commerce with France, accept privately owned vessels into the Navy, provide naval armament, defend merchant vessels against French deprivation, create the Marine Corps, authorize the borrowing power of the president during the emergency, encourage the capture of French vessels, and augment the army.[49] Only on the issue of giving Adams the authority to raise a standing army and a provisional army, did he oppose the administration in April, but as the likelihood of war advanced, he changed his vote in June.[50] He also opposed abrogating all the treaties between the two republics. These votes are consistent confirmations of a soldier of the Revolution who could be pragmatic in the face of zealotry.

For none of these votes was he criticized subsequently in North Carolina, but his support of a series of bills that came to be grouped as the Alien and Sedition Laws has been held as a black mark on his record as it has always been against President Adams. The Alien laws appeared first, at the end of April, early in the series of actions approved to prepare the country for war. Martin's wartime experience had been with a state nearly equally divided between Whigs and Tories. He had first come to the governor's office when the marauding Tories kidnapped the elected governor and most of the Council of State. He was forced to administer the remaining government of the state, and the supplying of a field army, in the face of a divided population. He appreciated that this infant republic had been inundated by 25,000 or more French émigrés—in Philadelphia alone there were French booksellers, restaurants, and schools.[51] The uncertainty about these people in case of war was not as much in their number as in their sophistication and penetration into society. The legislation sought to regulate the import of aliens, their freedom of action in America and to give the president the temporary power to expel aliens by executive order. One after another, amendments were proposed to this legislation in efforts by the Republicans to weaken the more suspect features of the alien laws and, on 13 ballots when the vote was recorded, Martin voted for the amendments nine times, indicating a very active effort to create a bill he could support. Concurrent with the consideration of the Alien legislation, the Senate was receiving daily petitions from cities and counties in every state in patriotic support for the administration. On May 17 Martin presented to the Senate a petition from the citizens of New Bern, signed by former Governor Richard Dobbs Spaight. Ultimately, on June 8, Martin turned his back on the core of seven Republican senators and voted with the 16-vote majority in passing the Alien legislation.

The day after the president signed the Alien Act, efforts began to bring forward legislation to redefine what would be considered treason and sedition and to re-establish the punishment for these crimes in the face of the crisis. Lacking common law in the United States, federal courts required statutory authority before they could consider either conspiracy against the government or libel against government officials. Beyond correcting this problem, the Sedition Act included a section making it a misdemeanor, punishable by fines and imprisonment, to speak or write against the president or Congress.[52] Adams and the administration justified the Sedition legislation as temporarily necessary in order to prosecute a war realistically. The Sedition Act passed early in July, with Martin again joining the 18-vote majority opposed by the 6-vote Republican opposition.[53] The judgment of history has characterized the Alien and Sedition legislation as expedient laws that contradicted the spirit of the Constitution and, in the case of the Sedition Act, the First Amendment. Adams considered them war measures that he really had not sought and that he would abrogate when the threat was gone.[54] Martin advanced the same justification to explain why he had gone, in one term, from demanding open access to debate in the Senate—because in the United States sovereignty lay in the people—to limits on free speech and the press. The full-blown emergence of an opposition press in America was mystifying to many Americans who sought consensus. Were there any limits, even common courtesies, that the press would not exceed? Martin's take was that "'the damn'd printers' had become so abusive they had to be checked, irrespective of the Constitution." The reporter of these words of exasperation from Martin also said that he reversed his earlier position and that his words today would "constitute grounds for imprisonment."[55] That is a classic case of measuring an eighteenth-century action by a twenty-first-century standard.

For Alexander Martin, the eight months that made up the second session of the 5th Congress constituted the zenith of his political career. He stood at the center of national crisis. He certainly confirmed his important place among the founding brothers who labored at the state and local level to create the foundation of the republic. He arrived at this Congress on the date it was scheduled,s aware that crisis loomed, and waited a week before enough senators arrived to make a quorum. For over eight months, from the freezing temperatures of November into the yellow fever days of July, his name was counted on every voice vote taken by the Senate save one.[56] His actions clearly move from opposition to a Federalist administration to support of a government in the face of outside threat. Those actions were not compromise but a consistent example of his capacity to bridge issues through reasoned debate. His was the first example of political bipartisanship necessitated by war, and there would be patriotic legislators in every future wartime experience of the United States who exemplified his actions in 1798. Measure his actions by those of some of his contemporaries. Jackson went home in April and Bloodworth in mid-June. By the time the special three-day executive session convened to approve the president's appointment of Washington as commander-in-chief, only one state, Massachusetts, had both senators present. New Hampshire and Georgia were not even represented. Virginia's senators, Tazewell and Mason, held blindly to support of the French republic even as it flaunted its insults on American envoys, commerce, and sailors. Tazewell went so far as to declare that he would join a French army if one were to land in America.[57] Hamilton used the crisis as his means of gaining control of the Federalists and isolating President Adams as a figurehead. Vice President Jefferson left for Monticello on December 18 and did not bother to return.

Martin's unequivocal actions at Philadelphia were not calculated to favor an incumbent. At least three other courses had been open to him in this critical Congress, each of which might have been a better guarantee in the face of re-election. Like Bloodworth, he might have come home early, avoided the tough choices and thus had no controversial record to defend. Jefferson had done that. Martin had left the Continental Congress early and had avoided the tough choices of the state ratification congresses when he was not elected a delegate. Had he left the Senate early, he might have confirmed a character flaw and justified the invective of his critics. Instead, he arrived early and he stayed late. Another choice might have been to vote solidly with the Republican minority in the 5th Congress, to return to North Carolina, claiming to have earned the Republican nomination in a state with a Republican majority, and then return for another term. Had he voted that way on every vote in the Congress, no legislative outcome would have been changed. Finally, he could have formally become a Federalist, supporting the president, and thus guaranteed his nomination by that party. Martin chose none of these expedients but returned to North Carolina confident that, in the fall, when he faced a re-election campaign, he could defend each of his actions as worthy of his public trust.

In North Carolina, the legislative elections were held in July, as Martin was preparing to leave Philadelphia and before he could do any courting of the electorate at meetings of county courts. The results of those elections have been called the high-water mark for the Federalists in North Carolina. They claimed a majority in the Senate and, although they failed to gain control, they increased their number in the Commons.[58] Martin could not sit isolated for long at Danbury. There was a new newspaper being printed in Salisbury but the old electioneering opportunities, on which Martin had formally depended, did little to assist his re-election.[59]

When the assembly met in Raleigh on November 19, there were few members who had served while Martin was governor, fewer still for the time when he had been speaker. One notable exception was William R. Davie, who was in the Commons and again representing the town of Halifax. The assembly would fill Martin's senate seat and elect a governor, Ashe's eligibility having run out.

Aside from their victory in the state senate, the Federalists claimed six of the ten House districts. Davie had double reason to rejoice since at the special session of the United States Congress called by Adams to staff the provisional army, Davie, with Martin's support, had been appointed a brigadier general. At this halcyon moment, Davie, in his usual self-righteous manner, wrote Iredell that "the Assembly will see the importance of appointing a man of business and energy Governor: in time of war it is the most important office in the State: in time of peace its duties may be performed by any body, even A. M. [Alexander Martin]."[60]

Davie, at his political pinnacle, was in a position to claim the governor's office. The letter exposes his fear of the one person who might now block him. If Martin had come home with the strong support of the Republicans, he would have had his choice of their support for re-election or to return to the governor's office for which he was again eligible. Samuel Johnston identified the political spin that the Federalists had against Martin. Johnston stated the legislature was "wonderful federal, I say wonderful because I never conceived it possible there could be so universal a conversion in so short a space." He even added that when Senator Alexander Martin arrived at the opening session of the assembly, he was "wonderfully federal."[61] Martin had supported the administration's preparations for war even to the extent of his support of the Alien and Sedition Acts. The bitter controversy supported by the Republican press against these acts had initiated only moderate interest in North Carolina so far. Martin had no desire to become a Federalist so Davie's supporters had to fill this issue with hyperbole in order to plant the seed of plausibility. Hence, the idea that, close to the seat of federal power in Philadelphia, Senator Martin had become "wonderfully federal" by socializing with Adams and Hamilton.

The office of senator gave Martin credibility at this moment but he did not have the clout of the governor's office anymore nor did he have a floor manager like James Taylor to advance his cause. He could expect some Federalist support from old military friends, who could appreciate his courage in support of the administration under the threat of war. The Republicans were in moderate disarray. The doubts, suggested by the Federalists of Martin's loyalty to the Republicans, were designed to have effect in that party, weakening any power of incumbency.

According to Johnston, Martin was available at the opening of the assembly. Davie, though a delegate, was not but he had the patriotic excuse, as brigadier general, of being involved in assembling troops for the defense of the nation. Davie did not appear until December 29 but on December 3 he had been nominated for governor along with Benjamin Williams; on the following day Davie was elected. Though he was not in Raleigh on that day, he was present the following day for a meeting of the university trustees but Martin was not.[62] In his later years in the Senate, Martin had not been active in the matters of the university and Davie clearly had. Davie's strategy therefore was to be about his business as trustee and general while his surrogates managed his election.

Balloting for the senate was concurrent with the gubernatorial vote. Martin was one of five nominated for his senate seat. The Federalists' caucus nominated the recent attorney general, Alfred Moore of Wilmington. The Republican caucus placed in nomination a former congressman from Surry, Jesse Franklin. Thus Martin was given opposition in both of the constituencies he had previously been able to transcend: the backcountry and the merchant east. In a surprise even to his contemporaries, Alfred Moore suddenly withdrew. The official explanation was that Moore had preferred being Superior Court judge to being United States senator and that post was given to him immediately after the election.[63] Spaight found Moore's actions dubious and admitted that he could not "see through the politics" that had motivated Moore, whom he judged "better qualified than Franklin." Spaight went on to explain his suspicion. He deduced that "there certainly must have been some juggling in it. Was Davie afraid of Martin and kept Moore out of sight as Senator, lest M[artin] should oppose him as Governor? What other reason could induce him to drop Moore for the Senate after so hard a struggle was made for him as senator four years ago, and the idea of his offering again has been uniformly kept up?"[64] Spaight's analysis was that it was not logical for Moore, who had fought so hard to be senator four years earlier, to now settle for a judgeship as more attractive. He further speculated that if Martin should feel he was a candidate in no-man's land in a five-way race for the senate, he might turn and, as a Republican, take on Davie in a less contested race for governor. So he speculated that Davie prevailed on Moore, using the consolation prize of the judgeship, to stand aside and make Martin the tacit Federalist candidate for senator. Such a maneuver was designed to dissuade Senator Martin from considering the post of governor, a job that he certainly preferred.

The election of Davie as governor was quickly over but the election for senator lasted 12 days. Martin was present and he did actively seek another term promoting his own candidacy.⁶⁵ Martin was the Federalist candidate.⁶⁶ The Republicans, who would not accept his reasoned explanation of his support of the administration, abandoned him, as they would damaged goods. If he were damaged goods in his own party, could he expect much solace in the other? Martin, who never appreciated the party system, was ill-served by it now.

On the seventh ballot his name was withdrawn. The contest narrowed to Benjamin Smith, the benefactor of the university, and Jesse Franklin, and the latter was elected on the ninth ballot. Five of the sets of ballots for this election have survived in the legislative papers and, on the four ballots on which his name appears, Martin had the fewest votes.⁶⁷

In little over a year, Alexander Martin had gone from the heady honor of membership in the American Philosophical Society, through spirited defense of the republic, to rejection by his own legislature. Martin's defeat did not come from his unwilling appreciation of the forming political party system, or from becoming "wonderfully federal," although those factors contributed. The truth was that in six years his absence from the North Carolina assembly had cut him off from the system that governed state elections to federal offices. Previously he had always been able to mold that consensus and bridge provincial interests. This form of personal politics faded as parties began to govern alliances. Martin never came to terms with political parties even though his philosophy of government prescribed him a Republican.

Davie's success was complete, coupled, as was his selection as governor, with the defeat of his nemesis. At the end of a year Davie resigned as governor to accept Adams' appointment, as substitute for Patrick Henry, as a commissioner to France. Ironically, this absence in France did to Davie's political viability precisely what Martin's senate term had done to him. Davie came home and was handed rejection in an election for Congress. His reaction to that defeat provided a revealing comparison of personalities. Davie wrote Richard Bennehan that his opponents, "raising the spirit of party into a flame, and alarming the ignorant and credulous with frightful stories" had produced the result that "thousands of these poor wretches sincerely believe they have saved their Country from these monsters by preventing my going to Congress."⁶⁸

Martin and Davie were proud men, purposeful and principled. Martin was active as a serving officeholder in the state but none of his personal papers survived nor any of his own reflections of his service. Davie was not only ultimately defeated in politics but, although he remained fiercely loyal, his Federalist Party was rejected. Disillusioned, he went back to his South Carolina plantation and wrote an autobiographical justification for the causes and opinions of his life.⁶⁹

Martin returned to Philadelphia as a lame-duck senator. This session was even more highly charged than had been the last as the national Republicans focused on repealing of the Alien and Sedition Laws. In the Virginia assembly, the Republicans, with their solid two-thirds majority, sought to present their opposition to the administration in such a way as to stimulate a national debate. Using a strategy that had worked before, they drew up a series of resolutions to be the points at issue and they drew up a second companion list planned for the North Carolina assembly as proof of extensive support. The Republicans, however, weakened as they were in North

Carolina in the August elections, were less than enthusiastic and when Republicans in the more solid majority in Kentucky offered to sponsor the resolution, it became theirs.[70] The Republicans were better prepared for the third session of Congress to confront the administration. Also, news was received soon after the Congress had convened that the British fleet under Nelson had crushed the French off the coast of Egypt, making war with France progressively less likely. Any moderates, who had supported the administration under the conditions of a threat of war, now had to gradually turn back into the party fold and party stalwarts intended to exact some penance. The evolution of party politics continued to be refined.

Martin did not arrive this time in Philadelphia until the 17th, which was 11 days after a quorum was reached, so he was no part of organization of the session. He arrived the same day the senate first formed itself "into a court of impeachment" for purposes of carrying out the impeachment of William Blount.[71] It was not a cheerful moment. Although Republicans would have been glad to see the question go away, more extreme Federalists still relished the possibility of a public embarrassment and the opportunity to structure the impeachment power as a centralizing force for their ends. With preliminaries over, the senate organized itself into a court on January 3. To no one's surprise, Blount had not appeared but was represented by able counsel. On the 14th, following debate behind closed doors, the senate held at 14 to 10 that they lacked jurisdiction over the case and the impeachment was dismissed. Martin does not appear to have been active in the debate and in the end he and all the Republicans, joined by a few moderate Federalists, held the majority.[72]

On roll call votes in this session, Martin and Bloodworth were more likely to deliver North Carolina's two votes in the Republican column. They opposed giving Adams authority to augment the army, or to be able to call up volunteers where he could call militia, and they opposed the majority in giving Adams further authority to suspend commercial intercourse with France. Because he had no electoral mandate, it is unclear whether Martin was one of those moderates returning to the fold as the war threat subsided or a bitter Republican outdone by Davie's Federalist maneuvering. Suffice it to say, he had gotten precious little respect from either side for putting the national welfare first.

Martin had opportunity to bid farewell to friends in New Jersey and at Princeton and to make final social calls on his friends in Philadelphia society. He attended his final meetings of the American Philosophical Society.[73] Had he been re-elected, he might have been positioned very well when Jefferson became president two years later but it would have been a daunting task to vindicate himself with the party. Virginia Republicans had turned viciously on George Washington and party loyalty was becoming more prized than patriotism or pragmatism. Martin's ride home, however, was not the skulking backroad escape of William Blount. He returned to Danbury in March 1799 to the life of a farmer and was received with reverence by his extended family.

18

Martin's Final Role as Governor

The spring thaws provided the normally deep-rutted roads with a spongy, slippery surface that gave some relief to the passenger but little to the two fine horses, Isaac and Jacob, or to the driver. The shiny carriage, which had been so functional in Philadelphia, was now mud-spattered and out of place on the roads of the southern Piedmont. Inside, a well-dressed man of 60 sat, surrounded by luggage and official-looking papers. On top sat Prince, the driver and servant, and more cases strapped to the roof. It was mid–March, the budding season. The grass and woods were new-growth green, more striking, he perceived, as he approached home. There is no record of the route Martin took from Philadelphia. He did not choose to go by way of Mt. Vernon to honor the one-year-old invitation from the president issued after he had sent his Columbia poem, a "little dramatic piece" honoring "the most prominent Characters in our late Revolution."[1] Perhaps he was still too disillusioned by his failure to win re-election. He had also missed the opportunity to inspect the new federal city under construction on the Potomac where he might have served in the new Senate chamber. Again, he had slipped into those morose thoughts. When he left Halifax on the final leg, it occurred to him that the court circuit had already started in his district. He would busy himself right away. Would they now call him senator or continue with governor, the title that had followed him all of his term in the Senate.

Martin mused on the previous trips he had made north. Some had been more memorable than others. The first time he had gone back was after he had been advised of the death of his father. In the summer of 1769 it had been by way of Montpelier when he had visited his brother, Thomas, and together they had persuaded old James Madison to allow his son to matriculate at the College of New Jersey. In the spring of 1777 it was as senior regimental commander of the Second North

Carolina Regiment that he had marched his troops north to join Washington outside Philadelphia. With equal vividness he recalled that return from Pennsylvania in November after the disaster at Germantown and his resignation from the army. Ten years later he went as the former governor of North Carolina, accompanied as he was now by his faithful Prince, to approach the uncharted territory of a constitutional convention, as one of five delegates. That time he had been introduced into Philadelphia society and he had learned to deport his Princeton training and his frontier habits to make entertaining companionship. He left the governor's office again to return to Philadelphia as the new senator from North Carolina and, at least once a year for six years, he had ridden this carriage to terms of the Congress. Philadelphia had become his second home, a place where he had developed a second persona. There he could be learned and literate. He could discuss books and debate crises beyond these shores. He met his friends from the military and those like himself who had risked everything for a vision of independence that was revolutionary. They had grown old together struggling with words and ideas to mold a nation worthy of their surroundings. Soon they would each have to let it go and they worried about those who would be their heirs.

He stopped briefly at Peter Terry's, just after entering North Carolina, and passed on news from Philadelphia that affected the Farley estate. Riders were dispatched to Danbury to announce his approach. The carriage crossed the Smith River at Island Ford and followed the Salem Road on the north side of the Dan to the fork. There he turned south on the Baggage Road, crossed the river again at Lone Island and he was home! Straining up the carriage-high depression that was the approach to the ford from the south, the horses turned expectantly off the main road and down the path to the plantation house. His 80-year-old mother led the greeting that must have included nearly 100 people—family, slaves, and neighbors who had been drawn to the community that gathered around this man.

It was open to him to choose Martinville for his retirement. He had a house there and other property. He might have built a house on his lot in the new capital city, Raleigh. Neither had many more residents than Danbury but they had more promise.[2] He could have gone back to Salisbury where he had many professional friends. Martin had built Danbury originally for his mother and his younger siblings almost a quarter of a century earlier. It had been clear for some time though, that it would be his to share with his mother as the family compound.

No description of the house at Danbury has survived.[3] Something of the surroundings can be imagined through the inventory of those things that Martin had in his home. There was enough fine furniture to be divided into three households. Tableware included multiple sets of export porcelain and Queensware, plain white and with blue or green rim.[4] The large silver service included a coffeepot with stand, teapot, milk pot, tea tray and sugar dish. There were silver-plated candlesticks to set off a table and two silver tumblers that he reserved for Pleasant Henderson and his brother, James Martin. In later generations the tradition grew that Washington gave those cups to Martin "when he left the army." The cup that is known to survive with descendents of James Martin is engraved "Presented to Conl. James Martin by Gov. Alexander Martin—1782."[5]

Pastel portrait of Alexander Martin by James Sharples, Sr., probably from life, 1797. The buttons on Martin's coat are similar to those found at Danbury. (Independence National Historical Park.)

Artifacts from Danbury. Eighteenth century ceramic and porcelain, two metal buttons, pieces of smoking pipes (includig a Moravian-made pipe with a face), bottle glass, and Queensware china with blue and green trim.

The personal objects were what demonstrated Martin's appreciation of fine things. His gold sleeve buttons, silver spurs, gold watch and seal, gold stock buckle, stone knee buckles, silver spectacle case, and gold-plated headed cane had little use on the Carolina frontier but they were reminders of his presence in Philadelphia society. His case of pistols and horseman's sword were memories of his military service. His surveyor compass with appendages and instruments and his blacksmith's tools were practical reminders of his necessary self-sufficiency.

Alexander Martin bookplate.

There was a portrait of Martin made earlier in Philadelphia and highly prized by his mother. Judge Robert Douglas described it in a later generation, while looking at "a large photograph of him [Martin] taken from the original portrait also in the possession of Colonel Martin."[6]

> The head is large and well shaped, and has the poise of conscious strength. The face is strong and attractive. The nose is long and straight, with full thin nostrils. The forehead is not unusually high, but is broad and well developed.

The jaw is square and massive, indicating, with the firm straight lips, extraordinary force of character, with an inflexible will and great concentration of purpose. The lips seem to be slightly compressed, which is sometimes the result of the habitual effort of self-control. The eyes, which are wide and wide apart, are looking straight at you and apparently through you, from lids that are slightly closed. It is not the laughing eyes of Erin, whose wrath "a word can kindle and a word assuage." It is rather the calm eye of the frontiersman, long used to danger, for which it was ever watchful, but from which it never shrank. ... The entire expression is one of repose.[7]

Martin's portrait has been attributed to James Sharples and does show a distinct similarity to the Sharples portrait of George Washington.[8] It is a pastel. Sharples charged $20 for his full-face portraits. He prided himself on his very exact likenesses and trained his wife and several of his children in the technique so that it was sometimes difficult to determine which family member was the original artist.[9]

The library at Danbury was extensive and testified to Martin's wide interests. There was a law library that descended to his two nephews, Thomas and Alexander M. Rogers. Of general interest were found John Hawksworth's *A New Voyage, round the World*; Oliver Goldsmith's *A History of the Earth*; Charles Varlo's *A New System of Husbandry*; and the sermons of Dr. Samuel Stanhope Smith. These books, and their uncle's urging in support of education, influenced James Martin's two eldest sons, James and Samuel A., to attend the University of North Carolina along with Alexander M. Rogers, several of the Hendersons and Alexander Martin, Jr. (James), who was listed as a student in 1799 but did not graduate.[10]

Alexander Martin owned 62 slaves at Danbury at the turn of the century. His several farms in Rockingham County totaled fewer than 2,000 acres. Tobacco was his main crop. He had owned slaves for 30 years and, even in his will, was reluctant to see family members separated, so natural increase accounted in large measure for the number that called his plantation their home. Like many of the founders who approached the end of their lives, Martin agonized over slavery—the issue that seemed to invalidate their revolution. He knew that no person should belong to another but he also knew that the agricultural economy of the South depended on human labor. He would leave his heirs and his "people" this unsettled paradox. In writing his will he tried to cure some ills but in doing for some he left even more unfulfilled.

Two of his slaves earned particular affection from their master. Prince was his personal servant and his true confidant when Martin was governor. He was the carriage driver and the one selected to care for Mrs. Martin when her health was not good. Prince had been told that, if the governor died before his mother, Prince would serve her until her death, and then he would be given his freedom.[11]

Benjamin Harris Martin had been given to Alexander Martin in 1777 by the will of his uncle, John Hunter. Benjamin had gone to war with Martin, before the bequest could be recorded, and had three years in "Continental service under my Command faithfully and with reputation as a soldier."[12] Ben Martin appears to have been treated by the governor in a manner much like slaves in the Caribbean. He had a full name including the Martin surname. He lived on a tract of his own with his family and, as Benjamin Martin, was counted as a head of household in the census.[13]

Alexander's enemies on occasion made fun of his remote plantation and his bachelor status and accused him of fathering many of the slaves at Danbury. In that era it was an accusation that was valid for most owners of slaves, and that could go toward explaining his intense efforts to consider the feelings of his slaves in his will. What he did for Prince and Ben, however, was motivated by their war service and personal service to him and reflected the legal terms in North Carolina at that time for freeing slaves.[14]

By 1800, Elizabeth Strong and Alexander Martin were listed as heads of separate households but 13-year-old Alexander Strong appears in the governor's household. In the previous decade, Elizabeth had maintained a home for her teenage sons across the river and when John Strong came of age, he bought 50 acres on Sharp Creek. Elizabeth and Alexander appear to have had "an arrangement" that served their mutual purposes. They shared the training of their son but did not use that as a pretext for contention. If there was not an enduring romance, there was closeness within the families.[15] The dissident influence in this arrangement very likely was the Governor's aging mother. She had always been acknowledged as the matriarch of Danbury. How hard it must have been for her to see her prized son, at an advanced age of 40, father a son with a local mother with a brood of sons. She made no secret of her preference for her elder son and would she not have insisted on spoiling his only son?

On December 14, 1799, General George Washington died at Mt. Vernon. The loss was universally mourned. Some wondered whether the nation could long survive him. There had been serious talk by Republican leaders in Virginia and Kentucky concerning the possibility of severing the union between North and South. Political parties were in their infancy but the intensity of public debate and the chicanery of leaders in exploiting the public trust tested the limits of a young democracy. Governor Davie, in advancing the call of reinforcing the army, had advised manipulatively that Federalists be commissioned wherever possible.[16] The governor's kinsman, John May, was buried with the defiant epitaph, "I am who was a federalist at first but now is a real republican."[17]

The deep suspicion of distant government that was so fundamental to the Scotch-Irish view of politics had been in their baggage when they began the settlement of Rockingham County and it would remain the majority opinion into the twenty-first century. This gave the Republicans solid political control. Robert Williams, who lived eight miles from Danbury, was elected to Congress from the Rockingham district in 1796, 1798 and 1800. When Jefferson was elected, he rewarded Williams with the commissionership attached to the Georgia Cession of 1802 and later made him governor of the Mississippi Territory.[18]

Among the Republicans there were identifiable factions that contested elections. One group formed around the Scots merchants like James and Robert Gallaway and the sheriffs John Menzies and John Mattocks. A local broadside called them "a set of designing demagogues" operating "under the mask of Republicans."[19] James Hunter, Theophilis Lacy, Thomas Henderson, and James Martin, Jr., headed another *cabal*, more Scotch-Irish in makeup. Another author referred to that group as auxiliaries and "effusions of our sage Squire Sneed," a reference to the author of the earlier insult.[20] This second group was more closely connected with the governor but together they preempted any Federalist influence.

From Danbury the governor observed the trial of the Glasgow Land Fraud defendants. The special court was made up of three Superior Court judges: Spruce Mccay, John Louis Taylor, and Samuel Johnston. Summoned at the end of 1799, the trial lasted through the middle of the next year. Glasgow was found guilty on two counts and fined $2,000 and, a few months after the trial ended, he and his family moved to Roane County, Tennessee.[21] Most of the accused remained in Tennessee, avoided trial, and kept the land they had acquired by fraud. Andrew Jackson, whose comments to Martin had exposed the fraud, tried unsuccessfully to incorporate, as a defendant, the popular Tennessee governor, John Sevier, and his efforts ended in a bloodless dual. In spite of the considerable land speculation that had swirled around Jackson, he was never charged with any crime. Stokely Donaldson, his brother-in-law, proved to be deeply involved in the fraud, connected through the family as Glasgow's son-in-law. Donaldson eventually owned 382 grants in Tennessee—a total of 562,000 acres.[22] Martin Armstrong was removed from administration of the Nashville Land Office, but he lost none of about 100 grants to a total of 260,000 acres. He retained his office as surveyor general of Tennessee.[23] William Blount died in March 1800 before the Glasgow trial opened. His brothers held grants to over 369,000 acres in Tennessee. They also held grants to nearly 1,000,000 acres in Buncombe County and over 1,800,000 acres in ten other counties in North Carolina. The Blount brothers were each acquitted.[24] There were about 50 others who were involved in receiving and attempting to receive land grants based on the use of fraudulent warrants and surveys.

Land dealings in which Martin was a participant did not always go smoothly. In 1778, he and his brothers, James and Robert, made entries for tracts in what was then Surry County with Joseph Winston, entry taker.[25] That was how James Martin acquired his original section on Snow Creek, including the lime kiln, where he built his home and, at the end of the Revolution, moved his family. One of the 640-acre sections that Alexander entered was on the north side of the Dan River near the mouth of Seven Island and Buck Island Creeks. It included improvements of John Slaton, William Mullins and George Slaton "being the said Martin's claim" and was "purchased from James Lankford in 1764." This was the grant that Alexander Martin gave as a wedding present on 1793 to his private secretary and nephew, Thomas Rogers.[26] Subsequently, a bank of iron ore was discovered within the survey that Rogers completed in 1795. Jonathan Harris brought a case in Salisbury District Court in 1803, claiming ten acres, including the ore bank, to have been his claim fraudulently included in the Rogers' survey. The governor gave his affidavit September 11, 1804, at the home of James Davis in Stokes County. It demonstrated that Martin had twice since 1764 amended his claim to satisfy poor settlers, the Slatons and Robert Mayab [Mabe], who had not properly processed their titles but had moved onto the land and built improvements.[27] Later, Rogers Ore Bank produced iron for several kilns in the area.[28] Governor Martin retained a passing interest in the development of the production of iron beginning as part of the Revolutionary War effort but his involvement was more an interest in what his brother, James, was up to.

Militia General Abraham Philips had represented Rockingham County in the state Senate since 1797.[29] In 1804, former governor Alexander Martin replaced him. In previous sessions Martin had been elected from Guilford but now he served Rockingham County. When he arrived in Raleigh, he found few old friends. He represented the founders among the heirs.

Martin was appointed to six committees and was much sought for advice. The question of slavery was exacerbated again when South Carolina re-instituted the slave trade.[30] Senator William Little introduced a bill in the North Carolina Senate to instruct the state congressional delegation to propose a constitutional amendment prohibiting the slave trade. There were abolitionists in the state but actually the slave trade was opposed in North Carolina more from fear of the slave population. This same Senate passed a prohibition on the right of free Negroes to vote, although that measure failed in the House, and denied by law the right of slaves to sell their free time.[31]

Jesse Franklin, victor over Martin in 1798, was at the end of his term as senator but he declined re-nomination. Others declined and the Senate elected Montford Stokes without first obtaining his agreement. By the time he communicated his rejection of the office, the assembly was in recess and the state was left with a single senator.

The assembly attempted to achieve better control of the financial system by incorporating the Bank of Cape Fear, headquartered in Fayetteville with its first branch in Wilmington. The following year, the Bank of North Carolina was chartered. These constructive actions were the exception in a state whose pervasive attitude was to make government as imperceptible as possible. The principal national advocate of obtuse government was North Carolina Congressman Nathaniel Macon, Speaker of the House. As successor to Willie Jones, his prevailing view was "that the function of government was simply to afford protection to individual rights" and Congress was instituted, in his opinion, "for observing the limitations of the Constitution."[32] That perspective was so unacceptable to a nation that had just acquired the unlimited potential of the Louisiana Purchase, through the act of an aggressive government, that Congress soon replaced Macon.

In North Carolina, however, Macon's was a majority view, combining as it did the fear of government exemplified by the Scotch-Irish in the west and the preponderant vote of the east always seeking to retain its dominance. This was the beginning of the sleep of the "Rip Van Winkle state," which would last for 30 years.[33] From his first executive pronouncements in 1783, Alexander Martin had consistently prodded the successive assemblies to advance education, improve navigation, lobby for a better post, and develop better roads and river transport. He had challenged his fellow westerner's inbred fear of government interference, to recognize themselves, the people, as the government and hence the source of the power to make better choices. Now, he was surrounded by self-interest and self-satisfaction and a growing paralysis creeping over every urgent need, as the country that had been initiated as a government of men became a government ensnared by laws. The new generation had not been called on to bet their lives on their actions. They did not remember those critical final years of the Revolution when the assembly was called to legislate on the edge of catastrophe.

The spirit of the "new democracy" threatened now to even destroy the university. In 1801, the assembly repealed the legislative acts of 1789 and 1794 that had respectively granted, for the birth and sustenance of the university, all unsold confiscated land and all escheated property. In the face of this threat of repeal, the trustees chose Alexander Martin to chair a committee. Martin prepared a defense of the university that he asked be presented directly to the people of the state. The trustees agreed. The florid Martin style claimed "literary institutions" to be the grand security of our liberties and that from them, in great measure, all civil and religious information flows; they prepare young citizens for their political duties with honor and reputation. He found regrettable the "want of resources and funds to complete the principal building, and the walls of which are yet incomplete." Then he turned to the grand provisions for funding, drawn by two separate assemblies, that had now been withdrawn by a third, causing the disagreeable necessity of resorting to lotteries, "a mode not the most honorable of raising money for the institution." He challenged the people "trusting in liberal and enlightened fellow citizens to complete the principal building that must soon fall to ruins unless supported by their aid. The Trustees therefore request such donations of money [as] you may think proper generously to grant."[34] Two years later, it was counter to the broad face of isolation and indifference that the last assembly in which Martin was to serve restored the proceeds of all escheated property to the university. This grant was "the 'source of the endowment of the University' up to the Civil War."[35] Martin was appealing to the public, confounding a reactionary assembly, to preserve the young university, while Davie, the so-called Father of the University, was lamenting "Poor No. Carolina," viewing its citizens as "thousands of these poor wretches" and planning his move to South Carolina.[36] Davie's attitude at this time had good justification but the contrast, under these circumstances, does enhance the record of Martin's lifelong contribution to the university.

In a final irony, Martin once more was called on to act as governor of North Carolina. The assembly met on November 15, 1805, and General Joseph Riddick, who had been Speaker of the Senate for the last five terms and whom Iredell called, "one of the family of the wrong heads" was late in arriving.[37] The Senate thereupon elected "Alexander Martin, LL.D" once more as Speaker. Then, in order to fill that United States Senate seat left vacant by Jesse Franklin, they chose Governor James Turner. To replace Turner, the legislature chose Congressman Nathaniel Alexander of Mecklenburg. Alexander sent word that he was unable to immediately assume his duties. At that point, Speaker Martin was asked to function in the governor's absence in a true déjà vu experience. Since Alexander was not vacating the office, this time Martin was authorized to act pro tempore. Alexander was technically not governor because he had not been sworn in before the legislature and Turner could not be considered still governor because North Carolina law prohibited double officeholding. The legislature then put Riddick back in the chair as Speaker pro tempore and so the government functioned. Martin was careful to sign documents "Alexander Martin *pro tempore* [sic] by inability of the Gov."[38]

The plot borders on public tragedy. The state was sliding away from leadership and public responsibility. When Martin returned to the Speaker's chair, having just held the function of the chief officer of the state for the eighth time, the assembly then proceeded, when presented the elected governor's message of encouragement for building inland navigation, public roads, and education, to respond, "for want of sufficient funds, an interference at this time would be inexpedient."[39] It was time to go home and Alexander Martin did. The session had lasted less than a month, the shortest since the end of the Revolution. It had produced little.

One final public service remained to Martin in 1806. Two years earlier, the Earl of Coventry, successor by devise of Earl Granville, brought suit in the United States Circuit Court at Raleigh against Josiah Collins and Nathan Allen and a similar suit against William R. Davie.[40] The Earl's claim was to all the acres of the Granville Grant that had not been sold by the Granville Land Office, contending that the Treaty of Paris had reserved this land to Granville. Potentially one of the most important cases ever to be argued before a court in the state, at that time, it drew universal public interest and concern.

Passing through several preliminary stages, the jury trial was heard in January 1806. On the 6th the case came to trial before Chief Justice John Marshall and District Judge Potter. Marshall removed himself. William Gaston opened with the case for the plaintiff and Duncan Cameron opened the case for the defense. Former attorney general Blake Baker and former governor Alexander Martin for the defense followed them.[41] Blake Baker was a first cousin of Elizabeth Strong and had drawn the indictment against James Glasgow in the fraud trial.[42] As friends and relations, Blake and Martin had worked together in the past. "Colonel Alexander Martin" volunteered his services and was heard next by the court for the defense as amicus curiae.[43] The verdict held for the defense. The case was not prosecuted further and some years later it was dropped from the docket. Before this court, Martin had a final public word defining issues of his time as the chief contemporary authority. Symbolically, that testimony tied up a last political loose end.

Danbury now seemed to be the place where he should be. He had been drained of all political fire. He thought a great deal about his slaves—his "persons of color," as they were popularly called. In the summer, he sent one of his Negroes, who had suffered from dropsy for some time, to be treated by the doctor at Salem. She died July 11 and the *Moravian Journal* recorded that "she was highly prized by her master for her fidelity."[44] Martin had closely observed the machinations within the state of the treatment of slaves and the great caution about "freedmen." So he gave considerable thought to the provisions he would have to make to preserve the freedom he intended to provide for Prince and Benjamin Harris Martin and the latter's family. He would have to tutor them about freedom and caution them about its dangers.[45]

In the February term of the Rockingham County Court of Pleas and Quarter Sessions in 1807, Governor Martin brought a petition that "Alexander Strong [age 19], otherwise called Alexander Strong Martin, the reputed son of Alexander Martin, Esq., and Elizabeth Strong, be allowed to be known by the name of Alexander Strong Martin." The governor had struggled for months with the terms of his will and he was almost finished. One final duty was to confirm in law that which had been routinely accepted in practice.[46] Martin was forging for this boy the future he deserved. He gave him property and objects of precious meaning and he left Elizabeth Strong with secure independence.[47]

The governor's last land purchase was in 1804 when, by grant, he acquired title to Lone Island, the three and a half acres in the middle of the Dan River at Danbury.[48] It had been Martin's fording point as far back as 1761 when he had first surveyed the claim for Danbury.[49] Now he looked to the disposal of all the property he had amassed between these, his first and last acquisitions. In structuring his will, Martin used his land to engineer security for his extended family and to make statements of appreciation to those who had shared his age. He provided cash for his surviving siblings by directing the sale of his miscellaneous acres in Montgomery, Anson, Rowan, Buncombe, and Wilkes counties. Danbury would be his mother's during her lifetime, and then it would go to Thomas and Jane Henderson and then to his nephew, James Martin, Jr. His land in Tennessee represented his major holdings. He divided the 5,000 acres given him as his bounty share, near the ore bank of the Mississippi, between Thomas Henderson, Pleasant Henderson, Sr., Robert Martin, James Martin, Sr., and James Hunter. They were his revolutionary brotherhood. He divided the 2,000 acres on Duck River and the Prewits Lick between his favorite nephews: Major Pleasant Henderson, Alexander Martin (James), Thomas Searcy, and Alexander M. Rogers. The tract on Harpath River went to Alexander Strong Martin and nephews Nathaniel Henderson, James, Samuel, and Robert Rogers.

His "Quarter lands called Ralston on Jacobs Creek" went to "my natural son, Alexander Strong, son of Elizabeth Strong, otherwise called and known by the name Alexander Strong Martin."[50] There it was—affirmed in his will and confirmed in the court. Subsequent generations would lock on this statement as one of scandal and amusement but for the governor it was a fact in his story. The Martin family confirmed "Aleck" and his descendents bore proudly their relationship to this pair. This particular bequest also gave to his son the land on which he and his mother had lived for years, referring to it as his "Quarter lands," a place set aside for living.

The furniture, china and silver were given to Martin's sisters and nieces. Alexander Strong was left many of the prized personal and military mementoes. Martin's portrait and chariot went to his brother, James. He remembered the Rev. David Caldwell with special books and he returned to Alex Frohock the small sword his father, Thomas, had given him when he was a young Salisbury lawyer.[51]

The hours he spent on his detailed will and codicils dated April, June, and September, and the court action to acknowledge Alexander Strong Martin as his son, seem to point to a debilitating illness that the governor, at some point, recognized as terminal. Alexander Martin died November 2, 1807, just as winter took hold, and when in former days he would have been setting off for a meeting of the assembly. His widowed mother died four days later.[52] In anticipation of death, the Governor had prepared a stone lined vault on a bluff on the south side overlooking the Dan River. In his will Martin directed that his funeral be "liberal not ostentatious at the discretion of my Executor [James Hunter]."[53] A significant effort was made in the will to make secure the remaining life of his mother, Jane Hunter Martin, that he had no reason to believe would be so short after his own death. So it is presumed that she was also buried in the vault with appropriate compliance with his wishes.

It is obvious to compare Martin's will and particularly his considerations about his family and slaves with Washington's will. The vault the governor had prepared for himself and his family was an even more obvious imitation of the one the Washington family had at Mt. Vernon. About 35 years after Martin and his mother were placed in the vault, it was damaged by water and erosion. The bodies, now joined by other members of the family, were removed and reburied; over time, however, the location of the grave of the governor was forgotten. Like his closest political friend, Governor Richard Caswell, no monument marks the grave of Alexander Martin.[54]

He was mourned and perhaps remembered best, beyond his family, by the Moravians at Salem. "We were deeply touched when the life of Mr. Alexander Martin, formerly governor of this state, came to an end in November of this year. In early time he was very friendly with the Brethren and did them many services, and we wish for him a place in the eternal house of Salem."[55]

Ignoring an inventory of his many accomplishments, Alexander Martin left his personal epitaph in the preamble of his will. "I, Alexander Martin LL.D., of the County of Rockingham in the State of North Carolina late Governor of the same. ..."

Epilogue:
The Final Resting Place of Alexander Martin

Martin was the most famous political figure of Piedmont North Carolina. He had served with Washington, six times been elected governor by the legislature and twice served as governor in an emergency capacity, was chosen Speaker of the North Carolina Senate for 13 sessions of the legislature, elected U.S. senator, and was a delegate to the Constitutional Convention. A graduate of Princeton, he was elected to the American Philosophical Society and was presented a doctorate degree of law by Princeton. Aside from land in excess of 10,000 acres throughout North Carolina and Tennessee, he devised gold sleeve buttons, a silver service, a chariot, gold stock buckles, a case of pistols, his portrait, silver tumblers given to him by George Washington and an extensive library. A family vault was a dignity consistent with the other objects in his estate even if it was certainly ostentatious when observed by the yeoman farmers who were his neighbors.

There was also the tradition that Martin's casket was placed in the vault in a standing position. Memorable for the neighbors, it was explained that he requested that detail because he passionately coveted the plantation across the Dan. This tradition has always been discounted since the plantation in question could have been purchased at any time. Eight years earlier, Washington was buried in his brick and stone vault at Mt. Vernon. Imitation of Washington would not have been lost on Martin but would have been alien to most of his neighbors who, some years later, might have to make up a reason to explain why the casket stood on end.[1]

In 1822, Robert Martin, Alexander's younger brother, died.[2] Robert's plantation was six miles from Danbury.[3] In his will he instructed, "my body to be discreetly

	1775	76	77	78	79	80	81	82	83	84	85	86	87	88	89	90	91	92	93	94	95	96	97	98	99	00
Alexander Martin						x	x	x	x	x	x	x	x	x	x	x	x	x	x	x	x	x	x	x	x	
Richard Caswell	x	x	x	x	x			x	x	x	x	x			x											
Thomas Burke		x	x		x		x																			
Samuel Johnston						x	x						x	x	x	x	x	x	x							
William R. Davie																								x		
William Blount								x			x	x														
Timothy Bloodworth										x	x	x			x	x	x	x			x	x	x	x	x	x
Benjamin Hawkins							x	x	x			x	x			x	x	x	x	x	x	x				
Hugh Williamson								x	x	x			x			x	x	x	x	x						

Alexander Martin as Officeholder. In the 18th Century, the highest offices in government in North Carolina were governor, Speaker of the Senate, U.S. senator and congressman.* In the last 25 years of that century, no one filled those offices in greater consistency than Alexander Martin.†

*Continental and U.S. Congress.

†Martin, David, Blount and Williamson were also elected as delegates to the Federal Convention in 1787. Before his death in 1807, Martin served once more as Speaker of the Senate and once more as acting governor.

interred in the family vault."⁴ Since there was no other vault, family or otherwise, in the region, this reference is to the governor's vault at Danbury. There is the further possibility that Alexander's sister, Jane, and her husband, Thomas Henderson, who died in 1821, may also have been buried in the family vault.⁵

In his will Martin bequeathed Danbury to Thomas and Jane Henderson on the condition that they maintain his mother, Jane Hunter Martin, in comfort for the rest of her life. At their deaths, the plantation was to go to his nephew, James Martin, Jr., of Snow Creek.⁶ In 1808, Thomas Henderson deeded to his son 2,000 acres on which the father lived. This may have included Danbury although Thomas did not have the right to deed his lifetime interest.⁷ In 1812, James Martin, Jr., deeded his residual interest in Danbury to Thomas Henderson's son, Alexander of New Bern, calling it 933 acres.⁸ This same Alexander Henderson then was deeded the 1,700-acre adjoining plantation, Mt. Pleasant, in 1816 by his uncle, Pleasant Henderson, who had owned that plantation since 1783.⁹ In 1835, Alexander Henderson gave a Deed of Trust to Rawley Gallaway for $4,000 with Mt. Pleasant and Danbury as security.¹⁰ Five years later Henderson, then living in Mobile, Alabama, gave Gallaway his Power of Attorney to sell Mt. Pleasant, "land of Major Pleasant Henderson," and Danbury. No sale came about and the sheriff foreclosed for debt to the Bank of the State of North Carolina on May 24, 1841. Less than a month later, June 16, the bank sold Danbury to Robert Martin for the foreclosure value of $5,137.50. This was Robert Martin, Jr., son of Robert Martin and nephew of Governor Alexander Martin. The plantation, including the family vault, was still in the family after a little over 30 years. Presumably all the various owners were heirs of Governor Alexander Martin and had been present at his burial and that of his mother and siblings.

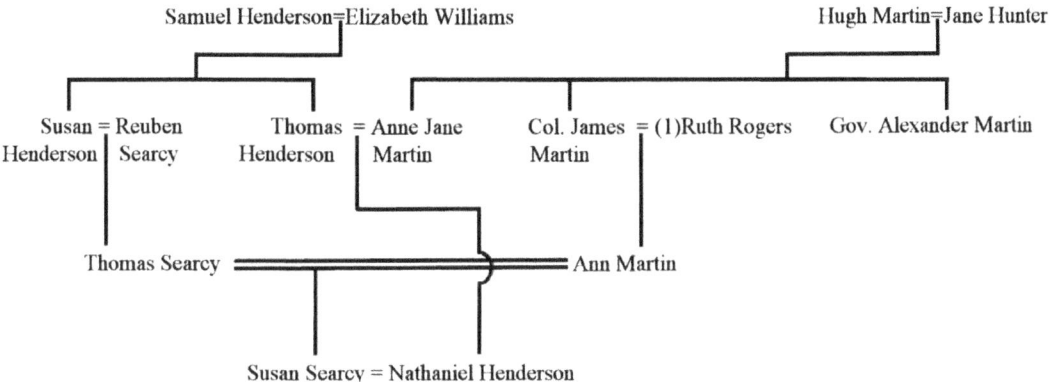

Interrelation of Martin, Searcy, and Henderson Families.

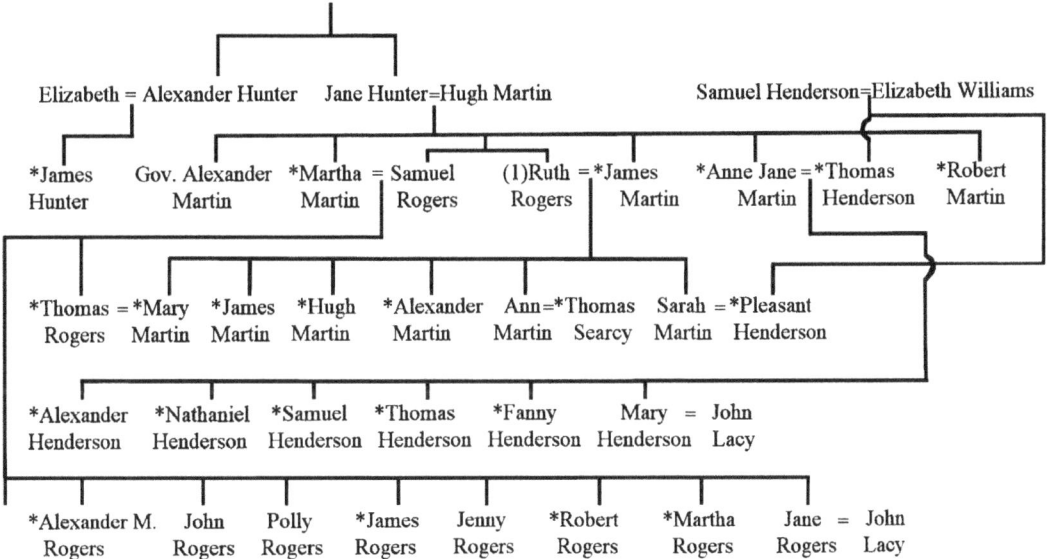

* indicates bequest from Gov. Alexander Martin

Family Heirs of Alexander Martin.

Repeatedly the story was told that the vault decayed. There are conflicting tales of water damage; it was far too high on the bluff to flood, however, general deterioration could be expected after about 30 years. The bodies were moved but the various accounts disagree widely on where and how. There is one explanation that they were moved to Georgia or South Carolina, unlikely in the logistics of the times. Several say vaguely that they were reburied nearby and one says a Negro was directed to dig a hole at the corner of the old vault and put them in the ground. The most prevalent assertion is that the bodies were "moved." Only in this century was a serious effort made to document the place to which they were moved.

In an address Robert Martin Douglas, great grandson of Robert Martin, gave July 4, 1898, at the battleground at Guilford Courthouse honoring the governor, he concluded, "as the vault was injured, his remains were moved and buried elsewhere, but at what spot no one seems to know." He went on to observe the irony that Martin and General Greene "should both sleep in unknown graves."[11]

In 1929, Mary M. Baker wrote about the re-interment of Governor Martin and its relationship to the family of Stephen A. Douglas. Her authority was two Napier sisters who had lived next to her, one actually living for seven years with her. "This one cousin was Miss Elizabeth Champion Napier, who with her brother Robert Martin Napier and John Napier, and two sisters, Martha Martin and Jane Hunter Napier, were the children of Sallie Martin Napier, wife of Moses Napier, and sister of Robert Martin, father of Mrs. Stephen A. Douglas." She concludes concerning the burial of Governor Martin: "[H]ere [on Dan River] a vault was constructed, in which, on the death of the Governor Martin, his body was placed. It remained here until the vault began falling to ruins. Then it was removed and the remains carried to the Settle-Martin burying ground and there interred."[12]

Avery Baker, son of Mary Madison Baker, worked at the post office and was an occasional writer for the *Reidsville Review*. In 1938, he wrote on the subject, qualifying his comments by noting that his mother "spent the first years of her married life in the house in which Governor Alexander Martin once lived, (but which has since been destroyed by fire)." He is the one who confirms the placing of the coffin in an upright position and the removal of the body. He repeats several conflicting speculations about the removal of the governor's body then concludes, "other accounts have it that after the removal of his body from the old vault, it was most likely removed to the old 'Settle-Reid' burying ground; about 18 miles to the east of old Danbury, now known as the 'Judge Thomas Settle Place,' about 3 miles east of Reidsville, and laid to rest among relatives there (for many of his kindred are buried there) in an unmarked grave."

Maude Reynolds was a writer and music and art teacher and produced a number of articles on local history. She made a concerted effort about 1930 to confirm a location for Martin's final resting place. She repeats the myth explaining the upright burial as necessary in order for Martin to keep an eye on his slaves and the other popular one about the river rising to flood the crypt. Then she says, "I was told, by good authority, after much inquiry, that the citizens of that part of the county came by wagon and on horseback and moved the remains to the Martin and Ellington graveyard several miles north of Reidsville just off the Yanceyville road, at the old Ellington home place. It is reasonable to believe this to be true since a brother and other members of the Martin family are buried there." Although she is confused with connecting this cemetery to the Ellington family, Miss Reynolds is describing the previously mentioned "Settle-Reid" cemetery.

The cemetery each of these writers is concluding to be the site of Martin's final burial was begun by the family of David Settle. His daughter, Mary, married Robert Martin, nephew of the governor and they lived near Danbury. This was the same Robert Martin who, in 1841, bought Danbury with the site of the family vault. In 1846, his daughter, Lucinda Martin, a young belle who had captivated chaperones in Washington, died and was buried in the cemetery of her mother's family.[13] A year later Robert Martin concluded his own carefully worded will tying up many details, not least of which was the ownership of his slaves, who would go to his surviving daughter, Martha, the young wife of the junior senator from Illinois, Stephen A. Douglas. It would seem logical that at this time of melancholy and while concluding arrangements of important family responsibilities, Robert Martin might also look to the deteriorating family vault on his Danbury plantation that at the very least contained his father, grandmother and very famous uncle, and saw to it that their bodies were properly buried with the family. His beloved daughter was buried with the Settles and he anticipated that he would soon join them, as would his wife. He could not have known that his daughter, Martha, would be buried there in 1853 at the age of 25.[14] The time line for these events seems logical and the motivation obvious. Robert brought them all to the Settle cemetery and he joined them there on his death a few months later on May 25, 1848. It may only be the result of his eminent death that prevented Robert Martin from properly marking the burial site of Governor Martin and the rest of his family. Had he lived longer, it is obvious from the care he took in other matters, that he would have had appropriate stones to mark their graves.

Chapter Notes

Chapter 1

1. Witherspoon was an aide to General Maxwell and was the son of Dr. John Witherspoon, President of Princeton. Martin knew James as the President's son when he was a student. McGuire, *The Surprise of Germantown*, 1994), 55.

2. When he was pulled from under the horse it was found that his leg had almost been blown off. A litter was made of poles and he was carried twenty miles to DeHaven's house where he died three days later. At the time he was hit by the artillery ball, it is said a musket ball, which grazed his head, also blinded him. *Ibid.*; Rankin, *The North Carolina Continental Line*, 30.

3. Flexner, *George Washington*, II, 235.

4. There is confusion concerning the date of his birth. The date of 1740 is often used by biographers but neither date has been positively confirmed. James Martin, Alexander's brother, records in his family history that his father was married when he was about 40 years old. Hugh Martin would have been 40 in 1738. James also says his mother was about 18 when she was married. Jane Hunter Martin was 18 in 1735. Since Alexander was their first child, it is likely that the earlier date of 1738 is the year of his birth. Hunter, *The Hunters of Bedford County*, 13–14; Hugh Martin's tombstone in Hunterdon County, NJ, says he died March 7, 1761, at the age of 63; Raleigh Register, November 19, 1807: "Died at his seat in Rockingham County 2nd inst. the Honorable Alexander Martin, LL.D. And on the 6th, his mother, at the advanced age of ninety years."

5. Manuscript of James Martin written late in his life (he died in 1834). Copies are preserved by his descendents.

6. Leyburn, *The Scotch Irish*, 273.

7. Dunaway, *The Scotch Irish*, 25.

8. "When my father came to years of discretion..." seems to indicate that Hugh came soon after he was 21, which would have been about 1718. Yates, "The Public Career of Alexander Martin."

9. "Mr. [Alexander] Hunter was one of the first settlers of this part of the country—he with about thirty other families arriving here from the north of Ireland in 1730." Hunter, *The Hunters of Bedford County*, 17; Dunaway, *Scotch Irish*, 55.

10. "He had already married Elizabeth Steele and had children born before they left Ireland." Yates, "The Public Career of Alexander Martin."

11. McLachlan, *Princetonians*, xviii.

12. McLachlan, *Princetonians*, 40.

13. Pomfrey, *Colonial New Jersey*, 204.

14. When Lewis Morris was appointed governor of New Jersey in 1738, he was the first to hold that post entirely separate from New York. He was a controversial figure, irascible in all his dealings.

15. Yates, "The Public Career of Alexander Martin."

16. Federal Writers' Project, *New Jersey*, 40.

17. Attributed to Lequear, *Traditions of Hunterdon*, 12–13.

18. Leyburn, *The Scotch-Irish*, 319.

19. Lomask, *Aaron Burr*, 17.

20. Findley was later president of Princeton. The "Log Colleges" were a product of the demand among Presbyterians for an educated clergy.

21. George William Pilcher, *Samuel Davies* (Knoxville: University of Tennessee Press, 1971), 10.

22. Ramsey, *Carolina Cradle*, 190; Foote, *Sketches of North Carolina*, 349.

23. Sarah Burr was born May 3, 1754, and Aaron Burr, Jr., was born February 6, 1756.

24. McLachlan, *Princetonian*, xviii.

25. Lomask, *Aaron Burr*, 17.

26. Moore, *The Madisons*, 28.

27. McLachlan, *Princetonians*, 157.

28. Moore, *The Madisons*, 38.

29. McLachlan, *Princetonians*, 186.

30. Some biographies list him as an Anglican and some as a Presbyterian. His brother was an Anglican priest and his mother was certainly Anglican. Martin was said to have been a member of the Presbyterian congregation of Dr. David Caldwell.

31. Lomask, *Aaron Burr*, 18.

32. Alexander Martin was also inoculated at this time for smallpox. He may have been inoculated again 18 years later when the North Carolina Continentals, arriving in Pennsylvania during a similar epidemic, were all inoculated.

33 For some years the story was repeated that on the first day of this year of his death, Burr preached a sermon on Jeremiah 27:16: "Thus saith the Lord, This year thou shalt die." Pilcher, *Samuel Davies*, 185. They marveled further when Edwards' replacement, Samuel Davies, preached from the same text in 1760, the year of his death.

Chapter 2

1. This was the year that the Presbyterian Church reunited. The competing Synods came together in May as the Synod of Philadelphia and New York. American Presbyterians, thus united, looked to be an even stronger force in colonial influence.

2. Davies died in February 1761, sending the college again into gloom. Wertenbaker, *Princeton*, 41.

3. This may have been Nicholas Davies but the relationship to the Rev. Davies is not clear. McLachlan, *Princetonians*, 157; Adair, "Autobiography of the Reverend Devereaux Jarrett," 346–393; Seeley G. Mudd Manuscript Library, Princeton University.

4. In 1761, this location fell into Buckingham County, which was separated from Albemarle. John Hunter bought his first land on Glovers Creek on February 13, 1749. He may have been in Virginia even as early as 1743. Hunter, *The Hunters of Bedford County*, 25.

5. Hunter's Settlement in Lower and Upper Mount Bethel Township of Northampton County originated about 1730 and was named after Alexander Hunter, a leader among the group. In 1738 they had organized Mount Bethel Presbyterian Church. Dunaway, *The Scotch-Irish*, 55. Alexander Hunter bought his first land on David's Creek in Albemarle on April 3, 1754. Hunter, *The Hunters of Bedford County*, 21.

6. The war sermons of the Rev. Davies had roused the Presbyterians to their duty in support of the British and colonial forces. Foote, *Sketches of Virginia*, 295.

7. Alexander Hunter may never have finalized his move to North Carolina. He died at his home in Bedford County, Virginia, between December 25, 1767, and March 22, 1768. Hunter, *The Hunters of Bedford County*, 22.

8. Henderson, "Although Governor Six Times He Is Neglected by Historians."

9. The county of Rowan was surveyed out of Anson in 1753. The original Act creating the county had been revoked by George II but re-established in 1756. In 1755, the county town of Salisbury was surveyed. Ervin, "A Colonial History of Rowan County," 16:I, 14–15.

10. Saunders, *Colonial Records of North Carolina*, 5:355.

11. Ramsey, *Carolina Cradle*, 112.

12. Frohock had been involved with an uncle in Maryland as a merchant and trader. Then he had become acquainted with Alexander and Henry Eustace McCulloch in land speculation. The McCullochs were cousins and Henry Eustace was the father-in-law of Thomas Frohock, brother of John. Henry Eustace McCulloch was sent from England in 1761 to act as land agent for his father's land. As part of the settlement between Henry McCulloch and Earl Granville, for the latter's service as agent, McCulloch received sixteen hundred acres between the Uwharrie and Catawba Rivers then all in Rowan County. In four years, after his arrival in America, Henry Eustace McCulloch had disposed of all his father's tracts in Rowan and had given deeds to all the purchasers. Ramsey, *Carolina Cradle*, 114.

13. Henderson, "Although Governor Six Times He Is Neglected by Historians."

14. Over Hugh Martin's grave is a white marble tablet.

15. The will was probated May 12, 1761. Based on the extreme weakness of his signature, Hugh Martin must have been very near death when he signed a codicil to his will on March 6, 1761. His brother-in-law, Thomas Rogers, wrote his will three days later and James Martin, Jr., witnessed both. The family urgency to sign wills may indicate the presence of an epidemic illness. Thomas Rogers did not die until 1766. Hunterdon County Wills #688J and Lot Number 11, folio 45. The grave of Hugh Martin has been moved twice. In 1946, it was moved a short distance when the road was widened. In 1975, the Interstate was completed and Martin's grave was moved to Clinton East Cemetery among a lot of more recent burials; Snell, *History of Hunterdon and Somerset Counties*, 538–539.

16. Tate's grants were on Dan River above Reedy Creek and on Great Rock House Creek, Granville Grant #4909, 21 December 1761 to Joseph Tate for 422 acres on the east side of Dan River, Granville Grant #4911, 21 December 1761 for 320 acres on Great Rock House Creek of Dan River. Alexander Martin was recording 436 acres on Dan River at Jacobs Creek, Granville Grant, Rowan County Deed Book 4, page 815–816, 21 December 1761. He also witnessed Granville Grant, Rowan County Deed Book 4, page 13, 14 September 1758, and Book 4, page 243, 26 January 1760. Joseph Tate already had Granville Grants to 1,296 acres, Granville Grants #4907, 4908, and 4910 all dated 27 June 1759; Uncle Alexander Hunter had 620 acres, Rowan County Deed Book 4, page 10, 14 September 1758; Uncle John Hunter had a deed to 1,000 acres, Rowan County Deed Book 4, page 11, 16 September 1758; Cousin John Hunter, Jr., had purchased 200 acres from Robert Jones, Rowan County Deed Book 4, page 13, 14 September 1758; and Cousin Edmund Hunter five tracts from Jones totaling 2,889 acres, Rowan County Deed Book 4, page 243, 26 September 1759. See also Linn, "Virginia–North Carolina Migrations," 30–35. One of these locations included "Hoop-hole Bottom" (1759) that was later associated derisively with Alexander Martin's frontier residence.

17. Hugh's brother, Robert Martin, was acting as

trustee and his other brother, James, was also available to assist, although he died in December. Estate of Hugh Martin, Hunterdon County, New Jersey, File 11, folio 45; Stokes County Court, June Session, 1802, Answer of James Martin to the Petition of Robert Martin.

18. Henderson, "Although Governor Six Times He Is Neglected by Historians"; Minutes of Rowan County Court Book 2, page 606, 8 October 1765.

19. Henderson, "The Creative Forces."

20. On October 13, 1766, he received his appointment as attorney for the Crown, Rowan County Court Records Book 2, page 647, 15 October 1766.

21. Henderson, "Although Governor Six Times He Is Neglected by Historians"; Rowan County Court Minutes Book 2, page 679, 16 January 1767.

22. Green, *To Colonize Eden*, 69.

23. Powell, *The Correspondence of William Tryon*, 1:467–468.

24. Lefler and Newsome, *History of a Southern State*, 172.

25. Henderson, *Conquest*, 141.

26. *Dictionary of North Carolina Biography*, s.v. "John Frohock."

27. Fries, *Moravians*, 2:353.

28. Henderson, *Conquest*, 148.

29. Martin became increasingly associated with the Henderson family beginning with this period in Salisbury.

30. James Martin married Ruth Rogers, "his cousin," in 1763. They had Sarah the following year, Jean in 1766 and Hugh in 1770. Family notes in Wall Collection, Special Collection, Rockingham Community College, Wentworth, NC.

31. "I order my two sons to wit are at college, to be brought through, out of the real estate, and after they are cleared at college, I order each of my sons, Alexander, James and Thomas to receive twenty pounds to be paid out of the real estate by the Executors."

32. *The North Carolina Booklet*, 14 January 1915, 129.

33. McLachlan, *Princetonians*, 394–395.

34. Brant, *James Madison*, 1:65.

35. McLachlan, *Princetonians*, 395.

36. Witherspoon ultimately accepted the position of president in December 1767. Wertenbaker, 48–51.

37. Brant, *James Madison*, 1:74.

38. Brant, *James Madison*, 1:70–71.

39. Moore, *The Madisons*, 27.

40. Brant, *James Madison*, 1:70–71.

41. Peterson, ed., *The Founding Fathers*, 19.

42. The Rev. Thomas Martin to James Martin, Virginia, June 20, 1770. Manuscript owned by Bob Upshur of Columbia, SC.

43. Brant, *James Madison*, 1:65.

44. Samuel Martin may have already gone on to Mecklenburg County where he located.

45. Mr. Madison had asked his son if it might be possible to employ another graduate of Princeton in the post. Nothing came of the effort. James Madison, Jr., to James Madison, Sr., July 23, 1770, Princeton, NJ.

46. Bethabara, February 24, 1771, Fries, *Moravians*, 1:451.

47. Brant, *James Madison*, 1:122–123.

Chapter 3

1. Richard Henderson to William Tryon, September 29, 1770, Public Records Office, London, Colonial Papers 5/314.

2. There is scholarly contradiction on the identity of James Hunter, who has been identified by history as "General" of the Regulators. During the 19th century, particularly late in the century when public efforts were under way to establish the Battleground at Alamance as a public memorial, James Hunter of Snow Creek in Stokes County was attributed as this leader. He was the first cousin of Alexander Martin and his identity in this question seemed to have been proven by an extensive exchange of letters from Dr. Robert Hunter Dalton, Hunter's grandson, who had known his grandfather and frequently talked to him about his exploits in the Regulation and the Revolution. However, there were at least two other James Hunters present among the Regulators and in recent years a case has been effectively made by Vearl Guymon Alger that James Hunter, a Quaker who lived on Stinking Quarter in what is now Randolph County, was the person Governor Tryon was actually pursuing following the Battle of Alamance as the Regulator provocateur. Whether it was in the Quaker character for that James Hunter to have been the aggressive petitioner at Hillsborough is in question. That he was a Regulator is not. Alger, "The Case for James Hunter," 70–83; *Dictionary of North Carolina Biography*, s.v. "James Hunter."

3. Rowan County Registry Book IV, p. 815; Book VIII, p. 134; Book VI, p. 337; Book VII, p. 110; Book VIII, p. 335–336.

4 Clark, *The State Records of North Carolina*, 23:810.

5. Saunders, *Colonial Records of North Carolina*, 8:477-479; Clark, *State Records of North Carolina*, 223:789-849.

6. Powell, *The Regulators in North Carolina*, 131–132.

7. Saunders, *Colonial Records of North Carolina*, 8:533-536.

8. Ibid.

9. Ibid.

10. Haywood, *Governor William Tryon*, 114–115.

11. William Tryon to Lord Hillsborough, April 12, 1771, Public Records Office, London, CO 5/314.

12. "He [Martin] must have been a member of the Buffalo congregation while he was living at Martinsville [sic], only four miles from the Church." It is an assumption. Conversely, had he been a member, considering his high profile, wouldn't it be more likely that there would be a corroborating record? Rankin, *Buffalo Presbyterian Church*.

13. Presbyterian Ministers to William Tryon, Hawfields, August 23, 1768, Saunders, *Colonial Records of North Carolina*, 7:813–814.

14. Presbyterian Pastors to Presbyterians of North Carolina, August 23, 1768, Saunders, *Colonial Records of North Carolina*, 7:814–815.

15. William Tryon to Lord Hillsborough, New Bern, March 12, 1771, Public Records Office, London, CO5/314.

16. Eli Carruthers, *David Caldwell*, 149.

17. Rankin, *Buffalo Presbyterian Church*, 31.

18. In the aftermath of the Battle of Alamance it

was said that both James Hunter of Stinking Quarter and James Hunter of Beaver Island Creek fled to Maryland. It was following his return from Maryland, in 1774, that James of Beaver Island is specifically identified as a Regulator by the Moravians. In November 1774, the Salem Diary records an incident where James Hunter steals back from the Moravians some cattle that Governor Tryon had taken from him after the Battle of Alamance and had sold to the Moravians. That same incident is recorded in a letter written in 1873 by Hunter's grandson, Dr. Robert Hunter Dalton, who as a child had heard the story from his grandfather. Since the Moravian diaries, written in German, were not translated until well into the 19th century, the two sources verify each other and confirm James Hunter of Beaver Island as a recognized Regulator. Hunter, *The Hunters of Bedford County*, 32–33; Dr. Robert Hunter Dalton to Maria Tidball, February 26, 1873, private papers, Linda Vernon, Madison, NC.

19. Andrew Jackson, John C. Calhoun, Ben Tillman, Huey Long, George Wallace, and Strom Thurmond are more notable examples.

20. In the first 20 years of the life of the College of New Jersey/Princeton only one student was born in North Carolina but eight students took residence in that state after graduation: Waightstill Avery (1766), Hezekiah James Balch (1766), Ephraim Brevard (1768), David Caldwell (1761), Hugh McAden (1753), Alexander Martin (1756), Adlai Osborne (1768), and Samuel Spencer (1759). Avery, Martin, and Spencer became lawyers. Balch, Caldwell, and McAden were Presbyterian ministers. Brevard was a doctor. Caldwell, Martin, and Spencer were members of the North Carolina provincial congress. Later, Avery, Martin, and Spencer were members of the state assembly. In the coming Revolution, Avery, Brevard, Martin, and Spencer all performed military service while the three ministers were active on behalf of the patriot cause. At the time of the regulation the Rev. Hugh McAden strongly opposed the regulation, as did Waightstill Avery and Adlai Osborne, who both signed the "Redressor" Association in opposition. Samuel Spencer actually fought at Alamance as a colonel under Governor Tryon.

Chapter 4

1. Wake came from Orange, Johnston, and Cumberland Counties.

2. Fries, *Moravians*, 1:451.

3. Henderson would become Martin's brother-in-law when he married Jane Martin. Sam Martin may have been Alexander's brother, Samuel, and this may have preceded his permanent move to Mecklenburg.

4. In 1771 the first members of the assembly from the new county of Guilford were John Kimborough and William Fields. Fields and his four sons had been among the Regulator leaders. Cheney, Jr., 90.

5. Robinson and Stoesen, *History of Guilford County*, 30–32.

6. Saunders, *Colonial Records of North Carolina*, 9:396, 497, 422, 444, 661; Clark, *State Records of North Carolina*, 23:928.

7. In 1752 the Moravians of Bethlehem, Pennsylvania, responded to the suggestion of Lord Granville and began an extensive settlement in North Carolina, which they designated Wachovia. The first settlers had arrived to establish the village of Bethabara in Rowan County on November 17, 1753.

8. Green, *To Colonize Eden*, 46.

9. Governor Tryon's palace at New Bern had done much to anger the Carolina farmers. Josiah Martin had interesting ties with James Parke Farley, Alexander Martin's near neighbor on Dan River. About the same age, both had grown up as children of prominent sugar planters in Antigua. In spite of the claims of at least one descendent (see Horton *Wasted Talents*, 109) that Alexander Martin and Governor Josiah Martin were related and that both were related to General Joseph Martin of Virginia, there is no support for the theory. It is repeated at times in poorly researched newspaper articles and sometimes in the family of one or the other of the men.

10. Moore, *History of North Carolina*, 151.

11. With Martin on the committee, it is unlikely that they would have struck his cousin's name [James Hunter] off the list of those being offered a pardon, thus indicating that this James Hunter was the Quaker living on Stinking Quarter in southern Guilford who appears to have been far more active as a Regulator. Yates, "The Public Career of Alexander Martin," 5.

12. Stumpf, *Josiah Martin*, 56.

13. Ibid., 60.

14. After being a leader among the Regulators, William Fields became a leading Tory in that part of Guilford that became Randolph County. Robinson and Stoesen, *History of Guilford County*, 34.

15. Stumpf, *Josiah Martin*, 61.

16. Ibid., 98.

17. Moore, *History of North Carolina*, 161.

18. Clark, *State Records of North Carolina*, 10:953.

19. First called for July 21, 1774, it was technically true that this provincial convention was "the first representative assembly of North Carolina and in all of America based on popular authority rather than royal." Stumpf, *Josiah Martin*, 85.

20. Saunders, *Colonial Records of North Carolina*, 10:136.

21. Richmond Courthouse, on the Armstrong land, was the second location for a courthouse in Surry County from 1774 until a new county called Stokes was taken from Surry in 1789. Fries, *Moravians*, 2:643.

22. In one of the early excesses of the mounting hostilities, Dunn and Boote were abducted by radicals and taken to South Carolina where they were detained for over a year. Both men were paroled and rehabilitated as citizens although at the appearance of Lord Cornwallis in 1781, Boote joined the British. *Dictionary of North Carolina Biography*, s.v. "John Ross Dunn."

23. The first decade of the court minutes of Guilford County are missing.

24. Robinson and Stoesen, *History of Guilford County*, 31–32.

25. Ibid., 32.

26. Sellers, Jr., "Making a Revolution," 26.

27. There are some authorities that feel that the 15 members of the congress who were not recorded

as delegates of the assembly represented a recording oversight since this was really one body meeting under two names – taking one name and then the other as subjects of debate required. Stumpf, *Josiah Martin*, 97. Martin is recorded as having to miss Anson County Court because he is at the congress.

28. James Hunter Chapter NSDAR, *Early Families*, 2:41–43.

29. This was a court of *oyer* and *terminer* for the Salisbury court. Hoyt, Jr., *Mecklenburg Declaration of Independence*, 87.

30. Henderson, "Although Governor Six Times He Is Neglected by Historians."

31. Hoyt, Jr., *Mecklenburg Declaration of Independence*, 65–66.

32. Moore, *History of North Carolina*, 187.

33. The fact that this court continued to function as a Crown court after the reading of Captain Jack's resolutions in open court is a factor used to argue that this was not a Declaration of Independence. Hoyt, Jr., *Mecklenburg Declaration of Independence*, 66.

34. *Dictionary of North Carolina Biography*, s.v. "James Jack."

35. Fries, *Moravians*, 2:634.

36. Fries, *Moravians*, 2:880.

37. Six months later Farley's father-in-law, William Byrd III, committed suicide and Farley returned with his family to Westover. In 1778, he died at Rosewell while visiting Mann Page. "In Glouchester, James Parke Farley, Esq., of North Carolina," *Virginia Gazette*, May 23, 1777.

38. Lefler and Newsome, *History of a Southern State*, 194.

39. This [James] Hunter was certainly not Alexander Martin's cousin; Samuel Johnson to James Iredell, August 14, 1775. McRee, *James Iredell*, 1:261–262.

40. Saunders, *Colonial Records of North Carolina*, 10:165, 175, 180.

41. In the Salisbury District two members of the new council were his Princeton friends, Samuel Spencer and Waightstill Avery.

42. Russell, *North Carolina in the Revolutionary War*, 12.

Chapter 5

1. Fries, *Moravians*, 2:884–943.

2. Retirement was postponed and finally abandoned until 8,000 paper dollars equaled one hard dollar. *Ibid.*, 2:849.

3. Saunders, *Colonial Records of North Carolina*, 22:145.

4. Fries, *Moravians*, 2:941.

5. *Ibid.*, 2:942.

6. Affidavit sworn by James Henderson, March 29, 1776, to events in November 1775, possibly in Mecklenburg County. Draper Collection, Library of Congress copy, reel 104, extracted from the Manuscript Papers of Waightstill Avery in reference to Arthur Graham vs. William Moore, Esq., 1776.

7. Some of the property that burned belonged to the father of James Parke Farley.

8. Likened by some authors to the Regulators in North Carolina, this group had some similarities, including the fact that many were Scotch-Irish. Russell, *North Carolina in the Revolutionary War*, 14; letter of Waightstill Avery, December 3, 1775, Draper Collection, reel 104, Library of Congress.

9. Lefler and Newsome, *History of a Southern State*, 198.

10. Moore, *History of North Carolina*, 200.

11. Stumpf, *Josiah Martin*, 159.

12. Moore, *History of North Carolina*, 203–204.

13. It is sometimes difficult to determine whether Alexander Martin or his brother, James, is being referred to when a reference is made to "Martin."

14. Clark, *State Records of North Carolina*, 22: 97, Col. Richard Allen; 128–129, Pleasant Henderson.

15. Robinson and Stoesen, *History of Guilford County*, 36.

16. This Colonel Martin appears to refer to Alexander as James, in his narrative, says he did not arrive at Cross Creek for a day or two after the battle. Rankin, "Moore's Creek Bridge," 52.

17. Pension application of James Martin, W-4728, National Archives, Washington, DC.

18. Rankin, "Moore's Creek Bridge," 59.

19. The Third under Colonel Jethro Sumner; the Fourth under Colonel Thomas Polk; the Fifth under Colonel Edward Buncombe; and the Sixth under Colonel Alexander Lillington.

20. Some authors do claim this distinction for the Mecklenburg Resolves and declaration. Hoyt, Jr., *Mecklenburg Declaration of Independence*.

21. Moore, *History of North Carolina*, 220.

22. Northampton County, PA, June 25, 1776, Will #693.

23. This clause remained in the North Carolina constitution until it was revised in 1835.

24. General James Moore to The President of the Provincial Congress, Headquarters Wilmington, March 29, 1776. Original in private collection of Raeford Cates, Reidsville, NC.

25. Clark, *State Records of North Carolina*, 22:917.

26. He and his brother, Judge Maurice Moore, both appear to have died of malarial fever.

27. Russell, *North Carolina in the Revolutionary War*, 52.

28. Fries, *Moravians*, 3:1057.

29. This was the second time Alexander Martin had been part of a mass inoculation; the first was at Princeton in his student days. Russell, *North Carolina in the Revolutionary War*, 52.

30. Alexander Martin to J[ohn] Hancock, near Fredericksburg, May 10, 1777, Papers of the Continental Congress, M247, r99, i78, v.15, p. 189.

31. Russell, *North Carolina in the Revolutionary War*, 114.

32. At times the line was 12 abreast. It took two hours to pass but citizens were less festive when they saw "much nakedness and that what hats existed were all cocked at different angles were bad omens." Flexner, *George Washington*, II:221–222.

33. Maxwell was of Scotch-Irish descent, having settled in Warren County, New Jersey, not far from the boyhood home of Martin.

34. Commager and Morris, *The Spirit of Seventy-Six*, 611–618.

35. Robert C. Lawrence, "Alexander Martin, Soldier–Statesman," 1941, manuscript, 2368, Southern

Historical Collection, University of North Carolina, Chapel Hill.

36. Boatner, *Encyclopedia of the American Revolution*, 687.

37. Commager and Morris, *The Spirit of Seventy-Six*, 617.

38. His poem on the death of General Nash was typical of the florid poetry of the age.

> Last flow our sorrows for a favorite son,
> Whom weeping Carolina claims her own;
> The gallant Nash, who with the fatal wound,
> Tho' tortured, weltering, on the hostile ground,
> "fight on my Troops," with smiling ardour said,
> "'Tis but the fate of war, be not dismay'd."
> High Heaven ordains for great designs this woe,
> Which till the destin'd period, none must know;
> Heroes of old thus for their country stood,
> Raised mighty empires founded with their blood;
> In this new World, like great events must come,
> Thus Athens rose, and thus imperial Rome.

Walser, "Alexander Martin, Poet," 55–61; Swain, "Stray Leaves of History, No. 2," 79–81.

39. Clark, *State Records of North Carolina*, 13:262–264.

40. Clark, *State Records of North Carolina*, 11:625–626.

41. Boatner, *Encyclopedia of the American Revolution*, s.v. "Adam Stephens."

42. Clark, *State Records of North Carolina*, 11:677–678, 13 November 1777.

43. *Ibid.*, 20 November 1777.

44. Jethro Sumner himself would be forced by illness to return to North Carolina in the spring of 1778.

45. After Germantown the Fourth Regiment was combined with the First Regiment under the command of Colonel Thomas Clark.

46. Clark, *State Records of North Carolina*, 13:262–264.

Chapter 6

1. He appeared before the Council in person and recommended Richard Caswell's son, William, in his place. Clark, *State Records of North Carolina*, 22:937.

2. Clark, *State Records of North Carolina*, 12:778, 832, 839.

3. As early as 1767, Governor Tryon had sent a Swiss mineralogist to look for minerals in this area and he had located iron in presumed abundance. Fries, *Moravians*, 1:360.

4. Pearse, *A Concise History*, 60.

5. Martha Martin, Alexander's sister, had married Samuel Rogers probably in New Jersey.

6. The Moravians purchased their burned lime from Duncan, then James Martin. Fries, *Moravians*, 1:375, 4:1819, 5:2025, 2028.

7. Clark, *State Records of North Carolina*, 24:978–979.

8. Phillips, "William Duane," 365.

9. Cheney, *North Carolina Government*, 340.

10. Clark, *State Records of North Carolina*, 24:123.

11. January 19, 1779.

12. Clark, *State Records of North Carolina*, 13:584.

13. Moore, *History of North Carolina*, 253; Randolph County was actually established by Act of 1778. Clark, *State Records of North Carolina*, 24:234–236.

14. Among them were Henry Eustice McCulloch, his father, Sir Nathaniel Dukinfield; William Tryon; Josiah Martin; Edmund Fanning; Edward Brice Dobbs and Justice Maurice Howard. Moore, *History of North Carolina*, 255.

15. *Ibid.*, 257.

16. April 17, 1780.

17. The office of lieutenant governor was not established until the constitution of 1868.

18. Roberts, *The Battle of Cowpens*, 29.

19. Russell, *North Carolina in the Revolutionary War*, 154.

20. Rankin, *The North Carolina Continental Line*, 60.

21. Moore, *History of North Carolina*, 280.

22. Fries, *Moravians*, 4:1558–1559.

23. Russell, *North Carolina in the Revolutionary War*, 171.

24. Fries, *Moravians*, 4:1561.

25. Moore, *History of North Carolina*, 285; Lefler and Newsome, *History of a Southern State*, 214, 231–232.

26. The original purpose of the Board was as a committee to keep records and help in recruiting and supply. The person eventually chosen by Congress to head the Board was none other than Horatio Gates. That Board became a stage for anti-Washington intrigue and the power base for Gates. Only as Washington's position strengthened after the Valley Forge winter did the Board become superfluous. Commager and Morris, *The Spirit of Seventy-Six*, 655–656.

27. Clark, *State Records of North Carolina*, 24:355.

28. Lefler and Newsome, *History of a Southern State*, 231.

29. Robinson, *William R. Davie*, 96.

30. Clark, *State Records of North Carolina*, 15:137; Gardner, *Alexander Martin*, 12.

31. Henderson, "How Famous Tar Heel Governor...."

32. Alexander Martin to General Sumner, October 13, 1780, Southern Historical Collection, Chapel Hill, PD#3406.

33. *Ibid.*

34. *Dictionary of North Carolina Biography*, s.v. "Oroondates Davis."

35. Thomas Jefferson to NC Board of War, Richmond, September 23, 1780. National Archives, M127, r72, p.109.

36. Moore, *History of North Carolina*, 295.

37. Another version reads, "Paddy Martin, a warrior of great fame." See Moore, *History of North Carolina*, 285; Robinson, *William R. Davie*, 82-83; Lefler and Newsome, *History of a Southern State*, 231-232.

38. Lefler and Newsome, *History of a Southern State*, 232.

39. *Dictionary of North Carolina Biography*, s.v. "Oroondates Davis."

40. Robinson, *William R. Davie*, 57.

41. Henderson, "How Famous Tar Heel Governor...."

42. Clark, *State Records of North Carolina*, 15:117.

43. Clark, *State Records of North Carolina*, 14:471.

44. Henderson, "How Famous Tar Heel Governor...."
45. Clark, *State Records of North Carolina*, 24:378–379.
46. *Ibid.*
47. Samuel Spencer to James Iredell, Halifax, February 15, 1781, in Higginbotham, *The Papers of James Iredell*, 2:211.
48. *Ibid.*, 218.
49. In 1992 a cannonball was uncovered in the area by employees of the Pine Hall Brick Company. The ball is property of the Rockingham County Historical Society.
50. This tradition comes through the Williams/Lowe family, which lived on the land in the 19th century (Miss Annie Williams to the author in 1991).
51. Robinson and Stoesen, *History of Guilford County*, 61.
52. *Ibid.*, 46. There are other claims that the militia was asked to take only two rounds and then they could withdraw. Clark, *State Records of North Carolina*, 21:145–150, pension application of James Martin.
53. Cheney, *North Carolina Government*, 207.
54. Russell, *North Carolina in the American Revolution*, 228.
55. *Dictionary of North Carolina Biography*, s.v. "Samuel Johnston."
56. He was originally trained as a doctor but became a lawyer because it was considered a more lucrative and respected position in the colonies.
57. Douglas, "Thomas Burke," 167–169.
58. Butler, *The Narrative of Colonel David Fanning*, 8, 9.

Chapter 7

1. Clark, *State Records of North Carolina*, 16:ix.
2. Fries, *Moravians*, 4:1695, June 5, 1781.
3. Massey, "The British Expedition to Washington," 66; Martin to Craig, September 22, 1781; Craig to Martin, September 29, 1781, PC/SA, Miscellaneous Papers, PC 21; *Royal Gazette*, October 27, 1781; Martin to Nathaniel Greene, November 17, 1781.
4. Clark, *State Records of North Carolina*, 19:869.
5. Conner, *History of North Carolina*, 187.
6. Douglas, "Thomas Burke," 26.
7. Alexander Martin to Thomas McKean, Williamsboro, October 10, 1781. National Archives M247, r86, i72, p. 127.
8. *Ibid.*, 526; Bute County was abolished in 1779 and divided into Warren and Franklin counties. The courthouse that was the home of General Sumner fell in Warren County. Corbitt, *The Formation of the North Carolina Counties*, 48; Wheeler, *Reminiscences of North Carolina*, 450.
9. Clark, *State Records of North Carolina*, 19:869.
10. Fries, *Moravians*, 4:1782.
11. Moore, *History of North Carolina*, 335.
12. Ashe, *History of North Carolina*, 703.
13. Morgan and Schmidt, *North Carolinians in the Continental Congress*, 109.
14. Marshall to Count Henry XXVIII of Reuss, March 7, 1782; Fries, *Moravians*, 4:1914.
15. The committee set up by the assembly was Colonel Joseph Taylor of Granville, Colonel Michael Rogers of Wake and Colonel William Sheppard of Surry, all of the Senate, and Samuel Cummins of Surry for the House. The Moravians were represented by "the leading men of the town." Fries, *Moravians*, 4:1705.
16. *Ibid.*
17. Clark, *State Records of North Carolina*, 22:211–212.
18. Massey, "The British Expedition to Washington," 408.
19. Crow, *Liberty Men and Loyalists*, 173.
20. Clark, *State Records of North Carolina*, 19:871.
21. Crow, *Liberty Men and Loyalists*, 171.
22. Butler, *The Narrative of Col. David Fanning*, 61–62.
23. Allen Jones to General Nathaniel Greene, December 28, 1781, William R. Davie Private Collection, State Archives, Division of Archives and History, Raleigh.
24. Conner, *A Documentary History of the University*, 1:493.
25. Pension applications, Pleasant Henderson, September 12, 1832, file S1912, National Archives, Washington.
26. In 1777 he was part of the survey party, which extended the North Carolina–Virginia line to the Tennessee River. He had fought against Tories in western Carolina and was a major under the Frenchman, Colonel Malmedy, at Guilford Courthouse and Eutaw Springs.
27. *Dictionary of North Carolina Biography*, s.v. "Pleasant Henderson."
28. Fries, *Moravians*, 4:1788.
29. Wheeler, *Reminiscences of North Carolina*, 325; Thomas Burke, *The Poems of Gov. Thos. Burke of NC* (private printing), 10.
30. Clark, *State Records of North Carolina*, 16:493–495; Clark, *State Records of North Carolina*, 16:529–530.
31. Martin to Robert Livingston, June 24, 1782, Clark, *State Records of North Carolina*, 16:342.
32. Graham, "Revolutionary History of North Carolina," 5.
33. Burke to Lillington, February 3, 1782, Clark, *State Records of North Carolina*, 16:181.
34. Davie to Burke, February 23, 1782, William R. Davie Private Collection, State Archives, Department of Archives and History, Raleigh; Robinson, *William R. Davie*, 129.
35. Robinson, *William R. Davie*, 128.
36. Clark, *State Records of North Carolina*, 24:391–392.
37. Robinson, *William R. Davie*, 130.
38. Governor Burke to Davie, February 22, 1782, William R. Davie Private Collection, State Archives, Department of Archives and History, Raleigh.
39. Ashe, *History of North Carolina*, 1:713.
40. Moore, *History of North Carolina*, 342.
41. Douglas, "Thomas Burke," 168–169.

Chapter 8

1. Clark, *State Records of North Carolina*, 19:iii.
2. Clark, *State Records of North Carolina*, 19:28.

3. Clark, *State Records of North Carolina*, 16:295–298.
4. Ekirch, *Whig Authority and Public Order*, 112, 117.
5. Malone, *Jefferson the Virginian*, 360–361.
6. Conner, *North Carolina Rebuilding*, 1:374.
7. Gilpatrick, *Jeffersonian Democracy*, 20–21.
8. Richard Caswell to Richard Caswell, Jr., May 4, 1783, Clark, *State Records of North Carolina*, 16:958.
9. Battle, "The Life and Services of Brigadier General Jethro Sumner," 131.
10. Clark, *State Records of North Carolina*, 24:263–264.
11. Thomas M. Devine, *The Tobacco Lords: A Study of the Tobacco Merchants of Glasgow and Their Trading Activities, c. 1740–1790* (Edinburgh: Donald, 1975), 14.
12. The governor was authorized to appoint a private secretary who was to make fair copies of all public correspondence and to receive a salary of £200 plus fees for such services as testimonials, commissions and grant sealing.
13. In 1756, the title to the original Wachovia Tract was vested in James Hutton, a London bookseller, because the Moravian church was not incorporated. Based on the same legal concern, title to 20 individual tracts sold to the Moravians by Granville's surveyor, William Churton, was vested in Charles Metcalf, a wealthy English Moravian. In 1773, Metcalf had sent deeds to his tracts to Marshall as *Oeconomus*, or superintendent of temporal affairs for the Brethren, along with a Power of Attorney allowing the sale of the land. It was under terms of the Confiscation Act that individuals claimed that Hutton and Metcalf, as Englishmen who did not appear to reclaim their title after October 1, 1778, had forfeited their land to confiscation. It was in this manner that a lame drummer was able to enter a claim on Salem itself; a militia officer claimed the mill, and an entry taker claimed the mills at Bethania and Bethabara. Fries, *Moravians*, 3:1206.
14. Fries, *Moravians*, 4:1794, 1797, 1824.
15. John Williams and Samuel Spencer acted as judges in this case. Moore, *History of North Carolina*, 348–349.
16. Higginbotham, *The Papers of James Iredell*, 2:346.
17. Each county had a senator and two members of the Commons and each borough had a member of Commons.
18. Gilpatrick, *Jeffersonian Democracy*, 19.
19. Malone, *Jefferson the Virginian*, 178.
20. Undated advice of Thomas Burke to the North Carolina assembly. Private collection of the late Raeford Cates, Reidsville, NC.
21. Clark, *State Records of North Carolina*, 16:707.
22. Ibid., 711–712.
23. Moore, *History of North Carolina*, 351.
24. Higginbotham, *The Papers of James Iredell*, 2:392–393.
25. Iredell may have authored this disdainful name for Martin's home on the Dan River. Easterners demonstrating the derision they held for people of the frontier frequently used it. In later years Martin gave the name to part of his lands, turning the joke on those who had sought to discredit. *Ibid.*, 2:388.

26. Martin arrived at Hillsborough on April 12, 1783.
27. Ashe, *History of North Carolina*, 1:723.
28. Risjord, *Chesapeake Politics*, 126–129.
29. A person was eligible to serve as governor three years out of every six years. Clark, *State Records of North Carolina*, 23:981.
30. Conner, *History of North Carolina*, 425.
31. Clark, *State Records of North Carolina*, 16:534.
32. Clark, *State Records of North Carolina*, 16:935.
33. Conner, *History of North Carolina*, 425.
34. *Ibid.*
35. Clark, *State Records of North Carolina*, 19:284–285.
36. Clark, *State Records of North Carolina*, 19:170.
37. Risjord, *Chesapeake Politics*, 90–91.
38. Robinson, *William R. Davie*, 125.
39. Risjord, *Chesapeake Politics*, 91–92.
40. Each one pound of the new money was equal to half of a Spanish milled dollar.
41. The description read, "beginning in the Virginia line whence Cumberland river intersects the same, thence south fifty miles, thence west to the Tennessee river, thence down the Tennessee to the Virginia line, thence with the said Virginia line to the beginning." Clark, *State Records of North Carolina*, 24:483.
42. Arnow, *Seedtime on the Cumberland*, 309.
43. Noncommissioned officers were allotted 1,000 acres, captains 3,800, colonels 7,200, and brigadier generals 12,000.
44. At least one source of questionable scholarship, Lucy Henderson Horton in her book *Wasted Talents*, quoting a Miss Josephine Robertson, says that "there were in the garret at 'Belmont,' home of her great-grandfather, General Joseph Martin, in Henry County, Virginia, letters from Governor Alexander Martin, which proved they were related. ... These letters were, however, lost in the fire."
45. Gerson, *Franklin*, 6.
46. The governor's brother, Robert Martin, living at the time in Rowan County, was clerk of the Salisbury District Court from September 15, 1782, until March 1788. Salisbury District Court Minutes.
47. Alexander Martin to R. R. Livingston, June 24, 1782, National Archives, m247, r99, i78, v.16, p. 295.
48. Livermore, *Early American Land Companies*, 90.
49. Clark, *State Records of North Carolina*, 24:530.
50. *Dictionary of North Carolina Biography*, s.v. "Samuel Henderson."
51. Keith, *The John Gray Blount Papers*, 1:28–29.
52. William Blount and Hugh Williamson to Governor Martin, October 22, 1782, Clark, *State Records of North Carolina*, 16:434–441; Risjord, *Chesapeake Politics*, 225.
53. Clark, *State Records of North Carolina*, 16:780.
54. Gerson, *Franklin*, 17.
55. Clark, *State Records of North Carolina*, 24:478–482.
56. Risjord, *Chesapeake Politics*, 223–224.
57. Alexander Martin to delegates in Congress, Guilford, January 28, 1783, Clark, *State Records of North Carolina*, 24:723.
58. This is the earliest letter that Martin addresses from "Danbury." Governor Martin to John Sevier,

February 11, 1784, Clark, *State Records of North Carolina*, 17:14–15.

59. *Ibid.*; Ramsey, *Annals of Tennessee*, 270.

60. Clark, *State Records of North Carolina*, 17:14–15.

61. Clark, *State Records of North Carolina*, 17:69.

62. Col. Joseph Martin to Governor Martin, September 2, 1784, Clark, *State Records of North Carolina*, 17:85.

63. The Creek had already put themselves under the protection of the Spanish and other tribes may have done the same. Clark, *State Records of North Carolina*, 17:91–92.

64. Ramsey, *Annals of Tennessee*, 270.

65. Higginbotham, *The Papers of James Iredell*, 434–435; Clark, *State Records of North Carolina*, 16:836–837.

66. Morgan and Schmidt, *North Carolina in the Continental Congress*, 107.

67. Higginbotham, *The Papers of James Iredell*, 434–435; Clark, *State Records of North Carolina*, 16:836–837.

68. Morgan and Schmidt, *North Carolina in the Continental Congress*, 107.

69. *Ibid.*, 109.

70. Clark, *State Records of North Carolina*, 16:434–441.

71. The 4th of July observance is now an enactment each year at Salem and it is a proud first for the state. See http://wkar.org/radio/hilites/2002-07/fourthofjuly.php.

Chapter 9

1. Clark, *State Records of North Carolina*, 14:Appendix.

2. Fries, *Moravians*, 5:2014.

3. Moore, *History of North Carolina*, 359.

4. Risjord, *Chesapeake Politics*, 95.

5. Clark, *State Records of North Carolina*, 19:Prefatory notes.

6. In his message to the assembly on April 20, 1784, praising General Washington on his retirement, Martin said, "the powers delegated to Congress by the Confederation must be exercised, and supported in the several States in their fullest extent, to give life and vigor to the American Union: Otherwise they will become disjointed, feeble and inadequate to bring to a point the federal Government." Clark, *State Records of North Carolina*, 16:36.

7. The North Carolina Society of the Cincinnati was founded October 25, 1783, at Hillsborough in the James Hogg house in response to a national call for each state to create a branch of a national organization. Davis, *Revolution's Godchild*, 3–9.

8. There is no manuscript list of these first honorary members. *Ibid.*, 21–22.

9. At the same organizational meeting at which Martin was voted an honorary membership the Society did not offer to Robert Howe, a major general and the state's highest active officer, the position of first president of the organization. There is no official explanation but there is speculation that their decision was due to his court-martial, from which he too was fully exonerated, and from his disreputable family life, indications of the degree to which the Cincinnati could make harsh, unyielding judgments.

10. Ashe, *History of North Carolina*, 2:28–29.

11. Cheney, *North Carolina Government*, 160.

12. Richard Caswell to Brigadier General Caswell, Clark, *State Records of North Carolina*, 17:138.

13. Clark, *State Records of North Carolina*, 16:36.

14. *Ibid.*

15. Ashe, *History of North Carolina*, 2:29.

16. The first of the institutions of higher learning chartered under the constitution of 1777 was Liberty Hall, which was Queen's College reborn. There followed Science Hall in Hillsborough in 1779, Morgan Academy in Burke County in 1783, and then, the same year, the first charter for a learning institution west of the Alleghenies was to be called Martin Academy, named for Governor Alexander Martin. Henderson, *The Campus of the First State University*, 5–6; Conner, *A Documentary History of the University of North Carolina*, 2:8; Clark, *State Records of North Carolina*, 24:536.

17. At the same time he introduced a bill to establish another academy at Salisbury to be called Liberty Hall after the academy in Mecklenburg, which was failing.

18. Henderson, *The Campus of the First State University*, 6.

19. Alexander Martin to Williamson, Spaight, delegates to Congress, Hillsborough, June 4, 1784. Clark, *State Records of North Carolina*, 17:78–79.

20. Ashe, *History of North Carolina*, 2:33.

21. Masterson, *William Blount*, 87.

22. Clark, *State Records of North Carolina*, 17:78–79.

23. Morgan and Schmidt, *North Carolinians in the Continental Congress*, 79.

24. Clark, *State Records of North Carolina*, 17:78–79.

25. Clark, *State Records of North Carolina*, 16:733.

26. Clark, *State Records of North Carolina*, 16:889.

27. Clark, *State Records of North Carolina*, 24:561–563.

28. The representatives were Joseph Martin, Samuel Mear, William Cocke, and James Robertson in the Senate and Ephraim McLaine, Elijah Robertson, William Cage, David Looney, Landon Carter, Charles Robertson, and Abraham Bledsoe in the Commons.

29. Clark, *State Records of North Carolina*, 17:601–603.

30. Clark, *State Records of North Carolina*, 17:446.

31. Ramsey, *Annals of Tennessee*, 286.

32. *Ibid.*, 288.

33. Williamson to Governor Martin, Edenton, July 5, 1784. Clark, *State Records of North Carolina*, 17:80–81.

34. Ramsey, *Annals of Tennessee*, 284.

35. Masterson, *William Blount*, 81.

36. Keith, *The Papers of John Gray Blount*, 1:124–125.

37. Masterson, *William Blount*, 77.

38. *Ibid.*, 69.

39. The 1782 law allotted land to each military rank as payment for service in the Continental Line for the entire 84 months of the war. The rank of lieutenant colonel commandant and colonel was given 7,200 acres each. A year later the law was modified to allow prorated amounts of land for service of at least two years.

40. Pruitt, *Glasgow Land Fraud Papers*, 3, preface; *Dictionary of North Carolina Biography*, s.v. "James Glasgow."
41. Carl S. Driver, *John Sevier: Pioneer of the Old Southwest* (Chapel Hill: University of North Carolina Press, 1932), 66. Governor Martin to the Cherokee Treaty Commissioners, September 20, 1782. Clark, *State Records of North Carolina*, 16:710–711.
42. Masterson, *William Blount*, 84.
43. *Ibid.*, 85.
44. Robinson, *William R. Davie*, 83.
45. Vote was 52 to 43 in favor. *Ibid.*, 170.
46. It is typical of some of the puffing of Davie's reputation in subsequent years by members of his family, that his son, Allen Jones, on July 25, 1826, writing to Judge Archibald Henderson made the claim that his father "also drew the Bill and promoted the secession of Tennessee, a measure then thought of a doubtful policy." Clark, *State Records of North Carolina*, 19:998–999; Philbrick, *The Rise of the West*, 120.
47. The October session of the assembly was the beginning of the shift to the winter meeting of the assembly and it had required another election.
48. Clark, *State Records of North Carolina*, 18:176.
49. Clark, *State Records of North Carolina*, 19:551–552.
50. Ashe, *History of North Carolina*, 2:37.
51. Lefler and Newsome, *History of a Southern State*, 259.
52. Clark, *State Records of North Carolina*, 18:77.
53. Robinson, *William R. Davie*, 171.
54. Ramsey, *Annals of Tennessee*, 290–291.
55. Governor Martin to the president of Congress, November 1784, Governor's Letter Book, Richard Caswell, 1785–1787, 6–7, State Department of Cultural Resources, Division of Archives and History, Raleigh.
56. Clark, *State Records of North Carolina*, 17:186.
57. Masterson, *William Blount*, 94.
58. Ramsey, *Annals of Tennessee*, 109.
59. Ashe, *History of North Carolina*, 2:37.
60. Ramsey, *Annals of Tennessee*, 304–305.
61. Long Island on the Holston River.
62. Ramsey, *The Annals of Tennessee*, 304-305.
63. Keith, *The Papers of John Gray Blount*, 1:185.
64. Ramsey, *Annals of Tennessee*, 304–305.
65. In 1782, Samuel Henderson wrote his friend and sometime employer, John Gray Blount, a pathetic letter describing the distress he had experienced economically in Kentucky. He was back in Guilford County at that time and hoped to make some kind of economic recovery. Keith, *The John Gray Blount Papers*, 1:28–29.
66. Instructions dated December 19, 1784. Yates, "The Public career of Alexander Martin," 46. Archibald Henderson, *North Carolina: The Old North State and New*, 5 vols. (Chicago: The Lewis Publishing Company, 1941), 1:388.
67. The white settlers who were attempting to justify Hubbard's actions were protecting this murderer. Ramsey, *Annals of Tennessee*, 303–305.
68. *Ibid.*, 306–307, 307–308. Henderson's younger brother, Pleasant, had been Martin's secretary.
69. Sevier also says that he received the letter by Major Henderson on February 27. Clark, *State Records of North Carolina*, 18:623.
70. Ashe, *History of North Carolina*, 2:38.
71. Masterson, *William Blount*, 96–97.
72. Ramsey, *Annals of Tennessee*, 309–313.
73. Clark, *State Records of North Carolina*, 18:435.
74. Alderman, *The Overmountain Men*, 198.
75. Ramsey, *Annals of Tennessee*, 309–313.
76. Ashe, *History of North Carolina*, 2:40; "The State of Franklin," *The North Carolina Booklet* 14/1 (July 1914): 36.
77. The session was also to debate the unrelated issue, referred to it by the Congress, of foreign credit. Ramsey, *Annals of Tennessee*, 313.
78. Alderman, *The Overmountain Men*, 201.
79. Williamson was sending messages, addressed to the governor, to Caswell, as delays in writing to Martin might "be fatal to the design." Hugh Williamson to Richard Caswell, March 28, 1785.
80. Walter Clark says that his term ended June 3. Clark, *State Records of North Carolina*, 17:368.
81. Cheney, *North Carolina Government*, 160.

Chapter 10

1. Governor Sevier to Governor Caswell, May 14, 1785. Ramsey, *Annals of Tennessee*, 314–316; Ashe, *History of North Carolina*, 2:42.
2. Ramsey, *Annals of Tennessee*, 317; Clark, *State Records of North Carolina*, 18:472.
3. Robert Martin Douglas, Martin's great nephew, 100 years later in a speech at Guilford Courthouse made the statement that Caswell was "personally antagonistic to Governor Martin." Speech delivered at the annual celebration of the Battle of Guilford Courthouse, July 4, 1898.
4. Masterson, *William Blount*, 98.
5. At this moment there was no Speaker of the Senate since Caswell had to surrender that office when he became governor and the assembly was not in session to elect his successor.
6. Masterson, *William Blount*, 97–98.
7. Thomas Searcy was the son of Reuben Searcy and Thomas Henderson's sister, Susan Henderson. He married Ann Martin, daughter of Col. James Henderson, and thus the governor's niece. Their daughter married Nathaniel Henderson, son of Thomas and Anna Jane Martin Henderson.
8. Commissioners chosen were William Dent, Ralph Gorrell, Richard Lindsey, John Hamilton, William Dick, and Barzella Gardner. Robinson, *History of Guilford County*, 64.
9. *Ibid.*, 63.
10. Martin and Nathaniel Williams gave bond for Henderson and Martin; Henderson and James Gallaway gave bond for Tate. Rockingham County Court Minutes.
11. In 1806, the Guilford County court minutes listed values of taxable property in Martinville. Although listed only as "Alexander Martin lot," the value of £275 was exceeded by only three other properties and indicated that there were significant improvements. *Ibid.*, 66.
12. Clark, *State Records of North Carolina*, 20:3.
13. Ashe, *History of North Carolina*, 2:43.
14. Risjord, *Chesapeake Politics*, 184–187.
15. *Religion and Public Spirit*. A valedictory address

to the senior class, delivered in Nassau Hall, September 21, 1760 (Philadelphia, 1761), 6–7.

16. Clark, *State Records of North Carolina*, 13:897.

17. Clark, *State Records of North Carolina*, 17:35.

18. Yates, "The Public Career of Alexander Martin," 39.

19. James Parke Farley died in May 1777 and his father died in 1778. James left a wife, Elizabeth Hill Byrd Farley, and four daughters.

20. Meade, *Old Churches, Ministers and Families of Virginia*, 318–320.

21. Rockingham County Court Minutes, August term, 1786.

22. Peculiarly, the first few pages of the first book of Rockingham County deeds are missing and may have been taken from the book during this long litigation. The first page left in the book is part of a Farley estate action. Rockingham County Deed Book, A.

23. September 1783, Benjamin Goin to Elizabeth Strong, Guilford County Deed Book C, p. 24.

24. Detailed notes provided to the author in 2001 by Francie Lane. The known children were William Strong, born ca. 1769; James Strong, born ca. 1770; John Strong, born ca. 1772; Thomas Strong, Jr., born 1774; and Samuel Strong, born ca. 1776.

25. It is known that Joseph Martin, the Crowley brothers, and the Strong brothers were "Long Hunters." *Virginia Historical Magazine*, VIII, 347-359; the small cluster of neighbors surrounding Thomas Strong in the Sandy River area were James and John Strong, his brothers; Benjamin Crowley, his brother-in-law; and Joseph Martin, later known as General Joseph Martin of Henry County, Virginia, who in 1769, was living in the home of John Strong.

26. Had there been proof of death of Thomas Strong, there should have been a record that the court had placed his orphans under court-supervised guardianship, bound out, etc. No such record has been found.

27. It is possible that seven years, or some specified time required after a person had been presumed dead, had elapsed, allowing Elizabeth to buy property in her own right even though there was no proof she was indeed a widow.

28. There are many circumstances under which they may have casually met. One interesting possibility might have been through two of Martin's bodyguards at the aborted meeting of the assembly at Salem in 1781, Abner and Gideon Johnson, Jr. Gideon married the daughter of Baker DeGraffenreidt.

29. Neither Elizabeth nor her brother-in-law, John Strong, could sign their name. August 30, 1787, Rockingham County Deed Book B, p. 212; February 23, 1788, Rockingham County Deed Book B, p. 28.

30. The original commission was Willie Jones; his brother-in-law, Henry Montfort; and Benjamin McCulloch. Jones resigned and had been replaced by John Macon. Each man was serving in the legislature at the time of his appointment.

31. Robinson, *William R. Davie*, 174–175.

32. Ashe, *History of North Carolina*, 2:50.

33. He was elected to Congress on December 16, 1786, along with John Ashe, Timothy Bloodworth, Benjamin Hawkins, Thomas Polk, and James White. Congress was in session between November 6, 1786, and October 30, 1787, in New York. There is no record of his attendance and he resigned the appointment on November 27, 1787.

Chapter 11

1. William Grayson to James Madison, May 28, 1786. William T. Hutchinson and William M.E. Rachal, editors, *Papers of James Madison* (Chicago: University of Chicago Press, 1960), 9:64; Rakove, *Beginnings of National Politics*, 373.

2. January 6, 1787.

3. Clark, *State Records of North Carolina*, 18:462.

4. Lycom, "Alexander Hamilton," 444.

5. William Blount to Richard Caswell, July 19, 1787. Keith, *The Papers of John Gray Blount*, 1:321–323.

6. Mee, Jr., *Genius of the People*, 148.

7. Alexander Martin to Governor Caswell, July 27, 1787. Clark, *State Records of North Carolina*, 20:753.

8. Although elected in December 1786 along with James White, John B. Ashe, Timothy Bloodworth, Benjamin Hawkins, and Thomas Polk, he never took his seat but did not resign the seat until October 1787, after the convention and after he had returned to North Carolina.

9. Governor Caswell to the Honorable Alexander Martin, Kinston, April 11, 1787. Clark, *State Records of North Carolina*, 20:666–667.

10. Robinson, *William R. Davie*, 179.

11. Clark, *State Records of North Carolina*, 20:666–667.

12. Masterson, *William Blount*, 125.

13. Martin owned what was certainly a fine carriage for the frontier but it may have been only ordinary in Philadelphia. Prince had been his personal servant since the Revolution and would be with him until his death, at which time Prince would be freed.

14. Tinling, *Correspondence of the Three William*, 2:834.

15. McLachlan, *Princetonians*, 118–124, 154–160, 243–244, 394–395.

16. Grayson to Madison, May 28, 1786. Hutchinson, *Papers of James Madison*, 9:64.

17. Carl Van Doren, *The Great Rehearsal*, 19; after two days Madison moved to a boarding house a block away at Fifth and Market run by Mrs. Mary House. Moore, *The Madisons*, 60.

18. Ibid., 19; Edmund Randolph lodged at Mrs. Mary House's boarding house along with Madison. Reardon, *Edmund Randolph*, 96–97.

19. Robert Hendrickson, *Hamilton I (1757-1789)*, New York: Mason/Charter, 1976), 456.

20. Mee, *Genius of the People*, 61.

21. Rakove, *Beginnings of National Politics*, 393–394.

22. Monroe to John Sullivan, August 16, 1786. Edmund C. Burnett, editor, *Letters to Members of the Continental Congress*, 7 vols. (Washington, D.C., 1921), 1:206; Rakove, *Beginnings of National Politics*, 372.

23. Ibid., 378–380.

24. Bowen, *Miracle at Philadelphia*, 20.

25. Major Reading Blount, brother of William Blount, Lt. Colonel William Polk, and Major Robert Ferrer were the elected representatives of the society from North Carolina. Martin, Davie, Spaight, and William Blount were all members of the society.

26. Mee, *Genius of the People*, 44.

27. Alexander Martin to Governor Caswell, August 20, 1787. Clark, *State Records of North Carolina*, 20:763–764.
28. Mee, *Genius of the People*, 62.
29. Their brother-in-law, Samuel Blair, had also been at the College of New Jersey with Martin.
30. He shared with Martin the bitterness of being subject to a court-martial in spite of a total acquittal.
31. Wills, *Cincinnatus*, 162.
32. *Federalist Papers*, 40; Wills, *Cincinnatus*, 161.
33. Rakove, *Beginnings of National Politics*, 395.
34. Bowen, *Miracle at Philadelphia*, 55.
35. Rossiter, *1787: The Grand Convention*, 128, 141.
36. He had nearly 40 slaves at "Danbury." Rossiter, *1787: The Grand Convention*, 143.
37. Mee, *Genius of the People*, 148.
38. That reality did not come until tabulation of the 1790 census.
39. Mee, *Genius of the People*, 144, 148.
40. Ibid., 156.
41. Craige, *The Federal Convention of 1787*, 85.
42. Bowen, *Miracle at Philadelphia*, 23.
43. McLachlan, *Princetonians*, 122.
44. Bowden, *Miracle at Philadelphia*, 19.
45. Constitution, Article 1, Section 6, Clause 2.
46. William Pierce found "that he never speaks without tiring the patience of all who hear him." Van Doren, *The Great Rehearsal*, 53; Mee, *Genius of the People*, 188.
47. McLachlan, *Princetonians*, 579–585.
48. Rossiter, *1787: The Grand Convention*, 181.
49. Collier and Lincoln, *Decision in Philadelphia*, 214–215.
50. Collier says Cutler arrived July 11 and Van Doren has his arrival on July 12. Van Doren, *Great Decision*, 128; Collier and Lincoln, *Decision at Philadelphia*, 215.
51. McClellan and Bradford, *Jonathan Elliot's*, 2: 266.
52. Bartram was a world famous botanist and author of *Travels in the Carolinas*, a search for botanical specimens.
53. Craige has suggested that the subject of speculation consumed all these particular delegates. "What dreams of speculation and empire building this breakfast company must have had!" Craige, *The Federal Convention of 1787*, 151.
54. Ibid., 285.
55. Recognizing an immediate need, the Negro had called for a barber to dress the Reverend's hair. Bowen, *Miracle at Philadelphia*, 181.
56. Collier and Lincoln, *Decision in Philadelphia*, 222.
57. Alexander Martin to Governor Caswell, July 27, 1787. Clark, *State Records of North Carolina*, 20:753–754.
58. Fries, *Moravians*, 5:2119, 2173.
59. Collier and Lincoln, *Decision in Philadelphia*, 214.
60. Bowen, *Miracle at Philadelphia*, 27.
61. McRee, *James Iredell*, 2:161.
62. Alexander Martin to Governor Caswell, August 20, 1787. Clark, *State Records of North Carolina*, 20:763–764.
63. Hugh Williamson to Governor Caswell, August 20, 1787. Ibid.

Chapter 12

1. Rakove, *Beginnings of National Politics*, 398.
2. Rockingham County Deed Book B, p. 212.
3. The 1790 census of Rockingham County lists no separate household for Elizabeth Strong. In the household of Governor Martin is found one child under 16, which had to be Alexander Strong, and three adult women, two of whom had to be Jane Hunter Martin and Elizabeth.
4. Fries, *Moravians*, 5:2173.
5. Ibid., 5:2190.
6. As political opinions began to coalesce into common factions, associations, and eventually into parties, terminology that adequately identified the political leanings of individuals was very difficult. Opinions over the ratification of the Constitution did provide a clear division on a domestic issue fundamental to the form of government; these two sides easily became the Federalists who supported ratification and the anti-Federalists who were in opposition. Beyond the issue of ratification, however, this simplistic labeling cannot be sustained.
7. Fries, *Moravians*, 5:2174.
8. Remini, *Andrew Jackson*, 431ff.
9. Clark, *State Records of North Carolina*, 20:313.
10. The ruling concerned the limit on speakers to two comments on a single issue.
11. Clark, *State Records of North Carolina*, 20:371.
12. Ibid., 372.
13. Lefler and Newsome, *History of a Southern State*, 265.
14. Masterson, *William Blount*, 137–138.
15. Cheney, *North Carolina Government*, 813.
16. Robinson, *William R. Davie*, 191.
17. Two days before his election as governor, he was chosen Grand Master of the North Carolina Masons. *Dictionary of North Carolina Biography*, s.v. "Samuel Johnston."
18. Masterson, *William Blount*, 140.
19. Fischer, *Albion's Seed, Four*, 830.
20. Gilpatrick, *Jeffersonian Democracy*, 30–31.
21. The Buffalo Presbyterian Church was located in Guilford County about 25 miles south of "Danbury" and the same distance east of the Moravians at Salem.
22. In his will Martin specifies a gift of his copy of the Jewish Historian Josephus and Chamber's *Encyclopedia and Supplements*, to Caldwell, and Caldwell, in his will, devises these same books as a treasured gift of the governor. (See Will of Alexander Martin.)
23. James repeats the local tradition that, while at Martinville, Jackson "organized the first known celebration of the anniversary of the Battle of Guilford Court House, with speeches, horse-races and a cockfight." Miss Katherine Hoskins, of Summerfield, North Carolina, a student of local history, to the writer, September 23, 1931. James, *Andrew Jackson*, 40–41, footnote; Remini, *Andrew Jackson*, 34.
24. Jackson arrived at the McNairy house in November 1787. Hoskins, "Jackson's Stay in Guilford."
25. In the next legislative session, after Martin had again become governor, McNairy and Jackson petitioned for an increase in compensation; Clark, *State Records of North Carolina*, 21:637, 696.
26. Masterson, *William Blount*, 143.

27. Robinson, *William R. Davie*, 194.
28. Rossiter, *1787: The Grand Convention*, 297ff.
29. Masterson, *William Blount*, 146.
30. Robinson, *William R. Davie*, 201.
31. *Ibid.*, 205.
32. *The Debate on the Constitution*, 2:908.
33. Fries, *Moravians*, 5:2223.
34. William Gowdy and John Hamilton.
35. Clark, *State Records of North Carolina*, 20:481–483.
36. Clark, *State Records of North Carolina*, 20:494.
37. Masterson, *William Blount*, 149.
38. *Ibid.*, 150–151.
39. The act specifically exempted Sevier from the pardon, placing him as a fugitive and leaving all his acts as "Governor" of Franklin, in the realm of treason. Clark, *State Records of North Carolina*, 20:503, 554.
40. Masterson, *William Blount*, 152.
41. Keith, *The Papers of John Gray Blount*, 1:438–440.
42. Masterson, *William Blount*, 154.
43. Clark, *State Records of North Carolina*, 20:593.
44. Walker, "The Gallaways of Rose Hill," 22–46.
45. Clark, *State Records of North Carolina*, 20:541–542.
46. Clark, *State Records of North Carolina*, 24:953–954.
47. Clerk of Court Thomas Searcy noted that Guilford County had appointed Patrick Haley as a collector of public taxes for the year 1785 and took no surety.
48. Clark, *State Records of North Carolina*, 20:429, 446, 449.

Chapter 13

1. Moore, *History of North Carolina*, 391.
2. Lefler and Newsome, *History of a Southern State*, 269–270.
3. Robinson, *William R. Davie*, 214.
4. McDonald, *E Pluribus Unum*, 268.
5. Judge J. F. Grimke to General Harrington, Charleston, July 16, 1789. Clark, *State Records of North Carolina*, 21:522.
6. Robert himself fathered two "natural children" who were later recognized matter-of-factly in Alexander Martin's will.
7. Elizabeth Strong's grandmother, Ruth Champe, widow of Henry Baker, married William Gunn.
8. John Odeneal was married to the governor's cousin, Sarah Tate, daughter of Joseph Tate and Elly Hunter.
9. This may explain calling the mother, Elizabeth Gunn. Someone knew her grandmother's name was Gunn and was not really sure what name she went by.
10. Fries, *Moravians*, 5:2271.
11. Moore, *History of North Carolina*, 393; *Dictionary of North Carolina Biography*, s.v. "Richard Caswell."
12. Clark, *State Records of North Carolina*, 21:590.
13. Clark, *State Records of North Carolina*, 22:48–49.
14. Clark, *State Records of North Carolina*, 21:253, 614.
15. McDonald, *E Pluribus Unum*, 269; the term "Redneck" was slang for Presbyterian, Fischer, *Albion's Seed*.
16. Clark, *State Records of North Carolina*, 21:617.
17. Clark, *State Records of North Carolina*, 21:320, 661.
18. Cheney, Jr., *North Carolina Government*, 813.
19. Clark, *State Records of North Carolina*, 21:660, 661.
20. Clark, *State Records of North Carolina*, 21:689.
21. Clark, *State Records of North Carolina*, 21:522–524.
22. Clark, *State Records of North Carolina*, 21:v.
23. Clark, *State Records of North Carolina*, 21:720.
24. Conner, *A Documentary History of the University of North Carolina*, I:23.
25. *Ibid.*, 45.
26. The land adjoined acreage owned by Martin Armstrong and Griffith Rutherford. *Ibid.*, 51.
27. *Ibid.*, 55.
28. He was not a member of a Blue Lodge. He was appointed Grand Pursuivant in 1804 and Junior Deacon in 1806. Speidel, *North Carolina Masons*, 66.
29. Macay was also the lawyer who trained many in the profession including Andrew Jackson.
30. Cheney, Jr., *North Carolina Government*, 164.
31. Clark, *State Records of North Carolina*, 21:426–429.

Chapter 14

1. Wagstaff, *The Papers of John Steele*, 1:71.
2. Fries, *Moravians*, 2025, 2028.
3. *Dictionary of North Carolina Biography*, s.v. "James Martin."
4. McBride, "Claims of British Merchants," 147.
5. She did not marry until after her grandmother died in 1807. It is possible that she was at least 16 in 1790 and was the other woman above that age living at "Danbury."
6. The 1790 census lists Thomas Henderson with 14 slaves.
7. Flexner, *George Washington*, 3:239–243.
8. Gilpatrick, *Jeffersonian Democracy*, 42.
9. *Ibid.*
10. Flexner, *George Washington*, 3:242.
11. The amendment fell on deaf ears when it reached Congress. Clark, *State Records of North Carolina*, 22:51–52.
12. Henderson, *Hamilton II*, 27.
13. Stewart, *The Opposition Press*, 57. In 1788, Robert Martin, at the end of his service as clerk of the Salisbury District Court, was doodling on the minute book and he wrote down this interesting assortment of places: Pennsylvania, Rockingham, Petersburg, Salisbury District, Amsterdam, leading to the supposition that the international speculators had already appeared on the frontier. Salisbury District Court Records, April 28, 1788.
14. *Ibid.*, 25–26.
15. Stewart, *The Opposition Press*, 274.
16. *New York Journal*, June 11, 1790.
17. *State Gazette of North Carolina*, November 26, 1790.

18. Lefler and Newsome, *History of a Southern State*, 275.

19. Two hundred years later the same debate and distrust of federal government was being voiced in precisely the same region, applied to tobacco.

20. Abernethy, *The South in the New*, 35.

21. Clark, *State Records of North Carolina*, 22:797.

22. Governor Alexander Martin to Senator Samuel Johnston, May 25, 1790. Alexander Martin, Governor's Letter Books, State Archives, Division of Archives and History, Raleigh; Governor Alexander Martin to Hugh Williamson, *Ibid.*

23. Governor Alexander Martin to John Steele, *Ibid.*

24. Clark, *State Records of North Carolina*, 22:74–575.

25. Montford Stokes of Rowan was later United States Senator (1816–1823). Wallace Alexander was the brother of Nathaniel Alexander, Governor (1805–1807).

26. Wagstaff, *The Papers of John Steele*, 1:59.

27. Moore, *History of North Carolina*, 307.

28. Clark, *State Records of North Carolina*, 16:181, 459; Henderson, *Washington's Southern Tour*, 312–313.

29. The springs lay in Rockingham County east of the border with Caswell. It was 18 miles south of the Virginia border that still was used as a line of safety for petty thieves escaping prosecution for actions in either state. It was about the same distance from the governor's home at Danbury on Jacobs Creek. About the time of this meeting of the council, Rockingham Springs had gained some attention as a modest health spa when Dr. John Coats Cox had located there and recommended the waters for their therapeutic value. Cox was a one-eyed Irishman, who, a decade earlier, while serving as a surgeon on a slave ship off the coast of West Africa, went ashore and was lost, and abandoned when his ship sailed. Having nearly died of exposure, he was taken by the natives to their city of Timbo and cared for in the house of the king. At the end of six months the natives, at his request, guided him back to the coast where miraculously he was found by his own ship on its return journey. By the time he got to Rockingham Springs he had practiced medicine in several places in Europe and in the West Indies. He introduced himself to the Moravians and they were soon sending people to him at Rockingham Springs for the cure.

John Lenox was a Scotsman, born in Dumfriesshire, who had come to Edenton before the war. He was related to the Lennox family of Woodhead that was involved, in its earlier generations, in the trade of the Scottish merchant houses. In 1790, John Lenox was visiting Rockingham Springs. His father had recently died and he had money to invest.

Peter Oneal was of Irish descent, born in Stafford, Virginia, about 1740. He had been a captain in a regiment of light infantry of the North Carolina Militia. Oneal owned the Rockingham springs and lived there with his wife, Elizabeth, and 11 children. He kept a kind of public house that could serve the family and accommodate those visiting the springs for the cure.

Brother John Jacob Ernst was the 60-year-old minister at the Moravian town of Bethabara. He had been ill for several months and fellow Moravians had advised a visit to the springs. His wife, the widowed Sister Anna Catherine Hienzmann, whom he had married four years earlier, accompanied Brother Ernst. Also in their party was Brother Peter Stoehr, who would wait on Brother Ernst and a servant, Samuel.

Thomas Henderson was there in his capacity as clerk of court along with Martin's nephew, Thomas Rogers, as private secretary to the governor. All these people were at the springs when the governor and council held their meeting in June 1790. Since there was only one place of public assembly, these guests and family had access to the meetings, many of which were probably held outside because of the otherwise cramped quarters.

30. *The Fayetteville Gazette*, September 15, 1790.

31. With the advice of the council, the debt to Martinique, which had been an unresolved claim against North Carolina since his first term as governor, "is so far put in train, I flatter myself, as will shortly be extinguished." Most financially menacing to the state, however, were the frauds against public credit practiced by the "nefarious villains" (the counterfeiters). The problem was so extreme that it might have been necessary to call in all paper currency and reissue. Nowhere did he mention the speculators in North Carolina securities and warrants accepting them as the necessary consequence of assumption.

32. Clark, *State Records of North Carolina*, 21:876–879.

33. William R. Davie to Alexander Martin, November 1, 1790. Clark, *State Records of North Carolina*, 22:800–801.

34. Conner, *A Documentary History of the University*, I:35–63.

35. Clark, *State Records of North Carolina*, 21:983; Conner, *A Documentary History of the University*, I: 88.

36. William Lenoir had been elected president pro-tem of the trustees on the 11th and thus, according to Dr. Kemp Battle's history of the university was the first president. The *Documentary History of the University*, published in 1953, points out that when Lenoir resigned on the 23rd his was a temporary office and the trustees unanimously elected as their first president, Governor Martin. Clark, *State Records of North Carolina*, 21:974–975; Conner, *A Documentary History of the University*, 1:66–67, 79.

37. *Ibid.*, 1:84.

38. They did not know that it would be nearly 25 years before the university actually realized income.

39. The 1790 census lists Taylor as agent for the family.

40. There are some key missing pages from the first deed book of Rockingham County and the initial pages remaining begin with a document concerning Sauratown that is signed by James Taylor and witnessed by John Louis Taylor. Wheeler says in his short biography of Justice John Louis Taylor, "he was deprived, at an early age, of his father, and was brought to this country by an elder brother, he enjoyed the advantages of education, and spent two years at William and Mary College in Virginia. He then came to this state, studied law, and settled at Fayetteville." Rockingham County Deed Book A, p. 15; Wheeler, *Reminiscences and Memoirs of North Carolina*, 146; Conner, *A Documentary History of North Carolina*, I:67.

41. Clark, *State Records of North Carolina*, 21:1007.
42. *Dictionary of North Carolina Biography*, s. v. "James Gallaway." In the summer of 1795, a boat arrived at Halifax from Upper Sauratown, a distance of 200 miles, captained by Jeremiah Wade. Carrying 5000 lbs., it demonstrated the commercial potential of river traffic on the Roanoke system. "The North Carolina Journal," May 11, 1795, Halifax, NC.
43. Clark, *State Records of North Carolina*, 21:961–962.

Chapter 15

1. Flexner, *George Washington*, 3:240.
2. Henderson, *Washington's Southern Tour*, 3.
3. Ibid., 7.
4. Ibid., 321.
5. Ibid., 74.
6. Within the decade (1798) the palace was burned. Some blame was directed at the St. John's Lodge No. 2 of the Masons but the accepted cause turned out to be a torch held by an old Negro woman hunting for eggs in the trash of the basement. Ibid., 93.
7. Washington had difficulty in understanding the motive of Shay's Rebellion in Massachusetts four years earlier. In another two years the Whiskey Rebellion in western Pennsylvania, rooted in the same disaffection he was hearing voiced here in North Carolina, still was beyond the rational grasp of the soldier president.
8. Washington may already have been aware that, in 1783, it was in response to the request of then-governor Alexander Martin, that the Moravians had held perhaps the first community-wide observation in the nation of July 4th as a day of thanksgiving and praise. Marilyn Gombosi, *A Day of Solemn Thanksgiving* (Chapel Hill: The University of North Carolina Press, 1977), 17–19.
9. Fries, *Moravians*, 5:2325.
10. Ibid., 5:2403–2404.
11. George Washington Visits Salem, 1791. http://www.fmoran.com/wash.html
12. Ibid.
13. Near present-day Kernersville.
14. Henderson, *Washington's Southern Tour*, 323.
15. Ibid., 421.
16. It is frequently asserted that Martin entertained Washington at his home at "Danbury" in Rockingham County. Confusing the plantation with the town of Danbury that was not established, until 1848, as a county seat in nearby Stokes County sometimes further compounds this error. First called Crawford, it was given the name Danbury by members of the James Martin family who were leaders and named it for the governor's home. Martinville was still used by the governor and it was convenient to the battlefield. Did Martin take this opportunity to introduce the president to either his mother or even to Elizabeth Strong? These women, by virtue of human nature, must have placed extreme pressure on Martin to allow them to meet the great man. There is no comment recorded. When Washington resumed his return to Virginia, he passed through Rockingham County but on a route about ten miles east of Danbury.

17. Yates, "The Public Career of Alexander Martin," 79.
18. Conner, *A Documentary History of the University of North Carolina*, 1:92–95.
19. Ibid., 1:107–109.
20. Clark, *State Records of North Carolina*, 21:876–878.
21. The British heirs of part of the Sauratown were again confirmed in their title.
22. Lefler and Newsome, *History of a Southern State*, 244.
23. Clark, *State Records of North Carolina*, 21:v.
24. McRee, *Life and Correspondence of James Iredell*, 270.
25. Conner, *A Documentary History of the University of North Carolina*, 1:92–95.
26. Battle, *Early History of Raleigh*, 99.
27. In an obituary on October 30, 1834, it is noted that he was perhaps a member of the electoral college and "he first proposed the name Raleigh." *Carolina Watchman*, November 8, 1834; *North Carolina Booklet*, 21:July 1921–April 1922, 110.
28. Conner, *A Documentary History of the University of North Carolina*, 161.
29. Ibid., 170–172.
30. Alexander Martin to Thomas Jefferson, August 24, 1791. McPherson, "Unpublished Letters."
31. Aaron Burr carried South Carolina, which would otherwise be called Anti-federalist.
32. Wagstaff, *The Papers of John Steele*, 1:xxv–xxvi.
33. Leigh was involved in an aborted attempt to establish the Episcopal Church in North Carolina. *Dictionary of North Carolina Biography*, s.v. "John Leigh."
34. Ibid., s.v. "Thomas Blount."
35. Wagstaff, *The Papers of John Steele*, 1:84–85.
36. Ibid., 1:59.
37. Ibid., 1:95–96.
38. Lycom, "Alexander Hamilton," 460; Robinson, *William R. Davie*, 284.
39. Ibid.
40. Gilpatrick, *Jeffersonian Democracy*, 56.
41. Robinson, *William R. Davie*, 284.
42. Gilpatrick, *Jeffersonian Democracy*, 57.
43. House Journal, 1792, 58.
44. Copy of a manuscript copy of his redemption bill in the possession of the author given to him by the late Raeford Cates of Reidsville.
45. Ashe, *History of North Carolina*, 1:137.

Chapter 16

1. House Journals 1792, 23; Gilpatrick, *Jeffersonian Democracy*, 30.
2. This is the more likely time at which he would have taken in his niece, his late brother Samuel's daughter, as the companion for her grandmother.
3. Her parents were James Martin of Snow Creek, brother of the governor, and Ruth Rogers, sister of the late Samuel. Thomas' mother was Martha Martin, sister of both James and Alexander.
4. Martin was fond of his Rogers nephews. The land in Stokes County had been acquired early and brother James had also ventured into the purchase of some of this land as a mineral speculation.

5. Conner, *A Documentary History of the University of North Carolina*, 1:254n.
6. Wertenbaker, *Princeton*, 109–111.
7. Powell, *Bring Out Your Dead*, 30–35.
8. *Ibid.*, 302.
9. It is not certain if this was Prince or Ben, the latter having been with him since 1774. In his will Martin make clear that Prince accompanied him to war but he is less clear on which one was in Philadelphia—possibly both at different times.
10. Remini, *Andrew Jackson*, 92.
11. Ellis, *Founding Brothers*, 16.
12. *Ibid.*, 13.
13. Gilpatrick, *Jeffersonian Democracy*, 62–63.
14. *Ibid.*, 13, 78.
15. In none of the Presidential cabinets until that of Jackson was there a North Carolinian. James Iredell comes closest to the national stage as one of Washington's appointees to the Supreme Court.
16. Williamson, *History of North Carolina*, 1:138–139.
17. *Ibid.*, 145.
18. Ellis, *Founding Brothers*, 104.
19. Senate Journal, 3rd Cong., 1st sess., December 2, 1793, National Archives, reel 6, M1251.
20. Clark, *State Records of North Carolina*, 22:961–962.
21. Annals of Congress, 3rd Cong., 1st sess., January 16, 1794, 33–34.
22. Gilpatrick, *Jeffersonian Democracy*, 66; Senator Martin to Governor Spaight, February 21, 1794, Governor's Letter Book, 11:186–187.
23. Senator Pierce Butler to James Iredell, April 3, 1794. McRee, *Life and Correspondence of James Iredell*, 2:407.
24. Annals of Congress, 4th Cong., 1st Sess., 14.
25. Senate Journal, 3rd Cong., 1st sess., March 4, 1794, National Archives, reel 6, M1251.
26. Flexner, *George Washington*, IV:162.
27. *Ibid.*, 163–164.
28. He had settled at Coffee Springs Farm in Somerset County, PA. Jackson and Twohig, *The Papers of George Washington*, The Diaries of George Washington, October 23, 1794, 6:195.
29. Although the session was scheduled to begin on the 3rd, Martin was not counted as present until the 7th and the senate did not reach quorum until November 18 with the arrival of Aaron Burr of New York. National Archives, Senate Journal 1251/128, Reel 7.
30. Caldwell had a daughter, Patsy, who is said to have had superior endowments but at about the time she came of age, she "gave evidence that reason had lost its dominion." She was born about 1773 so at this time she would have been about 21. Caldwell and Dr. Benjamin Rush had been students at Princeton together and it appears that this was the first of at least two times that Caldwell brought Patsy to Philadelphia to be treated by Dr. Rush. Carruthers, *David Caldwell*, 115; Arnett, *David Caldwell*, 25.
31. Moore, *History of North Carolina*, 137; Wheeler, *Reminiscences*, 2:249.
32. Lament, "Benjamin Rush," 452–453.
33. Ellis, *Founding Brothers*, 56.
34. Lefler and Newsome, *History of a Southern State*, 278.
35. Alexander Martin to William Lenoir, Philadelphia, February 3, 1794. Lenoir Papers, 1793–1794.
36. Risjord, *Chesapeake Politics*, 450–455.
37. Senate Journal, June 17–24, Library of Congress; Flexner, *George Washington*, 208–209.
38. Strong, *The Papers of James Madison*, 16:26.
39. Alexander Martin to Richard Dobbs Spaight, June 27, 1795. Governor's Letter Book, State Archives, Division of Archives and History, Raleigh.
40. Stewart, *The Opposition Press*, 193–194.
41. *Aurora* (Philadelphia), June 26, 1795.
42. *Argus* (New York), July 2, 1795.
43. Risjord, *Chesapeake Politics*, 456.
44. Alexander Martin to Richard Dobbs Spaight, June 27, 1795. Governor's Letter Book, State Archives, Division of Archives and History, Raleigh.
45. Fries, *Moravians*, 6:2540.
46. In 1775 James Parke Farley, his wife Elizabeth Carter Byrd, and their children had located on the Sauratown and started Bellview that would have been a Virginia plantation on the Carolina frontier. The outbreak of the Revolution brought them back to Westover and during the war James died.
47. Shippen House was built by old Dr. William Shippen and given as a wedding present to his son, Dr. William Shippen, on his marriage to Alice Lee of Stratford Hall. Their children had been raised in this house by particularly doting parents. The house stands today in Philadelphia.
48. Benjamin Rush and William Shippen had been at odds professionally during the Revolution. Although they frequently debated bitterly over treatment, Rush was the physician for the Shippen family, avoiding the concern of a physician caring for his own family. Shippen Family Papers, Thomas Lee Shippen Diary, Library of Congress.
49. Morison, *The Oxford History of the American People*, 346.
50. Ellis, *Founding Brothers*, 136.
51. Yates, "The Public Career of Alexander Martin," 89.
52. Ellis, *Founding Brothers*, 157.

Chapter 17

1. MacLachlan, *Princetonians*, 159.
2. Hawke, *Franklin*, 64.
3. From France he added La Rocheforecauld, Condorcet, Soulavie, Ingenhousz, LeRoy, LeVeillard, Cabanis, and from England, Benjamin Vaughn and Thomas Percival. Carl Van Doren, *Benjamin Franklin* (New York: Viking, 1938), 140.
4. Hendrickson, *Hamilton II*, 140.
5. Stewart, *The Opposition Press*, 12.
6. Malone, *Jefferson the Virginian*, 177–179.
7. Henderson, *Hamilton II*, 115–116.
8. *Ibid.*, 375.
9. Williamson, *The History of North Carolina*, 1:foreword.
10. Of the graduates of Princeton from 1748 to 1768, only 16 became members of the society. Of these, only three lived outside Philadelphia: the Rev. Jonathan Odell of New Jersey; Dr. David Ramsey, the doctor and historian of Charleston, South Carolina,

and Senator Alexander Martin of the Dan River in North Carolina.

11. Proceedings of the American Philosophical Society, Manuscript Minutes of Its Meetings, 1744–1838 (Philadelphia: American Philosophical Society, 1884), 252; along with John Guillemand, St. John's College in Oxford; William Bache, M.D., Philadelphia; and William Hamilton, of the Woodlands near Philadelphia.

12. Ibid., 261–262.

13. Ibid., Alexander Martin to Jonathan Williams, Esquire, January 1, 1798.

14. Ibid., 272, 278, 257. The examination of fragments from the wall was referred to Dr. Adam Seybert for study.

15. Joseph Ellis, PBS interview on *Founding Brothers*, June 2001.

16. Alexander Spotswood (1676–1740) Papers, 1710–1712, Box 24, Private Collections, State Archives, Division of Archives and History, Raleigh.

17. Battle, *History of the University of North Carolina*, 133.

18. Robert Walser, "Alexander Martin, Poet," 60.

19. Robert Martin Douglas, Address at Guilford Battleground, July 4, 1898.

20. Walser, "Alexander Martin, Poet," 56.

21. Ibid.

22. Another product of this period was an elegy "on the home-going of Br. Bagge." Traugott Bagge was the Salem storekeeper whom Martin had known for thirty years. Fries, *Moravians*, 2653–2654; Surratt, *Gottlieb Schober of Salem*, 29.

23. In fact it was a poor-quality history and only covered the period up to the end of royal rule under Governor Josiah Martin. Wagstaff, "Letters of William Barry Grove," 58.

24. Ibid., 59.

25. Adams, *The Adams Family*, 102.

26. Melton, Jr., *The First Impeachment*, 104–105

27. Senate Journal, June 1, 1797, Library of Congress.

28. Melton, *The First Impeachment*, 66.

29. Masterson, *William Blount*, 306.

30. Ibid., 317.

31. Melton, *The First Impeachment*, 106–107.

32. Masterson, *William Blount*, 313.

33. Melton, *The First Impeachment*, 107.

34. Masterson, *William Blount*, 318; Melton, *The First Impeachment*, 110.

35. Senate Journal, July 8, 1797, Library of Congress.

36. To date he is the only senator expelled from the Senate with the exception of the 14 Southern senators expelled at the beginning of the Civil War. Melton, *The First Impeachment*, 126fn.

37. Masterson, *William Blount*, 323.

38. Remini, *Andrew Jackson*, 87–91.

39. Pruitt, *Glasgow Land Fraud Papers*, ii, iii.

40. *Dictionary of North Carolina Biography*, s.v. "James Glasgow."

41. There is only secondhand proof of the authenticity of this remark as having originated with Ashe.

42. Remini, *Andrew Jackson*, 117.

43. *Dictionary of North Carolina Biography*, s.v. "James Glasgow."

44. Pruitt, *Glasgow Land Fraud Papers*, iv.

45. The term "Band of Brothers" comes from Shakespeare, *Henry V*. Martin used it in his speech, at the end of his sixth elected term as governor, when he made his most complete statement of his political philosophy (see p. 242).

46. Cartwright, *North Carolina Land Grants in Tennessee*.

47. Senate Journal, February 5, 1798; March 5, 1798; March 19, 1798, Library of Congress.

48. Senate Journal, March 1, 1798, 22 to 5, Library of Congress.

49. Senate Journal, April 12, 1798; May 23, 1798; June 7, 1798; June 14, 1798; June 19, 1798; June 20, 1798; July 7, 1798; July 10, 1798; July 11, 1798; July 13, 1798, Library of Congress.

50. Senate Journal, April 19, 1798; April 23, 1798; June 20, 1798, Library of Congress.

51. McCullough, *John Adams*, 505.

52. Morison, *Oxford History of the American People*, 353.

53. Senate Journal, July 4, 1798, Library of Congress.

54. McCullough, *John Adams*, 504–505.

55. Stewart, *The Opposition Press*, 479.

56. On June 2 he made the motion that the Senate attend the funeral of Col. Nathan Bryan, North Carolina congressman who had died of yellow fever. Senate Journal, June 2, 1798, Library of Congress.

57. Risjord, *Chesapeake Politics*, 535.

58. Robinson, *William R. Davie*, 300.

59. Gilpatrick, *Jeffersonian Democracy*, 95.

60. McRee, *Iredell*, 2:532.

61. Robinson, *William R. Davie*, 300-301; McRee, *Iredell*, 2:540.

62. Conner, *A Documentary History of the University*, 2:226–228.

63. Comment of Samuel Johnston in Robinson, *William R. Davie*, 302–303.

64. Richard Dobbs Spaight to John Haywood, June 6, 1799, Ernest Haywood Papers, Southern Historical Collection, University of North Carolina, Chapel Hill, NC.

65. Gilpatrick, *Jeffersonian Democracy*, 101.

66. Robinson, *William R. Davie*, 303.

67. Gilpatrick, *Jeffersonian Democracy*, 101.

68. Robinson, *William R. Davie*, 373–374.

69. His son added what he failed to record. Clark, *State Records of North Carolina*, 19:994, 998–999.

70. Risjord, *Chesapeake Politics*, 534–539.

71. Senate Journal, December 17, 1798, Library of Congress.

72. Melton, *The First Impeachment*, 209–232.

73. Proceedings of the American Philosophical Society, Manuscript Minutes of Its Meetings, 1744–1838, 278–279.

Chapter 18

1. Alexander Martin to George Washington, February 4, 1798; George Washington to Alexander Martin, February 22, 1798; Mt Vernon, George Washington Papers, Library of Congress; Linda Ayres, Associate Director for Collections, Mt. Vernon to Charles Rodenbough, August 3, 1999.

2. The most frequent and flagrant error in

thumbnail biographies of Alexander Martin confuses Danbury plantation with Danbury, the county seat of Stokes County, North Carolina, that about 1850 was given its name by Martin's nephews who had been involved in the division of that county. It is a giveaway to sloppy scholarship but it is even repeated in such places as the Library of Congress web page.

3. There is a line drawing of a complex of buildings executed about 1935 by a local historian, Nancy Watkins, that she records as Danbury Plantation. There is also a photograph in the Rockingham County Collection at Rockingham Community College at Wentworth that purports on the reverse to be Governor Martin's home. Butler, *Our Proud Heritage* (Bassett, VA: Bassett Printing Corp., 1971), 45.

4. The author has shards representing all these types of china found at the site of the Danbury plantation.

5. This cup has been traced in the James Martin family. It appears in the inscription to honor 1782, the year the fighting stopped and the year Alexander was first elected governor. It may be the same cup mentioned in Alexander's will—the one left to James. The other cup descended in the Henderson family.

6. Colonel Martin was Colonel James Martin, son of John Julius Martin, the youngest son of Alexander's brother, James Martin. Address of Robert M. Douglas AM, LL.D., "Upon the life and character of Governor Alexander Martin." Delivered at the Annual Celebration of the Battle of Guilford Courthouse, July 4, 1898.

7. The original was donated to Independence Hall in Philadelphia in 1983 by Dr. Thomas T. Upshur, a direct descendent of James Martin. It has frequently been copied in oils and as an engraving by Albert Rosenthal in 1902 commissioned by Mayor Ashbridge of Philadelphia and approved by James Martin, grandson of Colonel James Martin.

8. There were several portrait painters active in America during the time of Martin's Senate term including Gilbert Stuart, Charles Wilson Peale, John Trumbull, Adolph Ulric Wertmüller, Edward Savage, Matthew Pratt, John Johnston, and James Sharples. Knox, *The Sharples*, 11.

9. There is a surviving portrait of Alexander's brother, James, that has characteristics of Sharples but family tradition says it was executed by a member of the Martin family. Knox, *The Sharples*, 9; William Dunlap, *History of the Rise and Progress of Arts of Design in the United States*, 3 vols. (Boston: C. Goodspeed, 1918), 2:70-71, 101-111.

10. *Alumni History of the University of North Carolina*, 415.

11. Will of Governor Alexander Martin.

12. *Ibid.*; Rodenbough, "The Will of Alexander Martin," 34–37.

13. In the 1800 census, the person recorded as Benjamin Martin had a family whose ages and sexes appear to match those of Benjamin Harris Martin.

14. At the time of his death, North Carolina law recognized service during the Revolution as just grounds for freeing a slave but such service had to be proved to the court. Then sufficient money or land had to be provided the freed slave so that he could make his way as a free person.

15. Elizabeth's son John had a son named Alexander Martin Strong.

16. Robinson, *William R. Davie*, 304–305.

17. *Cemetery Records of Rockingham and Stokes County, North Carolina*, 24 (Wesley Chapel Cemetery); John May, Pension Application, W18476.

18. Receiving a total of only 102 votes in the district in 1803, the Federalists never again fielded a candidate in Rockingham. "North Carolina Congressional Elections 1803-10," NCHR, 10, (July 1933), 172–173.

19. James Campbell to Thomas Ruffin, July 26, 1809. Hamilton, *The Papers of Thomas Ruffin*, 2:122–124.

20. *Ibid.*

21. *Dictionary of North Carolina Biography*, s.v. "James Glasgow."

22. Pruitt, *Glasgow Land Fraud Papers*, xii.

23. *Ibid.*

24. *Ibid.*, xiii.

25. Joseph Winston Entry Book, Surry County, currently found in the State Archives.

26. By 1793 this area was in Stokes County. Rogers married his first cousin, the daughter of James Martin.

27. Salisbury District Court Records, 1804, North Carolina State Archives.

28. A partnership of James Martin, Peter Perkins, and Matthew Moore developed several of these kilns and ore was processed commercially until after the Civil War

29. *Dictionary of North Carolina Biography*, s.v. "Abraham Philips."

30. 40,000 slaves are believed to have been brought in through the port of Charleston in four years. Ashe, *History of North Carolina*, 2:194.

31. Taylor, *Slaveholding in North Carolina, An Economic View*, 28–29.

32. Ashe, *History of North Carolina*, 1:193.

33. Lefler and Newsome, *History of a Southern State*, 298–311.

34. University of North Carolina Trustee Minutes 1801–1810, 64–67; Henderson, *The Campus of the First State University*, 129–130.

35. Robinson, *William R. Davie*, 8.

36. *Ibid.*, 14.

37. McRee, *Life and Correspondence of James Iredell*, 481.

38. Manuscript copy of a commission so signed, in the collection of the late Raeford Cates of Reidsville, NC.

39. Ashe, *History of North Carolina*, 1:200.

40. *Ibid.*, 196.

41. January 20, 1806. North Carolina Journal, Raleigh, January 6.

42. *Dictionary of North Carolina Biography*, s.v. "Blake Baker"; Elizabeth Strong's mother was Ruth Baker, sister of Blake Baker, Sr. E-mail, February 6, 2001, to the author from Francie Lane, family historian.

43. *Wilmington Gazette*, 10, Tuesday, January 14, 1806.

44. Fries, *Moravians*, 6:2851.

45. Prince had been a Negro boy left by Hugh Martin to his son, James. At some point Alexander obtained Prince from his brother and Prince ended

his life as a free black property owner in Tennessee.

46. His will was signed February 20, 1807.

47. His horseman's sword, gold sleeve buttons, and broach with silver spurs.

48. The original entry had been for ten acres and was granted to Thomas Henderson, John Hamilton, James Hays and Isaac Wright, April 8, 1780. Guilford County Entry Book 2133: November 15, 1804, Plat No. 618.

49. Grant, Earl of Granville to Alexander Martin, December 21, 1761.

50. Robert Ralston was married to Frances Tate, daughter of Alley Hunter Tate, first cousin of Governor Martin. This tract immediately joined the "Danbury" tract on both sides of Jacobs Creek and on the south side of the Dan. Guilford County Deed Book 3, page 161, January 12, 1785.

51. Caldwell received the *Jewish Historian, Josephus* and *Chamber's Cyclopedia Supplements*. In 1822, Caldwell willed the books "presented me by Gov. Martin" to his son, Robert; Rodenbough, "The Will of Alexander Martin," 39–40.

52. Raleigh Register, November 19, 1807.

53. Rockingham County Will Book A, page 44, February 20, 1807.

54. The Rockingham County Historical Society is currently making plans to establish a site in the Martin-Settle Cemetery northeast of Reidsville as the "presumed" location of Governor Alexander Martin's relocated grave.

55. Fries, *Moravians*, 5:2884.

Epilogue

1. "His remains were placed in a vault, which he had built for himself in imitation of President Washington's tomb. This vault was built on a bluff, near to and overlooking Dan river. And it is said that his body was placed in this vault in a standing position in his coffin, facing the north, by his request; which was also in imitation of President Washington, whose body was placed in his vault in this position, at first." Avery Baker, *Reidsville Review*, 1938. The curator's office at Mount Vernon advised the author that they had no such record of Washington's burial position. Several traditions about the reason for this standing position have persisted concerning Martin.

2. Robert Martin died June 1, 1822. *Raleigh Register*, July 4, 1822.

3. South of Wentworth near Rock House Creek.

4. Rockingham County Will Book A, page 240.

5. Thomas Henderson died in Rockingham County, November 15, 1821. *Raleigh Register*, November 23, 1821. His will, found in Will Book A, page 175, indicates that his wife was already dead.

6. Son of Colonel James Martin of Snow Creek.

7. The deed is to the land on which Thomas lived (December 27, 1808).

8. Rockingham County Deed Book O, page 329.

9. Rockingham County deed, August 31, 1816, Pleasant Henderson of Orange to Alexander Henderson of New Bern. Pleasant Henderson had moved his family to Chapel Hill in 1797 when he was chosen steward of the University of North Carolina, *Dictionary of North Carolina Biography*, s.v. "Pleasant Henderson."

10. Deed of Trust, September 23, 1835.

11. Address of Hon. Robert Martin Douglas, Guilford Battleground, July 4, 1898.

12. *Reidsville Review*, February 25, 1929.

13. She died September 15, 1846, according to her tombstone, which survives.

14. She died in Washington, DC, survived by her husband and two infant sons, on January 19, 1853. Her grieving husband brought her by rail and coach back to North Carolina for burial. Today the two daughters lie between their parents, each grave marked with elaborate marble boxed stones.

Bibliography

Manuscript Collections

Abishai Thomas Papers, NC State Archives
Alexander Martin, Governor's Letter Book, NC State Archives
Alexander Spotswood Papers, NC State Archives
American Philosophical Society, Manuscript Minutes, 1744–1838
Aubrey Lee Brooks Collection, NC State Archives
Draper Manuscript, NC State Archives, Library of Congress
George Washington Papers, Library of Congress, 1741–1799
Joseph Winston Entry Book No. 27, Surry County, NC State Archives
Mecklenburg County, Draper Collection, Library of Congress (reel 104)
Papers of the Continental Congress, National Archives
Pension Application, National Archives
Richard Dobbs Spaight, Governor's Letter Book, NC State Archives
Richard Caswell, Governor's Letter Book, NC State Archives
Seeley G. Mudd Manuscript Library, Princeton University
Shippen Family Papers, Library of Congress
Southern Historical Collection, University of North Carolina, Chapel Hill, NC
Wall Papers, Special Collection, Rockingham Community College
William R. Davie Private Collection, NC State Archives

Books and Public Records

Abernethy, Thomas Perkins. *The South in the New Nation, 1789–1819*. New Orleans: Louisiana State University Press, 1961.
Adams, James Truslow. *The Adams Family*. Boston: Little, Brown and Company, 1930.
Agniel, Lucien. *The American Revolution in the South, 1780–1781*. Riverside, CT: The Chatham Press, 1972.

Alderman, Pat. *The Overmountain Men.* Johnson City, TN: The Overmountain Press, 1970.
Alford, Terry. *Prince Among Slaves.* New York: Oxford University Press, 1988.
Appleby, Joyce. *Inheriting the Revolution: The First Generation of Americans.* Cambridge, MA: 2000.
Armes, Ethel, ed. *Nancy Shippen: Her Journal Book.* New York: Benjamin Blom, 1968.
Arnett, Ethel Stephens. *David Caldwell.* Greensboro, NC: Media, Inc., 1976.
Arnow, Harriette Simpson. *Seedtime on the Cumberland.* New York: Macmillan, 1960.
Ashe, Samuel A. *History of North Carolina.* Greensboro, NC: C. L. Van Noppen, 1908–1925.
Battle, Kemp P. *The Early History of Raleigh, The Capital City of North Carolina. A Centennial Address Delivered by Invitation of the Committee on the Centennial Celebration of the Foundation of the City, October 18, 1892.* Raleigh: Edwards and Broughton, 1893.
____. *History of the University of North Carolina, 1789–1868.* Raleigh: Edwards & Broughton, 1907.
Binger, Carl. *Revolutionary Doctor: Benjamin Rush, 1746–1813.* New York: W. W. Norton & Company, 1966.
Blethen, H. Tyler, and Curtis W. Woods, Jr. *From Ulster to Carolina: The Migration of the Scotch-Irish to Southwestern North Carolina.* Raleigh: North Carolina Department of Cultural Resources, 1998.
Boatner, Mark Mayo. *Encyclopedia of the American Revolution.* New York: D. McKay, 1966.
Bowen, Catherine Drinker. *Miracle at Philadelphia: The Story of the Constitutional Convention.* Boston: Little, Brown, 1966.
Bradford, M. E. *Founding Fathers.* Lawrence: University Press of Kansas, 1981.
Brant, Irving. *James Madison, vols. 1–6.* Indianapolis: Bobbs-Merrill, 1941–61.
Brodie, Fawn M. *Thomas Jefferson: An Intimate History.* New York: W.W. Norton & Company, 1974.
Buchanan, John. *The Road to Guilford Courthouse: The American Revolution in the Carolinas.* New York: John Wiley & Sons, 1997.
Butler, Lindley S. *North Carolina and the Coming of the Revolution, 1763–1776.* Raleigh: North Carolina Department of Cultural Resources, 1976.
____, ed. *The Narrative of Colonel David Fanning.* Davidson, NC: Briarpatch Press, 1981.
Callahan, North. *Royal Raiders: The Tories of the American Revolution.* Indianapolis: Bobbs-Merrill, 1963.
Cartwright, Betty Goff Cook. *North Carolina Land Grants in Tennessee, 1778–1791.* Memphis, 1958.
Caruthers, Eli Washington. *A Sketch of the Life and Character of the Rev. David Caldwell.* Greensboro, NC: Swaim and Sherwood, 1842.
Cavanagh, John C. *Decision at Fayetteville: The North Carolina Ratification Convention and General Assembly of 1789.* Raleigh: Division of Archives and History, 1989.
Cheney, John L., Jr. *North Carolina Government, 1585–1974: A Narrative and Statistical History.* Raleigh: North Carolina Department of the Secretary of State, 1975.
Clark, Walter. *The State Records of North Carolina, Vols. 1–30.* Goldsboro, NC: Nash Brothers, 1902.
Collier, Christopher, and James Lincoln. *Decision in Philadelphia.* New York: Ballantine Books, 1986.
Commager, Henry Steele, and Richard B. Morris. *The Spirit of Seventy-Six: The Story of the American Revolution as Told by Participants.* New York: Harper & Row, 1967.
Conner, R. D. W., comp. *A Documentary History of the University of North Carolina, 1776–1799.* Vol. I. Chapel Hill: The University of North Carolina Press, 1953.
____. *A Documentary History of the University of North Carolina, 1776–1799*, Vol. II. Chapel Hill: The University of North Carolina Press, 1953.
____. *North Carolina: Rebuilding an Ancient Commonwealth 1584–1925.* 4 vols. Chicago: The American Historical Society, 1929.

Corbitt, David Leroy. *The Formation of the North Carolina Counties, 1663–1943*. Raleigh: Division of Archives and History, Department of Cultural Resources, 1950

Craige, Burton. *The Federal Convention of 1787: North Carolina in the Great Crisis*. Richmond: Expert Graphics, 1987.

Davidson, Chalmers Gaston. *Piedmont Partisan: The Life and Times of Brigadier General William Lee Davidson*. Davidson, NC: Davidson College, 1951.

Davis, Burke. *Old Hickory: A Life of Andrew Jackson*. New York: The Dial Press, 1977.

Davis, Curtis Carroll. *Revolution's Godchild: The Birth, Death, and Regeneration of the Society of the Cincinnati in North Carolina*. Chapel Hill: The University of North Carolina Press, 1976.

The Debate on the Constitution: Federalist and Antifederalist Speeches, Articles, and Letters during the Struggle over Ratification. 2 vols. New York: Library of America, 1993.

Dunaway, Wayland F. *The Scotch Irish of Colonial Pennsylvania*. Baltimore: Genealogical Publishing Co., 1981.

Duncan, Louis C. *Medical Men in the Revolution, 1775–1783*. Carlisle Barracks, PA: Medical Field Service Schools, 1931.

Ekirch, A. Roger. *Whig Authority and Public Order in Backcountry North Carolina, 1776–1783*. Charlottesville: U.S. Capital Historical Society by University Press of Virginia, 1985.

Elliot, Jonathan. *The Debates in the Several State Conventions of the Adoption of the Federal Constitution, Vol. I*. Philadelphia: J. B. Lippincott, 1863.

Ellis, Joseph J. *Founding Brothers: The Revolutionary Generation*. New York: Alfred A. Knopf, 2000.

Federal Writers' Project. *New Jersey: A Guide to Its Present and Past*. New York: The Viking Press, 1939.

Fischer, David Hackett. *Albion's Seed: Four British Folkways in America*. New York: Oxford University Press, 1989.

Fitzpatrick, John C., ed. *The Last Will and Testament of George Washington and Schedule of His Property*. Mount Vernon: The Mount Vernon Ladies' Association of the Union, 1939.

Flexner, James Thomas. *George Washington. Vol. I: The Forge of Experience, 1732–1775*. Boston: Little, Brown, 1965.

_____. *George Washington. Vol. II: In the American Revolution, 1775–1783*. Boston: Little, Brown, 1967.

_____. *George Washington. Vol. III: and the New Nation 1783–1793*. Boston: Little, Brown, 1969.

_____. *George Washington. Vol. IV: Anguish and Farewell, 1793–1799*. Boston: Little, Brown, 1969.

Foote, William Henry. *Sketches of North Carolina, Historical and Biographical, Illustrative of the Principles of a Portion of Her Early Settlers*. New York: R. Carter, 1846.

_____. *Sketches of Virginia Historical and Biographical*. Richmond: John Knox Press, 1966.

Fries, Adelaide L., ed. *Records of the Moravians in North Carolina*. 11 vols. Raleigh: State Department of Archives and History, 1968.

Ganyard, Robert L. *The Emergence of North Carolina's Revolutionary State Government*. Raleigh: North Carolina Department of Cultural Resources, 1976.

Gardner, Bettie Sue. *Alexander Martin and James Hunter of Rockingham County*, privately printed, 1953.

Garland, Hugh A. *The Life of John Randolph of Roanoke*. Vols. I, II. New York: D. Appleton & Co., 1859. Reprint ed., New York: Greenwood Press, 1969.

Gerson, Noel B. *Franklin: America's "Lost State."* New York: Crowell-Collier Press, 1968.

Gilpatrick, Delbert Harold. *Jeffersonian Democracy in North Carolina, 1789–1816*. New York: Octagon Books, 1967.

Gipson, Lawrence Henry. *The British Isles and the American Colonies: The Southern Plantations 1748–1754, Vol. II*. New York: Alfred A. Knopf, 1960.

_____. *The Triumphant Empire: The Rumbling of the Coming Storm, 1766–1770*. New York: Alfred A. Knopf, 1965.

Gombosi, Marilyn. *A Day of Solemn Thanksgiving: Moravian Music for the Fourth of July 1783, in Salem, North Carolina.* Chapel Hill: The University of North Carolina Press, 1977.

Green, Daniel. *To Colonize Eden: Land and Jeffersonian Democracy.* London: Gordon & Cremonesi, 1977.

Hamilton, J. G. de Roulhac, ed. *The Papers of Thomas Ruffin.* 4 vols. Raleigh: Edwards and Broughton, 1918–1920.

Hawke, David Freeman. *Franklin.* New York: Harper & Row, 1976.

Haywood, Marshall DeLancey. *Governor William Tryon and His Administration in the Province of North Carolina.* Raleigh: Edwards & Broughton, 1958.

Henderson, Archibald. *The Campus of the First State University.* Chapel Hill: The University of North Carolina Press, 1949.

———. *The Conquest of the Old Southwest.* New York: The Century Co., 1920.

———. *Washington's Southern Tour, 1791.* Boston: Houghton Mifflin Company, 1923.

Hendrickson, Robert. *Hamilton I (1757–1789).* New York: Mason/Charter Publishers, 1976.

———. *Hamilton II (1789–1804).* New York: Mason/Charter Publishers, 1976.

Higginbotham, Don. *The Papers of James Iredell. Vol. II: 1778–1783.* Raleigh: Division of Archives and History, 1976.

Hooker, Richard J., ed. *The Carolina Backcountry on the Eve of the Revolution: The Journal and Other Writing of Charles Woodmason, Anglican Itinerant.* Chapel Hill: The University of North Carolina Press, 1953.

Horton, Lucy Henderson. *Wasted Talents.* Charlottesville: Private printing, 1947.

Hoyt, William Henry, Jr. *The Mecklenburg Declaration of Independence.* New York: G. P. Putnam's Sons, 1907.

Hunter, Walter Marvin. *The Hunters of Bedford County, Virginia.* Cottonport, LA: Polyanthos, 1973.

Jackson, Donald, and Dorothy Twohig, eds. *The Papers of George Washington.* Charlottesville: University Press of Virginia, 1979.

Jackson, Joseph. *America's Most Historic Highway: Market Street, Philadelphia.* Philadelphia: John Wanamaker, 1926.

James, Marquis. *Andrew Jackson: The Border Captain.* Indianapolis: Bobbs-Merrill, 1933.

James Hunter Chapter NSDAR. *Early Families of the North Carolina Counties of Rockingham and Stokes With Revolutionary Service, Vols. I–II.* Madison, NC: 1977.

Kammen, Michael G. *A Rope of Sand: The Colonial Agents, British Politics, and the American Revolution.* New York: Cornell University Press, 1968.

Keith, Alice Barnwell, ed. *The John Gray Blount Papers.* 4 vols. Raleigh: State Department of Archives and History, 1952.

Kelly, Joseph J., Jr. *Life and Times in Colonial Philadelphia.* Harrisburg, PA: Stackpole Books, 1973.

Kennedy, Billy. *The Scots-Irish in the Carolinas.* Belfast: Ambassador Productions, Ltd., 1997.

Kerber, Linda K. *Federalists in Dissent.* Ithaca, NY: Cornell University Press, 1970.

Knox, Katherine McCook. *The Sharples.* New York: Kennedy Graphics, Inc., 1972.

Lefler, Hugh Talmage, and Albert Ray Newsome. *The History of a Southern State.* Chapel Hill: The University of North Carolina Press, 1954.

Lequear, John W. *Traditions of Hunterdon.* Flemington, NJ: D. H. Moreau, 1957.

Leyburn, James G. *The Scotch-Irish: A Social History.* Chapel Hill: The University of North Carolina Press, 1962.

Livermore, Shaw. *Early American Land Companies.* New York: Octagon Books, Inc., 1968.

Lomask, Milton. *Aaron Burr: The Years from Princeton to Vice President, 1756–1805.* New York: Farrar Straus Giroux, 1979.

Madison, James. *Notes of Debates in the Federal Convention of 1787.* New York: W. W. Norton & Company, 1987, bicentennial edition.

Malone, Dumas. *Jefferson and the Ordeal of Liberty.* Boston: Little, Brown, 1962.
_____. *Jefferson the Virginian.* Boston: Little, Brown, 1962.
Massengill, Stephen E. *North Carolina Votes on the Constitution.* Raleigh: Division of Archives and History, 1988.
Masterson, William H. *William Blount.* New York: Greenwood Press, 1954.
McBee, Mary Wilson, comp. *Anson County, North Carolina Abstract of Early Records.* Baltimore: Genealogical Books, 1978.
McClellan, James, and M. E. Bradford, eds. *Jonathan Elliot's Debates in the Several State Conventions on the Adoption of the Federal Constitution, Vol. III.* Richmond: James River Press, 1989.
McCullough, David. *John Adams.* New York: Simon & Schuster, 2001.
McDonald, Forrest. *E Pluribus Unum: The Formation of the American Republic, 1776–1790.* Boston: Houghton Mifflin Company, 1965.
McGuire, Thomas J. *The Surprise of Germantown: October 4, 1777.* Gettysburg, PA: Thomas Publications, 1994.
McLachlan, James. *Princetonians, 1748–1768.* Princeton, NJ: Princeton University Press, 1976.
McRee, Griffith John. *Life and Correspondence of James Iredell, One of the Associate Justices of the Supreme Court of the United States.* New York: D. Appleton, 1857.
Meade, William. *Old Churches, Ministers, and Families of Virginia.* Philadelphia: J. B. Lippincott, 1878.
Mee, Charles L., Jr. *The Genius of the People.* New York: Harper & Row, 1987.
Melton, Buckner F., Jr. *The First Impeachment: The Constitution's Framers and the Case of Senator William Blount.* Macon, GA: Mercer University Press, 1998.
Miller, John C. *Triumph of Freedom, 1775–1783.* Boston: Little, Brown, 1948.
Moore, John W. *History of North Carolina.* Vol. I. Raleigh: Alfred Williams & Co., 1880.
Moore, Virginia. *The Madisons: A Biography.* New York: McGraw-Hill Book Company, 1979.
Morgan, David T., and William J. Schmidt. *North Carolinians in the Continental Congress.* Winston-Salem, NC: John F. Blair Publishers, 1976.
Morison, Samuel Eliot. *The Oxford History of the American People.* New York: Oxford University Press, 1965.
Morris, Richard B. *The Forging of the Union, 1781–1789.* New York: Harper & Row, 1987.
Meyer, Duane. *The Highland Scots of North Carolina, 1732–1776.* Chapel Hill: The University of North Carolina Press, 1961.
Pearse, John B. *A Concise History of the Iron Manufacture of the American Colonies Up to the Revolution and of Pennsylvania Until the Present Time.* New York: Burt Franklin, 1876, reprint 1970.
Peterson, Merrill D., ed. *The Founding Fathers: James Madison, A Biography in His Own Words.* New York: Newsweek, 1974.
Philbrick, Francis S. *The Rise of the West, 1754–1830.* New York: Harper & Row, 1965.
Phillips, Kevin. *The Cousins' War.* New York: Basic Books, 1999.
Pomfrey, John F. *Colonial New Jersey: A History.* New York, Charles Scribner & Sons, 1973.
Powell, J. H. *Bring Out Your Dead.* New York: Time Reading Program, 1965.
Powell, William S., ed. *North Carolina Through Four Centuries.* Chapel Hill: The University of North Carolina Press, 1989.
_____. *Patrons of the Press.* Raleigh: State Department of Archives and History, 1962.
_____. *The Regulators in North Carolina.* Raleigh: State Department of Archives and History, 1971.
_____, ed. *The Correspondence of William Tryon. Vol. 1.* Raleigh: Division of Archives and History, Department of Cultural Resources, 1980.
_____, ed. *The Correspondence of William Tryon. Vol. 2, 1768–1818.* Raleigh: Division of Archives and History, 1981.
_____, ed. *Dictionary of North Carolina Biography, Vols. 1–5.* Chapel Hill: The University of North Carolina Press, 1979.

Proceedings of the American Philosophical Society, Manuscript Minutes of Its Meetings, 1744–1838. Philadelphia: American Philosophical Society, 1884.

Pruitt. *Glasgow Land Fraud Papers, 1783–1800: North Carolina Revolutionary War Bounty Land in Tennessee.* Privately printed, 1970.

Rakove, Jack N. *The Beginnings of National Politics: An Interpretive History of the Continental Congress.* New York: Alfred A. Knopf, 1979.

Ramsey, J. G. M. *The Annals of Tennessee to the End of the Eighteenth Century.* Charleston, SC: Walker & Jones, 1853.

Ramsey, Robert W. *Carolina Cradle: Settlement of the Northwest Carolina Frontier, 1747–1762.* Chapel Hill: The University of North Carolina Press, 1964.

Rankin, Hugh F. *Greene and Cornwallis: The Campaign in the Carolinas.* Raleigh: North Carolina Department of Cultural Resources, 1976.

———. *The North Carolina Continental Line in the American Revolution.* Raleigh: North Carolina Department of Cultural Resources, 1976.

Rankin, S. M. *History of Buffalo Presbyterian Church and Her People.* Greensboro: privately printed, ca. 1910.

Raynor, George. *Patriots and Tories in Piedmont Carolina.* Salisbury: Salisbury Printing Co., 1990.

Reardon, John J. *Edmund Randolph.* New York: Macmillan Publishing Company, 1974.

Remini, Robert V. *Andrew Jackson and the Course of American Empire, 1767–1821.* New York: Harper & Row, Publishers, 1977.

Risjord, Norman K. *Chesapeake Politics, 1781–1800.* New York: Columbia University Press, 1978.

Rives, William C. *History of the Life and Times of James Madison.* Boston: Little, Brown, 1859.

Roberts, Kenneth. *The Battle of Cowpens.* Garden City, NY: Doubleday & Company, Inc., 1958.

Robinson, Blackwell P. *The History of Escheats.* Chapel Hill: The University of North Carolina, 1955.

———. *The History of Guilford County, North Carolina, USA.* Guilford County: Bicentennial Commission, 1971.

———. *The Revolutionary War Sketches of William R. Davie.* Raleigh: North Carolina Department of Cultural Resources, 1976.

———. *William R. Davie.* Chapel Hill: The University of North Carolina Press, 1957.

———, and Alexander R. Stoesen. *The History of Guilford County, North Carolina, U.S.A. to 1980 A.D.* Greensboro, NC: Guilford County American Revolution Bicentennial Commission, 1976.

Rodenbough, Charles Dyson, ed. *The Heritage of Rockingham County, North Carolina.* Winston Salem, NC: Hunter Publishing Company, 1983.

Rossiter, Clinton. *1787: The Grand Convention.* New York: Macmillan, 1966.

Rouse, Parke, Jr. *The Great Wagon Road.* New York: McGraw-Hill Book Company, 1973.

Rowan County Court Minutes

Rowan County Registry Book

Royster, Charles. *The Fabulous History of the Dismal Swamp Company.* New York: Alfred A. Knopf, 1999.

Russell, Phillips. *North Carolina in the Revolutionary War.* Charlotte: Heritage Printers, Inc., 1965.

Salisbury District Court Minutes

Saunders, William L., ed. *The Colonial Records of North Carolina.* Vols. 1–10. Raleigh: State of North Carolina, 1866–1890.

Schmidt, Hubert S. *Rural Hunterdon.* New Brunswick, NJ: Rutgers University Press, 1945.

Sellers, Charles Grier, Jr. "Making a Revolution: The North Carolina Whigs, 1765–1775." In *Studies in Southern History*, J. Carlyle Sitterson, ed., The James Sprunt Studies in History and Political Science. Chapel Hill, NC: The University of North Carolina Press, 1957.

Sensbach, Jon F. *A Separate Canaan: The Making of an Afro-Moravian World in North Carolina, 1763–1840.* Chapel Hill: University of North Carolina Press, 1996.

Sitterson, J. Carlyle, ed. *Studies in Southern History.* Chapel Hill: The University of North Carolina, 1957.

Skinner, Constance Lindsey. *Pioneers of the Old Southwest.* New Haven, CT: Yale University Press, 1919.

Slaughter, Thomas P. *The Whiskey Rebellion.* New York: Oxford University Press, 1986.

Snell, James P. *History of Hunterdon and Somerset Counties, New Jersey.* Philadelphia: Everts & Peck, 1881.

Sosin, Jack M. *The Revolutionary Frontier, 1763–1783.* New York: Holt, Rinehart and Winston, 1967.

Speidel, Frederick G. *North Carolina Masons in the American Revolution.* Oxford, NC: Press of Oxford Orphanage, 1975.

Stagg, J. C. A., ed. *The Papers of James Madison, 1795–1797.* Vol. 16. Charlottesville: University Press of Virginia, 1989.

Stewart, Donald H. *The Opposition Press of the Federalist Period.* Albany: State University of New York Press, 1969.

Storing, Herbert J. *What the Anti-Federalists Were For.* Chicago: The University of Chicago Press, 1981.

Strong, J. C. A., ed. *The Papers of James Madison, 1795–1797.* Charlottesville: University Press of Virginia, 1989.

Stumpf, Vernon O. *Josiah Martin: The Last Royal Governor of North Carolina.* Durham, NC: Carolina Academic Press, 1986.

Surratt, Jerry L. *Gottlieb Schober of Salem.* Macon, GA: Mercer University Press, 1983.

Tagg, James. *Benjamin Franklin Bache and the Philadelphia Aurora.* Philadelphia: University of Pennsylvania Press, 1991.

Tarlton, Lieutenant-Colonel. *A History of the Campaign of 1780 and 1781 in the Southern Provinces of North America.* London: T. Cadell, 1837.

Taylor, Rosser Howard. *Slaveholding in North Carolina: An Economic View.* Chapel Hill, NC: University of North Carolina Press, 1926.

Thane, Elswyth. *The Fighting Quaker: Nathaniel Green.* New York: Hawthorn Books, 1972.

Tinkcom, Harry Marlin. *The Republicans and Federalists in Pennsylvania, 1790–1801.* Harrisburg: Pennsylvania Historical and Museum Commission, 1950.

Tinling, Marion, ed. *The Correspondence of the Three William Byrds of Westover, Virginia, 1684–1776.* Charlottesville: The University Press of Virginia, 1977.

Troxler, Carole Watterson. *The Loyalist Experience in North Carolina.* Raleigh: North Carolina Department of Cultural Resources, 1976.

Van Doren, Carl. *The Great Rehearsal: The Story of the Making and Ratifying of the Constitution of the United States.* New York: The Viking Press, 1948.

Van Every, Dale. *Ark of Empire: The American Frontier, 1784–1803.* New York: William Morrow and Company, 1962.

———. *A Company of Heroes: The American Frontier, 1775–1783.* New York: William Morrow and Company, 1962.

Wacker, Peter O. *The Musconetcong Valley of New Jersey.* New Brunswick, NJ: Rutgers University Press, 1968.

Wagstaff, H. M., ed. *The Papers of John Steele, Vols. 1, 2.* Raleigh: Edwards & Broughton, 1924.

Watson, Alan D. *Society in Colonial North America.* Raleigh: North Carolina Department of Cultural Resources, 1996.

Webster, Irene, comp. *Guilford County, North Carolina Will Abstracts, 1771–1841.* Madison, NC: Irene Webster, 1979.

Wertenbaker, Thomas Jefferson. *Princeton, 1746–1896.* Princeton, NJ: Princeton University Press, 1946.

Wheeler, John H. *Reminiscences and Memoirs of North Carolina and Prominent North Carolinians.* Baltimore: Genealogical Publishing Company, 1966.

Wilkins, Roger. *Jefferson's Pillow.* Boston: Beacon Press, 2001.

Williamson, Hugh. *The History of North Carolina.* Philadelphia: Fry and Kammerer, Printers, 1812.

Wills, Garry. *Cincinnatus: George Washington and the Enlightenment.* Garden City, NY: Doubleday & Company, 1984.

Wood, Gordon S. *The Creation of the American Republic, 1775–1787.* New York: W. W. Norton & Company, 1969.

Wright, Louis B. *The Atlantic Frontier, Colonial American Civilization, 1607–1763.* New York: Alfred A. Knopf, 1947.

Yates, Elizabeth Winston. "The Public Career of Alexander Martin" (unpublished master's thesis). University of North Carolina, 1943.

Yates, Robert. *Secret Proceedings and Debates of the Convention Assembled at Philadelphia, in the year 1787, for the Purpose of Forming the Constitution of the United States of America* (1821). Birmingham, AL: Birmingham Public Library, 1987.

ARTICLES

Adair, Douglass. "The Autobiography of the Reverend Devereaux Jarrett, 1732–1763." *William & Mary Quarterly* 9 (1952).

Alger, Vearl Guymon. "The Case for James Hunter of Stinking Quarter." *The North Carolina Genealogical Society Journal* III, No. 2 (May 1977).

Battle, Kemp B. "The Life and Services of Brigadier General Jethro Sumner." *The North Carolina Booklet,* vol. 8, no. 2 (October 1908).

Browning, Mary A. "John Tate Store Accounts, Guilford County, 1772–1778." *The Guilford Genealogist,* Spring 1992.

Conner, H. G. "James Iredell, 1751–1799." *The North Carolina Booklet* XI, No. 4 (April 1912).

Crow, Jeffery J. "Liberty Men and Loyalists: Disorder and Disaffection in the North Carolina Backcountry." In Ronald Hoffman, Thad W. Tate, and Peter J. Albert, Eds., *An Uncivil War: The Southern Backcountry in the American Revolution.* Charlottesville: University of Virginia Press, 1985.

Douglas, Elisha P. "Thomas Burke, Disillusioned Democrat." *North Carolina Historical Review* 26 (April 1949).

Douglas, Robert M. "Upon the Life and Character of Governor Alexander Martin." Address Delivered at the Annual Celebration of the Battle of Guilford Court House, July 4, 1898.

Ervin, Sam J. "A Colonial History of Rowan County, North Carolina." *The James Sprunt Studies in History and Political Sciences* XVI, No. 1 (1917). Chapel Hill: The University of North Carolina Press.

Golumbic, Lars C. "Who Shall Dictate the Law? Political Wrangling between 'Whig' Lawyers and Backcountry Farmers in Revolutionary Era North Carolina." *North Carolina Historical Review* LXXII, no. 1 (January 1996).

Graham. "Revolutionary History of North Carolina, British Invasion of 1780–1781." *North Carolina Magazine* V (1856).

Henderson, Archibald. "Although Governor Six Times He Is Neglected by Historians." *Greensboro Daily News.* (August 4, 1935).

———. "The Creative Forces in Westward Expansion—Henderson and Boone." *North Carolina Booklet* XIV, No. 3 (January 1915).

———. "Governor Martin Hailed as Guilford's First Realtor." *Greensboro Daily News* (December 22, 1935).

———. "How Famous Tar Heel Governor Quashed Whispering Campaign." *Greensboro Daily News* (August 11, 1935).

———. "Origin of the State of Franklin." *Greensboro Daily News* (June 5, 1939).

Hoskins, Joseph A. "Bruce's Cross Roads." *The North Carolina Booklet* XIX, No.1–2, (April–October, 1919).
Hoskins, Katherine. "Jackson's Stay in Guilford Was Turning Point in Career." *Greensboro Daily News* (June 26, 1938).
Lament, Paul F. "Benjamin Rush and American Independence." *Pennsylvania History, Quarterly Journal of the Pennsylvania Historical Association* 39 (October 1972).
Linn, Jo White. "Virginia–North Carolina Migrations As Identified in the First Ten Deed Books of Rowan County, NC." *Magazine of Virginia Genealogy.*
Lycom, Gilbert L. "Alexander Hamilton and the North Carolina Federalists." *North Carolina Historical Review* 25 (October 1944).
Massey, De Van. "The British Expedition to Washington." *North Carolina Historical Review* 66 (October 1989).
McBride, B. Ransom. "Claims of British Merchants after the Revolutionary War." *North Carolina Genealogical Society Quarterly* (August 1992).
McPherson, Elizabeth Gregory. "Unpublished Letters of North Carolinians to Jefferson." *North Carolina Historical Review* XII (1935).
Phillips, Kim T. "William Duane, Philadelphia's Democratic Republicans, and the Origins of Modern Politics." *The Pennsylvania Magazine of History and Biography* (July 1977).
Rankin, Hugh. "Moore's Creek Bridge Campaign, 1776." *North Carolina Historical Review* XXX (January 1953).
Rodenbough, Charles D. "General George Izard Visits the Sauratown, 1815–1823." *Rockingham County Journal of History and Genealogy* VIII (June 1983).
____. "The Will of Alexander Martin: A Reflection." *The Journal of Rockingham County History and Genealogy* VIII (June 1992).
Smith, Charles Lee. "David Caldwell—Teacher, Preacher, Patriot." *The North Carolina Booklet* XI, No. 4 (April 1912).
Swain, William. "Stray Leaves of History." *North Carolina University Magazine* I, No. 2 (1848).
Wagstaff, Henry McGilbert. "Federalism in North Carolina." *The James Sprunt Historical Publication* Vol. 9, No. 2 (1910).
____. *Letters of William Barry Grove. The James Sprunt Historical Publications.* Chapel Hill: University of North Carolina, 1910.
____. "State Rights in North Carolina Through Half a Century." *The North Carolina Booklet* IX, No. 2 (October 1909).
Walker, Marjorie T. "The Gallaways of Rose Hill." *The Journal of Rockingham County History and Genealogy* IV (June 1979).
Walser, Richard. "Alexander Martin, Poet." *Early American Literature* IV (Spring 1971).

Newspapers and Journals

Carolina Watchman
The Fayetteville Gazette
Greensboro Daily News
Journals of the Continental Congress, 1774–1789
The North Carolina Journal (Halifax, NC)
The Pennsylvania Gazette
Pennsylvania History Journal (Bloomsburg, PA)
Raleigh Register
Senate Journal 3rd Congress
State Gazette of North Carolina
The Three Forks of Muddy Creek (Salem, NC)
Virginia Gazette
Wilmington Gazette

Index

Adams, Abigail 176–177
Adams, John 157, 170, 174, 176–177, 179–185
Alamance, Battlefield of 37, 40, 44, 82, 168
Alamance Creek, NC 32, 78
Alamance Presbyterian 32–33, 57
Albemarle County, VA 19
Alexander, Col. 30
Alexander, Gov. Nathaniel 194
Alexander, Wallace 145, 148
Alexander, Gen. William (Lord Sterling) 9
Alexandria, VA 25
Alien and Sedition Act 180–182, 184
Alison, the Rev. Francis 15
Alison Academy 15
Allen, Nathan 195
Allen, Valentine 108
American Philosophical Society 173–174, 184–185, 199
Anglican 49
Annapolis Convention 110, 113
Anson County, NC 49, 107, 196
Anti-Federalists 133, 137–138, 141, 148–149, 157, 159
Antigua 36, 41
Appalachian Mountains 88, 99, 104
Armstrong, John 40, 46, 50, 85, 97, 178
Armstrong, Martin 47, 84, 97, 178, 192
Armstrong Land Office 157
Articles of Confederation 65, 92, 110–111, 113, 117, 127

Articles of Impeachment 179
Ashe, Judge Samuel 106, 178, 182
Assembly 75, 79, 95
Assumption 164
Atlantic Ocean 79, 84
Augusta, GA 152
Avery, Waightstill Avery 42, 91, 117

Bache, Benjamin Franklin 173, 175
Baggage Road 187
Bagge, Traugott 137
Baker, Avery 202
Baker, Blake 195
Baker, Mary Madison 158, 202
Balch, Hezekiah James 42, 117
Baltimore, MD 25
Band of Brothers 140
Barnes, Turbefield 108
Bartram, John 118
Bassett, Richard 112
Battle, Elisha 123
Battle of Alamance 32
Bedford, Gunning 113
Belcher, Gov. Jonathan (NJ) 17
Belfast 12
Bellview 170
Benbury, Thomas 71
Benigna, Countess (Baronnes von Watteville) 119
Bennehan, Richard 184
Beresford, Richard 99
Berger, Captain 30
Big Harpeth River 179
Bill of Rights 75, 137

Bingham, Anne 114
Bingham, William 114
Black Horse 112
Bladen County, NC 136
Blair, the Rev. Samuel 170
Blair family 170
Bloodworth, Timothy 76, 91, 125, 130, 135, 169–171, 177, 179, 181, 185, 200
Blount, John Gray 86, 96, 98, 100, 112, 130, 136
Blount, Joseph 80
Blount, Gen. Thomas 158
Blount, William 84–86, 91, 94–98, 100, 105, 111–112, 117–118, 120, 123, 126, 129–130, 134–135, 144, 148, 151–152, 154, 156–159, 176–179, 185, 192, 200
Blount family 91, 95, 192
Blount Hall 100
Board of Trade 29, 48, 93
Board of War (Continental Congress) 59
Board of War (NC) 54, 59–62, 64, 82
Boone, Daniel 24, 96, 119
Boone, Gov. Thomas 23
Boote, Benjamin Booth 40
Bostic, Joseph 155
Boston 39, 45–46, 151
Braddock, Gen. 14
Bradford, William 173
Brandywine Creek 50–51, 65
Brevard, Dr. Ephraim 42, 93
Brick Church 24–25
Brown, John 169

Brown, Thomas 136
Bruce, Charles 137–138
Brunswick County, NC 43–44, 46, 59
Bryan, Col. Samuel 77
Bryan, Ens. William 33
Bryan Settlement 23
Buchanan, James 105
Buchanan, Hastie and Company 77
Buck Island Creek 192
Bucks County, PA 20, 170
Buffalo Presbyterian Church 32–33, 57, 125–126
Buncombe County, NC 192, 196
Burgoyne, Gen. 47
Burke, Gov. Thomas 49–52, 65–75, 79, 82, 88, 200
Burke County, NC 130
Burr, Aaron 169, 172
Burr, the Rev. Aaron 15–19
Burr, Esther 15–16, 18
Bute Old Courthouse 68
Butler, Gen. 66, 71, 93
Butler, Pierce 167, 169
Byrd, Mary Willing 112, 114
Byrd, William, III 41, 114
Byrd/Farley family 114

Cabarrus, Stephen 134
Cage, John 101
Caldwell, the Rev. David 32–34, 37, 40, 49, 64, 125–127, 134, 168, 174, 196
Caldwell, David of Iredell 148
Camden, SC 58–61, 63–64, 81, 152
Cameron, Duncan 195
Campbell, Col. Arthur 86, 95
Campbell, David 99
Campbell, John 40
Canada 176
Cape Fear 42, 48, 50, 82, 159; Bank of 193
Capritz Bridge 156
Carey, James 175, 177
Caribbean 164
Carroll's Ferry 13
Carter, Landon 101
Caruthers, the Rev. Eli 32
Cary's Rebellion 174
Caswell, Richard 47, 49, 52, 55, 57–60, 62, 65, 69, 76, 81–82, 85–86, 88, 91–92, 96–101, 103–105, 109–111, 114, 116, 119–121, 123, 126, 128–130, 134, 136, 156–157, 174, 197, 200
Caswell, William (son of Richard Caswell) 57
Caswell, Winston 112
Caswell County 83, 126
Catawbas 97
Catholic 49

Centre Quaker Church 57
Cession of Western Lands 93–96, 98–99, 101, 106, 129, 147, 157
Chadd's Ford 50
Chambers, Maxwell 137
Chapel Hill, NC 156, 162
Chapel Royal (St. James Palace) 24
Charles II, Charter of 84
Charleston, SC 20–21, 48–49, 58–59, 63, 66, 69, 152, 164
Charlotte, NC 42, 59–61, 79, 147, 152, 156
Charlottesville, VA 23
Chatham County, NC 30, 35, 49
Cherokee Indians 23–24, 83–84, 88, 96–97, 100, 157
Chesapeake 81
Chester 51
Chew, Benjamin 10
Chickamauga 84, 88
Chowan 71
Christianity 127
Christmas 70
Church of England 36
Cincinnati, Society of 53, 91–92, 114
Circuit Court of United States 195
City Tavern 112
Clark, Walter 91, 136
Clarke, Col. 52
Clinton, Sir Henry 46–48, 58
Clinton, Robert 157
Cliveden 10
Cocke, William 177–178
Coercive and Intolerable Acts 39
Collins, Josiah 195
Columbia SC 152
Columbus 175
Committee of Safety 40–41
Committee of the Whole 149
Committee on Details 119–120
Committee on Military Claims 37
Committees of Correspondence 38
Confederation 94–95, 167
Confiscation Act 57, 76, 107, 155
Connecticut 99, 113–114, 118
Conners, R. D. W. 68, 137
Constable, William 143
Constitution, Federal 116, 119, 125, 127–128, 137, 157, 172, 181
Constitutional Convention 75, 109, 114, 120, 122, 124, 130, 145, 160, 163, 169, 174, 176, 199
Continental Congress 39–40, 42–43, 48–50, 57, 59–60, 62, 65, 68–69, 77, 85, 88, 93, 95, 98–99, 109–110, 112, 118, 164, 181
Continentals or Continental Line 43, 45, 50–51, 55, 61, 63, 68, 71, 74, 80, 83–85, 91, 96, 107, 109, 178, 190
Cooke, John 29, 176
Coor, James 106
Cornwallis, Lord 46, 48, 51, 58, 61–65, 67, 69, 152
Cortner, George 42
Council Extraordinary 62–66, 68
Council of State 50, 54,59, 66–68, 71, 77, 79, 82, 92, 99, 102, 137, 142, 146, 161, 180
County Antrim 11, 12
County Tyrone 11, 21
Couventry, Earl of 195; see also Granville, Earl
Craig, Maj. James H. 63–64, 67, 69
Craven County 106
Creek Indians 88
Cross Creek 46–47, 82
Crow, Jeff 71
Cumberland Company 85
Cumberland County, NC 49
Cumberland County, VA 19
Cumberland Gap 96
Cumberland River 83–84
Cunningham 46
Cutler, Manesseh 118–119, 125

Dan River 21, 27, 35–36, 41, 45, 50, 54–57, 64, 77, 80, 105, 108, 122, 142, 162, 170, 187, 192, 196, 199, 202
Danbury (Home of Gov. Alexander Martin) 70, 100–101, 104–105, 121–122, 137, 142, 147, 149, 170, 182, 185, 187, 190–192, 195–196, 199, 200, 202–203
Dartmouth, Earl of 35, 38
Davidson, George 46
Davidson County (TN) 95
Davie, William R. 61, 65, 68, 71–74, 76–77, 83, 92–93, 97–98, 107, 111, 117, 119–120, 122–123, 127–128, 132, 136, 138, 148, 152, 155–157, 159, 162, 182–184, 191, 194–195, 200
Davies, N. 19
Davies, the Rev. Samuel 19, 25, 107
Davis, James 192
Davis, Oroondates 59–61
de Bretigny, Marquis 83
Declaration of Independence 61, 166

Deep River Quaker Church 57
DeGraffenreidt, Baker 108
DeGraffenreidt, Sarah 108
Dekalb, Baron 58
Dekeyser's Tavern 137
Delaware 13, 58, 112, 114
Delaware River 19–20, 36, 116
Dent, William 42, 105
D'Estaing, Count 80
Deviney, Samuel 37
Dickson, Robert 148
Dinwiddie, Crawford and Company 77
Dismal Swamp 149–150
Dixon, John 114
Dobbins, Maj. 30
Dobbs, Gov. Arthur 20
Dodson 153
Donaldson, John 96
Donaldson, Stokely 178, 192
Double Creek 10
Douglas, Robert Martin 175, 189, 202
Douglas, Stephen A. 202
Drummond, Anne 13
Drummond, James 13
Dublin Society 173
Duck River 196
Dudley, Capt. 147
Duer, William 143
Duer-Constable Scheme 144
Dunbar, the Rev. Henry 108, 112
Duncan, James 55
Dunkards 77
Dunmore, Gov. 46
Dunn, John Ross 23, 40
Duplin County, NC 138
Duplin Rangers 47
Dutch Investors 145
Dutch Reformers 12

Easton (PA) 13
Edenton, NC 44, 79, 81–82, 151, 159, 170
Edwards, the Rev. Jonathan 15, 17–18
Egypt 185
Eighth North Carolina Regiment 50, 52
Elizabeth River 149
Elizabethtown, NJ 13
Elk River 50
Ellis, Joseph 171
Elsworth, Oliver 113
English Puritans 12
Ettwein, Brother 170
Eutaw Springs 68

Fanning, David 66–67, 70, 77–78
Fanning, Edmund 29–30, 94, 105, 107
Farley 170

Farley, Elizabeth Carter (wife of John Bannister, Thomas Shippen, James Izard) 114, 170
Farley, Francis 149
Farley, James Parke 41–42, 77, 108
Farley estate 108, 112, 114, 150, 187
Faulkner, William 159
Fayetteville, NC 82, 128, 130, 134–135, 137–138, 142, 147–149, 155, 165, 193
Federal Constitution 65, 123–124, 126–128, 132–133, 136, 138–141, 151–152, 155, 157, 164, 166
Federalist 73, 128–129, 132, 134, 138, 141, 144–145, 152–153, 157–159, 164–165, 171–172, 176, 179, 181–184, 191
Few, William 117–118
Fields, Jeremiah 28
Fields, John 108
Fields, Mary 108
Fields, William 35, 38
Fifth North Carolina Regiment 52
Findley, John 24
Finley, the Rev. Samuel 15, 25
Finley Log College 15
Fisher Creek 108, 121
Flexner, James Thomas 143
Florida 176–177
Ft. Johnston 41
Fort Moultrie 48
France 111, 168, 171, 176, 180–181, 184–185
Franklin (state of) 101–102, 104, 106, 119, 124, 129
Franklin, Benjamin 173
Franklin, Jesse 138, 149, 155, 183–184, 192, 194
Franklinites 101, 129, 136
Fredericksburg, VA 25, 50
French and Indian War 20, 23, 44, 52, 84
French Huguenots 12
French Republic 164
French Revolution 132
Frohock, Alex 196
Frohock, John 20, 23–24, 30–32, 35, 96
Frohock, Thomas 196

Gallaway, Charles 41, 50, 130, 156
Gallaway, James 124, 127, 130, 134–137, 143, 149–150, 191
Gallaway, Rawley 200
Gallaway, Robert 130, 191
Gallaway & Company 130
Gaston, William 195
Gates, Gen. Horatio 58–61

General Assembly 148, 160
Genet, Citizen Edmond 164
Georgetown, SC 50
Georgia 54, 85, 98–99, 102, 116, 118, 154, 157, 169, 181, 191, 201
Germantown, PA 9, 11, 51–53, 76, 170, 187
Gerry, Elbridge 112, 144, 179
Gillespie, James 138
Glasgow, James 148, 178, 195
Glasgow Land Fraud 178, 192
Glebe House, Montpelier 27
Gnadenhutten, PA 14, 170
Goldsmith, Oliver 190
Gorham, Nathaniel 112
Gorrell, Ralph 56
Governor's Palace (New Bern, NC) 41, 67
Gowdy, William 135
Grand Lodge 137
Granville, Lord (Earl) 20–21, 93, 170
Granville County, NC 126
Granville Land Office 131, 195
Gray, Col. 29
Grayson, William 110
Great Awakening 13
Great Britain 68, 107, 110–111, 139
Great Compromise 117, 120
Great Island of Holston (TN) 100
Great Lakes 169
Great Wagon Road 20
Green, Daniel 23
Greene, Gen. Nathanael 10, 50–51, 60–65, 68–69, 71–76, 79, 154, 202
Greene County (TN) 95, 102, 124
Grove, William Barry 175
Guilford County, NC 30, 32, 35–36, 38–42, 44–45, 47, 49, 55–57, 59, 64, 67, 79, 82, 85, 105, 121–122, 126, 128, 131, 135, 137, 142, 154–156, 193
Guilford Courthouse, NC 86, 153; Battle of 64, 71, 76, 82, 105, 202
Gunn, Elizabeth 133–134, 145

Halifax, NC 48–50, 57, 59–60, 63, 70–71, 79, 148, 152–182, 186
Halifax County, VA 108
Halifax Resolves 48
Hamilton, Alexander 112–113, 118, 142, 145, 147, 157–159, 163–165, 167, 170, 174, 179, 181, 183
Hamilton, John 137–138, 152
Hamilton Plan 142–145
Hampton, Lt. Col. John 77

Hancock, John 50, 151, 153
Hanging Rock, SC 59
Hannover Presbytery 18
Harnett, Cornelius 52
Harpath, River 196
Harris, Jonathan 192
Harris, Tyree 29
Hart, Thomas 29
Harvey, John 37–40
Hatteras, Cape 167
Haw River 105
Hawkins, Benjamin 88, 90–91, 93–94, 98, 134, 138, 155, 168, 177, 200
Hawkins, Philemon, Sr. 82
Hawkins, Wyatt 137, 146, 149
Hawkins County, TN 124
Hawksworth, John 190
Hazard, the Rev. Ebenezer 15
Heath, Maj. William 51
Henderson, Alexander 200–201
Henderson, Archibald 152
Henderson, Fanny 201
Henderson, James 46
Henderson, Mary 201
Henderson, Nathaniel 196, 201
Henderson, Pleasant 71, 82, 128, 179, 187, 196, 200
Henderson, Richard 24, 28–31, 71, 77, 82, 85, 96, 119
Henderson, Maj. Samuel 85, 100–103, 201
Henderson, Susan 201
Henderson, Thomas 35, 40–42, 54, 71, 85, 94, 105, 125, 138, 142, 191, 196, 200–201
Henderson Company 24
Henderson family 156
Henry, Patrick 84, 154, 184
Henry County 84
Hessians 50–51
Hewes, Joseph 76
Highlanders 36, 42, 46–47
Hillsborough, Lord 32
Hillsborough, NC 28–31, 35, 42–43, 57–62, 65, 70, 73, 79–80, 82, 91–92, 95, 100–102, 123, 126, 128, 134, 154, 156
Hillsborough Presbyterian Church 126
Holderness, James 108
Hollard Society of Science 174
Holt, Michael 29
Hooper, George 93
Hooper, William 63, 72, 76, 80, 93, 98, 125–126
Hoop-hole Bottom 80, 108
House of Commons 70
House of Representatives 177, 179
Howe, Robert 43–44, 45, 48–49, 88
Howe, Sir William 47, 50–51

Hubbard, Maj. John 101
Hunt, Memucan 137
Hunt, Thomas 24
Hunter, Alexander 12–13, 19
Hunter, Capt. Alexander 47
Hunter, James 29–30, 33, 37, 40, 57, 131, 137, 142, 179, 191, 196
Hunter, James of "Stinking Quarter" 33, 42
Hunter, Jane (mother of Alexander Martin) 11–14, 21, 23, 27, 30, 121, 190–191, 196–197, 200
Hunter, John 12, 19, 133, 190
Hunter family 12–13
Hunterdon County, NJ 11, 13–14, 20, 55
Husband, Herman 167–168

Independence Hall 16, 119
Indian Expeditions 99
Indian Mission 170
Indian Queen 112–113, 116–119, 125, 163
Indian Trading Path 20
Ingram, Lt. Col. 50
Iredell, James 72, 75, 80, 83, 90, 98, 105, 107, 110, 120, 125, 130, 138, 155, 167, 171
Ireland 12
Irion, Lewis 108
Irish Sea 11
Irishmen 36
Irvine, Lt. Col. 52
Isaac and Jacob 186
Island Ford 187

Jack, James 42
Jackson, Andrew 82, 125, 177–178, 181, 192
Jackson, James 169
Jackson, Maj. 154
Jacobs Creek 21, 27, 35, 196
James Island 68, 72
Jay, John 164, 168
Jay Treaty 168–171, 179
Jefferson, Thomas 60–61, 68, 79, 114, 127–128, 157, 164, 171–174, 177, 179, 181, 191
Jerusalem 122
Jews 127
Johnson, Charles 134–135, 158
Johnston, Samuel 45, 48, 65, 72–73, 76, 81, 83, 90, 92–93, 111, 123, 126, 128, 133–136, 145, 157–158, 160, 182–183, 192, 200
Jones, Gen. Allen 62, 72, 76, 124, 126
Jones, Thomas 76
Jones, Willie 72, 76, 80, 93, 108, 111, 115, 125, 127, 129, 130, 132–134, 137, 152, 193
Jonesboro, TN 95, 98, 101

Kenan, Gen. James 148
Kentucky 24, 85, 169, 185, 191
Kimbrough, John 31–32, 35–36, 38, 40
Kinchen, William 77
King George III 39, 80, 93
King's Bounty 24
King's Mountain 63, 102
Kinston 65
Knox, Gen. 164
Knoxville, TN 158

Lacy, John 201
Lacy, Theophilis 191
Lafayette, Gen. 51, 79–80
Land of Eden 41
Lane, Joel 156
Langdon, John 169
Langford, James 192
Lebanon Township 11,21
Lee, Gen. "Light Horse" Harry 48, 114, 164
Lee, Thomas 114
Leeward Islands 36
Leigh, John 158
Lemon Hill 114
Lenoir, William 135, 148, 158
Lewis, Ruth Baker 108
Lewis, Thomas 108
Lewis, William Tyrell 178
Liberty Hall 93
Lillington, Col. 47
Lindley's Mill 66
Little, William 193
Livingston family 170
Lloyd, Maj. 29
Lock, John 16
Locke, Matthew 76, 130, 158
Lockhart, Lt. Col. 52
Locust Street 170
London 29, 32–33, 37–39, 46, 93, 108
London Board of Trade see Board of Trade
Lone Island 63, 187
Long, Col. 47
Louis XVI 132, 164
Louisiana 176–177
Louisiana Purchase 193
Love, John 178
Lowland Scots 11
Loyalists 57, 66, 77, 83, 107
Lynd, Staunton 117–118

Mabe (Mayab), Robert 192
Macay, Spruce 82, 93, 125, 137, 192
Maclaine, Alexander 59–60, 76, 81–82, 90, 93, 98, 107, 125, 145
Maclay, William 143
Macon, John 109
Macon, Nathaniel 80, 82, 137, 149, 193

Madison, James 24–27, 110, 112–113, 118, 127–128, 130, 134, 165, 173, 186
Madison, James, Sr. 24–27, 186
Manifesto 102, 104, 106, 119, 124
"Marcus" 126
Marshall, the Rev. Friedrich Wilhelm 70, 77
Marshall, Justice John 179, 195
Martin, Agnes (sister of Hugh Martin, wife of Dawson) 12
Martin, Alexander 9–11; acting governor 66–70; and American Philosophical Society 173–175; birth 11, 201; birth of son 132–134; Board of War 59–62; cession 94–103; Constitutional Convention 111–121, 133; Council Extraordinary 62–64; court martial 51–53; Crown Attorney 38–43; in Danbury 105, 186, 189–192, 195; death 196–197, 199–200; Doctor of Laws 163; early life 11,14; early schooling 15–16; education of James Madison 25–27; family 142; governor 73–86, 89–103, 133–140, 142–160, 194–195; in Guilford 35–37; at home 55–56; Indians 87–88, 136; land dealings 192; lawyer 24; Martinville 106–109; Master Mason 137; meeting Washington 152–154; military 44–54; North Carolina Senate 56–57; opening Senate 166–167; poetry 175; at Princeton 16–19; Regulators 29–34; Rockingham County 105, 108–109, 121–122; in Salisbury 20–21, 23; Senator 160–171, 173–185; Society of Cincinnati 91; as Speaker 58–59, 65–66, 71 73, 106–108, 123–128, 130–131, 193–194; at university 136–137, 148, 162, 194; in Virginia 19–20
Martin, Alexander (brother of Hugh Martin) 13
Martin, Alexander (father of Hugh Martin) 11–12, 14
Martin, Alexander (son of James Martin) 190, 196, 201
Martin, Alexander Strong, 120, 191, 195–196
Martin, Ann 201
Martin, Anna Jane (sister of Alexander, wife of Thomas Henderson) 14, 27, 54, 142, 196, 200–201
[Martin], Ben (slave of Alexander Martin) 11

Martin, Benjamin Harris 190–191, 195
Martin, Ester (sister of Hugh Martin, wife of Francis Mason) 12
Martin, Henry (brother of Hugh Martin) 12–13, 16
Martin, Hugh (father of Alexander Martin) 11–15, 20–21, 23, 201
Martin, Hugh (son of James) 201
Martin, James (brother of Alexander) 14, 21, 23–25, 27, 40, 45, 47, 55, 64, 142, 154, 156, 179, 187, 190–192, 196–197, 201
Martin, James (brother of Hugh) 13
Martin, James (Indian agent) 102
Martin, James (son of James) 190, 196, 200–201
Martin, Joseph 103, 136, 156
Martin, Gov. Josiah 36–38, 41–42, 46, 48, 64, 67, 84
Martin, Lucinda 202
Martin, Luther 113, 117
Martin, Martha (sister of Alexander, wife of Thomas Rogers) 14, 142, 201
Martin, Martha (wife of Stephen A. Douglas) 203
Martin, Martha Coughran (mother of Hugh) 11, 12
Martin, Mary "Polly" (daughter of James and wife of Thomas Rogers) 162, 201
Martin, Robert (brother of Alexander) 14, 21, 27, 48–49, 54, 133, 142, 149, 192, 196, 199–202
Martin, the Rev. Robert (brother of Hugh) 12–13, 48
Martin, Robert, Jr. 200, 202–203
Martin, Ruth Rogers (wife of James) 142, 201
Martin, Sam 35
Martin, Samuel (brother of Alexander) 14, 21, 27, 35–36, 42
Martin, Samuel A. (son of James) 190
Martin, Sara (wife of Pleasant Henderson) 71, 201
Martin, Thomas (brother of Hugh) 12, 13
Martin, the Rev. Thomas (brother of Alexander) 14, 21, 24–27, 49, 117, 186
Martin-Ellington Cemetery 202
Martinique 83
Martin's Lime Kiln 55
Martinville, NC 40, 105–106, 125, 138, 177, 187
Maryland 58, 60, 102, 113, 117

Maryland, Col. 52
Mason, Francis 13
Mason, George 112, 118–120, 181
Mason, Steven 169–179
Masons 137, 152, 162
Massachusetts 99, 112, 118–119, 127, 151, 167, 181
Mattocks, John 191
Maubley, Middleton 78
Maxwell, William 50–52
May, John 191
Mazzei, Filippo 171
McAden, Hugh 40
McCauley, Maj. 73
McCorkle, the Rev. Samuel Eusebius 93
McCulloch 109
McCulloch, Henry Eustace 20, 93
McDowells, Joseph 130, 134, 148
McNairy, Francis 125
McNairy, John (son of Francis) 125
McNeill, "One-eyed" Hector 66
McWhorter, Dr. Alexander 93
Mebane, Alexander 98
Mecklenburg County, NC 24, 30, 35, 41, 45–46, 82–83, 93, 100, 126, 142, 196
Mecklenburg Resolves 42, 83
Mew, Charles 115
Mennonites 77
Menzies, John 191
Mero District, TN 125
Minute Men 46
Mirabeau 132
Mississippi River 79, 83–85, 99, 125, 176
Mississippi Territory 191
Mitchell, John 23
Mobile, AL 200
Monroe, James 113, 168
Montford 109
Monticello 173
Montpelier 24–25, 27, 30
Moore, Alfred 80, 183
Moore, James 43–44, 47–50, 73
Moore, William 46
Moore's Creek Bridge, Battle of 47–50, 59, 71
Moravians 35–36, 42, 45, 50, 63, 68–73, 77, 89–90, 119, 122, 124, 126, 137, 153, 170, 197
Morris, Robert 112, 114, 117–118
Morristown, NJ 49
Morse, Jedidiah 175
Mt. Pleasant 200
Mount Vernon 151–152, 176, 186, 191, 197, 199
Mrs. House's 117
Mullins, William 192
Muskingum River 170

Napier, Elizabeth Champion 202
Napier, Jane Hunter 202
Napier, John 202
Napier, Martha Martin 202
Napier, Moses 202
Napier, Robert Martin 202
Napier, Sallie Martin 202
Nash, Gov. Abner 58–60, 62, 65, 79, 81, 91, 93, 98, 156
Nash, Gen. Francis 9–10, 29, 44, 50–52, 174
Nashville, TN 178
Nashville Land Office 192
Nassau Hall 15–16, 18–19, 25, 27, 163
Neal, Col. Thomas 46
Nelson 185
New Bern, NC 23, 33, 37, 39, 41, 44, 54, 58, 64, 79, 83, 99–100, 102, 105, 151, 153, 157, 170, 180, 200
New Castle 12, 20
New England 165
New Garden Quaker Church 57
New Hampshire 152, 169, 181
New Hanover County, NC 43
New Hope 156
New Jersey 13–14, 21, 23–25, 27, 35–36, 113, 115, 117, 186
New Jersey, College of 14–15, 19, 25, 168, 185
New Jersey Plan 113, 117
New London PA 15
"New Side" Presbyterian 15–17
New York 33, 38, 94, 99, 111–112, 117–118, 120, 132, 143, 145, 157, 169
Newark, NJ 13
Newark Presbyterian Church 16
Ninety-six 46
Nollichucky 88
Norfolk 46, 151
North Carolina 23, 118
North Carolina, Bank of 193, 200
North Carolina House of Commons 57, 71, 79, 98, 104, 109, 158
Northampton County, NC 126
Northampton County, PA 13, 36
Northwest Ordinance 118
Northwest Territory 118
Nottingham Academy 15, 17

Obion County, TN 137
Ocracocke Island 167
Odeneal, John 133
Ohio 157
Ohio Company 118–119
Ohio River 118, 170
Old East 162
"Old Side" Presbyterian 15, 17

Old Tassel 100–101
Orange County, NC 28, 32–33, 35, 38, 126, 156
Orange County, VA 24–25, 27
Osbabrugs 45
Outlaw, Alexander 99–100

Pagans 127
Paine, Tom 173
Paisley, Scotland 25
Pardon and Oblivion, Act of 129
Paris 79–80
Parker, Sir Peter 46, 48
Parliament 39, 42–43, 150
Parrott, Benjamin 133
Pasquotank River 149
Patillo, Henry 40
Patterson, William 113–115
Patton, Lt. Col. 48
Pee Dee River 78
Penn, John 52, 59–61, 76, 82
Pennsylvania 38, 88, 119, 122, 143, 167, 170, 177, 187
Pennsylvania *Gazette* 20
Pennypacker's Mill 10
Pensacola, FL 86
Person, Thomas 76, 91, 93, 98, 123–124, 130, 134, 136
Petersburg, VA 41, 112, 165
Peterson, William 113, 117
Philadelphia 18, 25, 42, 48–51, 65, 80, 85, 88, 98, 100, 108–114, 116, 118–123, 125, 127–128, 130, 138, 144–145, 152–153, 160–161, 163, 166, 168–170, 174–178, 180, 182–187
Phillips, Gen. Abraham 135, 193
Pickering, Timothy 164
Piedmont 42, 57, 59, 63–64, 82, 105, 122, 125, 186, 199
Pierce, William 116–118
Pinckney, Charles 112–113, 176, 179
Pinckney, Thomas 172
Plato 16
Polk, Gen. Thomas 30, 45–47, 52, 83 59–60
Polk, William 135
Porter, William 149
Potomac River 165, 186
Potter, District Judge 195
Powell, Elizabeth 114
Powell, Samuel 114
Powell River 85
Pratt, John 108
Presbyterian Church 12, 24, 30, 34, 36–37, 48–49, 57–58, 61, 64, 138, 150, 163, 170
Presbyters 150
Presbytery of New York 13
Prince (slave of Alexander Martin) 21, 112, 186–187, 190–191, 195

Princeton College 15–18, 21, 25, 27, 32, 34, 42, 48, 61, 82, 93, 108, 112–114, 116–117, 136, 150, 162, 170, 174–175, 185, 187, 199
Proclamation of Pardon 70, 78
Prewits Lick 196
"Publicola" 126

Quakers 14, 20, 36, 40, 57, 77
Queen's College 93
Queensware 187, 189

Raleigh, NC 156, 178, 182–183, 187, 193
Ralston 196
Randolph, Edmund 164
Randolph County, NC 36, 47, 57, 105, 122, 126
Randolph Courthouse 78
Raritan River 13–14, 117
Rebels 31
Reddick, Joseph 194
Reed, Capt 67
Regulators 28–33, 35–37, 40, 42, 46–47, 57, 74, 77, 102, 167
Reidsville, NC 202
Renusson, Monsieur 50
Republicans 157, 164–166, 168–173, 175–177, 179–180, 182–185, 191
Reus, Brother 122
Reynolds, Maude 202
Rhode Island 60, 94, 129
Rhodes, James 121
Richardson (general of SC) 46
Richmond, VA 152
Richmond Courthouse 47, 59, 67, 69, 77, 122
Rip Van Winkle state 193
Risjord, Norman 81
Rives William Cabell 25
Roane County, TN 192
Roberts, Kenneth 58
Robertson, Elijah 129
Robertsons 129
Robinson, Moses 169
Rockingham County, NC 54, 105, 108, 121–122, 126, 130, 134, 138, 142, 156, 158, 165–166, 190–191, 193, 195, 197
Rockingham Springs 146–147
Rogers, Alexander M. 190, 196, 201
Rogers, James 196, 201
Rogers, Jane 201
Rogers, Jenny 201
Rogers, John 201
Rogers, Martha 201
Rogers, Polly 201
Rogers, Robert 196–201
Rogers, Ruth 142, 201
Rogers, Samuel 27, 55, 162, 196

Rogers, Thomas 154, 162, 190, 192, 201
Rogers family 142
Rogers Ore Bank 192
Rowan County, NC 20–21, 23–24, 30, 35, 38, 40, 46, 69, 78, 126, 158, 196
Rowan County Court 25, 32, 36, 41
Rowan Superior Court 77, 158
Royal Society in London 173
Rush, Dr. Benjamin 15, 163, 168, 170
Russia Drill 45
Russia Duck 45
Rutherford, Gen. Griffith 30, 46, 55, 69, 71, 82, 91, 96, 133, 138
Rutledge, Gov. John 63, 112, 118

St. Clair, Maj. Gen. 72
Saint James Palace, London 24
Saint Paul 132
Saint Thomas Parish 24
Salem, NC 36, 45, 68–72, 77, 79, 89–90, 119, 122, 126, 147, 153–154, 170, 174, 195, 197
Salem Road 187
Salisbury, NC 20, 23–24, 27, 30–33, 35–37, 39–40, 42, 44–47, 50, 63, 67, 77, 79, 82, 90, 93, 125, 137, 147, 152, 158, 182, 187
Salisbury Court District 84, 90, 120–122, 133–135, 145, 192
Saluda River 46
Sandy River 108
Santo Domingo 164
Sauratown, NC 64, 112, 149
Savannah, GA 152
Sawney (slave of James Madison, Sr.) 25, 27
Scales, Henry 156
Schuylkill River 50, 116, 118
Scotch-Irish 14–15, 19–20, 24, 28, 30, 34, 37, 40, 44, 49, 56–58, 116, 122, 125, 127, 191, 193
Scotland 130
Scottish Enlightenment 16, 34, 49, 78
Scottish Merchant Houses 41, 95
Scovillites 46
Searcy, Susan 201
Searcy, Thomas 105, 125, 196, 201
Second Regiment of NC Continentals 43, 47–48, 137, 179, 186
Senate 161, 163, 166–169, 171, 177, 180–183, 186, 194
Settle, David 202

Settle, Mary (daughter of Thomas Settle) 202
Settle, Judge Thomas 202
Settle-Reid Cemetery 202
Seven Island Creek 192
Sevier, John (Nallachucky Jack) 91, 95–96, 99–102, 104, 124, 129, 136, 144, 154, 178, 192
Shallow Ford 24
Sharpe, William 69, 73, 93
Sharpe's Creek 108, 191
Sharples, James 190
Shelby, Gen. Evan 102–103
Shelby, Isaac 91
Sherman, Roger 114
Shippen, Alice Lee 114
Shippen, Betsy 170
Shippen, Thomas 170
Shippen, Dr. William 18, 114, 170
Shippen family 112
Shippen House 114, 170
Sitterell, John 29
Slaton, George 192
Slaton, John 192
Smallwood, Gen. William 60, 62
Smith, Col. Benjamin 137, 148–149, 184
Smith, Robert 15
Smith, Samuel Stanhope 190
Smith River 187
Smithfield, NC 57, 156
Sneed, Squire 191
Snow Campaign 46
Snow Creek 55, 142, 192, 200
South Carolina 45–46, 48, 54, 57–59, 63, 65, 70, 72, 78, 102, 112, 127, 143, 167, 169, 184, 193–194, 201
Southerland, Ransom 42
Spaight, Richard Dobbs 80, 90–91, 111–112, 118, 122–123, 125, 135, 158, 161–162, 167, 174, 180, 183
Spain 111, 176
Spaniards 86
Speaker of the Senate (NC) 58, 68–70, 76, 98, 134, 194
Specific Act 73–74, 77, 79
Spencer, Elihu 18
Spencer, Samuel 63, 76, 106–107, 125
Spotswood, Gov. Alexander 174
Steele, John 76, 138, 141, 145, 158–159, 171
Stephens, Gen. Adam 10, 51–52
Sterling, Gen. 51
Stockbridge, MA 18
Stokes, John 135–136, 148–149
Stokes, Montford 145, 157–159, 193
Stokes County, NC 137, 142, 156, 162, 192
Stoltz, Brother 122

Stratford Hall 114
Strong, Alexander see Martin, Alexander Strong
Strong, Caleb 112, 118–119
Strong, Elizabeth Lewis 108, 121–122, 133–134, 191, 195–197
Strong, John 108, 122, 191
Strong, Thomas 108
Stuart, John 24
Sullivan, Gen. 51–52
Sullivan County, TN 86, 95, 102, 124
Sumner, Gen. Jethro 52, 60, 65, 68, 76
Superior Court 63, 145, 183
Surry County, NC 30, 35–36, 38–40, 42, 45, 47, 55, 59, 67, 69, 122, 126, 128, 142, 183, 192
Sussex County, NJ 14
Swarthout family 14
"Sylvius" 126

Tarboro, NC 122, 158
Tarlton, Col. Bannistre 68
Taswell, Henry 169–170, 181
Tate, Adam 105
Tate, James 125
Tate, Joseph 21
Taylor, James 133–138, 145, 148–149, 158–159, 183
Taylor, John Louis 149, 192
Taylor, Maj. 72
Tennent, the Rev. William 15
Tennessee 21, 23, 83, 96–97, 137, 170, 176–178, 192, 199
Tenth Amendment 65
Terry, Peter 187
Thackson, Col. 47
Thompson, James 163
Thompson, Robert 33
Tipton, John 102, 129
Tories 31, 40–41, 45–47, 54, 57, 59, 63–68, 70–73, 77–78, 93, 106–107, 180
Transylvania 85
Treaty of Paris 80, 84, 106–107, 123, 169, 195
Tremontaine 146
Trenton, NJ 50–51, 99
Troublesome Creek Ironworks 64
Tryon, Gov. William 23–24, 29–30, 32–33, 35–37, 40, 44, 46, 82, 102, 167
Turner, Gov. James 194
Tuscarora War 174
Tyrell, William 178

Ulster Scots 11, 12, 27
Union Forge (NC) 55
Union Furnace and Ironworks (NJ) 55

Union Square 156
Unitas Fratrum 77, 119
United States Congress 115, 132, 134, 142, 144–147, 149, 154, 157, 161, 163, 170–171, 174, 176, 179–182, 184–185, 187, 191
Unity Parish 35
University of North Carolina 61, 93, 136–137, 147, 155–156, 162, 190, 194
University of Pennsylvania 15
Upshur, Dr. Thomas 23
Utrecht Society of Arts and Sciences 174
Uwharrie 31

Van Scheelebeck and Marshall 83
Varlo, Charles 190
Vermont 169
Versailles 132
Virginia 35, 38, 41, 45, 52, 57, 60, 63, 75, 78, 84–85, 94, 96, 98–99, 102, 108, 110, 112–113, 118, 124, 127, 130, 136, 149, 154, 157, 165, 169–170, 174, 181, 191
Virginia Plan 113, 115
von Watteville, Baron Johannes 119

Wachovia 36
Waddell, Gen. Hugh 32–33
Wake County, NC 30, 35, 39, 65, 155–156
Walser, Dr. Richard 174
Walton, Jesse 47
Warren County, NC 82, 137
Washington, George 9–10, 49–54, 60, 75, 113–114, 132, 142, 146, 149, 151–155, 157, 164–165, 167–169, 171–172, 176–177, 179, 181, 185–187, 190–191, 197, 199
Washington, NC 152
Washington County (TN) 95, 102, 124
Washington Courthouse 101
Watt, Isaac 16
Wayne, Gen. Anthony 10, 52
West Harpath River 179
West Indies 42, 114, 165, 169
Westover 108, 112, 114
Whig 39–4, 44, 46–47, 49, 56–58, 64–65, 67, 70–73, 75, 78–79, 83–84, 107, 122, 180
Whiskey Rebellion 167–168
White, James 135
White, Maj. John 48
White, Capt. Nicholas 77
Whitney, Eli 165
Wilkes County, NC 47, 126, 196

William and Mary College 25
Williams, Benjamin 183
Williams, Elizabeth 201
Williams, John 24, 28, 73, 123, 126, 133–135
Williams, Jonathan 174
Williams, Nathaniel 42
Williams, Robert 191
Williamson, Hugh 76, 80, 86, 88, 94–95, 98–99, 111–112, 115, 118, 120, 125, 128, 134, 144–145, 147, 149, 174–175, 200
Willing, Thomas 112, 114
Wilmington, NC 41, 44, 63–66, 69, 71, 78, 152–153, 193
Wilmington Minutemen 47
Wilson, David 83
Winslow, Captain 147
Winston, Joseph 122, 137, 156, 192
Witherspoon, Maj. James 10
Witherspoon, the Rev. John 25, 163
Wright, Gideon 40, 42, 45

Yadkin River 20, 24
Yadkinville, NC 202
Yale 47
Yazoo Land Company 1954
Yorktown, VA 63, 69

www.ingramcontent.com/pod-product-compliance
Lightning Source LLC
Chambersburg PA
CBHW081550300426
44116CB00015B/2828